Also by the Editors at America's Test Kitchen

The America's Test Kitchen New Family Cookbook

The Complete Cooking for Two Cookbook

The Cook's Illustrated Meat Book

The Cook's Illustrated Baking Book

The Cook's Illustrated Cookbook

The Science of Good Cooking

Pressure Cooker Perfection

The America's Test Kitchen Cooking School Cookbook

The America's Test Kitchen Menu Cookbook

The America's Test Kitchen Quick Family Cookbook

The America's Test Kitchen Healthy Family Cookbook

The America's Test Kitchen Family Baking Book

THE AMERICA'S TEST KITCHEN LIBRARY SERIES

The How Can It Be Gluten-Free Cookbook

Healthy Slow Cooker Revolution

Slow Cooker Revolution Volume 2: The Easy-Prep Edition

Slow Cooker Revolution

The 6-Ingredient Solution

Comfort Food Makeovers

The America's Test Kitchen D.I.Y. Cookbook

Pasta Revolution

Simple Weeknight Favorites

The Best Simple Recipes

THE TV COMPANION SERIES

The Complete Cook's Country TV Show Cookbook

The Complete America's Test Kitchen TV Show Cookbook 2001–2015

America's Test Kitchen: The TV Companion Cookbook (2009 and 2011–2015 Editions)

Behind the Scenes with America's Test Kitchen

Test Kitchen Favorites

Cooking at Home with America's Test Kitchen

America's Test Kitchen Live!

Inside America's Test Kitchen

Here in America's Test Kitchen

The America's Test Kitchen Cookbook

AMERICA'S TEST KITCHEN ANNUALS

The Best of America's Test Kitchen (2007–2015 Editions)

Cooking for Two (2010–2013 Editions)

Light & Healthy (2010–2012 Editions)

THE COOK'S COUNTRY SERIES

From Our Grandmothers' Kitchens

Cook's Country Blue Ribbon Desserts

Cook's Country Best Potluck Recipes

Cook's Country Best Lost Suppers

Cook's Country Best Grilling Recipes

The Cook's Country Cookbook

America's Best Lost Recipes

THE BEST RECIPE SERIES

The New Best Recipe

More Best Recipes

The Best One-Dish Suppers

Soups, Stews & Chilis

The Best Skillet Recipes

The Best Slow & Easy Recipes

The Best Chicken Recipes

The Best International Recipe

The Best Make-Ahead Recipe

The Best 30-Minute Recipe

The Best Light Recipe

The Cook's Illustrated Guide to Grilling and Barbecue

Best American Side Dishes

Cover & Bake

Steaks, Chops, Roasts & Ribs

Italian Classics

American Classics

FOR A FULL LISTING OF ALL OUR BOOKS OR TO ORDER TITLES

CooksIllustrated.com

AmericasTestKitchen.com

or call 800-611-0759

Praise for Other America's Test Kitchen Titles

"Ideal as a reference for the bookshelf and as a book to curl up and get lost in, this volume will be turned to time and again for definitive instruction on just about any food-related matter."
PUBLISHERS WEEKLY ON *THE SCIENCE OF GOOD COOKING*

"A one-volume kitchen seminar, addressing in one smart chapter after another the sometimes surprising whys behind a cook's best practices . . . You get the myth, the theory, the science and the proof, all rigorously interrogated as only America's Test Kitchen can do."
NPR ON *THE SCIENCE OF GOOD COOKING*

"A wonderfully comprehensive guide for budding chefs . . . Throughout are the helpful tips and exacting illustrations that make ATK a peerless source for culinary wisdom."
PUBLISHERS WEEKLY ON *THE COOK'S ILLUSTRATED COOKBOOK*

"The perfect kitchen home companion . . . The practical side of things is very much on display . . . cook-friendly and kitchen-oriented, illuminating the process of preparing food instead of mystifying it."
THE WALL STREET JOURNAL ON
THE COOK'S ILLUSTRATED COOKBOOK

"If this were the only cookbook you owned, you would cook well, be everyone's favorite host, have a well-run kitchen, and eat happily every day."
THECITYCOOK.COM ON *THE AMERICA'S TEST KITCHEN MENU COOKBOOK*

"America's Test Kitchen spent two years reimagining cooking for the 21st century. The result is an exhaustive collection offering a fresh approach to quick cooking."
THE DETROIT NEWS ON *THE AMERICA'S TEST KITCHEN QUICK FAMILY COOKBOOK*

"This comprehensive collection of 800-plus family and global favorites helps put healthy eating in an everyday context, from meatloaf to Indian curry with chicken."
COOKING LIGHT ON *THE AMERICA'S TEST KITCHEN HEALTHY FAMILY COOKBOOK*

"There are pasta books . . . and then there's this pasta book. Flip your carbohydrate dreams upside down and strain them through this sieve of revolutionary, creative, and also traditional recipes."
SAN FRANCISCO BOOK REVIEW ON *PASTA REVOLUTION*

"This book upgrades slow cooking for discriminating, 21st-century palates—that is indeed revolutionary."
THE DALLAS MORNING NEWS ON *SLOW COOKER REVOLUTION*

"Forget about marketing hype, designer labels, and pretentious entrées: This is an unblinking, unbedazzled guide to the Beardian good-cooking ideal."
THE WALL STREET JOURNAL ON
THE BEST OF AMERICA'S TEST KITCHEN 2009

"Expert bakers and novices scared of baking's requisite exactitude can all learn something from this hefty, all-purpose home baking volume."
PUBLISHERS WEEKLY ON *THE AMERICA'S TEST KITCHEN FAMILY BAKING BOOK*

"Scrupulously tested regional and heirloom recipes."
THE NEW YORK TIMES ON *THE COOK'S COUNTRY COOKBOOK*

"If you're hankering for old-fashioned pleasures, look no further."
PEOPLE MAGAZINE ON *AMERICA'S BEST LOST RECIPES*

"This tome definitely raises the bar for all-in-one, basic, must-have cookbooks. . . . Kimball and his company have scored another hit."
THE OREGONIAN ON *THE AMERICA'S TEST KITCHEN FAMILY COOKBOOK*

"A foolproof, go-to resource for everyday cooking."
PUBLISHERS WEEKLY ON *THE AMERICA'S TEST KITCHEN FAMILY COOKBOOK*

"These dishes taste as luxurious as their full-fat siblings. Even desserts are terrific."
PUBLISHERS WEEKLY ON *THE BEST LIGHT RECIPE*

"Further proof that practice makes perfect, if not transcendent. . . . If an intermediate cook follows the directions exactly, the results will be better than takeout or Mom's."
THE NEW YORK TIMES ON *THE NEW BEST RECIPE*

"The best instructional book on baking this reviewer has seen."
THE LIBRARY JOURNAL (STARRED REVIEW) ON
BAKING ILLUSTRATED

The
Make-Ahead
Cook

8 Smart Strategies for Dinner Tonight

BY THE EDITORS AT
America's Test Kitchen

AMERICA'S TEST KITCHEN
17 Station Street, Brookline, MA 02445

Library of Congress
Cataloging-in-Publication Data

The make-ahead cook : 8 smart strategies for dinner tonight / by the editors at America's Test Kitchen.
    pages cm
 Includes index.
 ISBN 978-1-936493-84-5
1. Dinners and dining. 2. Make-ahead cooking. I. America's Test Kitchen (Firm)
 TX737.M366 2014
 641.5'55--dc23

2014014386

Manufactured in the United States of America

10 9 8 7 6 5 4 3 2

Distributed by America's Test Kitchen
17 Station Street, Brookline, MA 02445

EDITORIAL DIRECTOR: Jack Bishop

EDITORIAL DIRECTOR, BOOKS: Elizabeth Carduff

EXECUTIVE FOOD EDITOR: Julia Collin Davison

SENIOR EDITORS: Suzannah McFerran and Dan Zuccarello

ASSOCIATE EDITOR: Alyssa King

ASSISTANT EDITOR: Melissa Herrick

EDITORIAL ASSISTANT: Kate Edeker

TEST COOKS: Danielle DeSiato-Hallman, Sara Mayer, Sebastian Nava, Stephanie Pixley, and Meaghen Walsh

DESIGN DIRECTOR: Amy Klee

ART DIRECTOR: Greg Galvan

DESIGNER: Allison Pfiffner

PHOTOGRAPHY DIRECTOR: Julie Cote

ASSOCIATE ART DIRECTOR, PHOTOGRAPHY: Steve Klise

STAFF PHOTOGRAPHER: Daniel J. van Ackere

ADDITIONAL PHOTOGRAPHY BY: Keller + Keller and Carl Tremblay

CAST PHOTO: Christopher Churchill

FOOD STYLING: Catrine Kelty and Marie Piraino

PHOTO SHOOT KITCHEN TEAM:

    ASSOCIATE EDITOR: Chris O'Connor

    TEST COOK: Daniel Cellucci

    ASSISTANT TEST COOK: Cecelia Jenkins

PRODUCTION DIRECTOR: Guy Rochford

SENIOR PRODUCTION MANAGER: Jessica Quirk

SENIOR PROJECT MANAGER: Alice Carpenter

PRODUCTION AND TRAFFIC COORDINATOR: Britt Dresser

WORKFLOW AND DIGITAL ASSET MANAGER: Andrew Mannone

SENIOR COLOR AND IMAGING SPECIALIST: Lauren Pettapiece

PRODUCTION AND IMAGING SPECIALISTS: Heather Dube and Lauren Robbins

COPYEDITOR: Barbara Wood

PROOFREADER: Christine Corcoran Cox

INDEXER: Elizabeth Parson

PICTURED ON FRONT COVER: Moroccan Chicken Salad with Apricots and Almonds (page 144), Classic Beef Pot Roast (page 72), Meat Hand Pies (page 304), One-Pan Roast Chicken with Root Vegetables (page 38), Lemon-Herb Cod Fillets with Crispy Garlic Potatoes (page 179), Two Roast Chickens with Roasted Garlic and Herb Jus (page 209), Roasted Zucchini and Eggplant Lasagna (page 122), and Slow-Cooker Asian Braised Beef Short Ribs (page 262)

PICTURED ON BACK COVER: Roasted Spice-Stuffed Pork Loin (page 30), Overnight Kale Salad with Roasted Sweet Potatoes and Pomegranate Vinaigrette (page 152), and Spinach Manicotti (page 288)

Contents

Welcome to America's Test Kitchen

This book has been tested, written, and edited by the folks at America's Test Kitchen, a very real 2,500-square-foot kitchen located just outside of Boston. It is the home of *Cook's Illustrated* magazine and *Cook's Country* magazine and is the Monday-through-Friday destination for more than four dozen test cooks, editors, food scientists, tasters, and cookware specialists. Our mission is to test recipes over and over again until we understand how and why they work and until we arrive at the "best" version.

We start the process of testing a recipe with a complete lack of conviction, which means that we accept no claim, no theory, no technique, and no recipe at face value. We simply assemble as many variations as possible, test a half-dozen of the most promising, and taste the results blind. We then construct our own hybrid recipe and continue to test it, varying ingredients, techniques, and cooking times until we reach a consensus. The result, we hope, is the best version of a particular recipe, but we realize that only you can be the final judge of our success (or failure). As we like to say in the test kitchen, "We make the mistakes, so you don't have to."

All of this would not be possible without a belief that good cooking, much like good music, is indeed based on a foundation of objective technique. Some people like spicy foods and others don't, but there is a right way to sauté, there is a best way to cook a pot roast, and there are measurable scientific principles involved in producing perfectly beaten, stable egg whites. This is our ultimate goal: to investigate the fundamental principles of cooking so that you become a better cook. It is as simple as that.

If you're curious to see what goes on behind the scenes at America's Test Kitchen check out our daily blog, The Feed at AmericasTestKitchenFeed.com, which features kitchen snapshots, exclusive recipes, video tips, and much more. You can watch us work (in our actual test kitchen) by tuning in to *America's Test Kitchen* (AmericasTestKitchen.com) or *Cook's Country from America's Test Kitchen* (CooksCountryTV.com) on public television. Tune in to *America's Test Kitchen Radio* (AmericasTestKitchen.com) on public radio to listen to insights, tips, and techniques that illuminate the truth about real home cooking. Want to hone your cooking skills or finally learn how to bake—from an America's Test Kitchen test cook? Enroll in a cooking class at our online cooking school at OnlineCookingSchool.com. And find information about subscribing to *Cook's Illustrated* magazine at CooksIllustrated.com or *Cook's Country* magazine at CooksCountry.com. Both magazines are published every other month. However you choose to visit us, we welcome you into our kitchen, where you can stand by our side as we test our way to the best recipes in America.

facebook.com/AmericasTestKitchen
twitter.com/TestKitchen
youtube.com/AmericasTestKitchen
instagram.com/TestKitchen
pinterest.com/TestKitchen
americastestkitchen.tumblr.com
google.com/+AmericasTestKitchen

Preface

On my first day working for Vermont farmer Charlie Bentley, he asked me to do something simple—herd a cow and her newborn calf into the barn. So, with the sort of confidence born out of ignorance that only a 10-year-old can muster, I set out into the milkweed-speckled field to do what he had asked. Fifteen minutes later, bruised and my shirt torn by scuttling under barbed wire to escape being gored by the angry mother, I was rescued by Charlie, with a leather milking strap in one hand and the sort of confidence that is earned the hard way: through experience. The cow and calf ambled back to the barn without a hint of rebellion.

That experience taught me that many things that look easy are actually hard, including make-ahead cooking. It sounds easy—make enough for two meals and serve the same thing the next day. Or, freeze one batch and serve another. Or, use leftovers to make a hash or a soup. The problem is that many foods do not freeze well. Leftovers are notoriously second-class in terms of flavor. And all of this requires planning, test kitchen experimentation, and culinary know-how.

To bring some flavor and culinary adventure to make-ahead cooking, we have just published this book. To start with, this is eight cookbooks, not just one. Each chapter sings its own tune: "Prep Ahead," "Reheat and Eat," "Bake and Serve," "From Fridge to Table," "Shop Smart," "The Sunday Cook," "Come Home to Dinner," and "Stock the Freezer." And this volume is full of unexpected recipes, from Indian-Spiced Chicken with Yogurt Sauce to Overnight Kale Salad with Roasted Sweet Potatoes and Pomegranate Vinaigrette. Sure, you also get chilis, big roasts, and slow-cooker favorites, but we wanted to set the table with recipes that are fresher and more appealing.

To really deliver the goods, however, we had to solve the problem of dried-out freezer casseroles and pasta dishes such as lasagna (they need saucier sauces), casserole toppings that sink into the filling (use a foil shield between topping and filling), easier make-ahead stews (partially cook them the first day and let carryover cooking tenderize the meat), getting rice and chicken to cook at the same time (soak the rice overnight), and make-ahead fried chicken that loses its crunch (double-dipping in a low-protein flour coating works magic).

Specific recipes required tailored solutions. Baked Quattro Formaggio dried out when reheated, but when we added extra cream, it tasted heavy. The solution was to swap out most of the cream for evaporated milk for a silky, lighter texture. We also undercooked the pasta and cooled down the sauce before mixing for a perfectly al dente pasta dish. We even developed make-ahead pizza dough that would rise after freezing by adding baking powder. We also swapped in cornstarch for some of the flour for tenderness, and to freeze these make-ahead pizzas, we fitted them into disposable aluminum pizza pans and mixed the cheeses with a bit of half-and-half so they didn't dry out in the freezer.

Editors always have a favorite chapter, and ours is entitled "Shop Smart." We provide a shopping list of 12 ingredients that will produce three totally different dinners, not just slight variations on the same theme. How about Lemon-Herb Cod Fillets with Crispy Garlic Potatoes on day one followed by Sirloin Steak with Boursin Mashed Potatoes and then, on the third evening, Creamy Penne with Asparagus and Peas?

My mother was a farmer by nature, if not vocation. My sister Kate and I still have her calendar, the one that has reminders about repairing farm equipment in the winter, ordering seeds in January, painting just one side of the house each year (less expensive in the long run), sharpening tools at Thanksgiving, checking garden hoses in March, and pruning apple trees in the fall. Good cooking like good farming is mostly about planning. Although we all boast about that throw-together pantry pesto we made in a pinch, the odds are that most last-minute culinary endeavors are lackluster. It pays to think ahead.

So think of *The Make-Ahead Cook* as your personal guide to a well-planned culinary life, a place where your friends at America's Test Kitchen have removed the burden of meal planning and let you get on with the fun part, the cooking and eating.

CHRISTOPHER KIMBALL
Founder and Editor,
Cook's Illustrated and *Cook's Country*
Host, *America's Test Kitchen* and
Cook's Country from America's Test Kitchen

Make-Ahead 101

Introduction: 8 Smart Strategies for Dinner Tonight

What kind of cook are you? Do you like to cook all weekend just to stock your freezer? Do you like to prep Tuesday night's dinner on Monday night? Will you follow a precise shopping and prep plan that yields three great weeknight dinners with a minimum of fuss? Or would you rather do a little prep in the early morning, turn on your slow cooker, and have dinner waiting for you when you hit the door? While most make-ahead cookbooks focus entirely on stocking your freezer with complete meals or meal components, this book takes a new approach. Yes, you will find a chapter devoted to dinners from the freezer, but you will also find seven other creative chapters that show you how a little advance work can reap huge benefits. Here's a rundown of how we've set up the book so you can choose your style of make-ahead cooking depending on your temperament, your schedule, and your family's needs. You pick the lane. We've done all the planning for you, leaving nothing to chance.

PREP AHEAD: READY-TO-COOK MEALS

Oven-ready entrées that take a minimal amount of work the night before mean a great meal with little effort the next day. With these recipes, you can prep for tomorrow's meal while tonight's supper cooks or spend 20 minutes getting dinner ready in the morning, then pop it straight into the oven after work. We include a wide range of recipes, from grilled beef kebabs to tandoori chicken to vegetarian stuffed acorn squash. And we found smart ways to take advantage of the hands-off resting time—marinades and spice rubs infuse many of the dishes with great flavor as they sit. We also use the built-in rest to salt or air-dry larger cuts of meat for more tender, flavorful results.

REHEAT AND EAT: MAKE-AHEAD STEWS AND BRAISES

Stews and braises are some of the most time-intensive dishes to make because they require long, gentle cooking to tenderize tough cuts of meat and develop deeply flavored broths and sauces. But making these dishes ahead of time allows you to take advantage of the time the dish spends cooling and resting until you're ready to reheat it. We put this time to work, using carryover cooking during the cooling process so that we could cut back on the active cooking time. We also used the overnight resting time to develop complex flavor so we could simplify our ingredient lists, saving time and effort.

BAKE AND SERVE: OVEN-READY CASSEROLES

Casseroles are surefire crowd-pleasers, but between preparing the ingredients, assembling, and baking, they can be difficult to pull off on a busy weeknight. And storing and reheating usually results in dried-out sauces, mushy vegetables and noodles, and tough, dry meat. To make versions of all of our favorite casseroles—from chicken pot pie to classic lasagna—that could be made ahead, we had to reengineer our recipes. Parcooking pasta and vegetables so they'd turn tender as the casserole baked and making loose sauces that wouldn't overthicken in the oven were a couple of the tricks we used to keep our casseroles tasting just as good as traditional versions. And we also include fresh new classics that focus on whole grains and hearty vegetables, such as Hearty Vegetable and Orzo Casserole and Farro, White Bean, and Broccoli Rabe Gratin.

FROM FRIDGE TO TABLE: READY-TO-SERVE ENTRÉES

Whether you're in the mood for a healthy dinner, need something easy to bring to a potluck or picnic, or just want to avoid cranking up the oven on a hot summer night, dinners ready to serve straight from the fridge are great options to save time and energy. And you'd be surprised at the range of food that tastes great served cold—this chapter includes fried chicken, poached salmon, and chilled Asian noodle dishes along with a wide variety of fresh, inventive salads. Because cold dulls flavors, we made sure to season these dishes aggressively, to make bold dressings, and to finish the dishes with a little vinegar or lemon juice to ensure that the flavors were bright.

SHOP SMART: ONE GROCERY BAG MAKES THREE DINNERS

It's the eternal question: What's for dinner tonight? This chapter has the answer, with easy, thrifty plans that deliver three delicious weeknight dinners. For each three-day menu, we provide you with a shopping list of just 12 fresh ingredients plus a list of pantry staples you'll need. With such short ingredient lists, these menus required that we come up with clever ways to make ingredients do double duty while still delivering a menu with lots of variety. These easy weeknight meals come together quickly—with impressive results.

THE SUNDAY COOK: BIG ROASTS PLUS CREATIVE SECOND MEALS

Lazy Sundays are perfect for spending a little extra time in the kitchen pulling off a spectacular roast for a big family meal. We wanted to stretch that effort further by developing recipes using the leftovers to make a quick and easy weeknight meal. We include six roasts, each with two options for a creative meal that puts the leftovers to work. Rosy roast beef becomes beef and vegetable fajitas or a flavorful Vietnamese rice noodle soup, and leftover slow-roasted pork makes easy pork fried rice or a quick pork ragu with polenta.

COME HOME TO DINNER: EASY SLOW-COOKER FAVORITES

The massive popularity of the slow cooker is easy to understand. Thanks to its low, slow, and safe electric heat, many dishes can cook all day, so you can go to work and come home to a great-tasting hot dinner. But some slow-cooker recipes don't live up to that promise, with dull, washed-out flavors and mushy textures. So we looked for ways to build great flavor, adding lots of aromatics and savory ingredients like soy sauce and tomato paste and finishing our dishes with fresh herbs or a squeeze of lemon juice. And we made sure to keep the prep times short (some as quick as 15 minutes) and the cooking times long (at least 8 hours) so the recipes are easy to get started on a busy morning and ready to eat when you come home.

STOCK THE FREEZER: BIG-BATCH SUPPERS

There's no better antidote to a hectic schedule than a well-stocked freezer full of delicious, homemade, ready-to-heat meals. This chapter includes crowd-pleasing casseroles like shepherd's pie and macaroni and cheese (and each recipe makes two, so you get a big payoff for your time and effort). We also include big-batch stews, chilis, and pasta sauces plus individual items like burritos and chicken fingers that make it easy to feed any number of people. To ensure great results, we developed these recipes specifically for the freezer: For creamy freezer casseroles, we had to make the sauces looser. And to get crisp toppings for our casseroles, we used a foil shield to separate the topping from the moist filling.

Test Kitchen Discoveries

After months of developing make-ahead recipes, we learned a few tricks that made the effort to get organized and cook ahead well worth it. Whether you are stashing food in the freezer, holding it overnight in the fridge, or prepping entrées ahead so they are ready to cook the next day, here's what we discovered about how to be more efficient when cooking ahead and how to ensure great-tasting results.

1 Build Flavor Overnight

For our prep-ahead entrées, we used the storage time to our advantage. We turned to bold spice rubs and marinades to infuse meat with flavor as it rested overnight, giving us great results without any extra effort. And air-drying our chicken or letting crumb-coated pork chops and cod fillets rest uncovered gave us ultracrisp skin and crunchy coatings.

2 Make It Saucier

When we tried to freeze and reheat our favorite casseroles or hold dishes like risotto, lasagna, and pot roast in the fridge for a few days, the sauces ended up dry and overthickened. To compensate for the moisture lost during storage, we found that we had to make the sauces looser initially to get the perfect consistency in the finished dish.

3 Shield the Crust

For a freezer pot pie with a shatteringly crisp crust or a cornbread-topped tamale pie with a tender topping, we had to find a way to keep the moist filling from turning the topping soggy. We found that the solution was to use a simple foil shield to separate the topping and filling so that as the filling heated through, the topping could crisp. Then we simply slid out the greased foil shield before serving.

4 Chill Some Broth for Instant Cooling

It's important to cool food to room temperature before storing it in the fridge or freezer, but this step can add upward of an hour to some recipes. So we came up with a simple trick that rapidly cooled our stews and braises. Before we started cooking, we stashed some water, broth, or even canned tomatoes in the fridge, then once the dish was done cooking, we stirred in the chilled liquid to cool it to a safe temperature instantly.

5 Cut the Cooking Time

We reengineered long-cooking stews and braises to stagger the cooking across two days. We cooked them partway through, then let the meat continue to cook off the heat (no need to monitor the pot). During storage, the flavors continued to develop and deepen. Then we added fresh vegetables and herbs and finished the cooking on day two for weekend-worthy meals any night of the week.

6 Save Some Sauce

Tossing a dish with a marinade, sauce, or dressing before storing was a great way to build deep flavor, but we found that the flavors often needed refreshing before serving. So we saved some of the marinade to make a quick sauce or reserved some dressing to toss in just before serving. Brightening the sauce or dressing with some extra vinegar or citrus helped to reawaken the flavors of the dish on the second day.

7 Don't Worry About Thawing

We did a lot of testing to determine the best way to reheat a frozen casserole, and we found that the simplest method was actually the best—we put our frozen casseroles straight into a cold oven without defrosting. This method allowed the casserole to defrost gently as the oven came to temperature. Defrosting the casserole before baking took longer without giving us better results, and putting a frozen casserole into a hot oven resulted in casseroles with bubbling tops but icy centers.

8 Boost the Flavor Before Serving

The flavors of delicate ingredients like lemon juice and fresh herbs tend to dissipate as they sit, so we saved these ingredients to add just before serving. And reserving some of the marinade, sauce, or dressing in a dish to stir in before serving was a great way to refresh the flavors. We brightened the reserved marinade or dressing with vinegar or a little extra lemon juice to ensure that our make-ahead dishes never tasted dull.

Tips for Saving Prep Time

Prepping a few standard ingredients ahead of time is a great strategy for making weeknight cooking a little easier. When you bring home a load of groceries, try prepping some ingredients right away to use later in the week. Here are our favorite prep-ahead tricks that can save you time on a hectic night.

Chop and Freeze Onions

Onions are one of the most common ingredients, but unless you're a professional chef, they can be tedious to chop. Rather than pulling out a knife and cutting board and chopping an onion each time you cook, chop a bunch of onions at once and freeze them in portions in zipper-lock bags. They should last for about one month. When cooking, you can simply add the frozen onions right to the pan and add a few extra minutes of cooking time.

Shred Cheese

Having plenty of your favorite shredded cheese on hand is a great timesaver. Sure, you can buy the preshredded stuff at the grocery store, but it's more expensive, and it doesn't melt as well or taste as good because it's coated in powdered cellulose as a preservative. Buy the cheese in large blocks and use the food processor fitted with the shredding disk to prep it quickly all at once. Shredded cheese can be refrigerated in a zipper-lock bag for up to two weeks or frozen for up to one month.

Stem Herbs

Fresh herbs can be one of the most frustrating things to keep on hand because they spoil so quickly, but parsley, cilantro, and mint will last a surprisingly long time in the fridge if you wash and stem the leaves before storing. And prepping them ahead will save you time when you need to mince a few tablespoons to add to a dish. Store the leaves wrapped in a damp paper towel in a partially open zipper-lock bag for one to two weeks.

Wash Greens

Washing lettuce and hearty greens as soon as you get them home will not only save you time later, it will help prolong their freshness as well. Once you wash the greens, spin them dry in a salad spinner, then store them right in the spinner (lined with paper towels) or wrap them in paper towels and store them in a partially open zipper-lock bag. Hearty greens like kale and chard can even be chopped ahead of time so you can grab a handful to stir into a soup or pasta dinner.

Prep Hearty Vegetables

Broccoli, cauliflower, bell peppers, carrots, and leeks all can be washed and prepped ahead of time without browning or losing moisture like more delicate veggies. You can cut broccoli and cauliflower into florets, cut bell peppers into cubes or strips, and peel and chop carrots. Leeks require careful rinsing to remove grit, so prepping them ahead is a great timesaver. Store the chopped vegetables in an airtight container layered with damp paper towels for up to one week.

Freeze Wine

An opened bottle of wine is usable for only about a week, but recipes often call for just a few tablespoons to finish a sauce. To make it easy to keep wine on hand for cooking, measure 1 tablespoon into each well of an ice cube tray and freeze. The frozen cubes can be added straight to pan sauces, stews, and braises.

Mince and Freeze Chipotle Chiles

We love the smoky, spicy flavor of canned chipotle chiles in adobo, but we usually use just 1 or 2 teaspoons at a time. To avoid opening a can each time, then letting the rest mold in the fridge, mince the whole can at once, place teaspoonfuls onto a parchment paper–lined baking sheet, and freeze. Once frozen, transfer them to a zipper-lock bag, then add them to dishes as needed.

The Make-Ahead Cook's Checklist

When your goal is to cook ahead, regardless of which make-ahead approach you choose, there is one thing you must do: get organized and make sure you have the right containers, wrapping and labeling materials, and more.

Storage Containers

We reach for storage containers for stashing components of a recipe; prepped ingredients; and portions of sauces, soups, and stews. It's important to have lots of different sizes so you always have the right one on hand; storing food in a too-large container can allow it to spoil more quickly. Look for containers with a tight seal that are microwave-safe for quick thawing and dishwasher-safe for easy cleanup. We prefer reusable plastic storage containers, but you can also buy storage containers made of glass or disposable plastic. See page 10 for our complete testing of storage containers.

Zipper-Lock Bags

Disposable plastic zipper-lock bags are great for storing individual or odd-shaped items and marinating meat or vegetables. They are also handy for freezing sauces; they lie flat in the freezer and can be stacked upright once frozen. We recommend buying freezer-safe zipper-lock bags because they are made of thicker plastic than standard bags, so they are sturdier and better at protecting the food from off-flavors in the fridge or freezer. Our favorite brand is **Ziploc Brand Double Zipper Freezer Bags**, $3.99, which boasts a sturdy, leakproof double-zipper seal that kept foods fresh and held fast even through a tomato-sauce-drop test.

Plastic Wrap

When you want to stash a dish in the fridge or freezer without transferring it to a storage container, covering it with plastic wrap is the simplest way to keep the dish airtight. If the plastic doesn't adhere easily to the dish, dampen the edge of the dish with a wet paper towel to help the plastic stick. Plastic wrap can be made from two distinctly different substances. Some manufacturers use a food-safe version of PVC; others use low-density polyethylene (LDPE). The main difference? PVC clings but is not impermeable; LDPE is impermeable but has far less cling. Clingy PVC wraps are preferable if you are transporting food or are worried about spills and leaks, but to keep foods fresh longer, select plastic wraps made from LDPE. Our all-around winner is **Glad Cling Wrap Clear Plastic**, $1.20 per 100 square feet.

Aluminum Foil

We reach for aluminum foil constantly in the test kitchen. We use it to line baking sheets for easy cleanup, to cover dishes when baking to prevent them from drying out, to wrap food in a pouch so it will steam gently in the oven, and to protect dishes from off-flavors in the freezer. We find heavy-duty foil easier to work with and recommend you stock extra-long rolls as well as standard 12-inch rolls.

Disposable Aluminum Baking Pans

When making and freezing casseroles, we like the convenience of using inexpensive disposable aluminum pans. These lightweight pans, which are readily available at the grocery store, stack easily and ensure that our glass baking dishes aren't sitting in the freezer when we need them. We like to make casseroles in 8-inch square or 9-inch round pans because they heat through quickly and you can make two casseroles, giving you the option to bake one now and store one for later.

Casserole Dishes

Classic 13 by 9-inch casserole dishes are essential for casseroles of any sort, and make-ahead casseroles are no exception. While the straight sides and sharp corners of a metal baking pan are ideal for making bar cookies and sheet cakes, we prefer glass and ceramic dishes for casseroles. Our favorite is the **Pyrex Bakeware 9 by 13-Inch Baking Dish**, $12.99. Its tempered glass won't react with acidic foods such as tomatoes, and it's safe for use with metal utensils. Its transparency lets you track browning, and the rounded corners make it easy to scoop out soupy desserts and casseroles. However, this dish has one drawback—it's not broiler-safe. For a casserole dish that we can stick under the broiler, we like the **HIC Porcelain Lasagna Baking Dish**, $37.49. This dish has large, convenient handles and straight sides for easy serving.

Rimmed Baking Sheets

One of our favorite kitchen workhorses is the rimmed baking sheet. We frequently pull this piece of equipment into service for our make-ahead dishes; it's perfect for roasting a large cut of meat or for baking chicken pieces on top of hearty vegetables. Our prep-ahead All-American Meatloaf (page 24) is shaped right on the baking sheet and stashed in the fridge, ready to pop into the oven the next day. And spreading chicken fingers or veggie burgers on baking sheets and quick-freezing them for an hour before storing makes it easy to grab just what you need from the freezer later on. Our favorite baking sheet is the **Vollrath Wear-Ever Half-Size Heavy Duty Sheet Pan**, $14.99. This sturdy pan browns evenly and won't bend or warp. We recommend that you have at least two on hand.

Wire Cooling Racks

In the test kitchen, wire racks and rimmed baking sheets go hand in hand. Baking food on a wire rack set in a rimmed baking sheet allows air to circulate all around the food, helping it to brown evenly. We use this technique to get crisp bread-crumb-coated pork chops and fish fillets or to bake a big batch of meatballs for the freezer. We also use a wire rack set in a baking sheet to air-dry our prep-ahead chicken and Cornish game hens for ultracrispy skin. It's essential to get a wire rack that will fit inside your baking sheet; we like the **CIA Bakeware 12-Inch x 17-Inch Cooling Rack**, $15.95, for its sturdy central brace and extra feet.

Dutch Ovens

A good Dutch oven is essential for big-batch cooking. We put ours to work making pasta sauces to stash in the freezer and hearty reheat-and-eat stews and braises. Because it's heavier and thicker than a skillet, it retains and conducts heat more evenly and effectively, so it's perfect for dishes that have long simmering times. We like a Dutch oven that holds at least 6 quarts with a wide bottom for more efficient browning. Our favorite Dutch ovens are the **All-Clad Stainless 8-Quart Stockpot**, $279.95 (best if you prefer a lighter pot), and the **Le Creuset 7¼-Quart Round French Oven**, $304.95 (better for those who like a heavier pot). Our Best Buy, the Lodge Color Enamel 6-Quart Dutch Oven, $49.97, is a little smaller but offers excellent performance at an affordable price.

The Test Kitchen's Guide to Storage Containers

Packing up leftovers ought to be easy, but food storage containers are one of life's persistent little annoyances. Does it fit in the fridge or freezer? Will it leak if it tips over? Can you microwave in it? Do you have to remember to wash it only on the top rack of the dishwasher? Should you worry about possible health risks with plastics containing bisphenol-A (BPA)? In search of a storage container that would put these questions to rest, we bought eight 8-cup rectangular and square containers made from purportedly safer BPA-free plastic. We submerged, froze, refrigerated, and microwaved them. We dropped them and ran them through dozens of dishwasher cycles. Then we did all the tests again. In a separate series of tests, we tried out three containers made from glass, a worry-free yet heavy and breakable alternative to plastic and its reported health risk.

Our testing revealed disappointing containers that leaked, warped, melted, absorbed odors, and stained. But one container was easy to use, survived all our tests, and met all our long-term goals. Our winner sealed tightly and easily; resisted warping, stains, and smells; and fit easily among the contents of our refrigerator. It performed well before taking more than 50 trips through the dishwasher—and perfectly afterward. This might be the last container we'll have to buy for quite a while.

Methodology

We tested eight BPA-free plastic (according to manufacturers) food storage containers, choosing square or rectangular sizes as close as possible to 8-cup capacity. All were purchased online or in Boston-area retail stores. Here are the features we considered and how we tested them.

LEAKS We filled the containers with chicken noodle soup and shook them vigorously for 15 seconds, then filled them with sugar and pie weights and submerged them in water for 2 minutes. Containers that didn't leak in the soup test and that kept their contents dry when submerged received high marks.

MICROWAVE We froze chili in the containers, then reheated it in the microwave, checking for warping, staining, and plastic flavors or odors. Several had trouble sealing afterwards, and a "disposable" container softened, rehardening as it cooled.

ODORS We refrigerated oil-packed tuna in each container for three days, then ran containers through a home dishwasher and checked for odors. Only the "disposable" container failed this test.

DURABILITY After testing, including 50 cycles in a home dishwasher, we observed stains, warping, and wear and tear, then we froze water in the containers and dropped them from chest height.

DESIGN We considered features that made the containers easier to use, such as simple, intuitive seals and efficient shapes.

GLASS STORAGE CONTAINERS

Many consumers have decided to avoid plastic storage containers after learning about the possible ill effects of microwaving in plastic, leading to the resurgence of glass food storage. We chose three and ran them through the same tests as our plastic containers (with the exception of dropping them onto the floor). Two models were ovensafe, but other design flaws knocked them out of the running. A third aced all our tests and was equal to the top-ranked plastic containers—if it weren't considerably heavier and more prone to breakage, we'd consider choosing glass as our favorite storage container.

The **Kinetic Go Green GlassLock**, $7.99, had a neat, tight, reliable seal, good capacity, and solid performance in every test. It was heavier than the lightweight all-plastic containers, but if you are concerned about microwaving food in plastic storage containers, this is the one to choose. Downsides: The lid is washable only on the top rack of the dishwasher, and the container has a deep, tall shape, which is less preferable than a shallower, flatter shape for quick cooling, freezing, and heating.

HIGHLY RECOMMENDED	CRITERIA		TESTERS' COMMENTS

SNAPWARE
Airtight
PRICE: $7.99

	LEAKS	★★½
	ODORS	★★★
	DESIGN	★★★
	MICROWAVE	★★★
	DURABILITY	★★★

Simple snap-down lid sealed easily throughout testing. Though it allowed a few drops of water during its first submersion test, after dishwashing, seal was perfect. Flat, rectangular shape encourages quick cooling or heating and stacks easily, with lid attaching to bottom. *Since our testing, the company has changed its name from Snapware Mods (but that's all that's changed).

RECOMMENDED

LOCK & LOCK
Classic Food
Storage Container
PRICE: $7.49

	LEAKS	★★½
	ODORS	★★★
	DESIGN	★★
	MICROWAVE	★★
	DURABILITY	★★★

Sturdy, with secure seal. Performed dependably overall but leaked a few drops during first submersion test—though seal improved after dishwashing 50 times. Stained slightly more than others after microwaving chili, and has taller, deeper shape that we find less practical.

OXO
Good Grips
LockTop Container
PRICE: $7.99

	LEAKS	★★½
	ODORS	★★★
	DESIGN	★★
	MICROWAVE	★★
	DURABILITY	★★½

Instead of employing flaps, seal works by pressing down single piece of plastic trim around lid. Leaked when submerged when new, but after dishwashing 50 times, seal improved (though lid bowed, making it stiffer to seal). Stained slightly more than other containers and has taller, deeper shape than preferred.

RECOMMENDED WITH RESERVATIONS

GLADWARE
Deep Dish
PRICE: $5.97

	LEAKS	★★
	ODORS	★
	DESIGN	★★
	MICROWAVE	★
	DURABILITY	★

Performed acceptably new but became alarmingly soft in microwave. After 50 dishwasher washes, it degraded: Seal leaked profusely, chili stained, and fishy odor hung on. Best for a potluck; it's cheap and you won't care if you don't get it back.

NOT RECOMMENDED

STERILITE
Ultra-Seal
PRICE: $6.49

	LEAKS	★
	ODORS	★★★
	DESIGN	★
	MICROWAVE	★★
	DURABILITY	★

We had high hopes for this container, but seal was uneven; because lid lacked rigidity, corners leaked badly even when new. (Second new model had same flaws.) Flap popped open during drop test. Chili stained more than in other containers.

ZIPLOC
Snap 'N Seal
PRICE: $4.55 for set of 2

	LEAKS	★
	ODORS	★★★
	DESIGN	★
	MICROWAVE	★
	DURABILITY	★

Despite being roomy, felt cheap and flimsy. Extremely leaky in soup and submersion tests, both before and after 50 dishwasher cycles. Not on a par with better containers in lineup, or even with fellow "disposable" containers by Glad. Its only virtue: rock-bottom price.

RUBBERMAID
Lock-its
PRICE: $12.99

	LEAKS	★½
	ODORS	★★★
	DESIGN	½
	MICROWAVE	★
	DURABILITY	★

Usually dependable brand flopped—poorly made flap seals distorted in microwave, popping back up when pressed down, trapping us in an endless game of Whack-A-Mole. (Second model shared these flaws.) Top flew off in drop test. We like "Easy Find" lid, which sticks to bottom of container, but that was its only asset.

Storage 101

While developing recipes for this book, we wrapped dozens of casseroles; stashed countless stews and braises in the fridge overnight; and prepped, marinated, and stored all sorts of recipe components. Here's what you need to know about storing and wrapping food safely and so that it will retain its freshness.

Storing Cooked Food in the Fridge

To keep cooked food fresh, store it in an airtight storage container or zipper-lock bag or cover it tightly with plastic wrap. Or, to maximize your refrigerator space, seal a bowl with plastic wrap, then cover it with an appropriately sized plate and stack another dish on top. If you can't fit a large dish (such as a baking sheet or a Dutch oven) in your fridge, transfer the food to smaller containers. As an added bonus, this will help the food to cool faster by increasing its surface area. Never store cooked food near or below raw meat in the fridge.

How Long Will It Keep?

BEEF, PORK, AND LAMB	
Cuts and roasts	3 days
Ground meat	2 days
Defrosted	2 days
Cooked	2–3 days
Smoked ham and bacon	2 weeks once opened
POULTRY	
Parts or whole bird	2 days
Ground chicken or turkey	2 days
Defrosted	2 days
Cooked	2–3 days
FISH AND SEAFOOD	
Fresh	1–2 days
Cooked	2–3 days

Storing Raw Meat and Seafood in the Fridge

Raw meat should be refrigerated promptly after purchase in the back of the fridge where it's coldest; make sure that it is well wrapped and never stored on shelves that are above other food, especially when thawing. Fish and seafood should be stored on a bed of ice.

Storing Produce in the Fridge

In general, it's a good idea to store produce in the packaging in which it was sold. The ready-made packaging is specially designed to let out the ripening gases that cause spoilage while protecting the produce from the drying effects of the air. If you buy loose lettuce, greens, fresh herbs, berries, or mushrooms, store them in a partially open plastic bag lined with paper towels. If you wash produce before storing, be sure to dry it thoroughly; moisture promotes the growth of mold.

Stashing Food in the Freezer

For safety reasons, frozen foods should stay at 0 degrees or colder. It's best to cool food before freezing because the quicker foods freeze, the smaller the ice crystals that form. And remember to label everything you freeze with the contents and date so you don't end up with mystery soups or casseroles past their prime. To avoid defrosting big batches of stews or sauces when you want just a few servings, divide them into appropriate portions before freezing. The containers should be mostly full with about ½ inch of headroom to allow for expansion; if there's more than ½ inch of headroom in the container, place a piece of plastic wrap directly on the surface of the food to prevent freezer burn.

Freezing Individual Items

Quick-freezing individual items like chicken fingers and meatballs before storing makes it easy to grab just what you need without having to thaw the entire package. Simply freeze the items on a tray for about 1 hour, then transfer to a zipper-lock bag. Or place portions in a zipper-lock bag, press out the air so the portions do not touch, fold the bag over in the center, and freeze.

Avoid the Danger Zone

Keep in mind that within the "danger zone" of 40 to 140 degrees, bacteria double about every 20 minutes. As a general rule, food shouldn't stay in this zone for more than 2 hours (1 hour if the room temperature is over 90 degrees).

COOL ON THE COUNTER, NOT IN THE FRIDGE It might seem like a convenient shortcut to put a hot dish into the fridge to cool, but this will cause the temperature in the refrigerator to rise, potentially making it hospitable to the spread of bacteria. Always cool foods to room temperature (about 75 degrees) before transferring them to the fridge. The FDA recommends cooling foods to 70 degrees within 2 hours after cooking, and to 40 degrees within another 4 hours.

DEFROST IN THE FRIDGE Defrosting should always be done in the refrigerator, not on the counter, where bacteria can multiply rapidly. Always place food on a plate or in a bowl while defrosting to prevent any liquid it releases from coming in contact with other foods. Most food will take 24 hours to thaw fully.

REHEAT CAREFULLY When food is reheated, it should be brought through the danger zone quickly—don't let it come slowly to a simmer. Make sure that leftover sauces, soups, and casseroles reach at least 165 degrees, using an instant-read thermometer to determine when they're at the proper temperature.

Wrapping Casseroles and More

To wrap a casserole dish, large platter, or baking sheet, lay a piece of plastic wrap about twice as long as the dish on the counter, set the dish on top parallel to the plastic, then bring the edges together over the top. Lay a second piece of plastic about twice as wide as the dish on the counter, set the dish on top perpendicular to the plastic, then bring the edges together and press to seal tightly. Casseroles stored in the freezer require an added layer of protection; after wrapping the dish with plastic, wrap it again with a layer of aluminum foil; this will prevent odors in the freezer from affecting the dish.

Storing Food in a Zipper-Lock Bag

When storing food in a zipper-lock bag, be sure to press out as much air as possible before sealing the bag. To make it airtight, insert a straw into the bag, seal the bag around it, and suck out the remaining air before removing the straw and quickly sealing the bag (do not use this method with raw meat). When transferring raw meat to zipper-lock bags, it can be difficult to keep the opening from coming in contact with the meat. To guarantee a clean seal, fold back the last 2 to 3 inches of the bag into a cuff. Once the meat is in the bag, simply unfold the cuff and seal. Zipper-lock bags are also a space-saving way to store soups and sauces for the freezer: Fill the bag, seal it tightly, and freeze it flat on a baking sheet. Once frozen, the bags can be stacked or stored upright wherever there's room.

Getting to Know Your Refrigerator

Knowing the best place to store different items in the refrigerator is the best way to ensure that food will stay fresher longer. Here's what you need to know about storing food in the fridge.

Refrigerator Microclimates

We often think of our refrigerator as having a single temperature, but every refrigerator has its own microclimates, with warmer, cooler, and more humid zones. You can make this temperature variation work to your advantage by learning about the different temperature zones.

COLD ZONE: BACK, TOP TO MIDDLE The top and middle shelves at the back of the fridge are normally the coldest, with temperatures as low as 34 degrees. Meat, dairy, and produce that are not prone to chilling injury should be stored here.

MODERATE ZONE: FRONT, MIDDLE TO BOTTOM The areas at the front of the refrigerator, from the middle to the bottom shelves, are the most moderate, with temperatures above 37 degrees. Put eggs, butter, and fruits and vegetables that are sensitive to chilling injury here.

HUMID ZONE: CRISPER DRAWER Crispers provide a humid environment that helps keep produce with a high water content from shriveling and rotting. However, if the humidity is too high, water can accumulate and hasten spoilage. You can regulate humidity by adjusting the vents; the more cold air that is let in, the less humid the environment.

Track the Temperature

A thermometer will tell you if your fridge is cooling properly. Check regularly to ensure that your refrigerator is between 35 and 40 degrees. Different foods are safest at different temperatures; see the chart below for our recommendations. Our favorite thermometer is the **Maverick Cold-Chek Digital Refrigerator/Freezer Thermometer**, $19.99. Its clear digital display and simultaneous freezer/refrigerator readings earned this model a permanent spot in our cold storage.

FOOD	IDEAL TEMP
Fish and Shellfish	30 to 34 degrees
Meat and Poultry	32 to 36 degrees
Dairy Products	36 to 40 degrees
Eggs	38 to 40 degrees
Produce	40 to 45 degrees

Where to Store Produce

KEEP IN THE FRONT OF THE FRIDGE These items are sensitive to chilling injury and should be placed in the moderate zone in the front of the fridge.

Berries	**Melons**
Citrus	**Peas**
Corn on the cob	

CHILL ANYWHERE These items are not prone to chilling injury and can be stored anywhere in the fridge (including its coldest zones), provided the temperature doesn't freeze them.

Apples	**Cherries**	**Grapes**

BEST IN THE CRISPER These items do best in the humid environment of the crisper.

Artichokes	**Chiles**	**Mushrooms**
Asparagus	**Cucumbers**	**Peppers**
Beets	**Eggplant**	**Radishes**
Broccoli	**Fresh herbs**	**Scallions**
Cabbage	**Green beans**	**Summer squash**
Carrots	**Leafy greens**	**Turnips**
Cauliflower	**Leeks**	**Zucchini**
Celery	**Lettuce**	

ON THE COUNTER Some produce is sensitive to chilling injury and subject to dehydration, internal browning, and/or pitting if stored in the refrigerator.

Apricots	**Mangos**	**Pears**
Avocados*	**Nectarines**	**Pineapple**
Bananas*	**Papayas**	**Plums**
Kiwis*	**Peaches**	**Tomatoes**

Once they've reached their peak ripeness, these fruits can be stored in the refrigerator to prevent overripening, but some discoloration may occur.

Getting to Know Your Freezer

The most commonly asked question about freezers is "How long can I freeze [fill in the blank]?" From a safety standpoint, food that is frozen properly (kept at a constant temperature of 0 degrees Fahrenheit or lower) will be safe to eat for a long time. However, the quality of frozen food diminishes over time, so for the best results, we recommend eating frozen foods within one month. To extend the life of your frozen foods, keep your freezer as cold as possible and properly wrap foods for freezer storage.

Temperature

Many freezers can be too warm. Track the temperature of your freezer with an inexpensive refrigerator/freezer thermometer. According to food safety experts, your freezer should register 0 degrees Fahrenheit or colder at all times.

Air Flow

Keep foods away from the vents in the back wall and don't overpack the freezer; this allows the air to circulate more efficiently, freezing foods faster.

The Warmest Spot

The door shelves are the warmest spots in most freezers. They are good places to store frequently used items and foods less prone to spoiling, such as coffee beans, bread, butter, and nuts.

The Coldest Spot

The rear center is the coldest spot in a freezer, making it the best place to quick-freeze individual items or to store casseroles and containers of sauces while they freeze, because the foods will freeze rapidly, preventing moisture loss.

Shelf Space

Many top-mounted freezers are short on shelf space. Use portable wire cabinet shelving (available at most home goods stores) to organize your food and to maximize the air flow, ensuring a quick and thorough freeze. Clear some shelf space to quick-freeze individual items—the quicker they are frozen, the less moisture loss they will suffer when defrosted.

10 Things You Didn't Know You Could Freeze

The freezer is not just for stashing casseroles—some of the staples in your pantry or refrigerator can be better preserved in the freezer. Here are some of the surprising items we store in the test kitchen freezer.

Bacon	To make it easy to grab just a couple of slices, we roll up individual slices of bacon and stash them in a zipper-lock freezer bag.
Bananas	Ripe or overripe frozen bananas are great to have on hand for banana bread, muffins, or fruit smoothies; just be sure to peel them before freezing.
Butter	Butter quickly picks up off-odors in the fridge, so keep it frozen and transfer it to the fridge one stick at a time. To quickly soften frozen butter, cut it into small pieces.
Buttermilk	Fill small paper cups with ½ cup of buttermilk each; place on a tray in the freezer. Once the buttermilk is frozen, wrap each cup in plastic wrap and store in a large zipper-lock freezer bag.
Cheese	Hard and semifirm cheeses like Parmesan, cheddar, and Brie can be frozen for up to two months wrapped tightly in plastic wrap and sealed in a zipper-lock freezer bag.
Citrus zest	Place grated zest in ½-teaspoon piles on a plate and freeze; transfer to a zipper-lock freezer bag.
Dry goods	Stored in the freezer, whole-grain flours, bread crumbs, coffee, cornmeal, oats, and grains are protected from humidity, bugs, and rancidity.
Egg whites	Pour leftover egg whites (never yolks) into each well of an ice cube tray and freeze.
Herbs	Place 2 tablespoons of chopped rosemary, sage, parsley, or thyme in each well of an ice cube tray with water to cover and freeze. Add frozen cubes to pan sauces, soups, or stews.
Nuts	Due to their high fat content, nuts go rancid quickly. Freeze nuts in a zipper-lock freezer bag to keep them fresh for months—and there's no need to defrost before using.

GRILLED CHICKEN KEBABS

Prep Ahead

READY-TO-COOK MEALS

Grilled Teriyaki Steak Tips

SERVES 4 TO 6 • **TO PREP** 15 MINUTES • **STORE** 1 TO 24 HOURS • **TO FINISH** 35 MINUTES

✔ **WHY THIS RECIPE WORKS:** Marinating is an easy way to transform steak that's headed for the grill, lending bold flavor, keeping the meat moist, and seasoning it throughout. Traditionally marinades contain an acidic ingredient like lemon juice or vinegar, which is thought to tenderize the meat, but we've found that more often than not acids wreak havoc on the texture of the meat, turning it spongy and discolored. Instead, a high concentration of salt in a marinade is the real key to getting flavorful, tender meat because it acts like a brine as well as a flavor booster. With this in mind, we turned to a teriyaki marinade with a base of salty soy sauce to give our grilled steak tips great flavor. Along with the soy sauce, we added a good amount of oil to help coat the meat and bloom the spices. A little sugar brought our marinade into balance and encouraged a really great char on the grill. A small amount of reserved marinade poured over the finished steak tips refreshed their flavor, and a couple of teaspoons of mirin, a sweet rice wine, added a hint of brightness. Sirloin steak tips, also known as flap meat, are sold as whole steaks, cubes, and strips. To ensure uniform pieces that cook evenly, we prefer to purchase whole steak tips and cut them ourselves. For tender, juicy steak, be sure to let the finished steak tips rest for at least 5 minutes before slicing into them. For information on setting up a single-level fire, see page 51. We prefer this steak cooked to medium, but if you prefer it more or less done, see our guidelines on page 221.

½ cup vegetable oil
⅓ cup soy sauce
⅓ cup sugar
¼ cup water
2 scallions, chopped
2 garlic cloves, minced
2 tablespoons grated fresh ginger
⅛ teaspoon red pepper flakes
2 teaspoons mirin
2 pounds sirloin steak tips, trimmed

TO PREP

1. Process oil, soy sauce, sugar, water, scallions, garlic, ginger, and pepper flakes in food processor until smooth, about 20 seconds. Transfer ¼ cup marinade to small bowl, stir in mirin, and cover.

2. Pat beef dry with paper towels, prick all over with fork, then cut into 2½-inch pieces. Add beef and remaining marinade to 1-gallon zipper-lock bag, press out air, and seal; toss to coat.

TO STORE

3. Refrigerate beef and reserved marinade separately for at least 1 hour or up to 24 hours, flipping bag occasionally to ensure beef marinates evenly.

TO FINISH AND SERVE

4. Remove reserved marinade from refrigerator and bring to room temperature while cooking beef.

5. Pat beef dry with paper towels. Place beef over hot, single-level fire. Grill (covered if using gas), turning as needed, until beef is well browned on all sides and charred at edges and registers 130 to 135 degrees (for medium), 8 to 10 minutes.

6. Transfer beef to serving platter. Stir reserved marinade to recombine, then drizzle over beef. Tent loosely with aluminum foil and let rest for 5 to 10 minutes. Serve.

MAKE A DOUBLE-DUTY MARINADE
To streamline our teriyaki steak tips, we make a bold marinade to flavor the meat overnight and reserve some to make a sauce for the second day. A food processor makes quick work of the marinade, and pricking the steak tips all over with a fork helps them to soak up the flavor. Adding some mirin to the reserved marinade makes a bright, balanced sauce for serving.

Spice-Rubbed Flank Steak with Toasted Corn and Black Bean Salad

SERVES 4 • **TO PREP** 25 MINUTES • **STORE** 1 TO 24 HOURS • **TO FINISH** 30 MINUTES

✓ **WHY THIS RECIPE WORKS:** The big beefy flavor of flank steak is well suited to the grill, but to keep this recipe convenient for a weeknight, we set out to find a method for bringing it indoors with equally flavorful results. Broiling gave us a nicely browned crust, but it overcooked the meat. Roasting allowed us to turn out a perfect medium-rare steak, but it never developed a flavorful crust. In our search for the perfect sear, we browned the steak on the stovetop, then moved it to the oven to roast. To enhance the flavor of the steak, we wanted a spice rub that developed flavor as it sat overnight; a combination of chili powder, cumin, coriander, cinnamon, and red pepper flakes added just the right amount of heat and complexity. A bright black bean and corn salad complemented the steak. To bring out its sweet flavor, we browned the corn in the skillet while the steak rested. Be sure to use fresh corn here; canned or frozen corn will not brown well. For a spicier salad, use the larger amount of chipotle. We prefer this steak cooked to medium-rare, but if you prefer it more or less done, see our guidelines on page 221.

1½ teaspoons chili powder
1½ teaspoons ground cumin
1½ teaspoons packed dark brown sugar
¾ teaspoon ground coriander
  Salt and pepper
  Pinch ground cinnamon
  Pinch red pepper flakes
1 (1½- to 2-pound) flank steak, trimmed
2 tablespoons vegetable oil
2 tablespoons lime juice
2 scallions, sliced thin
1–2 teaspoons minced canned chipotle chile in adobo sauce
1 (15-ounce) can black beans, rinsed
1 red bell pepper, stemmed, seeded, and chopped fine
¼ cup minced fresh cilantro
3 ears corn, kernels cut from cobs

TO FINISH AND SERVE
4 teaspoons vegetable oil

TO PREP

1. Combine chili powder, cumin, sugar, coriander, ½ teaspoon salt, ½ teaspoon pepper, cinnamon, and pepper flakes. Rub steak with spice mixture; wrap tightly with plastic wrap.

2. Whisk oil, lime juice, scallions, and chipotle together in large bowl. Stir in beans, bell pepper, and cilantro; cover.

TO STORE

3. Refrigerate steak, bean mixture, and corn kernels separately for at least 1 hour or up to 24 hours.

TO FINISH AND SERVE

4. Remove black bean mixture from refrigerator and bring to room temperature while preparing steak. Adjust oven rack to middle position and heat oven to 450 degrees.

5. Pat steak dry with paper towels. Heat 1 tablespoon oil in 12-inch ovensafe skillet over medium-high heat until just smoking. Place steak in skillet and cook until well browned on first side, 3 to 4 minutes. Flip steak, transfer skillet to oven, and roast until steak is browned on second side and registers 125 degrees (for medium-rare), 4 to 5 minutes.

6. Carefully remove skillet from oven (skillet handle will be hot). Transfer steak to carving board, tent loosely with aluminum foil, and let rest for 5 to 10 minutes. Being careful of hot skillet handle, wipe out skillet using paper towels, then add remaining 1 teaspoon oil and heat over medium heat until shimmering. Add corn and cook, without stirring, until well browned and toasted, 5 to 7 minutes.

7. Stir toasted corn into bean mixture and season with salt and pepper to taste. Slice steak thin against grain and serve with corn and bean salad.

Grilled Beef Kebabs

SERVES 4 TO 6 • **TO PREP** 25 MINUTES • **STORE** 1 TO 24 HOURS • **TO FINISH** 35 MINUTES

✓ **WHY THIS RECIPE WORKS:** Juicy beef and fresh vegetable kebabs grilled to perfection make great summer fare. The problem is that they take quite a bit of time to put together, from cutting up the meat and vegetables to a lengthy marinade. Make-ahead beef kebabs seemed like the perfect solution. Trimming and cutting all the meat and vegetables then refrigerating them overnight didn't affect the finished product, and sitting overnight in the marinade gave the kebabs time to absorb as much flavor as possible. We turned to the food processor to make quick work of the marinade, combining soy sauce, Worcestershire sauce, garlic, brown sugar, and chives for an easy steak sauce that packed a lot of flavor. Kebabs cook in minutes on the grill, and while the red bell pepper softened in the time it took for the beef to cook through, the red onion pieces still tasted raw. Microwaving the red onion with oil before skewering proved to be the best solution; the microwave parcooked the onion so that after a short stint on the grill, it was tender and charred. To finish, we reserved ¼ cup of the marinade to pour over the kebabs to give them a bright hit of flavor. You will need eight 12-inch metal skewers for this recipe. For information on cutting up an onion for kebabs, see page 44. For information on setting up a single-level fire, see page 51. We prefer the beef cooked to medium, but if you prefer it more or less done, see our guidelines on page 221.

½	**cup soy sauce**
⅓	**cup plus 1 tablespoon extra-virgin olive oil**
¼	**cup Worcestershire sauce**
2	**tablespoons packed dark brown sugar**
2	**tablespoons minced fresh chives**
4	**garlic cloves, minced**
1½	**teaspoons pepper**
1	**large red onion, halved through root end, core discarded, each half cut into 4 wedges and each wedge cut crosswise into thirds**
2	**pounds blade steaks, trimmed and cut into 1½-inch pieces**
2	**red bell peppers, stemmed, seeded, and cut into 1-inch pieces**

TO PREP

1. Process soy sauce, ⅓ cup oil, Worcestershire, sugar, chives, garlic, and pepper in food processor until smooth, about 20 seconds. Transfer ¼ cup marinade to bowl; cover.

2. Gently toss onion pieces with remaining 1 tablespoon oil in separate bowl. Microwave, covered, until just tender, 3 to 5 minutes. Thread beef, onion, and bell peppers evenly onto eight 12-inch metal skewers. Arrange skewers in 13 by 9-inch baking dish, pour remaining marinade over top, and turn to coat; cover.

TO STORE

3. Refrigerate kebabs and reserved marinade separately for at least 1 hour or up to 24 hours, turning kebabs occasionally to coat evenly.

TO FINISH AND SERVE

4. Remove reserved marinade from refrigerator and bring to room temperature while preparing kebabs. Pat kebabs dry with paper towels. Place kebabs over medium, single-level fire. Grill (covered if using gas), turning often, until kebabs are well browned on all sides and beef registers 130 to 135 degrees (for medium), 8 to 12 minutes.

5. Transfer kebabs to serving platter. Stir reserved marinade to recombine, then drizzle over kebabs. Tent loosely with aluminum foil and let rest for 5 to 10 minutes. Serve.

TEST KITCHEN TIP **TRIMMING BLADE STEAKS**

Halve each steak lengthwise, leaving gristle on one half. Then, cut away gristle from half to which it is still attached.

All-American Meatloaf

SERVES 6 TO 8 • **TO PREP** 35 MINUTES • **STORE** UP TO 24 HOURS • **TO FINISH** 1 HOUR 40 MINUTES

✓ **WHY THIS RECIPE WORKS:** There is something comforting about having a meatloaf ready to go into the oven after a long day. But assembling a good meatloaf is more than throwing ingredients together; it requires getting out a skillet to sauté aromatics, making a panade, and assembling all of the ingredients. We wanted to do all of the work ahead of time so that we simply had to bake the meatloaf hands-off on day two. To create a rich and meaty meatloaf, we found that meatloaf mix was the right combination of juicy, tender meat and assertive beef flavor. We flavored our meatloaf with traditional seasonings: salt, pepper, Dijon mustard, Worcestershire sauce, thyme, parsley, sautéed onion, and garlic. Combining the mix-ins before adding the meat gave the loaf the most cohesive, tender structure. Next we needed to select the right binders; we settled on a panade of milk and saltines along with two eggs; this mixture added moisture, a nice texture, and did not suffer from a night in the fridge. When you are ready for dinner, all you have to do is shape, glaze, and bake the loaf for a hearty and satisfying dinner. For easy cleanup, we baked the loaf on a sheet of aluminum foil. Poking holes in the foil and placing it on a wire rack set in a rimmed baking sheet allowed excess grease to drain away as the loaf baked. If you are using round saltines, use 19 instead of 17. Place the saltines in a zipper-lock bag and use a rolling pin to crush them. Meatloaf mix is a prepackaged mix of ground beef, pork, and veal; if it's unavailable, use 1 pound each of ground pork and 85 percent lean ground beef. If you prefer, the meatloaf can be formed on day two.

½   cup ketchup
¼   cup packed light brown sugar
4   teaspoons cider vinegar
1   tablespoon vegetable oil
1   onion, chopped fine
2   garlic cloves, minced
2   teaspoons minced fresh thyme or
    ½ teaspoon dried
½   cup milk
17 square saltines, crushed (⅔ cup)
⅓   cup minced fresh parsley
2   large eggs, lightly beaten
2   teaspoons Dijon mustard
2   teaspoons Worcestershire sauce
1   teaspoon salt
½   teaspoon pepper
¼   teaspoon hot sauce
2   pounds meatloaf mix

TO PREP

1. Fold sheet of heavy-duty aluminum foil to form 10 by 6-inch rectangle. Center foil on wire rack set in rimmed baking sheet. Poke holes in foil with skewer (about ½ inch apart). Spray foil with vegetable oil spray. Combine ketchup, sugar, and vinegar in bowl; cover.

2. Heat oil in 8-inch skillet over medium heat until shimmering. Add onion and cook until softened, about 5 minutes. Stir in garlic and thyme and cook until fragrant, about 30 seconds; transfer to large bowl and let cool slightly.

3. Add milk and saltines to cooled onion mixture and mash with fork until chunky paste forms. Stir in parsley, eggs, mustard, Worcestershire, salt, pepper, and hot sauce until combined. Add meatloaf mix and knead with hands until thoroughly combined. Transfer meat mixture to foil rectangle and shape into 9 by 5-inch loaf using wet hands; cover.

TO STORE

4. Refrigerate glaze and meatloaf separately for up to 24 hours.

TO FINISH AND SERVE

5. Adjust oven rack to middle position and heat oven to 350 degrees. Brush top and sides of meatloaf with half of glaze and bake for 1 hour.

6. Brush loaf with remaining glaze and bake until it registers 160 degrees, 20 to 30 minutes. Let cool for 20 minutes before slicing and serving.

ALL ABOUT Infusing Meat with Flavor

For recipes with short cooking times or hands-off cooking methods, often the prep work is the most time-consuming part. In this chapter, you'll find a variety of recipes designed to be prepped and assembled up to a day ahead of time so that the next day you can pull dinner from the fridge and pop it straight into the oven or into a hot skillet. And because we knew these recipes would be stashed in the fridge overnight, we developed marinades and salt and spice rubs that would infuse the meat with great flavor while we went about our day. We also learned a few important tips to ensure that our marinades and spice rubs were as successful as possible.

The Benefits of Salting Meat

Salting certainly enhances flavor, but more importantly, it helps proteins retain their natural juices. When salt is applied to raw meat, it draws the juices inside the meat to the surface. The salt then dissolves in the exuded liquid, forming a brine that is reabsorbed by the meat. Once absorbed, the salt changes the structure of the muscle proteins, allowing them to hold on to more of their natural juices when cooked. If the salt has been combined with seasonings, such as in a rub, they are also absorbed by the meat and help to add even deeper flavor. Normally the downside of salting is that it requires a long resting time, but this worked to our advantage for our prep-ahead recipes.

Spice Rub Success

In our testing, the most successful rubs were those that were allowed to sit on the meat overnight. Rubs that were rubbed on the meat immediately before cooking tasted raw and harsh because there was little time for the spices to penetrate and flavor the meat. But during an overnight rest, the flavors of the seasonings melded and became complex, and the salt in the rub helped to draw the flavors of the spices and dried herbs into the meat as it sat, seasoning and flavoring the meat throughout. We also found that wrapping the meat tightly with plastic wrap helped the spices to absorb.

Getting the Most from Your Marinade

Traditionally marinades contain an acidic ingredient like citrus juice or vinegar, which is thought to tenderize the meat, but we've found that more often than not acids wreak havoc on the texture of the meat, turning it spongy—especially if the meat is left to soak for hours. Our solution? We remove the acid from the marinade and instead spike our marinade with salt—essentially making a flavorful brine, which both seasons and tenderizes the meat while it adds flavor. To streamline our recipes, we reserve some of the marinade before adding the meat, then we brighten the reserved marinade with lemon juice or fresh herbs and use it as a sauce once the meat comes off the grill or out of the oven.

Flip and Toss

For marinades to be successful, they need to stay in constant contact with the meat. We find the best way to ensure that the meat gets marinated evenly is to place the meat and marinade in a zipper-lock bag with as much air as possible squeezed out, then flip or gently toss the bag occasionally during the soaking time to ensure that the meat is thoroughly coated.

Dinner's in the Bag

Another way we have found to infuse meat with flavor is by cooking it *en papillote*, or in a pouch, which allows the meat to steam in its own juices, infusing it with flavor. This classic French technique works best for quick-cooking, delicate cuts such as fish or boneless, skinless chicken breasts. While parchment is typically used, we find aluminum foil easier to work with. Here's how to make a tidy foil packet that can be refrigerated for up to 24 hours.

1. Spray center of sheet of heavy-duty aluminum foil with vegetable oil spray. Arrange ingredients in center of foil. Bring short sides of foil together and crimp edges to seal.

2. Crimp open edges at either end of packet together to seal, leaving as much headroom as possible.

Lamb Kofte

SERVES 4 TO 6 • **TO PREP** 30 MINUTES • **STORE** 1 TO 24 HOURS • **TO FINISH** 25 MINUTES

✓ **WHY THIS RECIPE WORKS:** In the Middle East, kebabs called *kofte* are a go-to warm-weather grilling recipe that features ground lamb mixed with lots of warm spices and fresh herbs. The seasoned meat is shaped into logs, skewered, and refrigerated for up to a day to develop the flavors. This refrigerated resting period makes grilling easier, as it helps the meat to firm up and stick to the skewer—instead of the cooking grate. We loved the nuanced flavors of the traditional blend of spices, but swapping out a handful of spices for garam masala helped to streamline our recipe without sacrificing the overall flavor. Pine nuts are a typical addition: They lend great flavor and keep the kofte from becoming overly tough or springy. Traditionally a panade is used to help keep the small patties moist, but we found that it imparted a pasty texture and muted the flavor of the lamb and seasonings. Swapping it for a small amount of gelatin worked wonders; since gelatin holds up to 10 times its weight in water, the juices released during cooking were simply reabsorbed, giving us tender, juicy kofte. For the serving sauce, we stuck to the traditional combination of lemon, garlic, and yogurt but added a couple of tablespoons of tahini to give the sauce a deeper flavor profile. You will need eight 12-inch metal skewers for this recipe. For information on setting up a concentrated fire, see page 51. If grilling over charcoal, you will need a 13 by 9-inch disposable aluminum roasting pan. Serve with rice pilaf or make sandwiches with warm pita bread, sliced red onion, and chopped fresh mint.

YOGURT-GARLIC SAUCE
- 1 **cup plain whole-milk yogurt**
- 2 **tablespoons lemon juice**
- 2 **tablespoons tahini**
- 1 **garlic clove, minced**
- ½ **teaspoon salt**

KOFTE
- ½ **cup pine nuts**
- 4 **garlic cloves, peeled**
- 2 **teaspoons garam masala**
- 1½ **teaspoons hot smoked paprika**
- 1 **teaspoon salt**
- ½ **teaspoon pepper**
- 1½ **pounds ground lamb**
- ½ **cup grated onion, drained**
- ⅓ **cup minced fresh mint**
- ⅓ **cup minced fresh parsley**
- 1½ **teaspoons unflavored gelatin**

TO PREP
1. FOR THE YOGURT-GARLIC SAUCE: Whisk all ingredients together in bowl; cover.

2. FOR THE KOFTE: Process pine nuts, garlic, garam masala, paprika, salt, and pepper in food processor until coarse paste forms, 30 to 45 seconds. Transfer mixture to large bowl. Add lamb, onion, mint, parsley, and gelatin and knead with hands until thoroughly combined and mixture feels slightly sticky, about 2 minutes. Divide mixture into 8 equal portions. Shape each portion into 5-inch-long cylinder about 1 inch in diameter. Using eight 12-inch metal skewers, thread 1 cylinder onto each skewer, pressing gently to adhere, then transfer to lightly greased rimmed baking sheet; cover.

TO STORE
3. Refrigerate yogurt-garlic sauce and skewers separately for at least 1 hour or up to 24 hours.

TO FINISH AND SERVE
4A. FOR A BROILER: Adjust oven rack 8 inches from broiler element and heat broiler. Set wire rack in clean, aluminum foil–lined rimmed baking sheet and spray with vegetable oil spray. Arrange skewers evenly on prepared rack. Broil until browned and meat registers 160 degrees, 15 to 20 minutes, turning skewers halfway through broiling.

4B. FOR A GRILL: Place skewers over hot, concentrated fire (directly over coals if using charcoal) at 45-degree angle to bars. Cook (covered if using gas) until browned on first side and meat easily releases from grill, 4 to 7 minutes. Flip skewers and continue to cook until browned on second side and meat registers 160 degrees, about 6 minutes.

5. Transfer skewers to serving platter and serve, passing yogurt-garlic sauce separately.

KEEPING KOFTE MOIST
The panade that's traditionally used to keep lamb kofte moist gave the meat a pasty texture and dull flavor when stored overnight. Our solution was to knead some gelatin into the meat mixture; as the kofte cooked, the gelatin reabsorbed the meat's juices, keeping the meat moist and tender. A creamy yogurt-garlic sauce was a cool counterpoint to the juicy lamb.

Provençal Pork Tenderloin with Apples and Shallots

SERVES 4 TO 6 • **TO PREP** 10 MINUTES • **STORE** 1 TO 24 HOURS • **TO FINISH** 50 MINUTES

✔ **WHY THIS RECIPE WORKS:** Pork tenderloins are a great weeknight dinner option because they are endlessly variable and quick-cooking. Our prep-ahead version pairs the pork with a fragrant herb rub and roasted apples and shallots. We started by rubbing the tenderloins with herbes de Provence and letting them sit overnight. Herbes de Provence provided a nice blend of flavors. Crumbling it helped it to coat the pork more evenly. The hearty combination of apples and shallots nicely complemented the rich pork. With the flavors established, we turned to the cooking method. While roasting the tenderloins seemed like the easiest method, we were unable to produce the juicy, well-browned, and flavorful meat we were looking for. We moved the pork to a skillet, seared it all over, then transferred it to a plate while we browned the apples and shallots in the same pan, flavoring them with the fond from the pork. Then we nestled the browned pork into the apples and shallots to finish cooking gently in the oven. While the pork rested, we added butter to the apples and shallots for some extra richness. You can find herbes de Provence in most large grocery stores; however, 1 teaspoon each of dried thyme, dried rosemary, and dried marjoram can be substituted.

2 **(1-pound) pork tenderloins, trimmed**
1 **tablespoon herbes de Provence, crumbled**
   Salt and pepper
6 **shallots, sliced ½ inch thick**
3 **Golden Delicious apples, peeled, cored, and cut into ½-inch-thick wedges**
2 **tablespoons vegetable oil**
½ **teaspoon sugar**

TO FINISH AND SERVE
2 **tablespoons vegetable oil**
1 **tablespoon unsalted butter**

TO PREP

1. Season pork with herbes de Provence, salt, and pepper; wrap tightly with plastic wrap.

2. Place shallots, apples, oil, and sugar in 1-gallon zipper-lock bag, press out air, and seal; toss to coat.

TO STORE

3. Refrigerate pork and apple mixture separately for at least 1 hour or up to 24 hours.

TO FINISH AND SERVE

4. Adjust oven rack to lowest position and heat oven to 350 degrees. Pat pork dry with paper towels. Heat oil in 12-inch ovensafe skillet over medium-high heat until just smoking. Place both tenderloins in skillet, spaced at least 1 inch apart, and cook until well browned on all sides, 8 to 10 minutes; transfer to plate.

5. Add apple mixture to now-empty skillet, discarding any excess liquid. Cook, stirring occasionally, until shallots and apples begin to soften and are lightly browned, 10 to 12 minutes.

6. Off heat, nestle tenderloins into apple mixture side by side, alternating thicker end to thinner end, along with any accumulated juices. Transfer skillet to oven and roast pork until it registers 145 degrees, 15 to 20 minutes.

7. Carefully remove skillet from oven (skillet handle will be hot). Transfer pork to carving board, tent loosely with aluminum foil, and let rest for 5 to 10 minutes. Stir butter into apple mixture, season with salt and pepper to taste, and cover to keep warm. Slice pork into ½-inch-thick slices and serve with apple mixture.

Roasted Spice-Stuffed Pork Loin

SERVES 6 • **TO PREP** 30 MINUTES • **STORE** 1 TO 24 HOURS • **TO FINISH** 1 HOUR 20 MINUTES

✓ **WHY THIS RECIPE WORKS:** A roast pork loin can be a delicious dinner, but not if it comes out of the oven with so-so flavor and dry, tough meat. Salting the roast and letting it rest overnight gave the roast a flavorful crust and seasoned it throughout so it came out of the oven juicy and tender. To add even more flavor to our roast, we butterflied the loin and applied a spice rub to the inside before rolling it back up and rubbing the outside with our salt rub. This gave our meat bold flavor throughout, plus we were able to use the same flavors to make a quick pan sauce. After searing the roast in a skillet, we added maple syrup and more of the warm spices to the pan to make a flavorful glaze to coat the pork as it roasted. Finally, while the pork rested, we added a little chicken broth and vinegar to the glaze to make a luscious sauce to serve alongside our pork.

2 tablespoons packed brown sugar
  Salt and pepper
1 tablespoon vegetable oil
1 tablespoon paprika
¾ teaspoon cinnamon
  Cayenne pepper
1 (2½- to 3-pound) boneless pork loin roast, trimmed
⅓ cup maple syrup

TO FINISH AND SERVE
1 tablespoon vegetable oil
⅓ cup chicken broth
1 teaspoon cider vinegar

TO PREP

1. Combine sugar, 2 teaspoons salt, and 1½ teaspoons pepper in bowl; set aside. Microwave oil, paprika, 1 teaspoon salt, ¼ teaspoon cinnamon, and pinch cayenne in separate bowl until fragrant, about 30 seconds; let cool slightly.

2. With roast fat side up, cut horizontally through meat, one-third of way up from bottom, stopping ½ inch from edge. Open roast and press flat; 1 side will be twice as thick. Continue cutting thicker side of roast in half, stopping ½ inch from edge; open roast and press flat.

3. Rub cooled oil mixture on cut surface of meat, leaving ½-inch border on all sides. Starting from short side, roll roast into tight cylinder and tie with kitchen twine at 1-inch intervals. Rub tied roast with sugar mixture; wrap tightly with plastic wrap.

4. Combine maple syrup, remaining ½ teaspoon cinnamon, and pinch cayenne in small bowl; cover.

TO STORE

5. Refrigerate pork and maple syrup mixture separately for at least 1 hour or up to 24 hours.

TO FINISH AND SERVE

6. Adjust oven rack to lower-middle position and heat oven to 325 degrees. Pat pork dry with paper towels. Heat oil in 12-inch ovensafe skillet over medium-high heat until just smoking. Brown roast on all sides, about 6 minutes; transfer to plate. Pour off fat from skillet.

7. Add maple syrup mixture to now-empty skillet, return to medium heat, and cook, scraping up any browned bits, until fragrant, about 1 minute. Off heat, return roast to skillet along with any accumulated juices and turn to coat evenly with glaze. Turn roast fat side up, transfer skillet to oven, and roast pork until it registers 140 degrees, 45 to 60 minutes, turning roast to coat evenly with glaze twice during roasting.

8. Carefully remove skillet from oven (skillet handle will be hot). Transfer pork to carving board, tent loosely with aluminum foil, and let rest for 15 to 20 minutes. Meanwhile, being careful of hot skillet handle, skim foam from surface of pan juices using large spoon. Transfer skillet to stovetop, whisk in broth and vinegar, and bring to simmer over medium heat. Cook, whisking often, until slightly thickened, about 3 minutes. Season with salt and pepper to taste. Discard twine, then slice pork into ½-inch-thick slices. Serve with glaze.

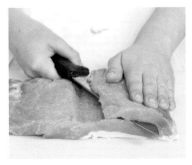

BUTTERFLY THE ROAST
To give our roast pork loin bold flavor throughout, we used a spice rub to impart flavor as it sat overnight. Butterflying the roast by making two horizontal cuts into the meat gave us a larger surface area for the rub, ensuring that we got some spice in every bite. Then we rolled up and tied the loin so that when we carved the roast, we had an attractive spice swirl.

Roasted Pork Loin with Potatoes and Mustard Sauce

SERVES 6 • **TO PREP** 25 MINUTES • **STORE** 1 TO 24 HOURS • **TO FINISH** 1 HOUR 20 MINUTES

✅ **WHY THIS RECIPE WORKS:** For our prep-ahead pork loin dinner, we wanted a make-ahead savory rub, an easy side dish, and a fragrant sauce. We rubbed our meat with savory spices and salt to infuse it with flavor as it sat overnight, and then we gently roasted the pork at a low temperature to keep it from drying out. This gave us tender, juicy pork, but we were looking for a crisper crust. Broiling the pork for just 5 minutes added the nicely browned exterior that we were missing. To round out our meal, we wanted an accompaniment that could hold up to being stored overnight and bake alongside the pork. Small red potatoes seemed like a good choice since we could roast them along with the pork in the same amount of time. To lend them some additional flavor, we tossed them with bacon pieces before storing them overnight. To prevent the potatoes from oxidizing as they sat, we added some oil to the bag as well. A quick mustard vinaigrette was an easy finishing touch. Use small red potatoes measuring 1 to 2 inches in diameter.

1½	teaspoons granulated garlic
1½	teaspoons dried oregano
1½	teaspoons ground coriander
1½	teaspoons ground cumin
	Salt and pepper
1	(2½- to 3-pound) boneless pork loin roast, trimmed
2½	pounds small red potatoes, unpeeled, halved
4	slices bacon, cut into ½-inch pieces
6	tablespoons extra-virgin olive oil
¼	cup minced fresh parsley
1	shallot, minced
2	tablespoons whole-grain mustard
1½	tablespoons white wine vinegar
	Pinch sugar

TO FINISH AND SERVE

1 tablespoon extra-virgin olive oil

TO PREP

1. Combine garlic, oregano, coriander, cumin, ½ teaspoon salt, and ½ teaspoon pepper. Rub pork with spice mixture; wrap tightly with plastic wrap.

2. Place potatoes, bacon, and 2 tablespoons oil in 1-gallon zipper-lock bag, press out air, and seal; toss to coat.

3. Combine remaining ¼ cup oil, parsley, shallot, mustard, vinegar, and sugar in bowl; cover.

TO STORE

4. Refrigerate pork, potatoes, and dressing separately for at least 1 hour or up to 24 hours.

TO FINISH AND SERVE

5. Remove vinaigrette from refrigerator and bring to room temperature while preparing pork. Adjust oven rack to upper-middle position and heat oven to 325 degrees. Line rimmed baking sheet with aluminum foil and brush with oil. Pat pork dry with paper towels and place fat side up in center of prepared sheet. Place bacon and potatoes, cut side down, on sheet around roast, discarding any excess liquid. Season potatoes with salt and pepper.

6. Roast pork and potatoes until pork registers 130 degrees, 40 to 60 minutes, rotating sheet halfway through roasting. Remove pork and potatoes from oven, adjust oven rack 6 inches from broiler element, and heat broiler. Broil pork and potatoes until pork is spotty brown and registers 140 degrees, 3 to 5 minutes.

7. Transfer pork to carving board, tent loosely with foil, and let rest for 15 to 20 minutes. Return potatoes to oven and continue to broil until lightly browned, 5 to 10 minutes. Slice pork into ½-inch-thick slices. Whisk dressing to recombine and serve with pork and potatoes.

Crispy Pan-Fried Pork Chops

SERVES 4 • **TO PREP** 25 MINUTES • **STORE** 1 TO 24 HOURS • **TO FINISH** 30 MINUTES

✓ **WHY THIS RECIPE WORKS:** Crispy pan-fried pork chops are delicious but time-consuming to make; usually they are coated first in flour, then in egg, then in bread crumbs before being pan-fried. We wanted to do all the prep work ahead so we could simply drop the pork chops into a hot skillet the next day, but when we tried to store the breaded chops overnight, the breading turned soggy and limp as the flour and bread crumbs absorbed moisture from the meat and the egg. Switching to cornstarch helped to lighten and crisp our coating. To help the coating stick, we swapped the egg for buttermilk, which created a tacky layer that more effectively bound the crust to the chops. For added insurance, we made shallow cuts in the chops to release juices and sticky meat proteins, further encouraging the coating to adhere. Bread crumbs also absorb moisture quickly, so we swapped them for crushed corn flakes; tossed with additional cornstarch, they stayed crisp even after sitting overnight in the refrigerator. You can substitute 1 cup of store-bought cornflake crumbs for the whole cornflakes; omit the processing step and mix the crumbs with the cornstarch, salt, and pepper.

- ⅔ **cup cornstarch**
- 1 **cup buttermilk**
- 2 **tablespoons Dijon mustard**
- 1 **garlic clove, minced**
- 4 **cups (4 ounces) cornflakes**
  Salt and pepper
- 8 **(3- to 4-ounce) boneless pork chops,**
  ½ to ¾ inch thick, trimmed

TO FINISH AND SERVE
- ⅔ **cup vegetable oil**
  Lemon wedges

TO PREP

1. Place ⅓ cup cornstarch in shallow dish. In second shallow dish, whisk buttermilk, mustard, and garlic together until combined. Process cornflakes, ½ teaspoon salt, ½ teaspoon pepper, and remaining ⅓ cup cornstarch in food processor until cornflakes are finely ground, about 10 seconds; transfer mixture to third shallow dish.

2. Pat chops dry with paper towels. Using sharp knife, cut 1/16-inch-deep slits on both sides of chops, spaced ½ inch apart, in crosshatch pattern. Season chops with salt and pepper. Working with 1 chop at a time, dredge in cornstarch, dip in buttermilk mixture, then coat with cornflake mixture, pressing gently to adhere. Transfer coated chop to large platter.

TO STORE

3. Cover and refrigerate chops for at least 1 hour or up to 24 hours.

TO FINISH AND SERVE

4. Adjust oven rack to middle position and heat oven to 200 degrees. Set wire rack in rimmed baking sheet and line large plate with triple layer of paper towels. Heat ⅓ cup oil in 12-inch nonstick skillet over medium-high heat until shimmering. Place 4 chops in skillet and cook until golden brown and crispy, 2 to 5 minutes.

5. Carefully flip chops and continue to cook until second side is golden brown and crispy and pork registers 145 degrees, 2 to 5 minutes. Transfer chops to paper towel–lined plate and let drain for 30 seconds on each side.

6. Transfer drained chops to prepared rack, then transfer to oven to keep warm. Discard oil in skillet and wipe clean with paper towels. Repeat with remaining ⅓ cup oil and remaining chops. Serve with lemon wedges.

TEST KITCHEN TIP **SCORING PORK CHOPS**

Using sharp knife, cut ½-inch-wide crosshatch pattern on both sides of each pork chop, about 1/16 inch deep.

Roasted Cornish Game Hens

SERVES 4 • **TO PREP** 25 MINUTES • **STORE** 4 TO 24 HOURS • **TO FINISH** 35 MINUTES

✔ **WHY THIS RECIPE WORKS:** Cornish game hens provide crisp skin and delicate meat and are an elegant alternative to chicken. Cornish game hens do present one significant challenge: By the time the skin is crisp and golden, the meat is dry and overcooked, and while brining encourages juicy meat, the added moisture prevents the skin from ever getting crisp. Our solution was to use a dry brining technique; this involved applying a salt rub on the skin and letting the meat rest to draw moisture from the surface of the hens to the meat inside. Adding some baking powder to the rub further dehydrated the skin, and poking holes in the fat on the breasts and thighs helped the fat to render. These hens came out moist and juicy, but even when we baked them in a hot oven on a preheated baking sheet, the skin still didn't get crisp. Typically we look to the broiler to achieve browning in a flash, but because of the hens' irregular shape, the broiler gave us uneven results. Instead, we decided to remove the backbone of the birds and press them flat, creating an even surface for the broiler to brown and crisp. After a brief 10 minutes in a hot oven, we turned on the broiler, and in 5 minutes more we had perfectly juicy hens with crisp, golden-brown skin. Our preferred brand of game hen is Bell and Evans. If your hens weigh 1½ to 2 pounds, cook three instead of four, and extend the initial cooking time in step 5 to 15 minutes.

4   (1¼- to 1½-pound) Cornish game hens, giblets discarded
    Kosher salt and pepper
¼   teaspoon vegetable oil
1   teaspoon baking powder

TO FINISH AND SERVE
1   tablespoon vegetable oil
    Pepper

TO PREP

1. Working with 1 hen at a time, use poultry shears to cut through bones on either side of backbone; discard backbone. Lay hen skin side up and flatten by pressing firmly on breastbone. Using sharp chef's knife, cut through center of breast to make 2 halves.

2. Combine 1 tablespoon salt and oil in small bowl and stir until salt is evenly coated with oil. Stir in baking powder until thoroughly combined. Pat hens dry with paper towels. Using fingers, carefully separate skin from breast and thighs. Using metal skewer or tip of paring knife, poke 10 to 15 holes in fat deposits on top of breast halves and thighs. Tuck wingtips underneath hens.

3. Sprinkle 1 tablespoon salt on underside (bone side) of hens. Turn hens skin side up and rub salt–baking powder mixture evenly over surface. Transfer hens, skin side up, to wire rack set in rimmed baking sheet.

TO STORE

4. Refrigerate hens, uncovered, for at least 4 hours or up to 24 hours.

TO FINISH AND SERVE

5. Adjust oven racks to upper-middle and lowest positions, place clean rimmed baking sheet on lower rack, and heat oven to 500 degrees. Brush skin of hens with oil and season with pepper. Carefully transfer hens, skin side down, to hot sheet and bake for 10 minutes.

6. Remove hens from oven and heat broiler. While broiler heats, flip hens skin side up. Transfer baking sheet with hens to upper rack and broil until well browned and breasts register 160 degrees and thighs register 175 degrees, about 5 minutes, rotating as necessary to promote even browning. Serve.

TEST KITCHEN TIP **BUTTERFLY THE BIRD**

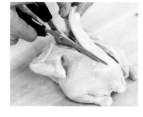
To remove backbone, use kitchen shears to cut along both sides of backbone. Then, flip bird breast side up and use heel of your hand to flatten breastbone.

Never-Fail Crispy Roast Chicken

SERVES 3 TO 4 • **TO PREP** 15 MINUTES • **STORE** 12 TO 24 HOURS • **TO FINISH** 1 HOUR 25 MINUTES

✓ **WHY THIS RECIPE WORKS:** In our minds, roast chicken is best when kept simple. Well-seasoned, juicy meat surrounded by crispy, flavorful skin is as good as it gets, but for all its simplicity, really good roast chicken is tough to get right. We've touted the benefits of brining chicken for years, but while a brined bird is guaranteed to be juicy and flavorful, it's usually at the expense of crispy skin. To overcome this challenge, we turned to a combination of salt and baking powder. A salt rub makes meat juicy in a process similar to brining, but unlike brining, it doesn't prevent the skin from crisping. And the lengthy rest that salting requires made it the perfect method for make-ahead roast chicken. Adding baking powder to the rub not only sped up the dehydration process that salting encourages (which is the cornerstone of crispy skin), it also accelerated browning during roasting, making for even crisper, more flavorful skin. Separating the skin from the meat and poking the fat deposits with a skewer allowed the rendered fat to flow freely from the roasting chicken and prevented the skin from becoming soggy. In search of the best roasting method, we found that placing the chicken breast side up in a preheated skillet gave the thighs a jump start on cooking, and turning the oven off while the chicken finished cooking slowed the evaporation of juices, ensuring moist, tender meat.

1½ **teaspoons salt**
⅛ **teaspoon vegetable oil**
1 **teaspoon baking powder**
½ **teaspoon pepper**
1 **(3½- to 4½-pound) whole chicken, giblets discarded**

TO PREP

1. Combine salt and oil in small bowl and stir until salt is evenly coated with oil. Stir in baking powder and pepper until thoroughly combined. Pat chicken dry with paper towels. Using fingers, carefully separate skin from breasts and thighs. Using metal skewer or tip of paring knife, poke 15 to 20 holes in fat deposits on top of breasts and thighs.

2. Rub salt–baking powder mixture evenly over surface of chicken. Tie legs together with twine and tuck wingtips behind back. Set chicken breast side up on wire rack set in rimmed baking sheet.

TO STORE

3. Refrigerate chicken, uncovered, for at least 12 hours or up to 24 hours.

TO FINISH AND SERVE

4. Adjust oven rack to middle position, place 12-inch ovensafe skillet on rack, and heat oven to 450 degrees. Carefully transfer chicken breast side up to preheated skillet in oven (skillet handle will be hot). Roast chicken until breasts register 120 degrees and thighs register 135 degrees, 25 to 35 minutes. Turn off oven and leave chicken in oven until breasts register 160 degrees and thighs register 175 degrees, 25 to 35 minutes.

5. Transfer chicken to carving board and let rest, uncovered, for 20 minutes. Carve chicken and serve.

TEST KITCHEN TIP LOOSENING CHICKEN SKIN

Use your fingers to carefully separate skin from breasts and thighs.

EASY TRICKS FOR CRISP SKIN
For the perfect roast chicken with shatteringly crisp skin, we needed a few tricks. To keep the meat moist, we used a salt rub instead of brining, which thwarts crisp skin by adding moisture. Mixing baking powder into the salt rub, then letting the chicken air-dry overnight further dehydrated the skin, and poking the fat deposits with a skewer helped the fat to render easily.

One-Pan Roast Chicken with Root Vegetables

SERVES 4 • TO PREP 25 MINUTES • STORE 1 TO 24 HOURS • TO FINISH 1 HOUR

✔ **WHY THIS RECIPE WORKS:** To transform classic roast chicken and vegetables into a make-ahead meal, we wanted a streamlined method that would take advantage of an overnight rest to build flavor. Tossing the chicken in oil flavored with thyme and rosemary before storing allowed it to develop deep herb flavor as it sat. To prevent the potatoes from oxidizing, we tossed them with more flavored oil and stored them in an airtight bag. To keep this dish simple enough for a weeknight, we wanted to eliminate a large cleanup by cooking the vegetables and chicken together in the same pan. Unfortunately, our first attempts produced unevenly cooked chicken and greasy, soggy vegetables. To get the chicken and vegetables to cook at the same rate, we swapped the whole chicken for chicken parts, which allowed the oven's heat to circulate to the vegetables underneath so they didn't steam in their own juices. The chicken parts also had less fat than a whole chicken, eliminating the excess grease. To ensure that the delicate white meat stayed moist while the darker meat cooked through, we placed the breasts in the center of the pan and the thighs and drumsticks around the perimeter where the heat was more intense. A similar treatment for the vegetables—leafy Brussels sprouts in the middle, hardier potatoes and carrots on the outside—also proved effective. Placing the chicken on top of the vegetables was a simple way to infuse the vegetables with savory flavor. Use Brussels sprouts no bigger than golf balls, as larger ones are often tough and woody.

12	ounces red potatoes, unpeeled, cut into 1-inch pieces
12	ounces Brussels sprouts, trimmed and halved
8	shallots, peeled and halved
4	carrots, peeled and cut into 2-inch pieces, thick ends halved lengthwise
¼	cup vegetable oil
6	garlic cloves, peeled
4	teaspoons minced fresh thyme
2	teaspoons minced fresh rosemary
3½	pounds bone-in chicken pieces (2 split breasts cut in half crosswise, 2 drumsticks, and 2 thighs), trimmed
	Salt and pepper

TO FINISH AND SERVE

1	teaspoon sugar

TO PREP

1. Place potatoes, Brussels sprouts, shallots, carrots, 2 tablespoons oil, garlic, 2 teaspoons thyme, and 1 teaspoon rosemary in 1-gallon zipper-lock bag. Press out air and seal; toss to coat.

2. Place chicken, remaining 2 tablespoons oil, remaining 2 teaspoons thyme, remaining 1 teaspoon rosemary, ¼ teaspoon salt, and ⅛ teaspoon pepper in separate 1-gallon zipper-lock bag. Press out air and seal; toss to coat.

TO STORE

3. Refrigerate chicken and vegetable mixture separately for at least 1 hour or up to 24 hours, flipping bag occasionally to ensure chicken marinates evenly.

TO FINISH AND SERVE

4. Adjust oven rack to upper-middle position and heat oven to 475 degrees. Spread vegetables in single layer in rimmed baking sheet, discarding any excess liquid and arranging Brussels sprouts in center. Season vegetables with sugar, ½ teaspoon salt, and ¼ teaspoon pepper.

5. Place chicken skin side up on top of vegetables, arranging breast pieces in center and leg and thigh pieces around perimeter of sheet. Bake chicken until breasts register 160 degrees and drumsticks and thighs register 175 degrees, 35 to 40 minutes, rotating sheet halfway through baking.

6. Transfer chicken to serving platter, tent loosely with aluminum foil, and let rest for 5 to 10 minutes. Return vegetables to oven and continue to bake until lightly browned, 5 to 10 minutes. Toss vegetables with any accumulated chicken juices and transfer to platter with chicken. Serve.

Easy Lemon–Goat Cheese Stuffed Chicken Breasts

SERVES 4 • **TO PREP** 20 MINUTES • **STORE** UP TO 24 HOURS • **TO FINISH** 1 HOUR

✔ **WHY THIS RECIPE WORKS:** It's hard to beat a juicy chicken breast stuffed with a flavorful cheesy filling. We wanted an easy make-ahead version of this classic, without the fuss of butterflying, pounding, rolling, and tying the chicken. Boneless, skinless chicken breasts were a nonstarter; they required too much knife work and didn't guarantee stellar results. Bone-in, skin-on chicken breasts, on the other hand, proved to be the right choice. To create a pocket for a dollop of our creamy, flavorful filling, all we needed to do was gently separate the skin from the meat. So far, so good—except for the flabby, inedible skin we were left with after baking. Cranking the oven up to 450 degrees solved that problem; this round of chicken baked up golden and crispy. It is important to buy chicken breasts with the skin still attached and intact or the stuffing will leak out.

4 **(12-ounce) bone-in split chicken breasts, trimmed and halved crosswise**
   Salt and pepper
3 **ounces goat cheese, softened**
2 **ounces cream cheese, softened**
2 **teaspoons minced fresh thyme**
1 **garlic clove, minced**
¼ **teaspoon grated lemon zest**
1 **tablespoon extra-virgin olive oil**

TO PREP

1. Pat chicken dry with paper towels and season with salt and pepper. Stir goat cheese, cream cheese, thyme, garlic, lemon zest, ⅛ teaspoon salt, and ⅛ teaspoon pepper together in bowl until combined.

2. Using fingers, carefully loosen center portion of skin covering each breast. Place about 1½ tablespoons filling under skin, directly on meat in center of each breast half. Brush skin with oil and transfer to large plate.

TO STORE

3. Cover and refrigerate chicken for up to 24 hours.

TO SERVE

4. Adjust oven rack to middle position and heat oven to 450 degrees. Set wire rack in aluminum foil–lined rimmed baking sheet. Place chicken skin side up on prepared rack and bake until chicken registers 160 degrees, 35 to 40 minutes. Let rest for 5 to 10 minutes. Serve.

TEST KITCHEN TIP
HALVING BONE-IN CHICKEN BREASTS

After smoothing skin to cover breast, cut breast in half until knife hits bone. To get through bone, rock knife back and forth, applying pressure from heel of your other hand, until separated.

Chicken Baked in Foil with Potatoes and Carrots

SERVES 4 • **TO PREP** 30 MINUTES • **STORE** 1 TO 24 HOURS • **TO FINISH** 40 MINUTES

✔ **WHY THIS RECIPE WORKS:** Baking food in packets, or *en papillote*, is both easy and healthy, because the steamy environment produces moist, tender results without lots of fat. And because you can prep the packets ahead of time and just pop them into the oven in time for dinner, they're a great choice for a make-ahead meal—if you can get the timing right. Our first attempts turned out overcooked chicken, mushy vegetables, and little flavor. To season the quick-cooking boneless chicken breasts throughout, we salted them before assembling the packets. Leaving some headroom in the packets allowed maximum steam circulation for even cooking, and checking the temperature of the chicken through the foil let us monitor its progress. To cook alongside the chicken, we chose hearty potatoes, carrots, and red onion. Layering the potatoes under the chicken insulated the chicken from the hot baking sheet and ensured that the potatoes turned tender in time. Garlic, fresh thyme, and a pinch of red pepper flakes gave the chicken and vegetables great flavor, and finishing the dish with chives and lemon juice added brightness. To ensure even cooking, buy chicken breasts of the same size. If using table salt, use only ⅛ teaspoon for each entire breast. For more information on making a foil packet, see page 25.

5	tablespoons extra-virgin olive oil
6	garlic cloves, sliced thin
1	teaspoon minced fresh thyme
¼	teaspoon red pepper flakes
12	ounces Yukon Gold potatoes, unpeeled, sliced ¼ inch thick
2	carrots, peeled, quartered lengthwise, and cut into 2-inch lengths
½	large red onion, sliced ½ inch thick, layers separated
	Kosher salt and pepper
4	(6-ounce) boneless, skinless chicken breasts, trimmed

TO FINISH AND SERVE

2	tablespoons lemon juice
2	tablespoons minced fresh chives

TO PREP

1. Spray centers of four 20 by 12-inch sheets of heavy-duty aluminum foil with vegetable oil spray. Microwave oil, garlic, thyme, and pepper flakes in small bowl until garlic begins to brown, 1 to 1½ minutes. Combine potatoes, carrots, onion, 1 teaspoon salt, and garlic oil in large bowl.

2. Pat chicken dry with paper towels. Sprinkle ⅛ teaspoon salt evenly on each side of each chicken breast, then season with pepper. Position 1 piece of prepared foil with long side parallel to edge of counter. In center of foil, arrange one-quarter of potato slices in 2 rows perpendicular to edge of counter. Lay 1 chicken breast on top of potato slices. Place one-quarter of vegetables around chicken. Repeat with remaining prepared foil, remaining potato slices, remaining chicken, and remaining vegetables. Drizzle any remaining oil mixture from bowl over chicken.

3. Bring short sides of foil together and crimp to seal tightly. Crimp remaining open ends of packets, leaving as much headroom as possible inside packets.

TO STORE

4. Place packets on large plate and refrigerate for at least 1 hour or up to 24 hours.

TO FINISH AND SERVE

5. Adjust oven rack to lowest position and heat oven to 475 degrees. Place packets on rimmed baking sheet and bake until chicken registers 160 degrees, 18 to 23 minutes. (To check temperature, poke thermometer through foil of 1 packet and into chicken.) Let chicken rest in packets for 3 minutes.

6. Transfer chicken packets to individual serving plates, open carefully (steam will escape), and slide contents onto plates. Drizzle lemon juice over chicken and vegetables and sprinkle with chives. Serve.

Chicken Baked in Foil with Sweet Potatoes and Radishes

SERVES 4 • **TO PREP** 30 MINUTES • **STORE** 1 TO 24 HOURS • **TO FINISH** 40 MINUTES

✔ **WHY THIS RECIPE WORKS:** For another version of our chicken baked in foil with some unconventional flavors, we combined radishes, celery, and sweet potatoes with ginger and toasted sesame oil. The hearty sweet potatoes protected the delicate chicken from the hot baking sheet and absorbed flavor from the chicken as it cooked. The crunch of celery and the bright, peppery flavor of the radishes were a nice complement to the earthy sweet potatoes. Fresh ginger punched up with spicy red pepper flakes gave the dish a bold, aromatic flavor that didn't fade in the fridge. Nutty sesame oil, sliced garlic, and red onion provided an aromatic flavor base. A couple of tablespoons of rice vinegar and cilantro added just before serving contributed brightness and a fresh flavor to round out this dish. To ensure even cooking, buy chicken breasts of the same size. If using table salt, use only ⅛ teaspoon for each entire breast. For more information on making a foil packet, see page 25.

¼ cup extra-virgin olive oil
6 garlic cloves, sliced thin
1 tablespoon grated fresh ginger
1 teaspoon toasted sesame oil
¼ teaspoon red pepper flakes
12 ounces sweet potatoes, peeled and sliced crosswise ¼ inch thick
4 radishes, trimmed and quartered
2 celery ribs, quartered lengthwise and cut into 2-inch lengths
½ large red onion, sliced ½ inch thick, layers separated
Kosher salt and pepper
4 (6-ounce) boneless, skinless chicken breasts, trimmed

TO FINISH AND SERVE
2 tablespoons rice vinegar
2 tablespoons minced fresh cilantro

TO PREP

1. Spray centers of four 20 by 12-inch sheets of heavy-duty aluminum foil with vegetable oil spray. Microwave olive oil, garlic, ginger, sesame oil, and pepper flakes in small bowl until garlic begins to brown, 1 to 1½ minutes. Combine potatoes, radishes, celery, onion, ½ teaspoon salt, and garlic oil in large bowl.

2. Pat chicken dry with paper towels. Sprinkle ⅛ teaspoon salt evenly on each side of each chicken breast, then season with pepper. Position 1 piece of prepared foil with long side parallel to edge of counter. In center of foil, arrange one-quarter of potato slices in 2 rows perpendicular to edge of counter. Lay 1 chicken breast on top of potato slices. Place one-quarter of vegetables around chicken. Repeat with remaining prepared foil, remaining potato slices, remaining chicken, and remaining vegetables. Drizzle any remaining oil mixture from bowl over chicken.

3. Bring short sides of foil together and crimp to seal tightly. Crimp remaining open ends of packets, leaving as much headroom as possible inside packets.

TO STORE

4. Place packets on large plate and refrigerate for at least 1 hour or up to 24 hours.

TO FINISH AND SERVE

5. Adjust oven rack to lowest position and heat oven to 475 degrees. Place packets on rimmed baking sheet and bake until chicken registers 160 degrees, 18 to 23 minutes. (To check temperature, poke thermometer through foil of 1 packet and into chicken.) Let chicken rest in packets for 3 minutes.

6. Transfer chicken packets to individual serving plates, open carefully (steam will escape), and slide contents onto plates. Drizzle rice vinegar over chicken and vegetables and sprinkle with cilantro. Serve.

TWO STEPS TO MOIST CHICKEN

Getting boneless, skinless chicken breasts to come out moist and tender is tricky, especially for a make-ahead meal. Our solution was to cook the chicken sealed in a foil packet, which allowed it to gently steam in its own juices. To make it a whole dinner in a packet, we added hearty sweet potatoes, peppery radishes, celery, and onion plus a flavorful Asian-inspired sauce.

Grilled Chicken Kebabs

SERVES 4 TO 6 • **TO PREP** 30 MINUTES • **STORE** 1 TO 24 HOURS • **TO FINISH** 35 MINUTES

✔ **WHY THIS RECIPE WORKS:** Grilled chicken kebabs should feature chunks of juicy chicken with lightly charred exteriors, but often they turn out dry and chalky on the grill. We thought an overnight marinade would be the perfect solution to this problem. We knew we wanted a salty base to act like a brine, seasoning the chicken and encouraging juiciness, and we wanted to give it fresh, bright flavors that would complement the chicken. We turned to a combination of fresh herbs, shallot, and a small amount of sugar, which we combined in a food processor to eliminate tedious chopping. While we didn't want the marinade to be overly sweet, we found that a little sugar encouraged the chicken to brown during its short time on the grill, and the sweetness also helped to temper the flavor of the raw shallot. We reserved some of the marinade to pour over the cooked kebabs to reinforce their flavor, and we found that adding a little lemon juice did wonders to brighten up the finished dish. You will need eight 12-inch metal skewers for this recipe. For information on setting up a single-level fire, see page 51.

½ cup plus 1 tablespoon extra-virgin olive oil

½ cup water

¼ cup fresh parsley leaves

2 tablespoons fresh thyme leaves

1 shallot, chopped

1 tablespoon sugar

1 teaspoon salt

¼ teaspoon pepper

1 tablespoon lemon juice

1 large red onion, halved through root end, core discarded, each half cut into 4 wedges, and each wedge cut crosswise into thirds

2 pounds boneless, skinless chicken breasts, trimmed and cut into 1½-inch pieces

2 red bell peppers, stemmed, seeded, and cut into 1-inch pieces

TO PREP

1. Process ½ cup oil, water, parsley, thyme, shallot, sugar, salt, and pepper in food processor until smooth, about 20 seconds. Transfer ¼ cup marinade to small bowl, stir in lemon juice, and cover.

2. Gently toss onion pieces with remaining 1 tablespoon oil in separate bowl. Microwave, covered, until just tender, 3 to 5 minutes. Thread chicken, onion, and bell peppers evenly onto eight 12-inch metal skewers. Arrange skewers in 13 by 9-inch baking dish, pour remaining marinade over top, and turn to coat; cover.

TO STORE

3. Refrigerate kebabs and reserved marinade separately for at least 1 hour or up to 24 hours, turning kebabs occasionally to coat evenly.

TO FINISH AND SERVE

4. Remove reserved marinade from refrigerator and bring to room temperature while preparing kebabs. Pat kebabs dry with paper towels and grill (covered if using gas) over medium, single-level fire, turning often, until kebabs are well browned on all sides and chicken registers 160 degrees, 14 to 18 minutes.

5. Transfer kebabs to serving platter. Stir reserved marinade to recombine, then drizzle over kebabs. Tent loosely with aluminum foil and let rest for 5 to 10 minutes. Serve.

TEST KITCHEN TIP CUTTING ONION INTO WEDGES

To make chunks of onion sized for skewering, first halve onion through root end and discard core. Cut each half into 4 wedges, then cut each wedge crosswise into thirds.

Indian-Spiced Chicken with Yogurt Sauce

SERVES 4 • **TO PREP** 20 MINUTES • **STORE** 1 TO 24 HOURS • **TO FINISH** 1 HOUR

✔ WHY THIS RECIPE WORKS: Tandoori chicken achieves its hallmark charred, crispy skin and juicy, flavorful meat from a combination of a three-day marinade and a superheated tandoori oven. We wanted to develop a make-ahead chicken dish inspired by this Indian classic. First we focused on the marinade; we chose a variety of traditional Indian spices and added oil to bloom them and a good amount of salt so that the marinade would have the effect of a brine, guaranteeing juicy meat. For the grilling method, we spread the coals over just half of the grill to create both a hot and a cooler zone; this allowed us to cook the chicken gently on the cooler side before transferring it to the hot side to sear and char the skin. And while grilling the chicken produced a great char and crispy skin, we wanted a recipe that we could make both indoors and out, so we adapted it to work in the oven as well. To replicate the heat of the grill, we used the broiler setting; starting the chicken on the lower-middle rack slowly cooked the chicken through without overcooking the exterior, and switching to a rack set 6 inches from the broiler to finish provided a final blast of heat to give the chicken the trademark char. To reinforce the flavors of the marinade, we created a quick yogurt sauce by reserving a few tablespoons of marinade and adding fresh cilantro and lime juice. For information on setting up a half-grill fire, see page 51.

½ cup vegetable oil
¼ cup water
1 tablespoon grated fresh ginger
1 tablespoon ground coriander
1½ teaspoons ground cumin
1½ teaspoons salt
1 teaspoon ground turmeric
½ teaspoon ground cinnamon
¼ teaspoon cayenne pepper
¼ cup plain whole-milk yogurt
2 tablespoons minced fresh cilantro
2 teaspoons lime juice
4 (12-ounce) bone-in split chicken breasts, trimmed and halved crosswise

TO PREP

1. Process oil, water, ginger, coriander, cumin, salt, turmeric, cinnamon, and cayenne in food processor until smooth, about 20 seconds. In small bowl, combine yogurt, cilantro, lime juice, and 2 tablespoons oil-spice mixture; cover.

2. Place chicken and remaining oil-spice mixture in 1-gallon zipper-lock bag, press out air, and seal; toss to coat.

TO STORE

3. Refrigerate chicken and yogurt mixture separately for at least 1 hour or up to 24 hours, flipping bag occasionally to ensure chicken marinates evenly.

TO FINISH AND SERVE

4. Remove yogurt mixture from refrigerator and bring to room temperature while preparing chicken. Pat chicken dry with paper towels.

5A. FOR A BROILER: Adjust 1 oven rack to lower-middle position and second rack 6 inches from broiler element; heat broiler. Set wire rack in aluminum foil–lined rimmed baking sheet and spray with vegetable oil spray. Arrange chicken skin side down on prepared wire rack. Broil on lower rack until chicken registers 150 degrees, 22 to 26 minutes, flipping chicken halfway through broiling. Transfer chicken to upper rack and broil until skin is spotty brown and crisp and chicken registers 160 degrees, about 3 minutes.

5B. FOR A GRILL: Prepare hot, half-grill fire. Place chicken skin side down on cooler side of grill with thicker ends of breasts facing hotter side of grill. Cook, covered, until chicken registers 145 to 150 degrees, 20 to 30 minutes. Slide chicken to hotter side of grill and cook, turning as needed, until chicken is browned and registers 160 degrees, about 10 minutes.

6. Transfer chicken to serving platter. Stir yogurt-marinade mixture to recombine, then drizzle over chicken. Tent loosely with aluminum foil and let rest for 5 to 10 minutes. Serve.

Turkey Burgers with Feta and Herbs

SERVES 4 • **TO PREP** 15 MINUTES • **STORE** UP TO 24 HOURS • **TO FINISH** 30 MINUTES

✓ **WHY THIS RECIPE WORKS:** Lean, mild ground turkey burgers are well suited to being dressed up with flavorful add-ins. But the added work can make them seem like a hassle for a busy weeknight, so we wanted a make-ahead version that we could grab from the fridge and throw into a skillet. We set out to create a turkey burger with a crisp, browned outside and a full-flavored, moist interior. Since getting moist and flavorful meat was crucial, we first tried grinding our own turkey thighs. But while this provided great flavor, it was more work than we wanted for this quick recipe. Luckily, we discovered that store-bought lean ground turkey enriched with a little ricotta cheese made an excellent burger. The cheese kept the burgers moist during the holding time without adding a lot of extra fat. To achieve a nicely browned, crusty exterior, we tried searing the burgers over high heat, but this resulted in an overbrowned crust and raw interior. To cook the burgers to a safe temperature without burning them or drying out the meat, we briefly seared them, then partially covered the pan and turned the heat down to gently cook them through. Finally, to elevate our basic turkey burger to company-worthy fare, we added fresh parsley and chives plus crumbled feta cheese. Ricotta cheese can burn easily, so keep a close watch on the burgers as they cook. Be sure to use ground turkey, not ground turkey breast (also labeled 99 percent fat-free), in this recipe. Serve with your favorite burger toppings.

1½	pounds ground turkey
4	ounces (½ cup) part-skim ricotta cheese
2	tablespoons minced fresh chives
1	tablespoon minced fresh parsley
¾	teaspoon salt
¼	teaspoon pepper
2	ounces feta cheese, crumbled (½ cup)

TO FINISH AND SERVE

1	tablespoon vegetable oil
4	hamburger buns

TO PREP

1. Break turkey into small pieces in bowl, then add ricotta, chives, parsley, salt, and pepper. Using your hands, knead mixture until thoroughly combined. Gently mix in feta until just combined.

2. Divide meat mixture into 4 equal portions. Form each into loose ball, then pat lightly into ¾-inch-thick burger; place on large plate.

TO STORE

3. Cover and refrigerate burgers for up to 24 hours.

TO FINISH AND SERVE

4. Heat oil in 12-inch nonstick skillet over medium heat until just smoking. Lay burgers in skillet and cook until crisp and lightly browned on first side, 3 to 4 minutes. Flip burgers and continue to cook until lightly browned on second side, 3 to 4 minutes. Reduce heat to low, partially cover, and continue to cook until burgers register 160 degrees, 14 to 18 minutes. Transfer burgers to serving platter and let rest for 5 minutes. Serve on hamburger buns.

Miso Salmon

SERVES 4 • **TO PREP** 10 MINUTES • **STORE** 5 TO 24 HOURS • **TO FINISH** 25 MINUTES

✓ **WHY THIS RECIPE WORKS:** Our miso-glazed salmon is marinated in an enticing salty-sweet mixture with savory, nutty miso that, once cooked, morphs into a deeply caramelized, almost candylike crust. This simple dish requires only five ingredients and just a few minutes of hands-on prep; its rich, complex flavor develops during the overnight marinade—which also makes it a perfect make-ahead dish. To ensure that we could make it year-round, we wanted to figure out how to cook the salmon both indoors and out. Broiling the salmon fillets turned out to be a straightforward procedure: 10 minutes was all it took to achieve a beautifully charred exterior and moist, flaky interior. Grilling the fillets proved trickier; because of the sticky marinade, we found that a combination of patting the fillets dry and brushing them with oil before grilling was integral to ensuring that the fish wouldn't stick to the cooking grate. We always recommend brushing your cooking grate with oil to create a nonstick surface, but we found that brushing the grate at least five times was the real key to ensuring that our fillets—and their flavorful crusts—made it from the grill to the serving platter in one piece. Look for center-cut salmon fillets of similar thickness so that they cook at the same rate. The best way to ensure uniformity is to buy a 1½- to 2-pound whole center-cut fillet and cut it into 4 pieces. It is important to keep the skin on during cooking; remove it afterward if you prefer not to serve it. For information on setting up a single-level fire, see page 51.

1   cup white miso
1   cup sugar
½   cup sake
4   (6- to 8-ounce) skin-on salmon fillets

TO FINISH AND SERVE
    Vegetable oil

TO PREP
1. Whisk miso, sugar, and sake together in bowl until sugar and miso are dissolved. Gently place salmon and miso mixture in 1-gallon zipper-lock bag, press out air, and seal; gently toss to coat.

TO STORE
2. Refrigerate salmon for at least 5 hours or up to 24 hours, flipping bag occasionally to ensure fish marinates evenly.

TO FINISH AND SERVE
3. Pat salmon dry with paper towels. Brush both sides of fish with thin coat of oil.

4A. FOR A BROILER: Adjust oven rack 6 inches from broiler element and heat broiler. Set wire rack in aluminum foil–lined rimmed baking sheet and spray with vegetable oil spray. Place salmon skin side down on prepared rack. Broil until center is still translucent when checked with tip of paring knife and salmon registers 125 degrees (for medium-rare), 7 to 10 minutes.

4B. FOR A GRILL: Prepare medium, single-level fire. Clean cooking grate, then repeatedly brush grate with well-oiled paper towels until grate is black and glossy, 5 to 10 times. Place salmon skin side down on grill at 45-degree angle to bars. Cook (covered if using gas), without moving salmon, until skin side is brown, well marked, and crisp, 3 to 5 minutes. (Try lifting gently with spatula after 3 minutes; if it doesn't lift cleanly off grill, continue to cook, checking at 20-second intervals, until it releases.) Using 2 spatulas, flip salmon to second side and continue to cook (covered if using gas) until center is still translucent when checked with tip of paring knife and salmon registers 125 degrees (for medium-rare), 6 to 9 minutes.

5. Transfer salmon to serving platter and serve.

ALL ABOUT Building the Right Fire

One of the biggest grilling mistakes happens before the food even hits the cooking grate: not building the proper fire. Just as you don't cook everything on high heat on your stovetop, you don't cook only on high heat on the grill. Shrimp need even, high heat to give them good color and cook them through, but if you tried that method with thick bone-in chicken breasts, the outside would be charred by the time they cooked through—different types of food need different types of fires. Here are the setups we use in this book and how to build them.

SINGLE-LEVEL FIRE

A single-level fire provides even heat and is used for small, quick-cooking foods like hamburgers and fish fillets.

For charcoal grill, open bottom and lid vents completely and pour lit coals (3 quarts for medium fire or 6 quarts for hot fire) evenly over grill; set cooking grate in place and preheat grill. For gas grill, turn all burners to high and preheat grill. Leave all burners on high for hot fire or turn all burners to medium for medium fire.

HALF-GRILL FIRE

A half-grill fire has two cooking zones: a hotter side for searing and a cooler side to cook food more gently. This setup is best for cuts like bone-in chicken breasts that require longer cooking times.

For charcoal grill, open bottom and lid vents completely and pour 6 quarts lit coals over half of grill, leaving other half empty; set cooking grate in place and preheat grill. For gas grill, turn all burners to high and preheat grill; leave primary burner on high and turn other burner(s) off.

CONCENTRATED FIRE

A concentrated fire creates a blazing-hot fire for food like scallops or lamb that needs to quickly get a good sear to avoid over-cooking the delicate meat.

For charcoal grill, poke 12 holes in bottom of 13 by 9-inch disposable aluminum roasting pan. Open bottom and lid vents completely and place pan in center of grill. Pour 4 quarts lit coals into pan, set cooking grate in place, and preheat grill. For gas grill, turn all burners to high and preheat grill; leave all burners on high.

Is Your Fire Hot Enough?

While grilling, we preheat charcoal grills, covered, for 5 minutes and preheat gas grills, covered, with all burners on high for 15 minutes. After preheating the grill, hold your hand about 5 inches above the cooking grate and count how long you can comfortably keep it there. You should be able to hold your hand over the fire for 5 to 6 seconds for a medium fire and 2 seconds for a hot fire.

Cleaning the Cooking Grate

Before placing food on the grill, it is important to clean and oil the cooking grate. After you've heated the grill, scrape the grate clean with a grill brush. Then dip a large wad of paper towels in vegetable oil, grab it with tongs, and wipe the grate thoroughly to lubricate it and prevent food from sticking. When grilling fish, it's important to repeat this process until the grate is black and glossy.

Salmon Burgers

SERVES 4 • **TO PREP** 20 MINUTES • **STORE** 1 TO 24 HOURS • **TO FINISH** 15 MINUTES

☑ **WHY THIS RECIPE WORKS:** We wanted moist, flavorful salmon burgers that tasted foremost like salmon and that could be made in advance and cooked up for a quick and delicious dinner. Many salmon burger recipes use canned salmon, but since the salmon is the star of this dish, we found that it was well worth the additional modest expense and effort required to make our burgers with fresh salmon. Burgers made with canned salmon were lackluster (to say the least) and mushy, while those made with fresh salmon were moist and full of flavor, with an appealing, chunky texture. A food processor made quick work of chopping the salmon into pieces. To keep the burgers together in the skillet, we used a light binder of mayonnaise and bread crumbs. Store-bought bread crumbs muddled the flavor of the salmon, so we made our own fresh crumbs from white sandwich bread. Minced shallot added aromatic depth, and some Dijon mustard provided moistness and flavor. With a little fresh parsley, we had a bright and meaty salmon burger that truly tasted like salmon. Be sure to process the fish in three separate batches and for no more than four pulses, or it will turn to paste and be impossible to shape. If you don't have a food processor, salmon is easy to chop by hand; to make it even easier, put the salmon in the freezer for 10 minutes before chopping.

1½ slices hearty white sandwich bread, torn into 1-inch pieces

1 pound skinless salmon, cut into 1-inch pieces

1 shallot, minced

3 tablespoons mayonnaise

2 tablespoons minced fresh parsley

2 teaspoons Dijon mustard

⅛ teaspoon salt

⅛ teaspoon pepper

TO FINISH AND SERVE

1 tablespoon vegetable oil

Lemon wedges

TO PREP

1. Pulse bread in food processor to coarse crumbs, about 4 pulses; transfer to large bowl. Working in 3 batches, pulse salmon in now-empty processor until coarsely chopped into ¼-inch pieces, about 2 pulses, transferring each batch to bowl with bread crumbs. Gently mix until thoroughly combined.

2. Whisk shallot, mayonnaise, parsley, mustard, salt, and pepper together in separate bowl, then gently fold into salmon mixture until just combined. Divide mixture into 4 equal portions. Form each into loose ball, then pat lightly into 1-inch-thick burger; place on large plate.

TO STORE

3. Cover and refrigerate burgers for at least 1 hour or up to 24 hours.

TO FINISH AND SERVE

4. Heat oil in 12-inch nonstick skillet over medium-high heat until shimmering. Gently lay burgers in skillet and cook until crisp and well browned on first side, 4 to 5 minutes. Gently flip burgers and continue to cook until golden brown on second side and burgers register 125 to 130 degrees, about 4 minutes. Serve with lemon wedges.

Baked Cod with Cherry Tomatoes and Chickpeas

SERVES 4 • **TO PREP** 20 MINUTES • **STORE** 1 TO 24 HOURS • **TO FINISH** 35 MINUTES

✔ **WHY THIS RECIPE WORKS:** For a make-ahead version of an oven-to-table cod fillet recipe, we wanted to infuse the cod with zesty flavors and bake it together with a savory side dish for a quick, complete dinner. We focused first on a rich spice rub for the cod that would impart flavor as it sat overnight. An oil-based rub with coriander and paprika provided aromatic flavor and nice color, and a small amount of cayenne added just the right amount of subtle heat. For the side dish, we tried many accompaniments from green beans to potatoes, but our favorite turned out to be a combination of chickpeas and cherry tomatoes. The chickpeas soaked up the spiced broth, and some of the tomatoes broke down in the oven, creating a bright sauce that complemented the cod nicely. We flavored the chickpeas and tomatoes with more coriander and paprika plus shallots, garlic, and lemon for a bright finish. When we were ready for dinner, we simply nestled the cod fillets into the chickpea and tomato mixture. To ensure that the tomatoes did not break down too much during a longer cooking time at a lower temperature, we baked the dish at 400 degrees; because cod is a relatively wet fish, it stood up well to the high heat. When it was cooked through, we drizzled the cod with some fruity olive oil and sprinkled it with fresh cilantro for an herbal note. You can substitute haddock or halibut for the cod.

3   **tablespoons extra-virgin olive oil**
2   **teaspoons ground coriander**
2   **teaspoons paprika**
⅛   **teaspoon cayenne pepper**
    Salt and pepper
4   **(6- to 8-ounce) skinless cod fillets, 1 to 1½ inches thick**
2   **(14-ounce) cans chickpeas, rinsed**
12 **ounces cherry tomatoes, halved**
¼   **cup chicken broth**
2   **shallots, minced**
5   **garlic cloves, minced**
1   **tablespoon grated lemon zest plus 1 tablespoon juice**

TO FINISH AND SERVE
2   **tablespoons extra-virgin olive oil**
2   **tablespoons chopped fresh cilantro**

TO PREP

1. Combine 2 tablespoons oil, 1 teaspoon coriander, 1 teaspoon paprika, cayenne, and ¾ teaspoon salt. Rub cod evenly with oil mixture. Place in 1-gallon zipper-lock bag, press out air, and seal; gently toss to coat.

2. Combine chickpeas, tomatoes, broth, shallots, garlic, lemon zest and juice, remaining 1 tablespoon oil, remaining 1 teaspoon coriander, and remaining 1 teaspoon paprika in 13 by 9-inch baking dish; cover.

TO STORE

3. Refrigerate cod and chickpea mixture separately for at least 1 hour or up to 24 hours, flipping bag occasionally to ensure cod marinates evenly.

TO FINISH AND SERVE

4. Adjust oven rack to middle position and heat oven to 400 degrees. Season chickpea mixture with ½ teaspoon salt and ¼ teaspoon pepper. Nestle cod into chickpea mixture and bake until cod flakes apart when gently prodded with paring knife and registers 140 degrees, 20 to 24 minutes. Drizzle with oil and sprinkle with cilantro. Serve.

ADD OIL TO THE SPICE RUB

Spice rubs are ideal for make-ahead dishes because the flavors improve as they sit, melding and deepening. We found that mixing the spices with oil increased this effect, keeping the spices from tasting dusty or harsh in the finished dish. To distribute the spices evenly, we gently tossed the fish with the rub in a zipper-lock bag before stashing it in the fridge.

Crispy Breaded Cod Fillets

SERVES 4 • **TO PREP** 35 MINUTES • **STORE** 1 TO 24 HOURS • **TO FINISH** 1 HOUR

✓ **WHY THIS RECIPE WORKS:** Baked fish with a crispy, flavorful crumb topping is a satisfying, delicious, and healthy meal. But could it be convenient, too? We wanted a recipe that would deliver fish with a crunchy crumb topping that actually stuck to the fish, and we wanted to be able to make it up to a day in advance. Keeping this lofty goal in mind, we began from the top: the breading. Traditional bread crumbs are prone to sogginess, but in the test kitchen we've had great success with extra-crispy panko bread crumbs. However, even panko lost its crispness after a night in the refrigerator. Toasting the panko on the stovetop with melted butter solved the problem; even a day later, the toasted topping was crispy and crunchy. To get it to stick to the fillets, we spread mayonnaise on top of the fish fillets before pressing on the crumbs. We had the texture down, but tasters thought that the dish tasted bland. Since we already had the skillet out to toast the panko, we decided to add aromatics to the skillet to bump up the breading's flavor. Adding an egg yolk, some lemon zest, and pepper to the mayonnaise enriched the flavor of the fish and rounded out the flavor profile of our dish. You can substitute haddock or halibut for the cod.

3 tablespoons unsalted butter
1 large shallot, minced
   Salt and pepper
1 garlic clove, minced
1 teaspoon minced fresh thyme or
   ¼ teaspoon dried
¾ cup panko bread crumbs
2 tablespoons minced fresh parsley
2 tablespoons mayonnaise
1 large egg yolk
½ teaspoon grated lemon zest
4 (6- to 8-ounce) skinless cod fillets,
   1 to 1½ inches thick

TO PREP

1. Melt butter in 12-inch skillet over medium heat. Add shallot and ½ teaspoon salt and cook until softened, about 3 minutes. Stir in garlic and thyme and cook until fragrant, about 30 seconds. Add panko and ¼ teaspoon pepper and cook, stirring constantly, until evenly browned, about 4 minutes. Transfer panko mixture to shallow dish and let cool for 10 minutes. Stir in parsley.

2. Whisk mayonnaise, egg yolk, lemon zest, and ¼ teaspoon pepper together in bowl. Pat cod dry with paper towels and season with salt and pepper. Brush tops of fillets evenly with mayonnaise mixture. Working with 1 fillet at a time, dredge coated side in panko mixture, pressing gently to adhere. Place fillets, crumb side up, on large plate.

TO STORE

3. Cover and refrigerate cod for at least 1 hour or up to 24 hours.

TO FINISH AND SERVE

4. Adjust oven rack to middle position and heat oven to 300 degrees. Set wire rack in rimmed baking sheet and spray with vegetable oil spray. Transfer cod to prepared rack and bake until fish flakes apart when gently prodded with paring knife and registers 140 degrees, 45 to 55 minutes, rotating sheet halfway through baking. Serve.

KEEPING BREADING CRISP
For a buttery bread-crumb topping that stayed crisp even overnight, we started with extra-crispy panko bread crumbs. Toasting them in butter kept them from turning soggy and gave them great flavor. To glue the topping securely to the cod fillets, we used mayonnaise whisked with an egg yolk and seasoned with lemon juice and pepper.

Thai-Style Fish and Creamy Coconut Couscous Packets

SERVES 4 • **TO PREP** 40 MINUTES • **STORE** UP TO 24 HOURS • **TO FINISH** 40 MINUTES

✔ **WHY THIS RECIPE WORKS:** Cooking fish *en papillote*, or folded in a pouch, is a classic French technique that, in addition to being incredibly easy, allows the fish to steam in its own juices and thus emerge moist and flavorful. It's a great option for a simple meal since you can cook a side right alongside the entrée in the pouch, allowing the flavors to meld. It's also a great choice for prepping ahead and stashing in the refrigerator until you are ready for dinner. To give the technique a fresh spin, we cooked the fish fillets on a bed of fluffy couscous with a flavorful, Thai-inspired sauce. We mixed coconut milk, ginger, fish sauce, a little cilantro for a fresh herbal touch, and red pepper flakes for a subtle hint of heat. The bold sauce transformed the couscous into a rich and creamy dish and infused the fish with flavor. We found that if we used too much sauce during cooking, the couscous soaked up all of the liquid and ended up gummy while the fish tasted bland. So we reserved some of the sauce to drizzle over the fish before serving. Any white fish will work here, but we prefer the thickness and meaty texture of cod or halibut. For an accurate measurement of boiling water, bring a full kettle of water to a boil and then measure out the desired amount. For more information on making a foil packet, see page 25.

1½   **cups couscous**
2   **cups boiling water plus ¼ cup room-temperature water**
   Salt and pepper
1   **cup canned coconut milk**
¼   **cup chopped fresh cilantro**
2   **tablespoons fish sauce**
1   **tablespoon grated fresh ginger**
3   **garlic cloves, minced**
⅛   **teaspoon red pepper flakes**
4   **(6- to 8-ounce) skinless halibut fillets, 1 to 1½ inches thick**

TO FINISH AND SERVE
2   **tablespoons rice vinegar**

TO PREP

1. Combine couscous and boiling water in medium bowl. Immediately cover with plastic wrap and let sit until liquid is absorbed and couscous is tender, about 5 minutes. Fluff couscous with fork and season with salt and pepper to taste. Let cool completely, about 20 minutes.

2. Combine room-temperature water, coconut milk, cilantro, fish sauce, ginger, garlic, and pepper flakes in small bowl.

3. Spray centers of four 14 by 12-inch sheets of heavy-duty aluminum foil with vegetable oil spray.

Pat halibut dry with paper towels and season with salt and pepper. Divide couscous evenly among foil pieces, mounding it in center of each piece. Place 1 fillet on top of each couscous mound and spoon 1 tablespoon sauce over top. Cover remaining coconut sauce.

4. Bring short sides of foil together and crimp to seal tightly. Crimp remaining open ends of packets, leaving as much headroom as possible inside packets.

TO STORE

5. Refrigerate packets and remaining coconut sauce separately for up to 24 hours.

TO FINISH AND SERVE

6. Adjust oven rack to middle position and heat oven to 400 degrees. Place packets in rimmed baking sheet and bake until fish flakes apart when gently prodded with paring knife and registers 140 degrees, 18 to 20 minutes. (To check temperature, poke thermometer through foil of 1 packet and into fish.) Let halibut rest in packets for 3 minutes.

7. Microwave coconut sauce, uncovered, until warmed through, about 1 minute. Stir in rice vinegar. Transfer fish packets to individual serving plates, open carefully (steam will escape), and slide contents onto plates. Drizzle warm sauce over fish and couscous. Serve.

Spice-Rubbed Shrimp with Lemon Aïoli

SERVES 4 TO 6 • **TO PREP** 30 MINUTES • **STORE** 1 TO 24 HOURS • **TO FINISH** 20 MINUTES

✔ **WHY THIS RECIPE WORKS:** For an updated version of classic shrimp cocktail, we skipped the poaching and used high heat and a flavorful spice rub to give the shrimp great flavor. We found that while an hour's rest was enough time to produce nicely seasoned and flavorful shrimp, after a full day the shrimp had developed even deeper, more balanced flavors. A little sugar added to the rub paired nicely with the fresh, sweet flavor of the shrimp, and it came in handy during cooking. The shrimp cooked through very quickly with the direct, intense heat of the grill or broiler, and the sugar helped by caramelizing quickly and adding a nice sear. Whether grilled or broiled, shrimp can turn from moist and juicy to rubbery and dry in the blink of an eye, but we found that tightly packing the shrimp onto the skewers helped to insulate the shrimp, slowing down the cooking and preventing the shrimp from overcooking and drying out. Other fresh herbs, such as dill, basil, cilantro, or mint, can be substituted for the tarragon. We prefer to use jumbo shrimp here, but extra-large shrimp (21 to 25 per pound) can be substituted; if using smaller shrimp, reduce the broiling time by about 2 minutes. You will need four 12-inch metal skewers for this recipe. For information on setting up a single-level fire, see page 51.

⅓   **cup mayonnaise**
1   **tablespoon lemon juice**
1   **scallion, minced**
1   **tablespoon minced fresh tarragon**
    Salt and pepper
½   **teaspoon ground coriander**
½   **teaspoon sugar**
⅛   **teaspoon cayenne pepper**
2   **pounds jumbo shrimp (16 to 20 per pound), peeled and deveined**
2   **tablespoons vegetable oil**

TO PREP

1. Combine mayonnaise, lemon juice, scallion, tarragon, ¼ teaspoon salt, and ⅛ teaspoon pepper in small bowl; cover.

2. Combine coriander, sugar, cayenne, ½ teaspoon salt, and ¼ teaspoon pepper in large bowl. Pat shrimp dry with paper towels. Add shrimp and oil to bowl with spice mixture and toss to coat evenly. Thread shrimp onto four 12-inch metal skewers (8 to 10 per skewer), alternating direction of heads and tails. Arrange skewers in 13 by 9-inch baking dish.

TO STORE

3. Cover and refrigerate skewers and lemon aïoli separately for at least 1 hour or up to 24 hours.

TO FINISH AND SERVE

4A. FOR A BROILER: Adjust oven rack 3 inches from broiler element and heat broiler. Set wire rack in aluminum foil–lined rimmed baking sheet and spray with vegetable oil spray. Pat shrimp dry with paper towels. Arrange skewers on prepared rack and broil shrimp until opaque throughout and edges begin to brown, 5 to 7 minutes.

4B. FOR A GRILL: Pat shrimp dry with paper towels. Grill shrimp (covered if using gas) over hot, single-level fire, turning as needed, until opaque throughout and edges begin to brown, 5 to 9 minutes.

5. Serve shrimp with lemon aïoli.

TEST KITCHEN TIP   **TIGHTLY SKEWERING SHRIMP**

For juicy shrimp, pass skewer through center of each shrimp, alternating direction of heads and tails for compact arrangement. Shrimp should be crowded and touching each other.

Quinoa Patties with Spinach and Sun-Dried Tomatoes

SERVES 4 • **TO PREP** 1 HOUR 10 MINUTES • **STORE** 1 TO 24 HOURS • **TO FINISH** 30 MINUTES

✔ **WHY THIS RECIPE WORKS:** We set out to develop a recipe for quinoa patties with bright, fresh flavors and enough add-ins to make them hearty and satisfying. To make these patties weeknight accessible, we wanted to distribute the work so you could come home and have a filling dinner in just 30 minutes. While we liked the earthy flavor of red quinoa, it did not soften enough to form cohesive patties. Classic white (or golden) quinoa performed much better, and upping the amount of cooking liquid delivered even more cohesive patties, since the quinoa was extra-moist from absorbing the extra liquid overnight. We skipped the usual toasting step because it encourages the individual grains to separate rather than stick together. As for the binder, we tried mashed beans and potatoes, a variety of cheeses, bread, and processing some of the quinoa itself, but only the duo of eggs and sandwich bread was successful. Chilling the patties ensured that they stayed together during cooking. Baking was an appealing hands-off cooking method, but the heat of the oven dried the patties out. It was much easier on the stovetop to get a crisp crust and moist interior. Because the patties needed at least 5 minutes on each side to set up and cook through, cooking them over medium-low heat prevented burning but still resulted in a nice crust. If you buy unwashed quinoa, rinse the grains in a fine-mesh strainer, drain them, then spread them in a rimmed baking sheet lined with a clean dish towel and let them dry for 15 minutes before proceeding with the recipe.

½ cup oil-packed sun-dried tomatoes, chopped coarse, plus 1 tablespoon packing oil

4 scallions, chopped fine

4 garlic cloves, minced

2 cups water

1 cup prewashed quinoa

1 teaspoon salt

2 slices hearty white sandwich bread

1 large egg plus 1 large yolk, beaten

½ teaspoon grated lemon zest plus 2 teaspoons juice

2 ounces (2 cups) baby spinach, chopped

2 ounces Parmesan cheese, grated (1 cup)

TO FINISH AND SERVE

2 tablespoons vegetable oil

TO PREP

1. Line rimmed baking sheet with parchment paper. Heat tomato oil in large saucepan over medium heat until shimmering. Add scallions and cook until softened, 3 to 5 minutes. Stir in garlic and cook until fragrant, about 30 seconds. Stir in water, quinoa, and salt and bring to simmer. Cover, reduce heat to medium-low, and simmer until quinoa is tender, 16 to 18 minutes. Off heat, let quinoa sit, covered, until liquid is fully absorbed, about 10 minutes. Transfer quinoa to large bowl and let cool for 15 minutes.

2. Pulse bread in food processor until coarsely ground, about 10 pulses. Add egg and yolk and lemon zest and pulse until mixture comes together, about 5 pulses. Stir bread mixture, tomatoes, lemon juice, spinach, and Parmesan into cooled quinoa until thoroughly combined. Divide mixture into 8 equal portions, pack firmly into ½-inch-thick patties (about 3½ inches wide), and place on prepared sheet.

TO STORE

3. Cover and refrigerate patties for at least 1 hour or up to 24 hours.

TO FINISH AND SERVE

4. Heat 1 tablespoon oil in 12-inch nonstick skillet over medium-low heat until shimmering. Gently lay 4 patties in skillet and cook until well browned on first side, 5 to 7 minutes. Gently flip patties and continue to cook until golden brown on second side, 5 to 7 minutes. Transfer patties to serving platter and tent loosely with aluminum foil. Return now-empty skillet to medium-low heat and repeat with remaining 1 tablespoon oil and remaining 4 patties. Serve.

Chickpea Cakes with Cucumber-Yogurt Sauce

SERVES 4 • **TO PREP** 30 MINUTES • **STORE** 1 TO 24 HOURS • **TO FINISH** 30 MINUTES

✔ **WHY THIS RECIPE WORKS:** Buttery, nutty chickpeas make a great foundation for a light yet filling vegetarian patty. They are protein-rich and just as satisfying as a beef burger, and they can be mixed and formed ahead of time and stored overnight for a quick dinner. To keep our recipe easy, we decided to use canned beans rather than dried, which would require an overnight soak before we could prep and form the patties. Pulsing the chickpeas in the food processor was quick and gave us just the right coarse texture for cohesive cakes. For the flavors, we started with the fragrant Indian spice mix garam masala. Tasters liked the aromatic flavor of onion, but it released moisture as it sat, making the cakes gummy. Swapping the onion for scallions fixed the problem, lending a nice onion flavor without excess moisture. Fresh cilantro added a bright complexity. For a cool, creamy counterpoint, we made a simple cucumber-yogurt sauce to top the cakes. Use a coarse grater to shred the cucumber. Be careful to avoid overprocessing the bean mixture, as it will cause the cakes to become mealy in texture.

1 cucumber, peeled, halved lengthwise, seeded, and shredded
Salt and pepper
1¼ cups plain Greek yogurt
6 scallions, sliced thin
¼ cup minced fresh cilantro
2 (14-ounce) cans chickpeas, rinsed
2 large eggs
6 tablespoons extra-virgin olive oil
1 teaspoon garam masala
⅛ teaspoon cayenne pepper
1 cup panko bread crumbs
1 shallot, minced

TO FINISH AND SERVE
¼ cup vegetable oil

TO PREP
1. Line rimmed baking sheet with parchment paper. Toss cucumber with ½ teaspoon salt in fine-mesh strainer and let drain for 15 minutes. Combine drained cucumber, ¾ cup yogurt, 2 tablespoons scallions, and 1 tablespoon cilantro in bowl and season with salt and pepper to taste; cover.

2. Meanwhile, pulse chickpeas in food processor to coarse puree with few large pieces remaining, about 8 pulses. Whisk eggs, 2 tablespoons oil, garam masala, cayenne, and ¼ teaspoon salt together in medium bowl. Stir in processed chickpeas, panko, shallot, remaining ½ cup yogurt, remaining scallions, and remaining 3 tablespoons cilantro until just combined. Divide mixture into 8 equal portions, pack firmly into 1-inch-thick patties, and place on prepared sheet; cover.

TO STORE
3. Refrigerate cucumber-yogurt sauce and chickpea cakes separately for at least 1 hour or up to 24 hours.

TO FINISH AND SERVE
4. Remove cucumber-yogurt sauce from refrigerator and bring to room temperature while preparing chickpea cakes. Heat 2 tablespoons oil in 12-inch nonstick skillet over medium heat until shimmering. Gently lay 4 patties in skillet and cook until well browned on first side, 6 to 8 minutes. Gently flip patties and continue to cook until golden brown on second side, 6 to 8 minutes. Transfer patties to serving platter and tent loosely with aluminum foil. Return now-empty skillet to medium heat and repeat with remaining 2 tablespoons oil and remaining 4 patties. Serve with yogurt sauce.

Stuffed Acorn Squash

SERVES 4   •   **TO PREP** 45 MINUTES   •   **STORE** UP TO 24 HOURS   •   **TO FINISH** 1 HOUR

✓ **WHY THIS RECIPE WORKS:** Stuffed acorn squash makes for a healthy meal, but who has time to roast the squash, make a filling, and assemble and bake the whole dish on a weeknight? We loved the thought of coming home after work and simply sticking the fully assembled squash in the oven, but we didn't want to be stuck in the kitchen for hours the day before. Parcooking the squash was necessary to prevent the filling from drying out in the time it took the squash to cook through; to cut down on kitchen time, we turned to the microwave, which softened the squash in under 15 minutes. For the filling, we turned to quick-cooking couscous and baby spinach as our base, but to bring the stuffing to life we added sautéed aromatics, along with cheese, pine nuts, and raisins. Sprinkling a little water over the couscous before baking moistened the filling and helped the squash to soften and become perfectly tender in the oven. A drizzle of olive oil was all that was needed to finish off this streamlined, make-ahead take on one of our favorite vegetarian meals. Be sure to look for similar-size squash (roughly 1½ pounds each) to ensure even cooking. For an accurate measurement of boiling water, bring a full kettle of water to a boil and then measure out the desired amount.

2	acorn squashes (1½ pounds each), halved pole to pole and seeded
3	tablespoons extra-virgin olive oil
⅔	cup couscous
⅔	cup boiling water
⅓	cup golden raisins
	Salt and pepper
1	small onion, chopped fine
3	garlic cloves, minced
5	ounces (5 cups) baby spinach
1	ounce Pecorino Romano cheese, grated (½ cup)
¼	cup pine nuts, toasted

TO FINISH AND SERVE

¼	cup warm tap water
½	ounce Pecorino Romano cheese, grated (¼ cup)
	Extra-virgin olive oil

TO PREP

1. Brush flesh of squash with 1 tablespoon oil, then place cut sides down on large plate. Cover and microwave until just softened, 12 to 15 minutes.

2. Meanwhile, combine couscous, boiling water, raisins, 1 tablespoon oil, and ¼ teaspoon salt in large bowl. Immediately cover with plastic wrap and let sit until liquid is absorbed and couscous is tender, about 5 minutes. Fluff couscous with fork.

3. Heat remaining 1 tablespoon oil in 12-inch skillet over medium heat until shimmering. Add onion and cook until softened, about 5 minutes. Stir in garlic and cook until fragrant, about 30 seconds. Stir in spinach, 1 handful at a time, and cook until wilted and most of liquid has evaporated, about 2 minutes. Gently fold spinach mixture, Pecorino, and pine nuts into couscous. Season with salt and pepper to taste and let cool for 10 minutes.

4. Arrange squash halves cut sides up in 13 by 9-inch baking dish and season with salt and pepper. Mound couscous mixture into squash, packing lightly with back of spoon.

TO STORE

5. Cover and refrigerate squash for up to 24 hours.

TO FINISH AND SERVE

6. Adjust oven rack to middle position and heat oven to 400 degrees. Unwrap dish, drizzle couscous mounds evenly with warm water, and cover tightly with greased aluminum foil. Bake squash until heated through, about 20 minutes. Remove foil, sprinkle squash with Pecorino, and bake, uncovered, until cheese is lightly browned, about 20 minutes. Drizzle with oil and serve.

INDIAN-STYLE VEGETABLE CURRY

Reheat and Eat

MAKE-AHEAD STEWS AND BRAISES

Easy Overnight Beef Stew

SERVES 4 TO 6 • **TO PREP** 1 HOUR 15 MINUTES • **STORE** UP TO 3 DAYS • **TO FINISH** 1 HOUR 20 MINUTES

✓ **WHY THIS RECIPE WORKS:** The appeal of a rich-tasting beef stew is undeniable, but developing the layers of flavor that are the hallmark of a great stew along with fork-tender beef requires lots of stovetop attention and hours of cooking. We set out to reengineer our classic beef stew recipe so that we could do the bulk of the work on day one and simply finish it the next day. Our hope was to make the most of the cooling time to tenderize the meat and the overnight rest to allow the flavors of the stew to develop further. We usually start by cutting up a big chuck roast, but this time we reached for boneless beef short ribs, which deliver big beefy flavor, require less prep, and turn tender faster than chuck roast—big advantages for this make-ahead stew. And rather than browning the meat in several batches, we saved time by throwing all the meat plus the onions into the pot at once. Although the meat didn't brown all over, this method left a good fond on the bottom of the pot, which was all we needed to build a flavorful base for our stew. After deglazing the pan with red wine, we added a portion of the broth to the pot and simmered the stew for just 30 minutes before taking it off the heat to cool. After 45 minutes of cooling time (during which the meat continued to cook), we added some chilled broth to quickly finish cooling the stew enough to store safely in the fridge. Adding the vegetables the next day ensured that they were bright and fresh. And since our stew needed additional cooking time, we found the fastest strategy was to bring it to a simmer on the stovetop and then transfer it to a preheated oven where it cooked through gently in less than an hour.

5   **cups chicken broth, plus extra as needed**

3   **pounds boneless beef short ribs, trimmed and cut into ¾-inch pieces**

2   **onions, chopped**

1   **tablespoon vegetable oil**

     Salt and pepper

2   **garlic cloves, minced**

2   **teaspoons minced fresh thyme or ½ teaspoon dried**

3   **tablespoons all-purpose flour**

2   **teaspoons tomato paste**

¾   **cup dry red wine**

TO FINISH AND SERVE

1   **pound Yukon Gold potatoes, unpeeled, cut into 1-inch pieces**

1   **pound carrots, peeled and cut into 1-inch pieces**

1   **cup frozen peas**

2   **tablespoons minced fresh parsley**

TO PREP

1. Refrigerate 3 cups broth. Combine beef, onions, oil, ¼ teaspoon salt, and ⅛ teaspoon pepper in Dutch oven over medium-high heat. Cook, stirring often, until released beef juices nearly evaporate and meat begins to brown, 20 to 25 minutes, reducing heat if necessary to prevent scorching.

2. Stir in garlic and thyme and cook until fragrant, about 30 seconds. Stir in flour and tomato paste and cook for 1 minute. Slowly stir in wine, smoothing out any lumps, and cook until slightly reduced, about 2 minutes. Stir in remaining 2 cups broth, scraping up any browned bits, and bring to simmer. Cover, reduce heat to low, and simmer for 30 minutes.

3. Remove pot from heat and let sit, covered, for 45 minutes. Stir in chilled broth to finish cooling.

TO STORE

4. Leave stew in pot or transfer to storage container. Cover and refrigerate for up to 3 days.

TO FINISH AND SERVE

5. Adjust oven rack to lower-middle position and heat oven to 400 degrees. Skim excess fat from surface of stew and transfer to Dutch oven, if necessary. Add potatoes and carrots and bring to simmer over medium heat, stirring often. Cover pot, transfer to oven, and cook until beef and vegetables are tender, 45 to 50 minutes. Remove pot from oven, stir in peas, and let sit until heated through, about 5 minutes. Adjust stew consistency with extra hot broth as needed. Stir in parsley and season with salt and pepper to taste. Serve.

SPEEDING UP BEEF STEW

Adding the beef and chopped onions to the pot all at once and cooking them just until the meat started to brown rather than cooking the beef in several batches gave us lots of flavorful fond in much less time. We also put carryover cooking to work during the cooling time to further tenderize the meat, then added chilled broth to finish cooling the stew rapidly.

Classic Beef Pot Roast

SERVES 6 TO 8 • **TO PREP** 5 TO 5½ HOURS • **STORE** UP TO 2 DAYS • **TO FINISH** 1 HOUR 10 MINUTES

✔ **WHY THIS RECIPE WORKS:** The ideal make-ahead dish is one that improves in flavor and texture from one day to the next. We found exactly that with our Classic Beef Pot Roast. The overnight rest not only made the roast more moist and easier to slice, but it also brought out deeper, beefier flavor. The key was to give the roast all the cooking time it needed on day one then let the proteins relax and the flavors intensify in the refrigerator. To start, we separated a boneless chuck-eye roast into two pieces, which allowed us to remove the knobs of fat that stubbornly refused to render and shortened the cooking time by about an hour. Next, we built a flavorful base with a *mirepoix* of onions, carrot, and celery plus garlic, tomato paste, red wine, thyme, and a bay leaf. Some recipes use water as the primary cooking liquid, but when we tried this, the gravy turned out as you'd expect— watery. We had better luck with beef broth. The resulting gravy boasted a rich, complex character. Sealing the pot with aluminum foil before securing the lid and moving the pot to the oven concentrated the steam for an even simmer and fork-tender meat. Chilling the whole cooked pot roast overnight made it much easier to slice before reheating, and the extra-long resting time improved the flavor of the meat and its gravy, which we made by blending all of the flavorful braising ingredients, not wasting an ounce of what went into the pot with the meat. The result—a meltingly tender roast sauced in savory, full-bodied gravy.

1 **(3½- to 4-pound) boneless beef chuck-eye roast, pulled into 2 pieces at natural seam and trimmed of large pieces of fat**
   Salt and pepper
2 **tablespoons unsalted butter**
2 **onions, halved and sliced thin**
1 **large carrot, peeled and chopped**
1 **celery rib, chopped**
2 **garlic cloves, minced**
1 **cup beef broth, plus extra as needed**
½ **cup dry red wine**
1 **tablespoon tomato paste**
1 **sprig fresh thyme**
1 **bay leaf**

TO FINISH AND SERVE
¼ **cup dry red wine**
1 **tablespoon balsamic vinegar**

TEST KITCHEN TIP **TYING A POT ROAST**

We divide the chuck-eye roast into two pieces so we can trim away the interior fat. Then we secure the roasts with twine at 1-inch intervals to promote even cooking.

TO PREP

1. Season beef with 1½ teaspoons salt, place on wire rack set in rimmed baking sheet, and let sit at room temperature for 1 hour.

2. Adjust oven rack to lower-middle position and heat oven to 300 degrees. Melt butter in Dutch oven over medium heat. Add onions and cook, stirring occasionally, until softened and beginning to brown, 8 to 10 minutes. Stir in carrot and celery and cook for 5 minutes. Stir in garlic and cook until fragrant, about 30 seconds. Stir in broth, wine, tomato paste, thyme sprig, and bay leaf and bring to simmer.

3. Pat beef dry with paper towels and season with pepper. Tie each piece of beef into even shape with kitchen twine at 1-inch intervals.

4. Nestle roasts on top of vegetables. Cover pot tightly with large piece of aluminum foil, then cover with lid; transfer pot to oven. Cook until beef is tender and fork easily slips in and out of meat, 3½ to 4 hours, turning meat halfway through cooking. Remove pot from oven and transfer roasts to storage container. Strain liquid through fine-mesh strainer into 4-cup liquid measuring cup. Discard bay leaf and thyme sprig; reserve vegetables. Allow liquid to settle for 5 minutes, then skim excess fat from surface. Add extra beef broth as needed to bring liquid amount to 3 cups. Transfer reserved vegetables and liquid to container with roasts. Let cool to room temperature, 1½ to 2 hours.

TO STORE

5. Cover and refrigerate for up to 2 days.

TO FINISH AND SERVE

6. Adjust oven rack to middle position and heat oven to 325 degrees. Transfer roasts to cutting board, remove twine, and slice against grain into ½-inch-thick slices. Shingle slices into 13 by 9-inch baking dish, cover tightly with foil, and bake until heated through, about 45 minutes.

7. While beef heats, process liquid and vegetables in blender until smooth, about 2 minutes. Transfer sauce to medium saucepan and bring to simmer over medium heat. Stir in wine and vinegar and season with salt and pepper to taste. Spoon half of sauce over meat. Serve, passing remaining sauce separately.

Onion-Braised Beef Brisket

SERVES 6 TO 8 • **TO PREP** 4½ TO 5 HOURS • **STORE** UP TO 2 DAYS • **TO FINISH** 40 MINUTES

✔ **WHY THIS RECIPE WORKS:** Brisket is the ideal cut for braising, as it takes hours of slow cooking to soften this otherwise tough-as-leather cut. Sadly, this patience is often rewarded with shreds of dry, chewy meat in dull, greasy sauce. Extending the preparation of our braised beef brisket recipe over two days solved several problems. After braising the brisket in an aluminum foil–lined pan, we let the meat stand overnight in the refrigerator in the braising liquid, which later became the sauce. This helped to keep the brisket moist and flavorful by allowing it to reabsorb some of the sauce, while creating a rich sauce that wasn't too thin. As the sauce cooled, the excess fat separated from it and solidified on top, making it a cinch to remove the next day. The overnight refrigeration also ensured that the cold brisket could be sliced easily without shredding. And because most of the work was now done ahead of time, our long-cooking brisket recipe could be easily reheated for the perfect midweek supper. If you prefer a spicy sauce, increase the amount of cayenne to ¼ teaspoon. You will need 18-inch-wide heavy-duty foil for this recipe. Serve over mashed potatoes or buttered egg noodles.

1   **(4- to 5-pound) beef brisket, flat cut preferred, fat trimmed to ¼ inch**
    Salt and pepper
1   **teaspoon vegetable oil**
3   **large onions, halved and sliced ½ inch thick**
1   **tablespoon packed brown sugar**
1   **tablespoon tomato paste**
3   **garlic cloves, minced**
1   **tablespoon paprika**
⅛   **teaspoon cayenne pepper**
2   **tablespoons all-purpose flour**
1   **cup chicken broth**
1   **cup dry red wine**
3   **sprigs fresh thyme**
3   **bay leaves**

TO FINISH AND SERVE
2   **teaspoons cider vinegar**

TO PREP

1. Adjust oven rack to lower-middle position and heat oven to 300 degrees. Line 13 by 9-inch baking dish with two 24-inch-long sheets of 18-inch-wide heavy-duty aluminum foil, positioning sheets perpendicular to each other and allowing excess foil to extend beyond edges of dish. Pat brisket dry with paper towels and place fat side up on cutting board. Using dinner fork, poke holes in meat through fat layer about 1 inch apart. Season both sides of brisket with salt and pepper.

2. Heat oil in 12-inch skillet over medium-high heat until just smoking. Place brisket fat side up in skillet (note that brisket will shrink as it cooks). Weight brisket with heavy Dutch oven or cast-iron skillet and cook until well browned, about 7 minutes. Remove Dutch oven, flip brisket, and cook on second side, without weight, until well browned, about 7 minutes. Transfer brisket to platter.

3. Pour off all but 1 tablespoon fat from skillet, add onions, sugar, and ¼ teaspoon salt, and cook over medium-high heat, stirring occasionally, until onions are softened and golden, 10 to 12 minutes. Stir in tomato paste and cook, stirring constantly, until paste browns, about 2 minutes. Stir in garlic, paprika, and cayenne and cook until fragrant, about 30 seconds. Sprinkle flour over onions and stir until well combined. Stir in broth, wine, thyme sprigs, and bay leaves, scraping up any browned bits. Bring mixture to simmer and cook until fully thickened, about 5 minutes.

4. Pour sauce and onions into prepared baking dish. Nestle brisket fat side up in sauce and onions. Fold foil extensions over and crimp to seal. Transfer to oven and cook until brisket is tender and fork slips easily in and out of meat, 3½ to 4 hours (when testing for doneness, open foil with caution as contents will be steaming). Carefully open foil and transfer brisket to storage container. Set fine-mesh strainer over container and strain sauce over brisket. Discard bay leaves and thyme sprigs and transfer onions to separate storage container. Let brisket and onions cool to room temperature, about 1 hour.

TO STORE

5. Cover brisket and onions and refrigerate for up to 2 days.

TO FINISH AND SERVE

6. Adjust oven rack to lower-middle position and heat oven to 350 degrees. Transfer brisket to cutting board. Skim excess fat from surface of sauce, then transfer to medium saucepan and heat over medium heat until warm (you should have about 2 cups sauce without onions; if necessary, simmer sauce over medium-high heat until reduced to 2 cups). Slice brisket against grain into ¼-inch-thick slices, trimming and discarding any excess fat, if desired. Shingle slices into 13 by 9-inch baking dish. Stir vinegar and reserved onions into warmed sauce and season with salt and pepper to taste. Pour sauce over brisket, cover baking dish with foil, and bake until heated through, 25 to 30 minutes. Serve.

Braised Boneless Beef Short Ribs

SERVES 4 TO 6 • **TO PREP** 2 TO 2½ HOURS • **STORE** UP TO 3 DAYS • **TO FINISH** 1½ HOURS

✔ **WHY THIS RECIPE WORKS:** Short ribs have great flavor and a luscious texture, but they can release a lot of fat during cooking. When we made this dish in advance, we found that the overnight rest in the refrigerator not only deepened the flavors of the meat and its braising liquid but also allowed the fat to solidify into an easy-to-remove layer. We chose boneless short ribs because they require less prep work, but without the bones' connective tissue to break down during cooking, our sauce was missing a silky, viscous texture. To restore the body that bones traditionally contribute, we sprinkled a bit of unflavored gelatin into the sauce at the end of cooking. After the initial braise, we stirred chilled broth into the pot to speed up the cooling process and protect the meat from drying out during storing and reheating. Adding the carrots to the pot the next day ensured that they were perfectly cooked and not overdone. To jump-start reheating, we brought the braise to a brief simmer on the stovetop, then finished it gently in the oven, which gave us deeply flavored, fork-tender ribs in a rich, luxurious sauce. Look for ribs that are at least 4 inches long and 1 inch thick. If boneless ribs are unavailable, substitute 7 pounds of bone-in beef short ribs that are at least 4 inches long with 1 inch of meat above the bone, and remove the meat from the bones. We recommend a bold red wine such as a Cabernet Sauvignon for this dish. Serve over buttered egg noodles or mashed potatoes or with roasted potatoes.

2	cups beef broth
3	pounds boneless beef short ribs, trimmed
	Kosher salt and pepper
1	tablespoon vegetable oil
2	onions, halved and sliced thin
1	tablespoon tomato paste
6	garlic cloves, peeled and smashed
2	cups dry red wine
4	sprigs fresh thyme
1	bay leaf

TO FINISH AND SERVE

4	carrots, peeled and cut into 1-inch pieces
½	teaspoon unflavored gelatin
¼	cup cold water

TEST KITCHEN TIP
TRIMMING BONELESS SHORT RIBS

Short ribs are notoriously fatty and need to be trimmed well before cooking. Using a sharp knife, trim away the large piece of fat on top and, if necessary, any fat on the bottom of each rib.

TO PREP

1. Refrigerate 1 cup broth. Adjust oven rack to lower-middle position and heat oven to 300 degrees. Pat beef dry with paper towels and season with 1½ teaspoons salt and 1 teaspoon pepper. Heat oil in Dutch oven over medium-high heat until just smoking. Brown beef well, 8 to 10 minutes; transfer to bowl.

2. Add onions to fat left in pot and cook over medium heat, stirring occasionally, until softened and beginning to brown, 8 to 10 minutes. Add tomato paste and cook, stirring constantly, until paste browns, about 2 minutes. Stir in garlic and cook until fragrant, about 30 seconds. Stir in wine, scraping up any browned bits. Increase heat to medium-high, bring to simmer, and cook until wine is reduced by half, 8 to 10 minutes.

3. Add remaining 1 cup broth, thyme sprigs, bay leaf, and beef with any accumulated juices and return to simmer. Cover pot, transfer to oven, and cook until beef is just tender, 1 to 1½ hours, turning meat halfway through cooking. Remove pot from oven and transfer beef to plate. To cool braising liquid, stir in chilled broth and let sit until cooled to room temperature, about 30 minutes.

TO STORE

4. Return beef to pot or transfer beef and braising liquid to storage container. Cover and refrigerate for up to 3 days.

TO FINISH AND SERVE

5. Adjust oven rack to lower-middle position and heat oven to 325 degrees. Skim excess fat from surface of braise and transfer to Dutch oven, if necessary. Stir in carrots and bring to simmer over medium heat. Cover pot, transfer to oven, and cook until beef is tender and fork slips easily in and out of meat, 45 to 60 minutes, gently turning meat halfway through cooking.

6. Sprinkle gelatin over cold water in bowl and let sit until gelatin softens, about 5 minutes. Remove pot from oven. Using slotted spoon, transfer meat and carrots to platter and tent loosely with aluminum foil. Strain braising liquid through fine-mesh strainer into bowl, pressing on solids to extract as much liquid as possible; discard solids. Return braising liquid to now-empty pot, bring to simmer over medium heat, and cook until reduced to 1 cup, 5 to 10 minutes. Off heat, stir in gelatin mixture until dissolved. Season with salt and pepper to taste, pour sauce over meat, and serve.

Texas Chili

SERVES 4 TO 6 • **TO PREP** 1 HOUR 15 MINUTES • **STORE** UP TO 3 DAYS • **TO FINISH** 1 HOUR 10 MINUTES

✓ **WHY THIS RECIPE WORKS:** Classic Texas chili features big chunks of beef in a fiery red sauce, but it often takes hours of simmering to get both tender meat and a flavorful sauce. We wanted all that in a chili that took less time to cook, was easy to prepare ahead, and had even more flavor when reheated. Boneless short ribs proved to be the best cut for our chili. They took less time to become tender and were easier to trim and prep than the traditional chuck roast. To add deep, smoky flavor, we tossed a few slices of bacon into the pot with our meat; leaving the slices whole and allowing them to break down throughout the cooking time saved us some prep time. These timesaving strategies allowed us to get everything into the pot quickly for a brief simmer on day one, and we took advantage of carryover cooking during the cooling time to ensure that the meat was tender. To cut down on cooling time while ensuring that the chili was cool enough to store in the fridge, we chilled the tomatoes and a portion of the chicken broth to stir into the pot right before we stored it. Bringing the chili to a simmer on the stovetop before finishing the cooking in the oven allowed us to keep the overall reheating time under an hour. A splash of lime juice before serving brightened all the flavors, and our chili delivered Texas-size flavor without a lot of work. Serve with chopped fresh cilantro, minced onion, diced avocado, shredded cheddar or Jack cheese, and sour cream.

1 (28-ounce) can crushed tomatoes
3 cups chicken broth, plus extra as needed
3 pounds boneless beef short ribs, trimmed and cut into 1-inch pieces
2 onions, chopped
4 slices bacon
5 garlic cloves, minced
3 tablespoons tomato paste
2 tablespoons chili powder
1 tablespoon ground cumin
2 teaspoons minced fresh oregano or ½ teaspoon dried
2 (15-ounce) cans pinto or kidney beans, rinsed
2 tablespoons packed dark brown sugar

TO FINISH AND SERVE
1 tablespoon lime juice

TO PREP

1. Refrigerate tomatoes and 1 cup broth. Combine beef, onions, and bacon in Dutch oven over medium-high heat. Cook, stirring often, until released beef juices nearly evaporate and meat begins to brown, 20 to 25 minutes, reducing heat if necessary to prevent scorching.

2. Stir in garlic, tomato paste, chili powder, cumin, and oregano and cook until fragrant, about 1 minute. Stir in remaining 2 cups broth, scraping up any browned bits, and bring to simmer. Cover, reduce heat to low, and simmer for 30 minutes.

3. Remove pot from heat and let sit, covered, for 45 minutes. Stir in chilled tomatoes and chilled broth to finish cooling. Stir in beans and sugar.

TO STORE

4. Leave stew in pot or transfer to storage container. Cover and refrigerate for up to 3 days.

TO FINISH AND SERVE

5. Adjust oven rack to lower-middle position and heat oven to 325 degrees. Skim excess fat from surface of chili and transfer to Dutch oven, if necessary. Bring to simmer over medium heat, stirring often. Cover pot, transfer to oven, and cook until beef is tender, about 45 minutes. Discard bacon. Adjust chili consistency with extra hot broth as needed. Stir in lime juice and season with salt and pepper to taste. Serve.

Pork Vindaloo

SERVES 4 TO 6 • **TO PREP** 1 HOUR 20 MINUTES • **STORE** UP TO 3 DAYS • **TO FINISH** 1 HOUR 10 MINUTES

✓ **WHY THIS RECIPE WORKS:** Vindaloo is a complex, spicy dish that originated on India's west coast, an area that once had a large population of Portuguese settlers, so the dish has both Indian and Portuguese influences. The hallmark of vindaloo is its interplay of sweet and sour flavors. It features tender meat in a thick, reddish-orange sauce with a delicately balanced flavor. The heat of the spices is tamed by the sweetness of the sugar and the acidity of the tomatoes and vinegar. Onions and garlic add pungency, and mustard seeds lend their unique flavor and punch. We tried to streamline this recipe by using boneless country-style ribs instead of the usual pork butt, but they tasted too lean and dry in our stew; the pork butt, on the other hand, turned meltingly tender and remained moist. We built flavor by blooming the spices in the fat from the pork, then simmered everything in a small amount of broth to build a base with depth and intensity of flavor. Cooling the stew with the lid on guaranteed that carryover cooking would further tenderize the meat. We then added chilled broth and tomatoes to help cool the stew down enough to store in the fridge quickly. Letting the sauce sit overnight (or for a few days) allowed the spices to bloom further, intensifying the fragrant sauce. Pork butt roast is often labeled Boston butt in the supermarket. Serve with basmati rice.

3   cups chicken broth
1   (14.5-ounce) can diced tomatoes
3   pounds boneless pork butt roast, trimmed
       and cut into 1-inch pieces
3   onions, chopped
1   tablespoon vegetable oil
       Salt and pepper
3   tablespoons paprika
8   garlic cloves, minced
4   teaspoons garam masala
⅛   teaspoon cayenne pepper
2   tablespoons all-purpose flour
1   tablespoon mustard seeds
2   teaspoons sugar

TO FINISH AND SERVE
2   tablespoons red wine vinegar
¼   cup minced fresh cilantro

TO PREP

1. Refrigerate 1 cup broth and tomatoes with their juice. Combine pork, onions, oil, ¼ teaspoon salt, and ⅛ teaspoon pepper in Dutch oven over medium heat. Cook, stirring often, until released pork juices nearly evaporate and meat begins to brown, 20 to 25 minutes, reducing heat if necessary to prevent scorching.

2. Stir in paprika, garlic, garam masala, and cayenne and cook until fragrant, about 1 minute. Stir in flour and cook for 1 minute. Slowly stir in remaining 2 cups broth, mustard seeds, and sugar, scraping up any browned bits and smoothing out any lumps. Bring to simmer, then cover, reduce heat to low, and cook for 30 minutes.

3. Remove pot from heat and let sit, covered, for 45 minutes. Stir in chilled broth and chilled tomatoes to finish cooling.

TO STORE

4. Leave stew in pot or transfer to storage container. Cover and refrigerate for up to 3 days.

TO FINISH AND SERVE

5. Adjust oven rack to lower-middle position and heat oven to 325 degrees. Skim excess fat from surface of stew and transfer to Dutch oven, if necessary. Stir in vinegar and bring to simmer over medium heat, stirring often. Cover pot, transfer to oven, and cook until pork is tender, about 50 minutes. Stir in cilantro and season with salt and pepper to taste. Serve.

Easy Pulled Pork

SERVES 4 TO 6 • **TO PREP** 4 HOURS • **STORE** UP TO 3 DAYS • **TO FINISH** 25 MINUTES

✔ **WHY THIS RECIPE WORKS:** Barbecued pulled pork has a lot of appeal—when made well, it features moist, tender, shreddable meat infused with deep smoky flavor. But getting that fall-apart-tender texture requires slow, gentle cooking whether you use the oven, your slow cooker, or your grill. The good news is that it is a relatively hands-off process, and because the flavor of the pork only deepens if it sits for a day or two in the sauce, it's a great recipe to make ahead. For our make-ahead version, we turned to the oven and chose to use boneless pork butt because of its generous marbling. We bloomed the spices in oil to give our simple homemade sauce depth of flavor. Cutting the meat into 2-inch pieces shortened the cooking time while still giving us the tenderness and hearty shredded texture we were after. Shredding the meat on day one and combining it with the sauce for storage kept the meat moist. Adding cider vinegar during the reheat brightened the sauce. Pork butt roast is often labeled Boston butt in the supermarket.

1 tablespoon vegetable oil
1 onion, chopped
3 tablespoons paprika
4 garlic cloves, minced
1 tablespoon ground cumin
¼ teaspoon cayenne pepper
1 cup water
1 cup ketchup
3 tablespoons molasses
1½ tablespoons packed brown sugar
1½ tablespoons Worcestershire sauce
  Salt and pepper
3 pounds boneless pork butt roast, trimmed and cut into 2-inch pieces

TO FINISH AND SERVE
1 tablespoon cider vinegar
4–6 hamburger buns

TO PREP

1. Adjust oven rack to lower-middle position and heat oven to 300 degrees. Heat oil in Dutch oven over medium heat until shimmering. Add onion and cook until softened, about 5 minutes. Stir in paprika, garlic, cumin, and cayenne and cook until fragrant, about 30 seconds. Stir in water, ketchup, molasses, sugar, Worcestershire, ½ teaspoon salt, and ½ teaspoon pepper.

2. Nestle pork into sauce and bring to simmer. Cover pot, transfer to oven, and cook pork until tender and fork slips easily in and out of meat, about 3 hours.

3. Remove pot from oven. Using slotted spoon, transfer pork to bowl and let cool slightly. Shred pork into bite-size pieces using potato masher or 2 forks. Let sauce cool to room temperature, about 45 minutes.

TO STORE

4. Transfer 1 cup sauce to small storage container. Stir shredded pork into remaining sauce in pot. Leave pork mixture in pot or transfer to separate storage container. Cover and refrigerate pork mixture and reserved sauce for up to 3 days.

TO FINISH AND SERVE

5. Skim excess fat from surface of pork mixture and reserved sauce. Transfer pork mixture to Dutch oven, if necessary. Stir in vinegar, bring to simmer over medium heat, and cook, stirring often, until heated through, about 10 minutes. Adjust consistency with hot water as needed and season with salt and pepper to taste. Meanwhile, bring reserved sauce to brief simmer in small saucepan, stirring often. Serve shredded pork on buns with reserved sauce.

Cider-Braised Pork Chops

SERVES 4 TO 6 • **TO PREP** 1 HOUR 10 MINUTES • **STORE** UP TO 3 DAYS • **TO FINISH** 1 HOUR 10 MINUTES

✔ **WHY THIS RECIPE WORKS:** Pork and apples are a tried-and-true pairing, but the apple flavor in cider-braised pork chops can be fleeting, and recipes often skimp on the time necessary for the pork to become fall-off-the-bone tender. We wanted tender, juicy chops infused with deep cider flavor that would only get better with time. Patting the chops dry before adding them to the hot oil helped them to develop a flavorful crust. After searing the chops, we simmered them in sweet, tart apple cider thickened with apple butter and infused with garlic and thyme. After 30 minutes of simmering, we took the chops off the heat and let carryover cooking continue to tenderize them as they cooled to room temperature. A slow, gentle reheat on day two finished tenderizing the chops and thickened the braising liquid. To reinforce the apple flavor and brighten the sauce, we whisked in more apple butter and some cider vinegar just before serving. The natural pectin in the apple butter also gave the sauce a rich, glossy consistency.

4   (10- to 12-ounce) bone-in blade-cut pork chops, about ¾ inch thick, trimmed
     Salt and pepper
2   tablespoons vegetable oil
1   onion, chopped
3   garlic cloves, minced
2   tablespoons all-purpose flour
2   tablespoons apple butter
2   cups apple cider
1   sprig fresh thyme

TO FINISH AND SERVE

2   tablespoons apple butter
1   tablespoon minced fresh parsley
1   tablespoon cider vinegar

TO PREP

1. Cut 2 slits, about 2 inches apart, through outer layer of fat and silverskin on each chop. Pat chops dry with paper towels and season with salt and pepper. Heat 1 tablespoon oil in Dutch oven over medium-high heat until just smoking. Brown 2 chops well on one side, about 4 minutes; transfer to plate. Repeat with remaining 1 tablespoon oil and remaining 2 chops; transfer to plate.

2. Pour off all but 1 tablespoon fat from pot, add onion, and cook over medium heat until softened, about 5 minutes. Stir in garlic, flour, and apple butter and cook until onion is coated and mixture is fragrant, about 1 minute. Stir in cider and thyme sprig, scraping up any browned bits.

3. Nestle chops into pot along with any accumulated juices and bring to simmer. Cover, reduce heat to medium-low, and simmer for 30 minutes. Uncover and let cool to room temperature, about 45 minutes.

TO STORE

4. Leave chops and braising liquid in pot or transfer to storage container. Cover and refrigerate for up to 3 days.

TO FINISH AND SERVE

5. Adjust oven rack to lower-middle position and heat oven to 325 degrees. Skim excess fat from surface of braise and transfer to Dutch oven, if necessary. Bring chops to gentle simmer over medium heat. Cover pot, transfer to oven, and cook until pork chops are tender and fork slips easily in and out of meat, about 45 minutes. Transfer chops to serving platter. Whisk apple butter, parsley, and vinegar into braising liquid and season with salt and pepper to taste. Pour sauce over chops and serve.

TEST KITCHEN TIP
PREVENTING CURLED PORK CHOPS

 As pork chops cook, the fat and silverskin around the edges contract and the chops curl. To prevent this, use a sharp knife to cut two slits, about 2 inches apart, into the fat and silverskin.

Chicken Cacciatore

SERVES 4 TO 6 • **TO PREP** 1 HOUR 25 MINUTES • **STORE** UP TO 3 DAYS • **TO FINISH** 30 MINUTES

☑ **WHY THIS RECIPE WORKS:** Chicken cacciatore is a rustic Italian dish featuring braised bone-in chicken with mushrooms in a robust tomato sauce. Like other braises, its flavors meld and deepen as it sits, making it a great candidate for a make-ahead dish. All too often, though, cacciatore recipes turn out overcooked chicken with a generic and greasy tomato sauce. Using chicken thighs and removing the skin after we had rendered the fat solved the problems of dry meat, greasy sauce, and soggy skin. We started with a basic sauce of canned diced tomatoes and chicken broth, but it was overly acidic and bland. Swapping the diced tomatoes for crushed tomatoes and the broth for dry red wine and adding thyme, garlic, and bay leaves gave us a well-balanced sauce with deeper flavor. We liked the meaty texture and flavor of portobello mushrooms, but we found that they muddied the sauce as the dish sat overnight, so we swapped in hearty cremini mushrooms instead. To brighten the flavors of the dish we added fresh sage before serving. An equal amount of minced fresh rosemary can be substituted for the sage.

4 **pounds bone-in chicken thighs, trimmed**
  Salt and pepper
1 **tablespoon vegetable oil**
6 **ounces cremini mushrooms, trimmed and quartered**
1 **red bell pepper, stemmed, seeded, and sliced ¼ inch thick**
1 **onion, halved and sliced ¼ inch thick**
4 **garlic cloves, minced**
2 **teaspoons minced fresh thyme or ½ teaspoon dried**
½ **cup dry red wine**
1 **(28-ounce) can crushed tomatoes**
2 **bay leaves**

TO FINISH AND SERVE
1 **teaspoon minced fresh sage**

TO PREP

1. Pat chicken dry with paper towels and season with salt and pepper. Heat oil in Dutch oven over medium-high heat until just smoking. Place half of chicken skin side down in pot and cook until well browned, about 5 minutes; transfer to plate. Repeat with remaining chicken; transfer to plate. Remove chicken skin.

2. Pour off all but 1 tablespoon fat from pot. Add mushrooms, bell pepper, onion, and ¾ teaspoon salt and cook, stirring occasionally, until softened and lightly browned, 10 to 12 minutes. Stir in garlic and thyme and cook until fragrant, about 30 seconds.

Slowly stir in wine, scraping up any browned bits, and cook until slightly reduced, about 1 minute. Stir in tomatoes and bay leaves.

3. Nestle chicken into pot along with any accumulated juices and bring to simmer. Cover, reduce heat to medium-low, and gently simmer until chicken registers 175 degrees, 30 to 40 minutes. Uncover and let cool to room temperature, about 45 minutes.

TO STORE

4. Leave cacciatore in pot or transfer to storage container. Cover and refrigerate for up to 3 days.

TO FINISH AND SERVE

5. Skim excess fat from surface of sauce and transfer to Dutch oven, if necessary. Discard bay leaves. Bring to simmer over medium-low heat and cook, stirring occasionally, until heated through, about 15 minutes (do not overcook chicken). Stir in sage and season with salt and pepper to taste. Serve.

TEST KITCHEN TIP **REMOVING CHICKEN SKIN**

Chicken skin is slippery, making it a challenge to remove by hand, even when the chicken has been browned. To simplify the task, use a paper towel to provide extra grip when pulling.

Marsala-Braised Chicken and Mushrooms

SERVES 4 • **TO PREP** 1 HOUR 10 MINUTES • **STORE** UP TO 3 DAYS • **TO FINISH** 1 HOUR

✔ **WHY THIS RECIPE WORKS:** Traditional chicken Marsala features flour-coated, sautéed cutlets dressed in a mushroom-laced pan sauce. We wanted to translate those flavors into a dish that could be made in advance, without sacrificing the texture of the chicken. We immediately skipped the step of coating the chicken in flour to avoid ending up with a soggy or slimy exterior. Instead, we gently poached the chicken in a combination of Marsala and chicken broth. When the breasts were just cooked through, we removed them from the braising liquid so they wouldn't overcook. Once cooled, we stored the cooked breasts and braising liquid in a baking dish covered tightly with aluminum foil so that it was oven-ready when it was time to reheat. Reheating the chicken in the oven ensured a gentle, even heat that kept the chicken moist and tender. With our cooking method set, we just needed to adjust the flavor of our sauce. The initial test turned out a bit too boozy, so we spent a little extra time reducing the Marsala with the browned mushrooms so that its flavor came through without being harsh. We preferred sweet (as opposed to dry) Marsala wine, which gave the sauce body and a smooth finish. Some lemon juice stirred in just before serving tempered the Marsala's sweetness, and a little cold butter whisked into the sauce gave it good body and richness.

1	tablespoon vegetable oil
2	ounces pancetta, chopped
8	ounces white mushrooms, trimmed and sliced thin
2	tablespoons all-purpose flour
1	garlic clove, minced
1	teaspoon tomato paste
1½	cups sweet Marsala
1	cup chicken broth
4	(6- to 8-ounce) boneless, skinless chicken breasts, trimmed and pounded to even thickness
	Salt and pepper

TO FINISH AND SERVE

2	teaspoons lemon juice
2	tablespoons unsalted butter, cut into 2 pieces and chilled
2	tablespoons chopped fresh parsley

TO PREP

1. Heat oil in 12-inch skillet over medium heat until shimmering. Add pancetta and cook until rendered and starting to brown, about 3 minutes.

2. Add mushrooms, increase heat to medium-high, and cook, stirring occasionally, until mushrooms are softened and lightly browned, about 8 minutes. Stir in flour, garlic, and tomato paste and cook until tomato paste begins to brown, about 1 minute. Off heat, stir in Marsala, scraping up any browned bits. Return skillet to high heat, bring mixture to vigorous simmer, and cook, stirring occasionally, until thick and syrupy, about 8 minutes. Whisk in broth until well combined.

3. Pat chicken dry with paper towels and season with salt and pepper. Nestle chicken into skillet and bring to simmer. Cover, reduce heat to low, and gently simmer until chicken registers 160 degrees, about 20 minutes, turning chicken halfway though cooking. Transfer chicken to 8-inch square baking dish and let cool. Let sauce cool to room temperature in skillet, about 30 minutes, then pour over chicken.

TO STORE

4. Cover dish tightly with aluminum foil and refrigerate for up to 3 days.

TO FINISH AND SERVE

5. Adjust oven rack to middle position and heat oven to 325 degrees. Place covered baking dish in oven and bake until chicken is heated through, 35 to 45 minutes (do not overcook chicken). Transfer chicken to serving platter and tent loosely with foil. Whisk lemon juice into sauce, then whisk in butter, 1 piece at a time, until incorporated. Whisk in parsley and season with salt and pepper to taste. Pour sauce over chicken and serve.

KEEPING LEAN CHICKEN MOIST
To make chicken Marsala ahead, we had to find a way to cook, cool, and reheat lean boneless, skinless chicken breasts without them ending up dry and overcooked. The trick was to poach them gently in a flavorful braising liquid, then take them out of the sauce and let them cool separately to protect them from the sauce's residual heat before reuniting the chicken and sauce.

Chicken Tagine

SERVES 4 TO 6 • **TO PREP** 1 HOUR 25 MINUTES • **STORE** UP TO 3 DAYS • **TO FINISH** 40 MINUTES

✔ **WHY THIS RECIPE WORKS:** Time-consuming techniques and esoteric ingredients make cooking authentic Moroccan chicken a daunting proposition. But this flavorful, assertively spiced dish is essentially a chicken stew, one that gets better and more flavorful with an overnight rest in the refrigerator. We wanted to keep the essence of this appealing dish while simplifying the ingredient list. Traditional olives and lemon were essential; for bold lemon flavor, we simmered strips of zest in the stew and added some fresh juice just before serving. Garam masala and cayenne proved to be the only spices we needed to achieve traditional flavor while streamlining our ingredient list. Dried apricots and fresh cilantro—both classic Moroccan ingredients—rounded out our dish. Searing the thighs with the skin on helped jump-start their cooking and created a flavorful fond with which to build our sauce. We then removed the skin to prevent it from making the stew overly greasy. If the olives are particularly salty, give them a rinse. If you cannot find pitted olives and don't want to pit them yourself, substitute pimento-stuffed green olives; be sure to rinse them very well under cold running water. Serve with couscous.

4	pounds bone-in chicken thighs, trimmed
	Salt and pepper
1	tablespoon vegetable oil
2	onions, halved and sliced ¼ inch thick
2	(2-inch) strips lemon zest
4	garlic cloves, minced
2	teaspoons garam masala
¼	teaspoon cayenne pepper
2	cups chicken broth
3	carrots, peeled and sliced ½ inch thick

TO FINISH AND SERVE

1	cup large pitted brine-cured green olives, halved
½	cup dried apricots, chopped
2	tablespoons lemon juice
1	garlic clove, minced
2	tablespoons minced fresh cilantro

TO PREP

1. Pat chicken dry with paper towels and season with salt and pepper. Heat oil in Dutch oven over medium-high heat until just smoking. Place half of chicken skin side down in pot and cook until well browned, about 5 minutes; transfer to plate. Repeat with remaining chicken; transfer to plate. Remove chicken skin.

2. Pour off all but 1 tablespoon fat from pot. Add onions, lemon zest, and ½ teaspoon salt and cook over medium heat, stirring occasionally, until onions are softened and lightly browned, 5 to 7 minutes. Stir in garlic, garam masala, and cayenne and cook until fragrant, about 30 seconds. Stir in broth, scraping up any browned bits.

3. Nestle chicken into pot along with any accumulated juices and bring to simmer. Cover, reduce heat to medium-low, and gently simmer until chicken registers 175 degrees, 30 to 40 minutes. Off heat, stir in carrots and let tagine cool, uncovered, to room temperature, about 45 minutes.

TO STORE

4. Leave tagine in pot or transfer to storage container. Cover and refrigerate for up to 3 days.

TO FINISH AND SERVE

5. Skim excess fat from surface of tagine and transfer to Dutch oven, if necessary. Discard lemon zest. Stir in olives and apricots, bring to simmer over medium-low heat, and cook, stirring occasionally, until carrots are tender and chicken is heated through, about 15 minutes (do not overcook chicken). Off heat, stir in lemon juice and garlic and let sit for 5 minutes. Stir in cilantro and season with salt and pepper to taste. Serve.

TEST KITCHEN TIP MAKING STRIPS OF ZEST

Using vegetable peeler, cut long, wide strips of zest from lemon, being careful not to remove any of bitter white pith beneath zest.

ALL ABOUT Cooling and Reheating Stews and Braises

Hearty stews and braises are ideal dishes to make ahead because their flavors and textures improve over time. But they require a lengthy simmer to tenderize the meat and fully develop the flavors—plus the time it takes to cool them before storing. So we re-engineered these recipes to put the hands-off cooling time to work, saving both time and effort. While developing these recipes, we also learned a few things about cooling and reheating these dishes that had a big impact on their overall success.

Cool Before Storing

Though it may seem like a convenient shortcut, never put hot food in the fridge immediately after cooking. This will cause the temperature of the refrigerator to rise, potentially making it hospitable to the spread of bacteria. To avoid this, keep a thermometer handy and make sure to cool food on the counter to room temperature (about 75 degrees) before transferring it to the fridge.

Take Advantage of Cooling Time

Cooling a stew or braise before storing it is necessary, but it can add a substantial amount of time to a recipe. So we looked for a way to put that time to work. For tougher cuts of meat that require long cooking times, like beef short ribs and pork butt, we found that the time spent cooling could be used to further tenderize the meat. That's because the residual heat in the pot continued to cook the meat gently as the stew or braise cooled. Taking advantage of the effects of carryover cooking also meant that we were able to reduce the active cooking time, saving us time overall.

Add Chilled Liquid for Quicker Cooling

It takes a long time for a braise or a big pot of stew to cool. Luckily, we found a great trick to speed up the cooling time so we could get our dish into the fridge without waiting up all night. While the dish cooked, we chilled some liquid (broth, water, and canned tomatoes all worked well). After allowing the dish to cool for just 45 minutes (so that the carryover cooking could further tenderize the meat), we added the chilled liquid to cool the dish to room temperature instantly. For chicken dishes that didn't benefit from carryover cooking, this trick allowed us to take the dish straight from the stovetop to the fridge without any cooling time at all. Finally, we kept delicate beans and vegetables from overcooking by adding chilled liquid to prevent them from continuing to cook off the heat.

Reheat Gently

Stews and braises require gentle reheating to prevent scorching. For dishes that needed to finish cooking on the second day, the fastest strategy was to bring them to a simmer on the stovetop, then transfer them to a preheated oven where they could finish cooking gently. We warmed chicken and vegetable dishes on the stovetop so that we could monitor them easily, avoiding overcooked chicken or mushy vegetables. Chicken Marsala was the exception; because it has less liquid, it scorched and dried out on the stovetop, so we gently reheated it in a shallow baking dish in the oven. We also used the reheating time to cook delicate, quick-cooking vegetables like bell peppers, corn, and Swiss chard.

Refresh Bright Flavors Before Serving

We often add fresh herbs, vinegar, citrus juice, and other aromatic ingredients to our stews and braises right before serving. While rich, meaty flavors are enhanced over time, bright, fresh flavors can become muted during storage and reheating. Refreshing the dishes with bright acidic and aromatic ingredients off the heat ensured that our dishes never tasted dull.

Classic Chicken Stew

SERVES 4 TO 6 • **TO PREP** 1 HOUR 20 MINUTES • **STORE** UP TO 3 DAYS • **TO FINISH** 40 MINUTES

✔ **WHY THIS RECIPE WORKS:** When we think of chicken stew, we imagine tender, moist chunks of chicken accompanied by potatoes, carrots, and peas, all enveloped in a glossy, flavorful sauce. It's the kind of supper that could easily take hours to prepare. But we wanted all those qualities in a hearty make-ahead stew that didn't require hours in the kitchen and could be quickly reheated when it was time for dinner. To ensure that our meat stayed moist and tender through storage and reheating, we chose chicken thighs, which have more fat than breasts. Traditionally, the meat is simmered on the bone and then shredded, but to save time we used boneless thighs and cut them into small pieces prior to cooking. Browning the chicken and sautéing the aromatics gave our recipe a flavorful base, and simmering the vegetables in white wine and chicken broth gave them complex flavor. We found that the best way to avoid overcooked vegetables when reheating the stew was to simmer them for only 10 minutes on the first day. Then we stirred in chilled broth to help cool the stew down faster so the vegetables didn't turn mushy. When we were ready to reheat, a quick 20-minute simmer gave us perfectly tender vegetables that still retained their shape and texture. Do not substitute boneless, skinless chicken breasts for the thighs in this recipe or the meat will taste very dry.

4 **cups chicken broth**
2 **pounds boneless, skinless chicken thighs, trimmed and cut into 1-inch pieces**
  Salt and pepper
2 **tablespoons vegetable oil**
1 **onion, chopped**
3 **garlic cloves, minced**
1 **teaspoon minced fresh thyme or ¼ teaspoon dried**
⅓ **cup all-purpose flour**
1 **cup dry white wine**
2 **bay leaves**
1 **pound red potatoes, unpeeled, cut into ¾-inch pieces**
4 **carrots, peeled and sliced ½ inch thick**

TO FINISH AND SERVE
⅔ **cup frozen peas**
3 **tablespoons minced fresh parsley**

TO PREP

1. Refrigerate 1½ cups broth. Pat chicken dry with paper towels and season with salt and pepper. Heat 1 tablespoon oil in Dutch oven over medium-high heat until just smoking. Brown chicken lightly on all sides, 6 to 8 minutes; transfer to bowl.

2. Add remaining 1 tablespoon oil to fat left in pot and return to medium heat until shimmering. Add onion and ¼ teaspoon salt and cook until softened, about 5 minutes. Stir in garlic and thyme and cook until fragrant, about 30 seconds. Stir in flour and cook for 1 minute. Slowly whisk in wine, scraping up any browned bits.

3. Slowly whisk in remaining 2½ cups broth, smoothing out any lumps. Stir in bay leaves and chicken with any accumulated juices and bring to simmer. Cover, reduce heat to medium-low, and gently simmer for 20 minutes. Stir in potatoes and carrots and continue to simmer until chicken is tender, about 10 minutes.

4. Remove pot from heat. To cool, stir in chilled broth and let sit, uncovered, until cooled to room temperature, about 45 minutes.

TO STORE

5. Leave stew in pot or transfer to storage container. Cover and refrigerate for up to 3 days.

TO FINISH AND SERVE

6. Skim excess fat from surface of stew and transfer to Dutch oven, if necessary. Remove bay leaves. Bring to simmer over medium heat. Cover, reduce heat to medium-low, and simmer, stirring often, until potatoes and carrots are tender and chicken is heated through, 15 to 20 minutes (do not overcook chicken). Off heat, stir in peas and let sit until heated through, about 5 minutes. Stir in parsley and season with salt and pepper to taste. Serve.

White Chicken Chili

SERVES 4 TO 6 • **TO PREP** 1 HOUR 20 MINUTES • **STORE** UP TO 3 DAYS • **TO FINISH** 25 MINUTES

✓ **WHY THIS RECIPE WORKS:** White chicken chili promises a lighter, fresher alternative to the tomato-based kind, but often recipes turn out bland and watery with chalky chicken. To ensure that the chicken in our chili stayed moist and tender, we started with bone-in chicken breasts. We browned them to develop fond (the flavorful bits on the bottom of the pot) and render their fat, which we used to sauté the aromatics. Then we gently poached the chicken until it was just cooked through. It was easiest to shred the chicken while it was still warm, but to prevent it from becoming dried out and overcooked, we cooled the chili base before stirring the shredded chicken back in for storage. Bite-size shreds also reheated quickly, so it didn't take much time to bring the chili up to serving temperature. A trio of jalapeño, poblano, and Anaheim chiles brought the perfect balance of flavor, complexity, and modest heat to our chili. For more heat, include the jalapeño seeds and ribs. If you can't find Anaheim chiles, substitute an additional poblano and an additional jalapeño. Serve with sour cream, tortilla chips, and lime wedges.

3   cups chicken broth
1   onion, chopped
1   jalapeño chile, stemmed, seeded, and chopped
2   poblano chiles, stemmed, seeded, and chopped
2   Anaheim chiles, stemmed, seeded, and chopped
2   pounds bone-in split chicken breasts, trimmed
     Salt and pepper
1   tablespoon vegetable oil
4   garlic cloves, minced
2   teaspoons ground cumin
1   teaspoon ground coriander
2   (15-ounce) cans cannellini beans, rinsed

TO FINISH AND SERVE
3   tablespoons minced fresh cilantro
3   scallions, sliced thin
1   jalapeño chile, stemmed, seeded, and minced
2   tablespoons lime juice

TO PREP

1. Refrigerate 1½ cups broth. Pulse onion and jalapeño together in food processor to consistency of chunky salsa, about 12 pulses. Transfer mixture to medium bowl. Pulse poblanos and Anaheims together in now-empty food processor to consistency of chunky salsa, about 12 pulses; transfer to bowl with onion and jalapeño.

2. Pat chicken dry with paper towels and season with salt and pepper. Heat oil in Dutch oven over medium-high heat until just smoking. Brown chicken well on all sides, 7 to 10 minutes; transfer to plate.

3. Pour off all but 1 tablespoon fat from pot, add chile-onion mixture, garlic, cumin, coriander, and 1 teaspoon salt, cover, and cook over medium heat until vegetables are softened, 8 to 10 minutes.

4. Remove pot from heat and transfer 1 cup cooked vegetables to now-empty food processor. Add 1 cup beans and ½ cup broth to food processor and process mixture until smooth, about 20 seconds. Stir processed bean mixture and remaining 1 cup broth into pot, scraping up any browned bits, and bring to simmer over medium heat. Nestle chicken into pot along with any accumulated juices and bring to simmer. Cover, reduce heat to low, and gently simmer until chicken registers 160 degrees, about 20 minutes.

5. Transfer chicken to cutting board, let cool slightly, then shred into bite-size pieces using 2 forks, discarding skin and bones. Meanwhile, remove pot from heat. To cool, stir in chilled broth and let sit, uncovered, until cooled to room temperature, about 30 minutes. Stir in remaining beans and shredded chicken.

TO STORE

6. Leave chili in pot or transfer to storage container. Cover and refrigerate for up to 3 days.

TO FINISH AND SERVE

7. Transfer chili to Dutch oven, if necessary. Bring chili to simmer over medium heat. Cover, reduce heat to medium-low, and simmer, stirring often, until heated through, about 10 minutes. Off heat, stir in cilantro, scallions, jalapeño, and lime juice. Season with salt and pepper to taste and serve.

BUILDING FRESH FLAVOR
The bold, warm spices in traditional tomato-based chilis improve with time, but the lighter, fresher flavors of white chicken chili can fade during storage and reheating, so we used three types of fresh chiles for layers of flavor. We sautéed them in oil before simmering them in the chili to develop deep flavor, then added a fresh jalapeño on day two for a bright, spicy kick.

Black Bean Chili

SERVES 4 TO 6 • **TO PREP** 1 HOUR • **STORE** UP TO 3 DAYS • **TO FINISH** 1 HOUR

✓ **WHY THIS RECIPE WORKS:** Packed with chiles, garlic, tomatoes, pork, and plenty of chili powder, Latin-inspired black bean chili should be hearty and satisfying, with bold flavors that deepen over a few days in the fridge. To develop a make-ahead version of this dish, our biggest challenge would be getting perfectly cooked beans. We applied what we had learned when developing our White Bean and Kale Stew, simmering the black beans with baking soda and salt for just 30 minutes on day one to ensure that they would turn tender in less than an hour when reheated. Adding ⅛ teaspoon of baking soda to the chili when reheating helped to speed up the reheating time further. Tomatoes are a key component of this chili, but their acidity can prevent beans from softening. To avoid this, we added the tomatoes toward the end of the cooking time, once the beans were nearly tender, then simmered the chili until thickened. Chunks of red bell pepper went in along with the tomatoes so that they would retain their firm texture and add freshness to the chili. To round out the chili, spicy chorizo and smoky paprika added depth of flavor, and chili powder lent lingering heat. If you can't find Spanish chorizo, you can substitute andouille sausage. In addition to lime wedges, this chili is great served with sour cream, shredded cheddar or Monterey Jack cheese, chopped tomatoes, and minced onion.

9	**cups water**
1	**pound (2½ cups) dried black beans, picked over and rinsed**
	Salt and pepper
1	**tablespoon baking soda**
1½	**teaspoons cumin seeds**
2	**tablespoons vegetable oil**
6	**ounces Spanish chorizo sausage, quartered lengthwise and sliced ¼ inch thick**
1	**onion, chopped**
4	**garlic cloves, minced**
1	**tablespoon chili powder**
2	**teaspoons smoked paprika**
2	**cups chicken broth**
2	**bay leaves**

TO FINISH AND SERVE

⅛	**teaspoon baking soda**
1	**(28-ounce) can crushed tomatoes**
1	**red bell pepper, stemmed, seeded, and cut into ½-inch pieces**
¼	**cup minced fresh cilantro**
	Lime wedges

TO PREP

1. Refrigerate 1 cup water. Bring remaining 2 quarts water, beans, 1½ tablespoons salt, and baking soda to boil in Dutch oven over high heat. Reduce heat to medium-high and simmer briskly for 30 minutes. Drain and rinse beans in colander. Wipe pot clean.

2. Toast cumin seeds in now-empty Dutch oven over medium heat, stirring constantly, until fragrant, about 1 minute. Stir in oil, chorizo, and onion and cook until onion is softened and lightly browned, 5 to 7 minutes. Stir in garlic, chili powder, and paprika and cook until fragrant, about 1 minute. Stir in broth and bay leaves, scraping up any browned bits. Let cool for 30 minutes. Stir in chilled water to finish cooling, then stir in drained beans.

TO STORE

3. Leave chili in pot or transfer to storage container. Cover and refrigerate for up to 3 days.

TO FINISH AND SERVE

4. Transfer chili to Dutch oven, if necessary. Stir in baking soda and bring to simmer over medium heat. Cover, reduce heat to medium-low, and simmer, stirring often, until beans are almost tender, about 30 minutes. Stir in tomatoes and bell pepper and cook, uncovered, until beans are tender, 10 to 15 minutes. Discard bay leaves. Stir in cilantro and season with salt and pepper to taste. Serve with lime wedges.

ADD BAKING SODA FOR TENDER BEANS

Tender, evenly cooked beans are an essential part of a good chili—but a time-consuming one. We found that adding baking soda to the water helped to break down the cell structure of the beans, giving us tender beans in much less time. We added the tomatoes on the second day to keep their acidity from counteracting the baking soda.

White Bean and Kale Stew

SERVES 4 TO 6 • **TO PREP** 45 MINUTES • **STORE** UP TO 3 DAYS • **TO FINISH** 1 HOUR

☑ **WHY THIS RECIPE WORKS:** The first step in cooking dried beans to tender, creamy perfection is usually soaking them overnight in salted water. With this built-in make-ahead strategy, bean stew seemed like a perfect choice to stash in the fridge for a busy weeknight. We thought it would be easy to build our stew base, soak the beans separately, and then marry them together when reheating. However, a big drawback to this method was the amount of time the soaked beans needed to fully cook—upward of two hours—which was longer than we wanted to spend reheating a make-ahead stew. To get perfectly cooked, richly flavored beans and a quick reheat, we needed a different approach. We tried partially cooking the beans on day one to shorten the reheating time, but that gave us inconsistent results—some beans were undercooked and others blown out and broken apart. We found the trick was to add baking soda, which helped to break down the cell structure of the beans, resulting in tender beans in less time. Swapping the traditional cannellini beans for smaller navy beans gave us more consistent results. To finish the stew, we stirred in chopped kale for the last 15 minutes of simmering, giving it enough time to become just tender but retain a hearty texture. If you can't find pancetta, you can substitute 3 ounces of bacon.

10	**cups water**
8	**ounces (1¼ cups) dried navy beans, picked over and rinsed**
	Salt and pepper
2	**teaspoons baking soda**
1	**tablespoon extra-virgin olive oil, plus extra for serving**
4	**ounces pancetta, chopped fine**
1	**onion, chopped**
1	**celery rib, chopped**
6	**garlic cloves, minced**
6	**cups chicken broth**
1	**bay leaf**

TO FINISH AND SERVE

2	**carrots, peeled and sliced ½ inch thick**
⅛	**teaspoon baking soda**
6	**ounces kale or collard greens, stemmed and cut into 1-inch pieces**
1	**sprig fresh rosemary**

TO PREP

1. Refrigerate 2 cups water. Bring remaining 2 quarts water, beans, 1 tablespoon salt, and baking soda to boil in Dutch oven over high heat. Reduce heat to medium-high and simmer briskly for 20 minutes. Drain and rinse beans in colander. Wipe pot clean.

2. Heat oil in now-empty Dutch oven over medium-high heat until shimmering. Add pancetta, onion, and celery and cook until pancetta has rendered and vegetables are softened and lightly browned, 5 to 7 minutes. Stir in garlic and cook until fragrant, about 30 seconds. Off heat, stir in broth, bay leaf, and drained beans. Stir in chilled water to finish cooling.

TO STORE

3. Leave stew in pot or transfer to storage container. Cover and refrigerate for up to 3 days.

TO FINISH AND SERVE

4. Transfer stew to Dutch oven, if necessary. Stir in carrots and baking soda and bring to simmer over medium heat. Cover, reduce heat to medium-low, and simmer, stirring occasionally, until beans and carrots are almost tender, about 30 minutes. Stir in kale and rosemary, cover, and cook until beans and vegetables are tender, about 15 minutes. Discard bay leaf and rosemary sprig and season stew with salt and pepper to taste. If desired, use back of spoon to mash some beans against side of pot to thicken stew. Serve, drizzling individual portions with extra oil.

Butternut Squash and Swiss Chard Stew

SERVES 4 • **TO PREP** 45 MINUTES • **STORE** UP TO 3 DAYS • **TO FINISH** 35 MINUTES

WHY THIS RECIPE WORKS: Classic creamy butternut squash soup is an easy make-ahead dish, but we wanted something that could stand alone as a heartier vegetarian meal. To create a velvety base for our stew, we simmered a portion of the butternut squash with aromatics and vegetable broth, then pureed it until smooth. We wanted substantial chunks of butternut squash in the finished stew, so we stirred the remaining raw squash into the pureed mixture just before cooling it down. This ensured that the squash remained intact and didn't turn to mush when reheated. To round out the stew, we stirred in a hearty amount of Swiss chard before reheating. As soon as the squash and chard were tender, we stirred in some coconut milk to produce a rich-tasting, creamy broth. A small amount of smoky chipotle chile balanced the sweetness of the coconut milk and added a kick of heat. If you prefer the stew less spicy, use the smaller amount of chipotle.

4	cups vegetable broth
1	tablespoon vegetable oil
2	onions, chopped fine
4	scallions, minced
4	garlic cloves, minced
1–2	teaspoons minced canned chipotle chile in adobo sauce
1	teaspoon minced fresh thyme or ¼ teaspoon dried
1	pound butternut squash, peeled, seeded, and cut into ½-inch pieces (3 cups)

TO FINISH AND SERVE

1	pound Swiss chard, stemmed and cut into 1-inch pieces
1	cup canned coconut milk
	Salt and pepper

TO PREP

1. Refrigerate 2 cups broth. Heat oil in Dutch oven over medium heat until shimmering. Add onions and scallions and cook until softened, 5 to 7 minutes. Stir in garlic, chipotle, and thyme and cook until fragrant, about 30 seconds.

2. Stir in 1 cup squash and remaining 2 cups broth, scraping up any browned bits. Bring to simmer and cook until squash is tender, 10 to 15 minutes.

3. Process squash mixture in blender until smooth, about 30 seconds. Return mixture to now-empty pot. Stir in remaining squash. To cool, stir in chilled broth and let stew sit, uncovered, until cooled to room temperature, about 30 minutes.

TO STORE

4. Leave stew in pot or transfer to storage container. Cover and refrigerate for up to 3 days.

TO FINISH AND SERVE

5. Transfer stew to Dutch oven, if necessary. Stir in Swiss chard and bring to simmer over medium heat. Cover, reduce heat to medium-low, and simmer, stirring occasionally, until squash is tender, 10 to 15 minutes. Off heat, stir in coconut milk and let sit until heated through, about 5 minutes. Season with salt and pepper to taste. Serve.

TEST KITCHEN TIP
CUTTING UP BUTTERNUT SQUASH

When preparing butternut squash, we find it easiest to divide it into two sections—the long neck and the curved bottom—then cut each section lengthwise, then crosswise into pieces.

Indian-Style Vegetable Curry

SERVES 4 TO 6 • **TO PREP** 1 HOUR 15 MINUTES • **STORE** UP TO 3 DAYS • **TO FINISH** 40 MINUTES

✔ **WHY THIS RECIPE WORKS:** Vegetable curries can be complicated affairs, with lengthy ingredient lists and fussy techniques meant to compensate for the lack of meat. We wanted a curry that we could make easily without sacrificing flavor or overloading the dish with harsh spices. Toasting store-bought curry powder in a skillet turned it into a flavor powerhouse, and garam masala added warm, complex flavor. Because the spices' flavors mellowed overnight, we found we needed generous amounts. To build the rest of our flavor base, we sautéed onions, garlic, ginger, and fresh jalapeño with some tomato paste for sweetness. Chickpeas made the curry feel more substantial. For the vegetables, we liked hearty potatoes plus cauliflower and peas for texture and color. Sautéing the potatoes along with the onions allowed them to take on golden-brown color and great flavor. We added the cauliflower off the heat to prevent it from ending up mushy and overcooked. As the curry rested overnight, its flavors melded and deepened. Before serving, we added peas, cilantro, and a splash of coconut milk for richness and fresh flavor. For more heat, include the jalapeño seeds and ribs. Serve with basmati rice and plain whole-milk yogurt.

5	cups water
2	tablespoons curry powder
1½	teaspoons garam masala
1	(14.5-ounce) can diced tomatoes
¼	cup vegetable oil
2	onions, chopped
12	ounces red potatoes, unpeeled, cut into ½-inch pieces
3	garlic cloves, minced
1	tablespoon grated fresh ginger
1	jalapeño chile, stemmed, seeded, and minced
1	tablespoon tomato paste
1	(14-ounce) can chickpeas, rinsed
	Salt
½	head cauliflower (1 pound), cored and cut into 1-inch florets

TO FINISH AND SERVE

1½	cups frozen peas
½	cup canned coconut milk
2	tablespoons minced fresh cilantro

TO PREP

1. Refrigerate 3 cups water. Toast curry powder and garam masala in small skillet over medium-high heat, stirring constantly, until spices darken slightly and become fragrant, about 1 minute. Transfer to small bowl and set aside. Pulse tomatoes with their juice in food processor until coarsely chopped, 3 to 4 pulses; set aside.

2. Heat 3 tablespoons oil in Dutch oven over medium-high heat until shimmering. Add onions and potatoes and cook, stirring occasionally, until onions are caramelized and potatoes are golden brown on edges, about 10 minutes.

3. Reduce heat to medium and push vegetables to sides of pot. Add remaining 1 tablespoon oil, garlic, ginger, jalapeño, and tomato paste to center of pot and cook, stirring constantly, until fragrant, about 30 seconds. Add toasted spices and cook, stirring constantly, for 1 minute.

4. Stir in remaining 2 cups water, pulsed tomatoes, chickpeas, and 1 teaspoon salt, scraping up any browned bits; bring to boil. Cover, reduce heat to medium, and simmer briskly, stirring occasionally, until vegetables are almost tender, about 20 minutes.

5. Off heat, stir in cauliflower and let sit, uncovered, for 30 minutes. Stir in chilled water to finish cooling.

TO STORE

6. Leave stew in pot or transfer to storage container. Cover and refrigerate for up to 3 days.

TO FINISH AND SERVE

7. Transfer stew to Dutch oven, if necessary. Bring to simmer over medium heat. Cover, reduce heat to medium-low, and simmer, stirring often, until cauliflower is tender, 20 to 25 minutes. Off heat, stir in peas and coconut milk and let sit until heated through, about 5 minutes. Adjust curry consistency with hot water as needed. Stir in cilantro and season with salt to taste. Serve immediately.

STAGGER THE VEGETABLES
A great vegetable curry should feature a variety of perfectly tender vegetables, but different vegetables need different cooking times. So we added them to the curry in stages, starting with hearty potatoes. To keep the cauliflower from ending up mushy, we added it off the heat on the first day so it would soak up flavor overnight. Then we stirred in the delicate peas just before serving.

Quinoa and Vegetable Stew

SERVES 4 TO 6 • **TO PREP** 45 MINUTES • **STORE** UP TO 3 DAYS • **TO FINISH** 35 MINUTES

✔ **WHY THIS RECIPE WORKS:** A staple in Peru, quinoa stew typically includes a good mix of vegetables, with potatoes and corn at the forefront. We found that red potatoes most closely resembled the flavor and texture of native Peruvian potatoes. While there was no exact substitute for the chewy, nutty Andean corn, sweet locally grown corn worked just fine. Paprika was similar in color and flavor to hard-to-find annatto powder, and cumin and coriander rounded out the spice profile for rich, balanced flavor. Adding the spices with the aromatics allowed time for their flavors to develop. We partially cooked the potatoes to give them a jump start, but adding the quinoa at the same time as the potatoes left it overcooked by the time the stew was cooled and reheated. Instead, we cooked the potatoes until just tender, then added the quinoa off the heat. As the stew cooled, the residual heat partially cooked the quinoa, allowing it to release some starch, which thickened the stew. On the second day, it took just 15 minutes to reheat the stew and finish cooking the potatoes and quinoa. This stew tends to thicken as it sits; add additional warm vegetable broth as needed before serving to loosen. If you buy unwashed quinoa, rinse the grains in a fine-mesh strainer, drain them, then spread them on a rimmed baking sheet lined with a clean dish towel and let them dry for 15 minutes before proceeding with the recipe. Do not omit the queso fresco or feta, avocado, and cilantro; these garnishes are important to the flavor of the stew.

5	cups vegetable broth, plus extra as needed
2	tablespoons vegetable oil
1	onion, chopped
1	red bell pepper, stemmed, seeded, and cut into ½-inch pieces
4	garlic cloves, minced
1	tablespoon paprika
2	teaspoons ground coriander
1	teaspoon ground cumin
10	ounces red potatoes, unpeeled, cut into ½-inch pieces
⅔	cup prewashed quinoa

TO FINISH AND SERVE

1	tomato, cored and chopped coarse
½	cup fresh or frozen corn
	Salt and pepper
6	ounces queso fresco or feta cheese, crumbled (1½ cups)
1	avocado, halved, pitted, and cut into ½-inch pieces
⅓	cup minced fresh cilantro

TO PREP

1. Refrigerate 3 cups broth. Heat oil in Dutch oven over medium heat until shimmering. Add onion and bell pepper and cook until softened, about 5 minutes. Stir in garlic, paprika, coriander, and cumin and cook until fragrant, about 1 minute. Stir in remaining 2 cups broth and potatoes, scraping up any browned bits, and bring to simmer. Reduce heat to low and gently simmer until potatoes are just tender, 10 to 15 minutes.

2. Off heat, stir in quinoa and let sit, covered, for 20 minutes. Stir in chilled broth to finish cooling.

TO STORE

3. Leave stew in pot or transfer to storage container. Cover and refrigerate for up to 3 days.

TO FINISH AND SERVE

4. Transfer stew to Dutch oven, if necessary. Stir in tomato and corn, bring to simmer over medium-low heat, and cook, stirring occasionally, until quinoa is tender, 13 to 15 minutes. Adjust stew consistency with extra hot broth as needed. Season with salt and pepper to taste. Sprinkle individual portions with queso fresco, avocado, and cilantro before serving.

ROASTED ZUCCHINI AND EGGPLANT LASAGNA

Bake and Serve

OVEN-READY CASSEROLES

Chicken Pot Pie with Crumble Topping

SERVES 6 TO 8 • **TO PREP** 1 HOUR 40 MINUTES • **STORE** UP TO 24 HOURS • **TO FINISH** 1 HOUR

✔ **WHY THIS RECIPE WORKS:** We wanted a recipe for a casserole-size chicken pot pie that could be made a day ahead and go straight from fridge to oven. For a flavorful base that wouldn't get muted in the fridge, we created a tasty sauce from the usual onions, carrots, and celery and added tomato paste and thyme to deepen the flavor. Gently simmering the chicken in this sauce gave the sauce savory flavor and kept the chicken juicy. We used chicken thighs here because the long cooking and cooling times tended to dry out lean chicken breasts. The topping for our make-ahead pot pie proved to be our biggest hurdle by far. Pie dough was hard to roll out large enough to fit our casserole dish. We tried rolling two crusts together to make this feat easier, but the crust browned unevenly and it never lost its soggy center. So to give our pot pie a hassle-free, crisp, buttery top, we swapped the pie dough for a crumble crust made with a quick, biscuitlike dough. It was a snap to prepare, and baking it on day one ensured that the savory crumble crust cooked through and stayed crisp when baked on top of the pot pie filling.

FILLING

- 1 **tablespoon unsalted butter**
- 2 **onions, chopped fine**
- 1 **pound carrots, peeled and sliced ¼ inch thick**
- 2 **celery ribs, sliced ¼ inch thick**
  Salt and pepper
- 2 **teaspoons tomato paste**
- 2 **teaspoons minced fresh thyme or ½ teaspoon dried**
- ½ **cup all-purpose flour**
- 2½ **cups chicken broth**
- 3 **pounds boneless, skinless chicken thighs, trimmed**
- ½ **cup heavy cream**
- 2 **tablespoons dry sherry**
- 1 **cup frozen peas**
- ¼ **cup minced fresh parsley**

CRUMBLE TOPPING

- 2 **cups (10 ounces) all-purpose flour**
- 2 **teaspoons baking powder**
- ¾ **teaspoon salt**
- ½ **teaspoon pepper**
- ⅛ **teaspoon cayenne pepper**
- 6 **tablespoons unsalted butter, cut into ½-inch pieces and chilled**
- 1 **ounce Parmesan cheese, grated fine (½ cup)**
- ¾ **cup plus 2 tablespoons heavy cream**

TO PREP

1. FOR THE FILLING: Melt butter in Dutch oven over medium-high heat. Add onions, carrots, celery, 1 teaspoon salt, and ½ teaspoon pepper and cook until softened and lightly browned, 8 to 10 minutes. Stir in tomato paste and thyme and cook until browned, about 2 minutes. Stir in flour and cook for 1 minute.

2. Slowly whisk in chicken broth, scraping up any browned bits and smoothing out any lumps. Add chicken and bring to simmer. Reduce heat to medium-low, cover, and simmer, stirring occasionally, until chicken registers 175 degrees and sauce has thickened, 25 to 30 minutes. Remove pot from heat. Transfer chicken to cutting board, let cool slightly, then shred into bite-size pieces using 2 forks.

3. Stir heavy cream and sherry into sauce, then stir in shredded chicken along with any accumulated juices. Season with salt and pepper to taste. Transfer filling to 13 by 9-inch baking dish and let cool to room temperature, about 45 minutes. Stir in peas and parsley.

4. FOR THE CRUMBLE TOPPING: While filling cools, adjust oven rack to upper-middle position and heat oven to 450 degrees. Line rimmed baking sheet with parchment paper. Combine flour, baking powder, salt, pepper, and cayenne in large bowl. Sprinkle butter pieces over flour mixture. Using fingers, rub butter into flour mixture until it resembles coarse cornmeal. Stir in Parmesan. Add cream and stir until just combined. Crumble mixture into irregularly shaped

pieces ranging from ½ to ¾ inch each onto pre-pared sheet. Bake until crumbles are fragrant and starting to brown, 10 to 13 minutes. Let cool to room temperature, about 20 minutes.

TO STORE

5. Place crumble topping in zipper-lock bag, press out air, and seal bag. Store topping at room temperature for up to 24 hours. Wrap dish tightly with plastic wrap and refrigerate for up to 24 hours.

TO FINISH AND SERVE

6. Adjust oven rack to middle position and heat oven to 425 degrees. Unwrap dish, sprinkle evenly with crumble topping, and place on aluminum foil–lined rimmed baking sheet. Bake casserole until hot throughout and bubbling around edges and topping is browned, 30 to 40 minutes. Let cool for 10 minutes. Serve.

Curried Chicken and Brown Rice with Red Peppers

SERVES 6 • **TO PREP** 40 MINUTES • **STORE** 8 TO 24 HOURS • **TO FINISH** 1 HOUR 45 MINUTES

✔ **WHY THIS RECIPE WORKS:** Looking to develop a chicken and rice dish that was out of the ordinary, we paired meaty chicken thighs and hearty brown rice with a fragrant curry sauce. For a complexly flavored sauce that was easy to throw together, we used store-bought red curry paste enhanced with sautéed onion and scallion. Blooming the scallions and curry paste in oil brought out their flavors further. Left to soak overnight, the rice tenderized and absorbed some of the flavor of the sauce. We seasoned the chicken thighs and marinated them overnight with oil and fresh lemon grass, which infused the chicken with flavor. To give the sauce richness and a silky texture, we stirred in coconut milk on the second day. Using boneless, skinless chicken thighs meant we could avoid the need to sear the chicken and eliminated the problem of soggy skin; we simply nestled the chicken into the rice before reheating and by the time the rice was fully tender, the chicken was perfectly cooked. Using light coconut milk was important because it kept the rice from becoming too greasy.

2 tablespoons extra-virgin olive oil
1 onion, chopped
  Salt and pepper
2 scallions, minced
2 tablespoons red curry paste
2½ cups chicken broth
1½ cups long-grain brown rice, rinsed
2 red bell peppers, stemmed, seeded, and cut into ½-inch pieces
2 pounds boneless, skinless chicken thighs, trimmed
1 lemon grass stalk, trimmed to bottom 6 inches and minced (2 tablespoons)

TO FINISH AND SERVE
½ cup canned light coconut milk
1 tablespoon minced fresh cilantro
  Lime wedges

TO PREP

1. Heat 1 tablespoon oil in 12-inch skillet over medium heat until shimmering. Add onion and ½ teaspoon salt and cook until softened and lightly browned, 5 to 7 minutes. Stir in scallions and curry paste and cook until fragrant, about 30 seconds. Stir in 1 cup broth, scraping up any browned bits.

2. Transfer broth mixture to 13 by 9-inch baking dish, stir in rice and remaining 1½ cups broth, and let cool to room temperature, about 20 minutes. Stir in bell peppers.

3. Pat chicken dry with paper towels, season with salt and pepper, and place in zipper-lock bag. Add lemon grass and remaining 1 tablespoon oil to bag, press out air, and seal; toss to coat chicken.

TO STORE

4. Wrap dish tightly with plastic wrap and refrigerate rice mixture and chicken separately for at least 8 hours or up to 24 hours.

TO FINISH AND SERVE

5. Adjust oven rack to middle position and heat oven to 375 degrees. Unwrap dish and nestle chicken into rice. Cover dish tightly with greased aluminum foil and bake casserole until liquid is almost fully absorbed and rice and chicken are tender, about 1 hour, stirring thoroughly 3 times during baking. Stir in coconut milk and bake, covered, until liquid is fully absorbed, about 15 minutes. Let sit, covered, for 10 minutes. Sprinkle with cilantro and serve with lime wedges.

TEST KITCHEN TIP **PREPPING LEMON GRASS**

Trim and discard all but bottom 6 inches of lemon grass stalk. Remove tough outer sheath to reveal tender inner stalk. Cut trimmed and peeled stalk in half lengthwise, then slice thin crosswise.

MARRYING CHICKEN AND RICE
It took a few tricks to get perfectly cooked boneless, skinless chicken thighs and hearty brown rice in a single dish. Marinating the chicken overnight infused it with flavor, then we nestled it into the rice before baking. Soaking the rice overnight meant that it needed less time to cook through, and stirring it a few times as it baked ensured that all the grains came out tender.

Chicken Enchiladas

SERVES 4 TO 6 • **TO PREP** 1 HOUR • **STORE** UP TO 24 HOURS • **TO FINISH** 50 MINUTES

✔ **WHY THIS RECIPE WORKS:** Making enchiladas is quite an undertaking, from preparing the sauce and the filling to assembling and baking everything. We wanted a make-ahead version of this popular casserole, and we hoped to streamline the process a little too. We tried making the enchiladas with straight-from-the-package tortillas and adding the sauce before holding it overnight. The result was mushy and lackluster. To solve this, we prepped the tortillas, brushing both sides with vegetable oil and warming them in the microwave. The warmed tortillas were easy to fill and roll, and the oil sealed the surface of the tortillas, preventing them from becoming soggy so they held up overnight. We also found it best to store the enchiladas separately from the sauce so that we could bake the enchiladas partway through before adding the sauce, giving the top of the casserole a chance to crisp and brown. For the sauce, we wanted to make our own quick but flavorful enchilada sauce. Canned tomato sauce provided a convenient base. Then, to punch up the flavor of the sauce (which became watery and dull overnight), we bloomed a full 3 tablespoons of chili powder in oil along with garlic, cumin, and coriander. If you prefer, Monterey Jack cheese can be used instead of cheddar, or for a mellower flavor and creamier texture, try substituting an equal amount of *queso fresco*. Serve with sour cream, diced avocado, shredded romaine lettuce, and/or lime wedges.

¼ cup vegetable oil

1 onion, chopped fine

3 tablespoons chili powder

3 garlic cloves, minced

2 teaspoons ground coriander

2 teaspoons ground cumin

2 teaspoons sugar

½ teaspoon salt

1 pound boneless, skinless chicken thighs, trimmed and cut into ¼-inch-wide strips

2 (8-ounce) cans tomato sauce

⅓ cup water

½ cup minced fresh cilantro

⅓ cup jarred jalapeños, rinsed, patted dry, and chopped

8 ounces sharp cheddar cheese, shredded (2 cups)

12 (6-inch) corn tortillas

TO FINISH AND SERVE

Vegetable oil spray

2 ounces sharp cheddar cheese, shredded (½ cup)

TO PREP

1. Heat 2 tablespoons oil in large saucepan over medium heat until shimmering. Add onion and cook until softened and lightly browned, 5 to 7 minutes. Stir in chili powder, garlic, coriander, cumin, sugar, and salt and cook until fragrant, about 30 seconds. Stir in chicken, tomato sauce, and water. Bring to gentle simmer and cook, stirring occasionally, until chicken is tender and flavors blend, 8 to 10 minutes.

2. Pour mixture through medium-mesh strainer into medium bowl, pressing on strained chicken mixture to extract as much sauce as possible. Transfer chicken mixture to large plate and freeze for 10 minutes to cool. Combine cooled chicken with cilantro, jalapeños, and cheddar in separate bowl. Transfer strained sauce to storage container.

3. Brush both sides of tortillas with remaining 2 tablespoons oil. Stack tortillas, wrap in damp dish towel, and place on plate; microwave until warm and pliable, about 1 minute. Working with 1 warm tortilla at a time, spread ⅓ cup of chicken mixture across center of tortilla, roll tortilla tightly around filling, and place seam side down in greased 13 by 9-inch baking dish.

TO STORE

4. Wrap dish tightly with plastic wrap and refrigerate enchiladas and sauce separately for up to 24 hours.

TO FINISH AND SERVE

5. Adjust oven rack to middle position and heat oven to 400 degrees. Unwrap dish and spray top of enchiladas with vegetable oil spray. Bake enchiladas uncovered (without reserved sauce) until lightly toasted on top, 10 to 15 minutes. Pour sauce over enchiladas, covering tortillas completely, then sprinkle cheddar across center of enchiladas. Cover dish tightly with greased aluminum foil and bake until enchiladas are hot throughout and bubbling around edges and cheese is melted, 20 to 25 minutes. Serve immediately.

Spicy Beef Taco Bake

SERVES 6 TO 8 • **TO PREP** 1 HOUR • **STORE** UP TO 24 HOURS • **TO FINISH** 1 HOUR

✓ **WHY THIS RECIPE WORKS:** Our spicy beef taco bake packs all the great texture and flavor of taco night into an easy one-dish meal. We used 93 percent lean ground beef instead of the usual 90 percent because we found that excess grease pooled on the bottom of the dish overnight. We flavored the beef with onion, garlic, chili powder, and oregano, blooming the seasonings in oil to bring out their complex flavors. A good amount of chili powder and Ro-tel tomatoes gave this dish a multilayered heat that built up during the overnight sit. We included refried beans to give this meal another hearty layer of flavor. Layers of Colby Jack cheese helped to bind the beans and the meat. Taco shells broken into pieces and even more cheese made the perfect topping. If you can't find Ro-tel tomatoes, substitute one 14.5-ounce can diced tomatoes, drained, and one 4-ounce can chopped green chiles, drained, reserving 6 tablespoons of the tomato juice and 2 tablespoons of the chile juice. Colby Jack cheese is also known as CoJack; if unavailable, substitute Monterey Jack cheese. Be sure to buy 93 percent lean ground beef or the finished casserole will be too greasy. Serve with your favorite taco toppings such as shredded lettuce, sour cream, chopped red onion, and/or salsa.

1	tablespoon vegetable oil
1	onion, chopped fine
	Salt and pepper
3	tablespoons chili powder
4	garlic cloves, minced
2	teaspoons minced fresh oregano or
	½ teaspoon dried
1½	pounds 93 percent lean ground beef
2	(10-ounce) cans Ro-tel Diced Tomatoes & Green Chilies, drained with ½ cup juice reserved
2	teaspoons cider vinegar
1	teaspoon packed brown sugar
1	(16-ounce) can refried beans
¼	cup minced fresh cilantro
4	ounces Colby Jack cheese, shredded (1 cup)

TO FINISH AND SERVE

12	taco shells, broken into 1-inch pieces
2	ounces Colby Jack cheese, shredded (½ cup)
2	scallions, sliced thin

TO PREP

1. Heat oil in 12-inch skillet over medium heat until shimmering. Add onion and ½ teaspoon salt and cook until softened, about 5 minutes. Stir in chili powder, garlic, and oregano and cook until fragrant, about 1 minute. Add ground beef and cook, breaking up meat with wooden spoon, until no longer pink, 3 to 5 minutes.

2. Stir in half of tomatoes, reserved tomato juice, vinegar, and sugar. Bring to simmer and cook until mixture is very thick, about 5 minutes. Season with salt and pepper to taste. Let cool to room temperature, about 30 minutes.

3. Mix remaining tomatoes, refried beans, and cilantro together, then spread in 13 by 9-inch baking dish. Sprinkle ½ cup Colby Jack over top. Spread cooled beef mixture in dish and sprinkle with remaining ½ cup Colby Jack.

TO STORE

4. Wrap dish tightly with plastic wrap and refrigerate for up to 24 hours.

TO FINISH AND SERVE

5. Adjust oven rack to middle position and heat oven to 400 degrees. Unwrap dish, scatter taco shell pieces over top, and sprinkle with Colby Jack. Cover dish tightly with greased aluminum foil and bake casserole until hot throughout and bubbling around edges, about 25 minutes. Remove foil and continue to bake until topping is spotty brown, about 10 minutes. Let cool for 10 minutes. Sprinkle with scallions and serve.

BUILD BALANCED HEAT
For a boldly spicy taco bake that still had balanced flavor, we started with a generous amount of chili powder and bloomed it in oil. Ro-tel tomatoes were a convenient way to add tomatoes and fresh chopped chiles in one step. The overnight rest in the fridge allowed a complex, multilayered heat to develop hands-off.

Mexican Lasagna with Turkey

SERVES 6 TO 8 • **TO PREP** 1 HOUR 15 MINUTES
STORE UP TO 24 HOURS • **TO FINISH** 1 HOUR 10 MINUTES

✓ **WHY THIS RECIPE WORKS:** For a comfort food classic that married the best qualities of two international favorites, we set out to create a hearty, make-ahead Mexican lasagna. Mild-flavored and convenient ground turkey made a good base for our filling; it paired well with all the ingredients and flavors of the dish and provided a meaty backbone for the green enchilada sauce and the smoky chipotles. Plus, it could be cooked in minutes along with the aromatics, keeping things easy. We added corn and pinto beans to make this dish feel satisfying. For the layers of cheese, we used Monterey Jack, which melted beautifully. To form the layers, we used corn tortillas; brushing them with oil and heating them briefly in the microwave kept them from turning to mush as the lasagna cooked. We added a bit of flour to thicken the sauce, which made it harder for the tortillas to soak up liquid overnight. Be sure to use ground turkey, not ground turkey breast (also labeled 99 percent fat-free), in this recipe. Serve with salsa, diced avocado, sour cream, scallions, and/or lime wedges.

¼	cup vegetable oil
4	scallions, sliced thin
4	garlic cloves, minced
4	teaspoons minced canned chipotle chile in adobo sauce
½	teaspoon salt
¼	teaspoon pepper
1½	pounds ground turkey
3	tablespoons all-purpose flour
2	cups chicken broth
1	(10-ounce) can green enchilada sauce
1	(15-ounce) can pinto beans, rinsed
2	cups frozen corn, thawed
⅓	cup minced fresh cilantro
18	(6-inch) corn tortillas
12	ounces Monterey Jack cheese, shredded (3 cups)

TO FINISH AND SERVE

2	tablespoons minced fresh cilantro

TO PREP

1. Heat 2 tablespoons oil in Dutch oven over medium heat until shimmering. Add scallions, garlic, chipotle, salt, and pepper and cook until fragrant, about 1 minute. Add turkey and cook, breaking up meat with wooden spoon, until no longer pink, 3 to 5 minutes. Stir in flour and cook for 1 minute.

2. Stir in broth, enchilada sauce, and beans. Bring to simmer and cook until mixture is slightly thickened and flavors blend, about 10 minutes. Stir in corn and cilantro and let cool to room temperature, about 30 minutes.

3. Brush both sides of tortillas with remaining 2 tablespoons oil. Stack tortillas, wrap in damp dish towel, and place on plate; microwave until warm and pliable, about 1 minute.

4. Spread one-third of cooled turkey mixture on bottom of 13 by 9-inch baking dish. Arrange 6 tortillas on top of filling, overlapping as needed, and sprinkle with 1 cup Monterey Jack. Repeat layering of filling, tortillas, and Monterey Jack once more. Spread remaining filling in dish. Cut remaining 6 tortillas into quarters and scatter over filling. Sprinkle with remaining 1 cup Monterey Jack.

TO STORE

5. Wrap dish tightly with plastic wrap and refrigerate for up to 24 hours.

TO FINISH AND SERVE

6. Adjust oven rack to middle position and heat oven to 400 degrees. Unwrap dish and cover tightly with greased aluminum foil. Bake casserole until hot throughout and bubbling around edges, about 30 minutes. Remove foil and continue to bake until topping is golden brown, about 15 minutes. Let cool for 10 minutes. Sprinkle with cilantro and serve.

Baked Quattro Formaggio

SERVES 6 • **TO PREP** 40 MINUTES • **STORE** 8 TO 24 HOURS • **TO FINISH** 50 MINUTES

✓ **WHY THIS RECIPE WORKS:** We love macaroni and cheese (who doesn't?), but sometimes we want a more adult version. Enter the classic Italian iteration of macaroni and cheese, *pasta ai quattro formaggi*, made with four cheeses and heavy cream. We wanted a make-ahead version of this dish that still delivered creamy sauce, properly cooked pasta, and a crisp bread-crumb topping. For the best cheese flavor and texture, we used Italian fontina, Gorgonzola, Pecorino Romano, and Parmesan cheeses. We started with a classic roux-based béchamel—cooking butter with flour and then adding cream—but the amount of cream needed to keep the sauce creamy for reheating left the dish too rich and dense for our tasters. Instead, we swapped out most of the cream for evaporated milk, which delivered a silky texture without being too heavy. To preserve the flavors of the cheeses, we stirred them in off the heat, then cooled the sauce to room temperature before combining it with the pasta. Knowing the pasta would rest in the sauce then bake in the oven, we cooked it just shy of al dente, then rinsed it with cold water to stop the cooking. This allowed it to turn perfectly tender as it baked in the sauce. To keep the sauce from turning gloppy or separating during reheating, we kept the oven temperature low and gave the mixture a thorough stir a few times during baking. Topped with toasted panko bread crumbs and a little more Parmesan, our pasta dinner was silky smooth and rich but not heavy.

1	cup panko bread crumbs
2	tablespoons unsalted butter, melted, plus 4 tablespoons unsalted butter
	Salt and pepper
1½	ounces Parmesan cheese, grated (¾ cup)
1	pound penne
2	tablespoons all-purpose flour
2	(12-ounce) cans evaporated milk
1	cup heavy cream
6	ounces fontina cheese, shredded (1½ cups)
4	ounces Gorgonzola cheese, crumbled (1 cup)
1½	ounces Pecorino Romano cheese, grated (¾ cup)

TO PREP

1. Adjust oven rack to middle position and heat oven to 350 degrees. Toss panko with melted butter and season with salt and pepper. Spread evenly in rimmed baking sheet and bake, stirring occasionally, until golden brown, about 10 minutes; let cool to room temperature. Combine cooled panko mixture and ¼ cup Parmesan; transfer to storage container.

2. Meanwhile, bring 4 quarts water to boil in large pot. Add pasta and 1 tablespoon salt and cook, stirring often, until just beginning to soften, about 5 minutes. Reserve 1½ cups cooking water, then drain pasta. Rinse pasta with cold water and drain again, leaving pasta slightly wet; leave in colander.

3. Dry now-empty pot, add remaining 4 tablespoons butter, and melt over medium-low heat. Add flour and cook, stirring constantly, until golden, about 1 minute. Slowly whisk in evaporated milk, cream, ¼ teaspoon salt, and ¼ teaspoon pepper and bring to bare simmer, whisking often. Off heat, gradually whisk in fontina, Gorgonzola, Pecorino, and remaining ½ cup Parmesan until melted and smooth. Let cool to room temperature, about 30 minutes.

4. Stir reserved cooking water and pasta into cooled sauce; transfer to 13 by 9-inch baking dish.

TO STORE

5. Wrap dish tightly with plastic wrap and refrigerate pasta and panko mixture separately for at least 8 hours or up to 24 hours.

TO FINISH AND SERVE

6. Adjust oven rack to middle position and heat oven to 300 degrees. Unwrap dish and stir pasta mixture thoroughly. Cover dish tightly with greased aluminum foil and bake pasta, stirring thoroughly every 10 minutes, until hot throughout, about 30 minutes. Remove foil, stir pasta once more, then sprinkle with panko mixture. Bake, uncovered, until topping is heated through, about 3 minutes. Serve immediately.

Baked Chicken and Penne with Broccoli and Sun-Dried Tomatoes

SERVES 6 • **TO PREP** 1 HOUR • **STORE** 8 TO 24 HOURS • **TO FINISH** 1 HOUR

✔ **WHY THIS RECIPE WORKS:** For an easy and flavorful chicken and broccoli pasta bake that could be assembled in advance, it was important to consider each component separately—pasta, chicken, broccoli, and sauce. We started by parcooking the pasta until it was just beginning to soften so that it wouldn't overcook when reheated. Next, we traded the typical cream-laden sauce for a lighter broth-based sauce with white wine and flavor-packed aromatics, thickened slightly with flour and a handful of Pecorino Romano cheese. Leaving the sauce a bit loose ensured that there was enough liquid to finish cooking the pasta during reheating. To keep prep easy and deliver tender, flavorful chicken, we decided to poach bite-size pieces of chicken directly in the sauce. The last task was to find a way to keep the broccoli fresh and bright in the finished dish. We tried stirring raw broccoli into the pasta mixture before reheating, but the broccoli was still crunchy by the time the pasta was done. Instead, we quickly blanched the broccoli in the boiling pasta water before cooking the pasta, then stored it separately. The broccoli needed only a few more minutes of cooking on the second day, so we stirred it into the dish during the last 10 minutes of baking. Stirring in a little extra Pecorino Romano after baking ensured that all the components were perfectly coated in our rich and flavorful sauce.

2½	cups chicken broth
12	ounces broccoli florets, cut into ¾-inch pieces
	Salt and pepper
12	ounces (3¾ cups) penne
2	tablespoons extra-virgin olive oil
1	onion, chopped fine
½	cup oil-packed sun-dried tomatoes, rinsed, patted dry, and sliced ¼ inch thick
8	garlic cloves, minced
1	tablespoon minced fresh thyme or 1 teaspoon dried
¼	teaspoon red pepper flakes
3	tablespoons all-purpose flour
1	cup dry white wine
1	pound boneless, skinless chicken breasts, trimmed and cut into 1-inch pieces
2	ounces Pecorino Romano cheese, grated (1 cup)

TO FINISH AND SERVE

1	ounce Pecorino Romano cheese, grated (½ cup)

TO PREP

1. Refrigerate 1 cup broth. Bring 4 quarts water to boil in large pot. Fill large bowl halfway with ice and water. Add broccoli and 1 tablespoon salt to boiling water and cook until just tender, about 2 minutes. Using slotted spoon, transfer broccoli to ice water and let cool. Drain broccoli well and transfer to paper towel–lined storage container.

2. Return water to boil, add pasta, and cook, stirring occasionally, until just beginning to soften, about 5 minutes. Reserve 1 cup cooking water, then drain pasta. Rinse pasta with cold water and drain again, leaving pasta slightly wet; leave in colander.

3. Dry now-empty pot, add oil, and return to medium heat until shimmering. Add onion and tomatoes and cook until onion is softened, about 5 minutes. Stir in garlic, thyme, and pepper flakes and cook until fragrant, about 30 seconds. Add flour and cook, stirring constantly, for 1 minute. Slowly whisk in wine, scraping up any browned bits and smoothing out any lumps. Bring to simmer and cook until liquid is almost completely evaporated, about 2 minutes. Slowly whisk in remaining 1½ cups broth and ¼ teaspoon pepper.

4. Add chicken, bring to gentle simmer, and cook, stirring occasionally, until chicken is just cooked

through, about 4 minutes. Off heat, gradually stir in Pecorino until melted. To cool, stir in chilled broth and let sit until cooled to room temperature, about 30 minutes. Stir in reserved cooking water and pasta; transfer to 13 by 9-inch baking dish.

TO STORE

5. Wrap dish tightly with plastic wrap and refrigerate pasta and broccoli separately for at least 8 hours or up to 24 hours.

TO FINISH AND SERVE

6. Adjust oven rack to middle position and heat oven to 400 degrees. Unwrap dish, cover tightly with greased aluminum foil, and bake pasta until sauce begins to bubble around edges, about 25 minutes. Stir in broccoli, cover, and bake until pasta is hot throughout and broccoli is tender, about 10 minutes. Stir in Pecorino until thoroughly combined and sauce is slightly thickened and coats pasta. Season with salt and pepper to taste. Let cool slightly before serving.

Cheeseburger Pasta Bake

SERVES 6 • **TO PREP** 45 MINUTES • **STORE** 8 TO 24 HOURS • **TO FINISH** 1 HOUR

✓ **WHY THIS RECIPE WORKS:** We wanted an easy make-ahead pasta bake that combined all the bright, tangy, meaty flavors of our favorite burger—juicy ground beef, mustard, dill pickles, and American cheese—with the heartiness and convenience of a macaroni casserole. Tomato sauce, with its smooth texture and long-cooked flavor, provided the perfect base for our sauce, which we seasoned with Worcestershire sauce, dry mustard, and garlic. Stirring in chopped dill pickles gave the sauce the same sweetly pungent flavor as pickle relish and great crunch. We found that the small, delicate macaroni quickly overcooked during storage and reheating, so we undercooked it initially. Then, to keep the pasta from absorbing too much liquid overnight, we reserved a portion of the tomato sauce and stirred it in before putting the casserole in the oven. This added the right amount of liquid to finish cooking the pasta and also freshened the tomato flavor in the dish. Slices of American cheese melted briefly over the top and a sprinkling of chopped fresh tomato and onion gave this casserole all the mouthwatering appeal of a cheeseburger with the works. Be sure to buy 93 percent lean ground beef. Using fattier beef will make the finished casserole overly greasy.

12	ounces (3 cups) elbow macaroni
	Salt and pepper
1	tablespoon extra-virgin olive oil
1	onion, chopped fine
1	garlic clove, minced
1	pound 93 percent lean ground beef
1	(15-ounce) can tomato sauce
½	cup chopped dill pickles
1	tablespoon Worcestershire sauce
1	tablespoon dry mustard

TO FINISH AND SERVE

1	(15-ounce) can tomato sauce
8	thin slices deli American cheese (4 ounces)
1	tomato, cored and chopped
1	small onion, chopped fine

TO PREP

1. Bring 4 quarts water to boil in large pot. Add macaroni and 1 tablespoon salt and cook, stirring often, until just beginning to soften, about 2 minutes. Reserve 1 cup cooking water, then drain pasta. Rinse pasta with cold water and drain again, leaving pasta slightly wet; leave in colander.

2. Dry now-empty pot, add oil, and return to medium heat until shimmering. Add onion and cook until softened, about 5 minutes. Stir in garlic and cook until fragrant, about 30 seconds. Add ground beef and cook, breaking up meat with wooden spoon, until no longer pink, about 3 minutes. Stir in tomato sauce, pickles, Worcestershire, mustard, ½ teaspoon salt, and ½ teaspoon pepper. Bring to simmer and cook until flavors blend, about 5 minutes. Let cool to room temperature, about 30 minutes.

3. Stir reserved cooking water and pasta into cooled sauce; transfer to 13 by 9-inch baking dish.

TO STORE

4. Wrap dish tightly with plastic wrap and refrigerate for at least 8 hours or up to 24 hours.

TO FINISH AND SERVE

5. Adjust oven rack to middle position and heat oven to 400 degrees. Unwrap dish and stir in tomato sauce. Cover dish tightly with greased aluminum foil and bake pasta until hot throughout and bubbling around edges, about 25 minutes, stirring thoroughly halfway through baking. Remove foil, lay cheese slices evenly over top, and bake, uncovered, until cheese is melted, about 5 minutes. Let cool for 10 minutes. Sprinkle with tomato and onion and serve.

TEST KITCHEN TIP CORING TOMATOES

To remove tough core and stem from tomato, use tip of paring knife to cut around stem, angling tip of knife slightly inward, then remove cone-shaped piece of hard core from tomato.

Classic Meat Lasagna

SERVES 8 • **TO PREP** 1 HOUR 20 MINUTES • **STORE** 8 TO 24 HOURS • **TO FINISH** 1½ HOURS

✓ **WHY THIS RECIPE WORKS:** With all of the components that go into a great lasagna, making it can be a labor-intensive endeavor, but that also makes it the ideal make-ahead dish. We started our testing by simply assembling our favorite lasagna recipe and refrigerating it overnight. While rich and cheesy, this version baked up a bit too dry the next day. In the test kitchen, we prefer no-boil lasagna noodles, but we found that the secret to getting perfectly tender no-boil noodles is to leave your tomato sauce a little on the watery side, especially when refrigerating the lasagna overnight. Because no-boil noodles rely primarily on the liquid in the sauce to rehydrate and soften, we had to get the moisture content just right. If the sauce was too thick, the noodles would be dry and crunchy; too loose, and they would turn limp. We started building the sauce with pureed tomatoes, but tasters found that this sauce was too heavy and overwhelmed the other flavors. Using all diced tomatoes yielded too thin a sauce, but a combination of pureed and diced tomatoes gave us a luxurious sauce with chunks of tomatoes. We added the tomatoes to browned meatloaf mix and simmered it to meld the flavors. In about 15 minutes, the sauce was just the right consistency. We found that it was important to cool the sauce before assembling the lasagna so the noodles didn't overcook before they reached the oven. Meatloaf mix is a prepackaged mix of ground beef, pork, and veal; if it's unavailable, use 8 ounces each of ground pork and 85 percent lean ground beef.

2	tablespoons extra-virgin olive oil
1	onion, chopped fine
6	garlic cloves, minced
1	pound meatloaf mix
	Salt and pepper
¼	cup heavy cream
1	(28-ounce) can tomato puree
1	(28-ounce) can diced tomatoes, drained
½	cup chopped fresh basil
24	ounces (3 cups) whole-milk or part-skim ricotta cheese
2	ounces Parmesan cheese, grated (1 cup)
1	large egg, lightly beaten
12	no-boil lasagna noodles
12	ounces mozzarella cheese, shredded (3 cups)

TO FINISH AND SERVE

4	ounces mozzarella cheese, shredded (1 cup)
1	ounce Parmesan cheese, grated (½ cup)

TO PREP

1. Heat oil in Dutch oven over medium heat until shimmering. Add onion and cook until softened, about 5 minutes. Stir in garlic and cook until fragrant, about 30 seconds. Add meatloaf mix, 1 teaspoon salt, and 1 teaspoon pepper and cook, breaking up meat with wooden spoon, until no longer pink, about 3 minutes. Stir in cream and simmer until liquid evaporates and only fat remains, about 4 minutes. Stir in tomato puree and diced tomatoes, bring to simmer, and cook until flavors blend, about 5 minutes. Off heat, stir in ¼ cup basil and season with salt and pepper to taste. Let cool to room temperature, 30 to 45 minutes.

2. Meanwhile, combine ricotta, Parmesan, egg, ½ teaspoon salt, ½ teaspoon pepper, and remaining ¼ cup basil in bowl.

3. Spread 1 cup cooled sauce on bottom of 13 by 9-inch baking dish (avoiding large chunks of meat). Lay 3 noodles in dish, spread ⅓ cup of ricotta mixture over each noodle, sprinkle with 1 cup mozzarella, and top with 1 cup sauce; repeat layering of noodles, ricotta, mozzarella, and sauce 2 more times. Lay remaining 3 noodles in dish and top with remaining sauce.

TO STORE

4. Wrap dish tightly with plastic wrap and refrigerate for at least 8 hours or up to 24 hours.

TO FINISH AND SERVE

5. Adjust oven rack to middle position and heat oven to 400 degrees. Unwrap dish and cover tightly with greased aluminum foil. Bake lasagna until hot throughout and bubbling around edges, 50 to 60 minutes. Remove foil, sprinkle with mozzarella and Parmesan, and bake, uncovered, until cheese is melted and begins to brown, about 10 minutes. Let cool for 10 minutes. Serve.

ALL ABOUT Oven-Ready Casseroles

Classic casseroles like chicken pot pie, lasagna, and baked ziti are guaranteed crowd-pleasers, but they can be hard to pull off on an already hectic weeknight. So the ability to make these favorites ahead of time and stash them in the fridge has lots of appeal. For this chapter, we baked through our favorites plus several inventive new cover-and-bake dishes. We found that most casseroles couldn't stand up to overnight storage without adverse effect—pasta turned to mush, vegetables became flavorless and drab, and chicken dried out. To make these dishes taste just as good when made ahead, we needed to rethink some of our techniques for preparing casseroles. Here's what we learned.

Parcook the Pasta

For most pasta casseroles, parcooking is necessary to ensure that the pasta turns tender once reheated. But it's easy to cook the pasta too much, leaving it mushy by the time it gets to the table. For the best results, it was important to cook the pasta just until it began to soften, then drain it and rinse it with cold water to stop the cooking. As the casserole baked the next day, the undercooked pasta soaked up some of the liquid from the sauce, turning perfectly tender. To ensure that the sauce wouldn't end up overly thick and dry as the dish reheated and the pasta finished cooking, we thinned it with some pasta cooking water before assembling the casserole.

Treat Chicken Gently

For our chicken casseroles, we used two different approaches to ensure that the chicken stayed moist and tender throughout cooling and reheating. For casseroles using cubed or shredded chicken, we found that poaching the chicken in the casserole base before assembling the dish boosted the moistness of the chicken and improved its flavor. For our classic chicken and rice casseroles, we wanted to use larger pieces of chicken. To flavor the chicken and keep it from overcooking, we salted the raw chicken and marinated it overnight to help it retain its juices and allow it to absorb flavor, then we simply baked the chicken through in the casserole on the second day.

Wrap Tightly and Heat Gently

To ensure that make-ahead casseroles emerge from the oven moist and saucy, it is important to cover them tightly with aluminum foil to trap steam and prevent moisture loss. Heating casseroles gently in a moderate oven prevents uneven cooking. For pasta, rice, and grain casseroles, it is also necessary to stir the ingredients occasionally; this helps to redistribute the liquid so that it is uniformly absorbed and the dish cooks evenly.

Soak Rice and Grains Overnight

We wanted to develop hearty, healthy rice and grain casseroles that would be moist and flavorful and easy to make. The trick was to find a way to get perfectly tender, evenly cooked rice and grains in a casserole. We knew we would need to avoid fully cooking the rice and grains before assembling and storing the casseroles to prevent the grains from getting blown out and mushy overnight. Soaking them overnight proved to be an ideal solution. First we created a flavorful base by sautéing plenty of aromatics, then we transferred the mixture to a casserole dish and stirred in the uncooked rice or grains along with plenty of broth and/or water. As the rice and grains soaked in the fragrant broth mixture overnight, they absorbed some of the broth, which both tenderized and flavored them and helped to shorten their cooking time in the oven. Stirring the dish a few times while it baked the next day ensured that the grains cooked through evenly.

Keep Broccoli Bright and Fresh

To keep broccoli and broccoli rabe bright and fresh in our casseroles, we tried stirring them in raw before reheating, but they didn't cook fully before the casseroles were done. Instead, we quickly blanched and shocked the broccoli, then stored it separately. The broccoli needed only a few more minutes of cooking, so we stirred it into the dish during the last 10 minutes of baking, preserving its crisp-tender texture and bright color.

Roasted Zucchini and Eggplant Lasagna

SERVES 8 • **TO PREP** 1 HOUR 20 MINUTES • **STORE** 8 TO 24 HOURS • **TO FINISH** 1 HOUR 20 MINUTES

✓ **WHY THIS RECIPE WORKS:** Vegetable lasagna recipes are often filled with watery, tasteless vegetables and weighed down by excess cheese. We wanted a flavorful vegetable lasagna that didn't fall into any of the usual traps—and could withstand an overnight rest in the fridge. Eggplant and zucchini are easy to prep, making them excellent choices for our make-ahead lasagna. Roasting the vegetables not only drove off excess liquid that would otherwise water down the sauce, but it also caramelized the vegetables, adding a savory depth. Ricotta cheese is traditional in lasagna, but we found that it muted the roasted vegetable flavor, so we layered our lasagna with only mozzarella and Parmesan, which lent plenty of rich cheese flavor and gooey texture. No-boil noodles made quick work of the assembly. Since the noodles absorbed almost all the sauce during overnight storage, we reserved some of the sauce to spread over the casserole before baking. This kept the lasagna saucy and prevented the top layer of noodles from drying out during baking. Be sure to grease the baking sheets before spreading the vegetables so they don't stick during roasting.

1½   pounds zucchini, cut into ½-inch pieces
1½   pounds eggplant, cut into ½-inch pieces
5   tablespoons extra-virgin olive oil
9   garlic cloves, minced
    Salt and pepper
1   onion, chopped fine
1   (28-ounce) can crushed tomatoes
1   (28-ounce) can diced tomatoes
2   tablespoons chopped fresh basil
12   no-boil lasagna noodles
8   ounces mozzarella cheese, shredded (2 cups)
3   ounces Parmesan cheese, grated (1½ cups)

TO FINISH AND SERVE
4   ounces mozzarella cheese, shredded (1 cup)
1   ounce Parmesan cheese, grated (½ cup)

TO PREP

1. Adjust oven racks to upper-middle and lower-middle positions and heat oven to 400 degrees. Toss zucchini and eggplant with 3 tablespoons oil, two-thirds of garlic, 1 teaspoon salt, and 1 teaspoon pepper. Spread vegetables in 2 greased rimmed baking sheets and bake, stirring occasionally, until softened and golden brown, 35 to 45 minutes; set aside to cool.

2. Meanwhile, heat remaining 2 tablespoons oil in large saucepan over medium heat until shimmering. Add onion and cook until softened, about 5 minutes. Stir in remaining garlic and cook until fragrant, about 30 seconds. Stir in crushed tomatoes and diced tomatoes with their juice, bring to simmer, and cook until flavors blend, about 5 minutes. Off heat, stir in basil and season with salt and pepper to taste. Let cool to room temperature, 30 to 45 minutes. (You should have 7 cups sauce. Add water as needed to reach 7 cups.)

3. Spread 1 cup cooled sauce on bottom of 13 by 9-inch baking dish. Lay 3 noodles in dish, spread one-quarter of cooled vegetables over noodles, and top with 1 cup sauce. Sprinkle ⅔ cup mozzarella and ½ cup Parmesan over sauce. Repeat layering of noodles, vegetables, sauce, and cheeses 2 more times. Lay remaining 3 noodles in dish and top with remaining vegetables and 1 cup sauce. Transfer remaining 2 cups sauce to storage container.

TO STORE

4. Wrap dish tightly with plastic wrap and refrigerate lasagna and reserved sauce separately for at least 8 hours or up to 24 hours.

TO FINISH AND SERVE

5. Adjust oven rack to middle position and heat oven to 400 degrees. Unwrap dish and spread reserved sauce over top. Cover dish tightly with greased aluminum foil and bake lasagna until hot throughout and bubbling around edges, about 45 minutes. Remove foil, sprinkle with mozzarella and Parmesan, and bake, uncovered, until cheese is melted and begins to brown, about 10 minutes. Let cool for 10 minutes. Serve.

BALANCE THE MOISTURE
Vegetable lasagnas often turn out soggy and bland, yet make-ahead lasagnas end up dried out, so the key to this dish was controlling the moisture. Roasting the vegetables kept their moisture from watering down the dish (and gave them caramelized flavor). We reserved some sauce to spread on top before baking to keep the top layer from drying out in the oven.

Stuffed Shells with Amatriciana Sauce

SERVES 6 TO 8 • **TO PREP** 1½ HOURS • **STORE** 8 TO 24 HOURS • **TO FINISH** 1 HOUR

✓ **WHY THIS RECIPE WORKS:** Being able to prepare a satisfying weeknight pasta dish ahead of time is a lifesaver for any time-crunched cook. We wanted a stuffed shells recipe that could be assembled in advance and go from refrigerator to oven without sacrificing flavor or texture. But when we reheated a batch of basic stuffed shells with marinara sauce, we found that the ricotta had turned watery, and the flavor of the sauce was washed out. A little Parmesan cheese and two eggs helped to bind the filling and prevent it from getting watery overnight, and mozzarella cheese gave the filling a rich, creamy texture. To amp up the flavor of our sauce, we were inspired by the bold flavors of Italian Amatriciana sauce, with its smoky pancetta and kick of red pepper flakes. Those few simple ingredients ensured that the sauce was rich and flavorful once the casserole was baked. Crushed tomatoes provided a smooth sauce base with just the right amount of texture. When buying pancetta, ask to have it sliced ¼ inch thick. If you can't find pancetta, you can substitute 6 ounces of thick-cut, or slab, bacon.

1   tablespoon extra-virgin olive oil
6   ounces pancetta, cut into 1 by ¼-inch pieces
1   onion, chopped fine
     Salt and pepper
¼   teaspoon red pepper flakes
2   (28-ounce) cans crushed tomatoes
12   ounces jumbo pasta shells
12   ounces (1½ cups) whole-milk or part-skim
     ricotta cheese
6   ounces mozzarella cheese, shredded
     (1½ cups)
2   ounces Parmesan cheese, grated (1 cup)
2   large eggs, lightly beaten
¼   cup chopped fresh basil
2   garlic cloves, minced

TO FINISH AND SERVE
4   ounces mozzarella cheese, shredded (1 cup)
1   ounce Parmesan cheese, grated (½ cup)
2   tablespoons chopped fresh basil

TO PREP

1. Heat oil in large saucepan over medium heat until shimmering. Add pancetta and cook until lightly browned and crisp, about 8 minutes. Using slotted spoon, transfer pancetta to paper towel–lined plate.

2. Pour off all but 3 tablespoons fat from saucepan, add onion and ¼ teaspoon salt, and cook until softened, about 5 minutes. Stir in pepper flakes and cook until fragrant, about 30 seconds. Stir in tomatoes, bring to simmer, and cook until slightly thickened, about 10 minutes. Let cool to room temperature, about

45 minutes. Stir in pancetta and season with salt and pepper to taste.

3. Meanwhile, line rimmed baking sheet with clean dish towel. Bring 4 quarts water to boil in large pot. Add pasta and 1 tablespoon salt and cook, stirring occasionally, until just beginning to soften, about 8 minutes. Drain pasta and transfer to prepared baking sheet. Using dinner fork, pry apart any shells that have clung together, discarding any that are badly torn (you should have 30 to 33 good shells).

4. Combine ricotta, mozzarella, Parmesan, eggs, basil, garlic, and ½ teaspoon salt in bowl; transfer to zipper-lock bag. Using scissors, cut off 1 corner of bag and pipe 1 tablespoon filling into each shell.

5. Spread 2 cups cooled sauce on bottom of 13 by 9-inch baking dish. Arrange filled shells seam side down in dish. Spread remaining sauce over shells.

TO STORE

6. Wrap dish tightly with plastic wrap and refrigerate for at least 8 hours or up to 24 hours.

TO FINISH AND SERVE

7. Adjust oven rack to middle position and heat oven to 400 degrees. Unwrap dish and cover tightly with greased aluminum foil. Bake shells until sauce begins to bubble around edges, 25 to 30 minutes. Remove foil, sprinkle with mozzarella and Parmesan, and bake, uncovered, until shells are hot throughout and cheese is melted and begins to brown, about 10 minutes. Let cool for 10 minutes. Sprinkle with basil and serve.

MAKING A STURDY FILLING
Stuffing pasta shells with our usual ricotta filling and storing them overnight left us with a bland and watery filling. To keep it creamy through storing and reheating, we added Parmesan to thicken it and to lend richness, plus two eggs to bind the cheeses. Fresh basil and garlic rounded out the flavor, and a zipper-lock bag made it easy to pipe the filling into the shells.

Baked Ziti with Italian Sausage

SERVES 6 TO 8 • **TO PREP** 50 MINUTES • **STORE** 8 TO 24 HOURS • **TO FINISH** 1 HOUR

✔ **WHY THIS RECIPE WORKS:** Baked ziti should be a simple pasta casserole, but too often it turns out dry, bland, and downright unappealing, especially when made ahead. We wanted to find a way to prepare this dish in advance and still have it taste fresh the next day. Since the tomato sauce is key to keeping the casserole moist, we started there. A combination of crushed tomatoes and tomato sauce gave us a smooth consistency with just the right amount of chunky texture. We found that loosening the sauce with some of the pasta cooking water prevented the casserole from drying out in the fridge. To conquer any soggy pasta problems, we made sure to undercook our pasta, so that once the casserole had baked, the ziti would be perfectly al dente. For meaty flavor, we added Italian sausage to the sauce. Chewy, stringy mozzarella is a crucial part of baked ziti, but shredded cheese seemed to disappear into the sauce when reheated. Cutting the mozzarella into chunks ensured that we had luscious pockets of gooey cheese throughout the casserole. Ricotta cheese is also a classic ingredient, but we found that mixing it in before storage left us with a watery, grainy mess. Instead, we dolloped the ricotta mixture on top of the partially baked casserole and just heated it through so that it stayed creamy. We prefer hot Italian sausage in this recipe, but sweet Italian sausage will work fine as well. To remove the sausage from its casing, cut it open at the end and simply squeeze out the ground sausage.

1 **pound ziti or other short, tubular pasta**
  Salt and pepper
¼ **cup extra-virgin olive oil**
1 **pound hot or sweet Italian sausage, casings removed**
4 **garlic cloves, minced**
1 **(28-ounce) can crushed tomatoes**
1 **(15-ounce) can tomato sauce**
4 **ounces mozzarella cheese, cut into ¼-inch pieces**
2 **tablespoons chopped fresh basil**
8 **ounces (1 cup) whole-milk or part-skim ricotta cheese**

TO FINISH AND SERVE
4 **ounces mozzarella cheese, shredded (1 cup)**
1 **ounce Parmesan cheese, grated (½ cup)**
2 **tablespoons chopped fresh basil**

TO PREP

1. Bring 4 quarts water to boil in large pot. Add pasta and 1 tablespoon salt and cook, stirring occasionally, until just beginning to soften, about 5 minutes. Reserve 1½ cups cooking water, then drain pasta. Rinse pasta with cold water and drain again, leaving pasta slightly wet; leave in colander.

2. Dry now-empty pot, add 1 tablespoon oil, and return to medium-high heat until shimmering.

Add sausage and cook, breaking up meat with wooden spoon, until no longer pink, about 5 minutes. Stir in garlic and cook until fragrant, about 30 seconds. Stir in crushed tomatoes and tomato sauce, bring to simmer, and cook until slightly thickened, about 5 minutes. Let cool to room temperature, 30 to 45 minutes.

3. Stir reserved cooking water, pasta, mozzarella, and basil into cooled sauce; transfer to 13 by 9-inch baking dish. Combine ricotta, remaining 3 tablespoons oil, ½ teaspoon salt, and ¼ teaspoon pepper in bowl; cover.

TO STORE

4. Wrap dish tightly with plastic wrap and refrigerate ziti and ricotta separately for at least 8 hours or up to 24 hours.

TO FINISH AND SERVE

5. Adjust oven rack to middle position and heat oven to 400 degrees. Unwrap dish and cover tightly with greased aluminum foil. Bake casserole until beginning to bubble around edges, about 20 minutes. Remove foil and dollop rounded tablespoons of ricotta mixture evenly over top. Sprinkle with mozzarella and Parmesan and bake, uncovered, until casserole is hot throughout and cheese is melted and begins to brown, 15 to 20 minutes. Let cool for 10 minutes. Sprinkle with basil and serve.

Hearty Vegetable and Orzo Casserole

SERVES 6 • **TO PREP** 45 MINUTES • **STORE** 8 TO 24 HOURS • **TO FINISH** 1 HOUR 15 MINUTES

✓ **WHY THIS RECIPE WORKS:** Looking for a hearty vegetarian casserole that was a little different, we turned to orzo. For texture and flavor, we added mushrooms, butternut squash, and arugula, sautéing the mushrooms and squash in some butter. To give the dish a creamy, risotto-like texture, we toasted the orzo in the butter to give it a rich, nutty flavor and to help keep it from becoming mushy overnight. A combination of white wine, vegetable broth, and water made a bright, balanced base for the sauce. Stirring with abandon during the reheat was the key to this recipe—it helped release the starch in the orzo, which made the dish creamy and cohesive. Adding the arugula and some more Parmesan at the end of cooking helped keep the arugula bright, giving the dish an overall freshness. A sprinkling of pine nuts added a nice complementary crunch.

3   tablespoons unsalted butter

8   ounces (1½ cups) butternut squash, cut into ½-inch pieces

¾   teaspoon salt

1   onion, chopped fine

8   ounces cremini mushrooms, trimmed and quartered

3   garlic cloves, minced

1   pound (2⅔ cups) orzo

½   cup dry white wine

2½ cups vegetable broth

2   cups water

TO FINISH AND SERVE

3   ounces Parmesan cheese, grated (1½ cups)

3   ounces (3 cups) baby arugula

2   tablespoons pine nuts, toasted

TO PREP

1. Melt butter in Dutch oven over medium heat. Add squash and salt and cook until beginning to soften, about 10 minutes. Stir in onion and mushrooms and cook until vegetables are softened and lightly browned, about 15 minutes. Stir in garlic and cook until fragrant, about 30 seconds. Add orzo and stir until coated with butter, about 2 minutes. Stir in wine and cook until completely evaporated, about 1 minute.

2. Transfer orzo mixture to 13 by 9-inch baking dish, stir in broth and water, and let cool to room temperature, about 45 minutes.

TO STORE

3. Wrap dish tightly with plastic wrap and refrigerate for at least 8 hours or up to 24 hours.

TO FINISH AND SERVE

4. Adjust oven rack to middle position and heat oven to 350 degrees. Unwrap dish, cover tightly with greased aluminum foil, and bake casserole until orzo is tender, about 40 minutes, stirring thoroughly 3 times during baking. Vigorously stir in 1 cup Parmesan until melted and orzo mixture is thickened and creamy. Stir in arugula, 1 handful at a time, until wilted, then sprinkle with remaining ½ cup Parmesan and pine nuts. Bake, uncovered, until cheese is melted, about 5 minutes. Let cool for 10 minutes. Serve.

TEST KITCHEN TIP **TOASTING PINE NUTS**

Toast pine nuts in dry skillet over medium heat, shaking pan occasionally to prevent scorching, until slightly darkened in color, 3 to 5 minutes.

PERFECTING BAKED ORZO

Parcooking delicate orzo in boiling water gave us mushy, blown-out pasta when we baked it the next day. Instead we sautéed it briefly, then soaked it in liquid overnight to tenderize it slightly. Stirring the orzo a few times as it baked helped it cook evenly, then we added Parmesan and stirred the orzo vigorously to release its starches for a rich and creamy casserole.

Rustic Polenta Casserole with Sausage

SERVES 6 TO 8 • **TO PREP** 1 HOUR 10 MINUTES
STORE UP TO 24 HOURS • **TO FINISH** 1 HOUR 10 MINUTES

☑ **WHY THIS RECIPE WORKS:** Polenta provides a hearty, flavorful backdrop to a ragout-style topping of tomatoes, meat, and vegetables. Since the polenta would be cooked twice, we initially cooked it on the stovetop until it was smooth but still very loose so that it wouldn't end up gluey and dry when it was baked. A combination of milk and water ensured a creamy consistency, and a little Parmesan and butter boosted flavor and richness. For the topping, we liked sweet Italian sausage paired with tomatoes and spinach. Canned diced tomatoes contributed sweet bites of tomato as well as juice that cooked down into a sauce and kept our topping moist. To keep the spinach fresh, we stirred it into the topping off the heat until it was just wilted. During reheating, we topped the casserole with smooth mozzarella cheese for a cheesy final touch. Hot Italian sausage works equally well in this recipe, but consider adjusting the amount of red pepper flakes to suit your taste. To remove the sausage from its casing, cut it open at the end and simply squeeze out the ground sausage.

5	cups water
1⅓	cups whole milk
	Salt and pepper
1	cup coarse-ground polenta
2	ounces Parmesan cheese, grated (1 cup)
3	tablespoons unsalted butter
1	tablespoon extra-virgin olive oil
1	onion, chopped fine
1½	pounds sweet Italian sausage, casings removed
3	garlic cloves, minced
¼	teaspoon red pepper flakes
1	(28-ounce) can diced tomatoes
8	ounces baby spinach

TO FINISH AND SERVE

4	ounces mozzarella cheese, shredded (1 cup)

TO PREP

1. Bring water and milk to boil in large saucepan over medium-high heat. Stir in 1 teaspoon salt, then very slowly pour polenta into boiling liquid while stirring constantly in circular motion with wooden spoon. Reduce to gentle simmer, cover partially, and cook, stirring often and making sure to scrape bottom and sides of pot clean, until polenta no longer has raw cornmeal taste, all liquid has been absorbed, and mixture has uniformly smooth but very loose consistency, 15 to 20 minutes.

2. Off heat, stir in Parmesan and butter and season with salt and pepper to taste. Pour polenta into 13 by 9-inch baking dish and let cool to room temperature, about 30 minutes.

3. Meanwhile, heat oil in 12-inch skillet over medium-high heat until shimmering. Add onion and ½ teaspoon salt and cook until softened, about 5 minutes. Add sausage and cook, breaking meat into large chunks with wooden spoon, until lightly browned, about 10 minutes. Stir in garlic and pepper flakes and cook until fragrant, about 30 seconds.

4. Stir in tomatoes and their juice, bring to simmer, and cook, stirring occasionally, until sauce has thickened, about 10 minutes. Off heat, stir in spinach, 1 handful at a time, until wilted. Season with salt and pepper to taste. Let cool to room temperature, about 30 minutes. Spread cooled sausage mixture evenly over cooled polenta.

TO STORE

5. Wrap dish tightly with plastic wrap and refrigerate for up 24 hours.

TO FINISH AND SERVE

6. Adjust oven rack to middle position and heat oven to 400 degrees. Unwrap dish and cover tightly with greased aluminum foil. Bake casserole until hot throughout and bubbling around edges, about 30 minutes. Remove foil, sprinkle with mozzarella, and bake, uncovered, until cheese is melted, 10 to 15 minutes. Let cool for 10 minutes. Serve.

KEEPING POLENTA LOOSE

When we tried storing our polenta casserole overnight, we ended up with a dense, gluey mess since it thickens as it sits. For polenta that could withstand an overnight rest, we had to add extra liquid and undercook it drastically, until it was smooth but still very loose. Then we topped the polenta with a fresh and flavorful ragout of tomatoes, spinach, and sausage.

Rustic Polenta Casserole with Mushrooms and Swiss Chard

SERVES 6 TO 8 • **TO PREP** 1½ HOURS • **STORE** UP TO 24 HOURS • **TO FINISH** 1 HOUR 10 MINUTES

✔ **WHY THIS RECIPE WORKS:** For a vegetarian version of our polenta casserole, we substituted hearty sliced mushrooms for the sausage. To bring out the mushrooms' flavor, we sautéed them until all their liquid evaporated and they began to brown. Garlic and thyme added depth of flavor to our sauce. To bulk up this dish, we replaced the spinach with heartier Swiss chard, which we cooked briefly to take away its raw bite before cooling the mixture. This ensured that the chard was perfectly cooked when the reheated casserole emerged from the oven. Since the chard continues to cook in the oven during reheating, we found that it was important to reduce all the liquid from our ragout first, so the extra moisture from the chard didn't turn our sauce watery. Sprinkled with flavorful fontina cheese, this combination of creamy polenta, meaty mushrooms, tomatoes, and Swiss chard was every bit as satisfying as our sausage version.

5	cups water
1⅓	cups whole milk
	Salt and pepper
1	cup coarse-ground polenta
2	ounces Parmesan cheese, grated (1 cup)
3	tablespoons unsalted butter
3	tablespoons extra-virgin olive oil
1	onion, chopped fine
1	pound white mushrooms, trimmed and sliced
3	garlic cloves, minced
1	tablespoon minced fresh thyme or 1 teaspoon dried
1	(28-ounce) can diced tomatoes
8	ounces Swiss chard, stemmed and cut into 1-inch pieces

TO FINISH AND SERVE

4	ounces fontina cheese, shredded (1 cup)

TO PREP

1. Bring water and milk to boil in large saucepan over medium-high heat. Stir in 1 teaspoon salt, then very slowly pour polenta into boiling liquid while stirring constantly in circular motion with wooden spoon. Reduce to gentle simmer, cover partially, and cook, stirring often and making sure to scrape bottom and sides of pot clean, until polenta no longer has raw cornmeal taste, all liquid has been absorbed, and mixture has uniformly smooth but very loose consistency, 15 to 20 minutes.

2. Off heat, stir in Parmesan and butter and season with salt and pepper to taste. Pour polenta into 13 by 9-inch baking dish and let cool to room temperature, about 30 minutes.

3. Meanwhile, heat oil in 12-inch skillet over medium heat until shimmering. Add onion and ½ teaspoon salt and cook until softened, about 5 minutes. Add mushrooms and cook until mushrooms have released their liquid and are well browned, about 15 minutes. Stir in garlic and thyme and cook until fragrant, about 30 seconds.

4. Stir in tomatoes and their juice, bring to simmer, and cook, stirring occasionally, until sauce has thickened, about 10 minutes. Stir in chard, 1 handful at a time, and cook until wilted, 2 to 4 minutes. Season with salt and pepper to taste. Let cool to room temperature, about 30 minutes. Spread cooled mushroom mixture evenly over cooled polenta.

TO STORE

5. Wrap dish tightly with plastic wrap and refrigerate for up 24 hours.

TO FINISH AND SERVE

6. Adjust oven rack to middle position and heat oven to 400 degrees. Unwrap dish and cover tightly with greased aluminum foil. Bake casserole until hot throughout and bubbling around edges, about 30 minutes. Remove foil, sprinkle with fontina, and bake, uncovered, until cheese is melted, 10 to 15 minutes. Let cool for 10 minutes. Serve.

White Bean Casserole with Spinach and Feta

SERVES 6 TO 8 • **TO PREP** 1 HOUR • **STORE** UP TO 24 HOURS • **TO FINISH** 1 HOUR

✓ **WHY THIS RECIPE WORKS:** We wanted to create a modern white bean casserole with fresh flavors and the simplicity of an easy pasta bake. We changed up our usual flavor profile by incorporating traditional Greek ingredients but kept this hearty, satisfying dish simple to make ahead. Using canned beans kept our dish quick-cooking and convenient. To give the casserole a thick, cohesive base, we pureed some of the beans with broth and Parmesan. For a layer of freshness, we topped the beans with a quick sauté of tomatoes and spinach. A little dill complemented the bright vegetables. Finally, to give our dish the rich flavor and attractive presentation of a gratin, we sprinkled it with feta and Parmesan and baked it until the cheese was golden brown. This dish can be a wonderful vegetarian main course or a delicious accompaniment to a main dish, such as a leg of lamb.

3	tablespoons extra-virgin olive oil
2	onions, chopped fine
3	garlic cloves, minced
1	(28-ounce) can diced tomatoes, drained
18	ounces spinach, stemmed
	Salt and pepper
3	(15-ounce) cans cannellini beans, rinsed
½	cup vegetable broth
1	ounce Parmesan cheese, grated (½ cup)
2	tablespoons minced fresh dill

TO FINISH AND SERVE

4	ounces feta cheese, crumbled (1 cup)
1	ounce Parmesan cheese, grated (½ cup)
	Lemon wedges

TO PREP

1. Heat 1 tablespoon oil in Dutch oven over medium heat until shimmering. Add onions and cook until softened and lightly browned, 5 to 7 minutes. Stir in garlic and cook until fragrant, about 30 seconds. Transfer half of onion mixture to large bowl; set aside. Stir tomatoes into pot with remaining onion mixture and cook over medium heat until dry, about 2 minutes. Stir in spinach, 1 handful at a time, and cook until wilted, about 4 minutes. Season with ½ teaspoon salt and ¼ teaspoon pepper. Let cool to room temperature, about 30 minutes.

2. Meanwhile, process one-third of beans, broth, Parmesan, ½ teaspoon salt, and remaining 2 tablespoons oil in food processor until smooth, about 2 minutes, scraping down sides of bowl as needed; transfer to bowl with onion mixture. Stir in dill and remaining beans until combined. Spread bean mixture on bottom of 13 by 9-inch baking dish, then spread cooled tomato-spinach mixture over top.

TO STORE

3. Wrap dish tightly with plastic wrap and refrigerate for up to 24 hours.

TO FINISH AND SERVE

4. Adjust oven rack to middle position and heat oven to 400 degrees. Unwrap dish, cover tightly with greased aluminum foil, and bake casserole until hot throughout and bubbling around edges, 20 to 25 minutes. Remove foil, sprinkle with feta and Parmesan, and bake until cheese is melted and golden brown, about 10 minutes. Let cool for 10 minutes. Serve with lemon wedges.

TEST KITCHEN TIP **RINSING CANNED BEANS**

The starchy, salty water that canned beans are packed in can affect the flavor and texture of a dish, so it's best to rinse the beans in a fine-mesh strainer before using.

Farro, White Bean, and Broccoli Rabe Gratin

SERVES 6 • **TO PREP** 35 MINUTES • **STORE** 8 TO 24 HOURS • **TO FINISH** 1 HOUR 40 MINUTES

✔ **WHY THIS RECIPE WORKS:** For this recipe, we set out to create a new kind of casserole, one that was hearty, healthy, and vegetarian with nutty, satisfying whole grains. We looked to Italian flavors, utilizing nutty farro, creamy white beans, slightly bitter broccoli rabe, and salty Parmesan—the hearty ingredients and bold flavors made this dish a natural make-ahead meal. Toasting the farro in the aromatics and oil gave it extra nuttiness and jump-started the cooking process, helping it to bake through more evenly. We liked small white beans in this dish as they blended in with the farro, lending creaminess and added protein, making this a hearty meal. We found that blanching the broccoli rabe in salted water tamed its bitterness. We tried adding it with all the other ingredients as the gratin went into the oven but found it emerged dull and overcooked. Adding it to the casserole during the last 10 minutes kept it bright green and perfectly tender. Sun-dried tomatoes gave us the extra pop of flavor we were after in this dish.

1   pound broccoli rabe, trimmed and cut into
      2-inch pieces
      Salt
1   tablespoon extra-virgin olive oil
1   onion, chopped fine
6   garlic cloves, minced
⅛   teaspoon red pepper flakes
1½   cups farro
3   cups vegetable broth
1   cup water
1   (15-ounce) can small white beans, rinsed
2   ounces Parmesan cheese, grated (1 cup)

TO FINISH AND SERVE
½   cup oil-packed sun-dried tomatoes, chopped
2   ounces Parmesan cheese, grated (1 cup)
2   tablespoons extra-virgin olive oil

TO PREP

1. Bring 4 quarts water to boil in large pot. Fill large bowl halfway with ice and water. Add broccoli rabe and 1 tablespoon salt to boiling water and cook until wilted and just tender, about 2 minutes. Drain broccoli rabe, then transfer to ice water and let cool. Drain broccoli rabe well and transfer to paper towel–lined storage container.

2. Meanwhile, heat oil in 12-inch skillet over medium heat until shimmering. Add onion and ½ teaspoon salt and cook until softened and lightly browned, 5 to 7 minutes. Stir in garlic and pepper flakes and cook until fragrant, about 30 seconds. Add farro and cook, stirring often, until lightly toasted, about 2 minutes

3. Transfer farro mixture to 13 by 9-inch baking dish, stir in broth, water, and beans, and let cool to room temperature, about 30 minutes. Stir in Parmesan.

TO STORE

4. Wrap dish tightly with plastic wrap and refrigerate farro mixture and broccoli rabe separately for at least 8 hours or up to 24 hours.

TO FINISH AND SERVE

5. Adjust oven rack to middle position and heat oven to 350 degrees. Unwrap dish, cover tightly with greased aluminum foil, and bake casserole until farro is just tender and liquid is almost completely absorbed, 60 to 75 minutes, stirring twice during baking. Stir in broccoli rabe and tomatoes, then sprinkle with Parmesan and bake, uncovered, until farro is completely tender and remaining liquid is thickened, about 10 minutes. Let cool for 10 minutes. Drizzle with oil and serve.

MOROCCAN CHICKEN SALAD WITH APRICOTS AND ALMONDS

From Fridge to Table

READY-TO-SERVE ENTRÉES

Picnic Fried Chicken

SERVES 4 • **TO PREP** 2 HOURS 20 MINUTES • **STORE** UP TO 24 HOURS • **TO FINISH** 15 MINUTES

✔ **WHY THIS RECIPE WORKS:** Fried chicken is always delicious hot out of the oil, but it usually turns soggy and unappealing as it sits. We wanted fried chicken that we could make ahead and grab right from the fridge for a last-minute meal. First, we brined the chicken to season it and keep it moist and juicy. A combination of Wondra flour (a low-protein, finely ground flour), baking powder, and cornstarch made for an ultralight, crispy coating that kept its crunch. Mixing some water into the coating to create clumps of dough, then dredging the chicken twice (with a water dip in between) created a thick, craggy crust that gave us even more crunch. Letting the coated chicken rest for at least 30 minutes hydrated the coating, preventing dry spots from getting soggy when they hit the oil. Double-frying the chicken with a brief rest in between let extra moisture evaporate from the skin, and storing it uncovered in the refrigerator further guarded against sogginess. Finally, since cold dulls flavors, extra seasonings were very important in this recipe—we liked a combination of thyme, sage, garlic powder, and cayenne. You will need at least a 6-quart Dutch oven for this recipe.

Salt and pepper
3 pounds bone-in chicken pieces (split breasts cut in half crosswise, drumsticks, and/or thighs), trimmed
1½ cups Wondra flour
1½ cups cornstarch
2 teaspoons white pepper
1½ teaspoons baking powder
1 teaspoon dried thyme
1 teaspoon ground sage
1 teaspoon garlic powder
¼ teaspoon cayenne pepper
3 quarts peanut or vegetable oil

TO PREP

1. Dissolve ¼ cup salt in 1 quart cold water in large container. Submerge chicken in brine, cover, and refrigerate for 1 hour.

2. Whisk flour and cornstarch together in large bowl. Transfer 1 cup flour mixture to shallow dish; set aside. Whisk 1 tablespoon pepper, white pepper, baking powder, thyme, sage, garlic powder, 1 teaspoon salt, and cayenne into remaining flour mixture. Add ¼ cup water to seasoned flour mixture. Rub flour mixture and water together with your fingers until water is evenly incorporated and mixture contains craggy bits of dough. Pour 2 cups cold water into medium bowl.

3. Set wire rack in rimmed baking sheet. Working with 2 pieces of chicken at a time, remove chicken from brine and dip in unseasoned flour mixture, pressing to adhere; dunk quickly in water, letting excess drip off; and dredge in seasoned flour mixture, pressing to adhere. Place chicken on prepared wire rack and refrigerate for at least 30 minutes or up to 2 hours.

4. Add oil to large Dutch oven until it measures about 2 inches deep and heat over medium-high heat to 350 degrees. Fry half of chicken until slightly golden and just beginning to crisp, 5 to 7 minutes. Adjust burner, if necessary, to maintain oil temperature between 300 and 325 degrees. (Chicken will not be cooked through at this point.) Return parcooked chicken to wire rack. Return oil to 350 degrees and repeat with remaining raw chicken. Let each batch of chicken rest for 5 to 7 minutes.

5. Return oil to 350 degrees. Return first batch of chicken to oil and fry until breasts register 160 degrees and thighs/drumsticks register 175 degrees, 5 to 7 minutes. Transfer chicken to clean wire rack set in rimmed baking sheet. Return oil to 350 degrees and repeat with remaining chicken. Let chicken cool to room temperature and transfer to paper towel–lined plate.

TO STORE

6. Refrigerate chicken, uncovered, for up to 24 hours.

TO FINISH AND SERVE

7. Remove chicken from refrigerator and let sit at room temperature for 15 minutes. Serve.

DOUBLE UP FOR AN ULTRACRUNCHY COATING
For fried chicken that kept its crunch overnight, we double-dipped the chicken in low-protein flour, baking powder, and cornstarch. Rubbing water into the flour mixture created a craggy coating that fried up extra-crunchy. Then we fried the chicken, let it rest, and returned it to the pot for maximum evaporation and the crispest possible coating.

Herb-Poached Salmon with Cucumber and Dill Salad

SERVES 4 • **TO PREP** 1 HOUR 10 MINUTES • **STORE** UP TO 2 DAYS • **TO FINISH** 35 MINUTES

✔ **WHY THIS RECIPE WORKS:** Chilled poached salmon is an easy make-ahead dinner, and our simple hands-off oven-poaching method delivers salmon with an ultrasilky texture. Wrapped in a foil packet, the fish slowly steamed in a little lemon juice and the moisture from the salmon itself, keeping the fish moist and tender when chilled. This method gave us rich salmon flavor that wasn't washed out by poaching liquid. Because the gently cooked fish can appear to have a semitranslucent orange hue, like that of smoked salmon, even though it is fully cooked (the normal opaque color returns after it is chilled), taking its temperature through the foil was the best way to determine when the salmon was perfectly cooked. A simple paste of extra-virgin olive oil, fresh herbs, and lemon zest infused the salmon with flavor overnight. A fresh cucumber-dill salad dressed with tangy Greek yogurt was the perfect light counterpart to our rich and meaty salmon. However, we found that storing the cucumbers in the dressing turned the salad too watery. Slicing and stirring in the cucumbers just before serving helped eliminate excess moisture, keeping the salad fresh and creamy when served. Use center-cut salmon fillets of similar thickness so that they cook at the same rate. The best way to ensure uniformity is to buy a 1½- to 2-pound whole center-cut fillet and cut it into four pieces. It is important to keep the skin on during cooking; remove it afterward if you prefer not to serve it.

¼   cup minced fresh dill
1   tablespoon minced fresh parsley
1   tablespoon extra-virgin olive oil
1   teaspoon lemon zest plus 2 tablespoons juice
    Salt and pepper
4   (6- to 8-ounce) skin-on salmon fillets
¼   cup plain Greek yogurt
2   tablespoons mayonnaise

TO FINISH AND SERVE
2   cucumbers, peeled, halved lengthwise, seeded, and sliced thin
    Lemon wedges

TO PREP

1. Adjust oven rack to middle position and heat oven to 250 degrees. Spray center of 18-inch square sheet of heavy-duty aluminum foil with vegetable oil spray. Combine 2 teaspoons dill, parsley, oil, lemon zest, ¼ teaspoon salt, and ¼ teaspoon pepper in small bowl.

2. Pat salmon dry with paper towels and season both sides with salt. Arrange fillets side by side in center of foil. Sprinkle salmon with 1 tablespoon lemon juice and spread herb mixture over top. Bring opposite sides of foil together and crimp to seal tightly. Crimp remaining open ends of packet, leaving as much headroom as possible inside packet, then place in 13 by 9-inch baking dish. Cook until color of flesh has turned from pink to orange and thickest part of fillet registers 135 to 140 degrees, 45 to 60 minutes. (To check temperature, poke thermometer through foil of packet and into fish.) Transfer foil packet to large plate. Carefully open foil packet (steam will escape) and let salmon cool to room temperature on foil, about 30 minutes.

3. Meanwhile, whisk yogurt, mayonnaise, remaining 1 tablespoon lemon juice, and remaining dill together in bowl; cover.

TO STORE

4. Pour off any accumulated liquid from foil packet and reseal salmon in foil. Refrigerate salmon and yogurt mixture separately for up to 2 days.

TO FINISH AND SERVE

5. Remove foil packet from refrigerator and let sit at room temperature for 30 minutes. Unwrap salmon and brush away any gelled poaching liquid. Carefully transfer fish to serving platter. Add cucumbers to reserved yogurt mixture and toss to combine. Season with salt and pepper to taste. Serve salmon with cucumber-dill salad and lemon wedges.

OVEN-POACH FOR SILKY SALMON

For the ultimate moist and tender salmon fillets, we relied on the gentle, even heat of the oven. Brushing the salmon with a flavorful herb oil and gently baking it wrapped in foil allowed the fish to poach in its own juices, giving it exceptionally rich flavor. To ensure that the salmon was perfectly cooked, we used an instant-read thermometer to check for doneness.

Thai Marinated Steak Salad

SERVES 4 • **TO PREP** 45 MINUTES • **STORE** UP TO 2 DAYS • **TO FINISH** 20 MINUTES

✓ **WHY THIS RECIPE WORKS:** We liked the idea of a flavorful steak salad that could be made ahead of time, but we didn't want to spend hours marinating a steak before we could cook it. So we swapped the steps and marinated the meat in a spicy Thai-style dressing after cooking. Searing the steak in a hot skillet gave the outside a great crust but kept the inside medium-rare. We let the steak rest briefly, then sliced it thinly against the grain to keep it tender before tossing it with the dressing. As the steak cooled, it soaked up the flavor of the dressing. For the dressing, we started with salty, savory fish sauce, bright lime juice, and sugar. A mix of toasted cayenne and paprika added an earthy, fruity red pepper flavor, and a Thai chile provided extra heat. We also made our own toasted rice powder, a traditional ingredient that lends a satisfying crunch. Just before serving, we refreshed the steak with a bit more dressing and tossed it with bright, fresh mint and cilantro leaves, then spread the mixture on a bed of freshly sliced cucumber. If a fresh Thai chile is unavailable, substitute half of a serrano chile. This dish is traditionally quite spicy, but if you prefer a less spicy dish you can leave out the chile. We prefer this steak cooked to medium-rare, but if you prefer it more or less done, see our guidelines on page 221.

1	teaspoon paprika
1	teaspoon cayenne pepper
1	tablespoon white rice
1	pound flank steak, trimmed
	Salt and pepper
1	tablespoon vegetable oil
3	tablespoons lime juice (2 limes)
2	tablespoons fish sauce
½	teaspoon sugar
4	shallots, sliced thin
1	Thai chile, stemmed and sliced thin into rounds

TO FINISH AND SERVE

1½	cups fresh mint leaves, torn
1½	cups fresh cilantro leaves
1	English cucumber, sliced ¼ inch thick on bias

TO PREP

1. Heat paprika and cayenne in 12-inch skillet over medium heat and cook, shaking skillet, until fragrant, about 1 minute. Transfer to small bowl. Return now-empty skillet to medium-high heat, add rice, and toast, stirring frequently, until deep golden brown, about 5 minutes. Transfer to second small bowl and let cool for 5 minutes. Grind rice in spice grinder, mini food processor, or mortar and pestle until it resembles fine meal, 10 to 30 seconds (you should have about 1 tablespoon rice powder). Wipe out skillet.

2. Pat steak dry with paper towels and season with salt and pepper. Heat oil in now-empty skillet over medium-high heat until just smoking. Brown steak well on first side, about 5 minutes. Flip steak and continue to cook until it registers 120 to 125 degrees (for medium-rare), 3 to 6 minutes. Transfer to carving board, tent loosely with aluminum foil, and let rest 5 to 10 minutes.

3. Meanwhile, whisk together lime juice, fish sauce, sugar, ¼ teaspoon toasted paprika mixture, and 2 tablespoons water in small bowl; set aside.

4. Slice steak about ¼ inch thick against grain on bias, cutting long pieces in half if necessary. Transfer sliced steak to large bowl and toss with shallots, chile, half of dressing, and half of toasted rice powder. Let steak cool to room temperature, about 20 minutes; cover. Cover remaining dressing.

TO STORE

5. Refrigerate steak mixture and dressing separately for up to 2 days. Cover remaining toasted rice powder and toasted paprika mixture separately and store at room temperature.

TO FINISH AND SERVE

6. Remove steak mixture and dressing from refrigerator and let sit at room temperature for 15 minutes. Whisk dressing to recombine, then drizzle over steak mixture. Add mint and cilantro and toss to combine. Lay cucumber slices on serving platter and top with steak mixture, pouring any accumulated dressing over top. Serve, passing remaining toasted rice powder and toasted paprika mixture separately.

Moroccan Chicken Salad with Apricots and Almonds

SERVES 4 TO 6 • **TO PREP** 1 HOUR • **STORE** UP TO 2 DAYS • **TO FINISH** 20 MINUTES

✔ **WHY THIS RECIPE WORKS:** For a creative take on a fresh chicken salad, we were inspired by the flavors of Morocco—apricots, lemon, and warm spices. Instead of pulling out half the spice cabinet to flavor our dressing, we reached for garam masala, a traditional spice blend of coriander, cumin, ginger, cinnamon, and black pepper that gave the dressing complex flavor without any fuss. We fortified the dressing with a little more coriander, honey, and a pinch of smoked paprika for depth. Microwaving the spices in a little oil was a quick and easy way to bloom them, deepening their flavors for an even bolder dressing. Chickpeas further echoed the Moroccan theme and lent heartiness, and fresh, crisp romaine combined with slightly bitter watercress made the perfect bed of greens to complement our toppings. Tossing the chicken mixture with a little extra dressing refreshed the flavors before serving, and a sprinkling of toasted almonds lent the perfect crunch to the finished salad.

1½ **pounds boneless, skinless chicken breasts, trimmed**
   Salt and pepper
¾ **cup extra-virgin olive oil**
1 **teaspoon garam masala**
½ **teaspoon ground coriander**
   Pinch smoked paprika
¼ **cup lemon juice (2 lemons)**
1 **tablespoon honey**
1 **(14-ounce) can chickpeas, rinsed**
1 **shallot, sliced thin**
¾ **cup dried apricots, chopped coarse**
2 **tablespoons minced fresh parsley**
2 **romaine lettuce hearts (12 ounces), cut into 1-inch pieces**
4 **ounces (4 cups) watercress**
½ **cup whole almonds, toasted and chopped coarse**

TO PREP

1. Pat chicken dry with paper towels and season with salt and pepper. Heat 1 tablespoon oil in 12-inch skillet over medium-high heat until just smoking. Brown chicken well on first side, 6 to 8 minutes. Flip chicken, add ½ cup water, and cover. Reduce heat to medium-low and continue to cook until chicken registers 160 degrees, 5 to 7 minutes. Transfer chicken to carving board, let cool slightly, then slice ½ inch thick on bias. Let cool to room temperature, about 15 minutes.

2. Meanwhile, microwave 1 tablespoon oil, garam masala, coriander, and paprika in medium bowl until oil is hot and fragrant, about 30 seconds. Whisk 3 tablespoons lemon juice, honey, ¼ teaspoon salt, and ¼ teaspoon pepper into spice mixture. Whisking constantly, drizzle in remaining oil.

3. In large bowl, combine cooled chicken, chickpeas, shallot, apricots, parsley, and half of dressing and toss to coat; cover. Whisk remaining 1 tablespoon lemon juice into remaining dressing; cover.

4. Toss romaine, watercress, and almonds together in separate bowl; cover.

TO STORE

5. Refrigerate chicken mixture, dressing, and lettuce mixture separately for up to 2 days.

TO FINISH AND SERVE

6. Remove chicken mixture, dressing, and lettuce mixture from refrigerator and let sit at room temperature for 15 minutes. Whisk dressing to recombine, drizzle 2 tablespoons dressing over chicken mixture, and season with salt and pepper to taste. Toss lettuce mixture with remaining dressing and season with salt and pepper to taste. Transfer lettuce mixture to serving platter and top with chicken mixture. Serve.

SAVE SOME DRESSING
To flavor our fresh chicken salad, we made a bold dressing of lemon juice, honey, and warm spices. We used half the dressing to marinate the chicken overnight, infusing it with flavor, and stored the remaining dressing and the lettuce separately. We brightened the remaining dressing with a squeeze of lemon juice before adding it to the salad on day two.

Chinese Chicken Salad

SERVES 6 • **TO PREP** 50 MINUTES • **STORE** UP TO 2 DAYS • **TO FINISH** 20 MINUTES

✔ **WHY THIS RECIPE WORKS:** To keep this restaurant-classic salad fresh and bright, we prepped and stored its components separately and assembled the salad just before serving. We also nixed anything from a can, as well as the typical salad bar pile-ons like chow mein noodles and fried wonton strips, which only weighed down the salad's fresh flavors. Instead, we started with crisp romaine lettuce, napa cabbage, bell peppers, and peanuts, which we combined and stored without dressing to keep the greens crisp. For moist, flavorful chicken, we poached boneless, skinless chicken breasts in a mixture of soy sauce, orange juice, rice vinegar, and ginger. We whisked more of the same mixture with sesame and vegetable oils to make a bright, bold dressing. Just before we served the salad, we tossed the dressing with the lettuce mixture and some scallions and fresh cilantro, then topped it off with the flavorful chicken and juicy fresh orange segments. You can substitute one minced garlic clove and ¼ teaspoon of cayenne pepper for the Asian chili-garlic sauce.

2	oranges
¼	cup rice vinegar
¼	cup soy sauce
3	tablespoons grated fresh ginger
3	tablespoons sugar
1	tablespoon Asian chili-garlic sauce
3	tablespoons ~~vegetable~~ oil *peanut*
2	tablespoons toasted sesame oil
2	pounds boneless, skinless chicken breasts, trimmed
2	romaine lettuce hearts (12 ounces), sliced thin
½	small head napa cabbage, cored and sliced thin (6 cups)
2	red bell peppers, stemmed, seeded, and cut into 2-inch-long matchsticks
1	cup salted dry-roasted peanuts, chopped

TO FINISH AND SERVE

6	scallions, sliced thin
1	cup fresh cilantro leaves

TO PREP

1. Cut thin slice from top and bottom of oranges, then slice off rind and pith. Working over bowl to catch juice, cut orange segments from thin membrane and transfer segments to storage container; cover. Squeeze juice from membrane into bowl (juice should measure ¼ cup). Whisk in vinegar, soy sauce, ginger, sugar, and chili-garlic sauce. Transfer ½ cup orange juice mixture to 12-inch skillet. Whisk vegetable oil and sesame oil into remaining orange juice mixture; cover.

2. Bring orange juice mixture in skillet to boil. Add chicken, reduce heat to medium-low, cover, and simmer until chicken registers 160 degrees, 10 to 15 minutes, flipping halfway through cooking. Transfer chicken to plate and let rest for 10 minutes.

3. Meanwhile, boil pan juices until reduced to ¼ cup, 1 to 3 minutes; set aside. Using 2 forks, shred chicken into bite-size pieces. Off heat, add chicken and any accumulated juices to skillet, toss to coat, then let cool to room temperature, about 30 minutes. Transfer to separate storage container; cover.

4. Toss romaine, cabbage, bell peppers, and peanuts together in large bowl; cover.

TO STORE

5. Refrigerate orange segments, dressing, chicken, and lettuce mixture separately for up to 2 days.

TO FINISH AND SERVE

6. Remove orange segments, dressing, chicken, and lettuce mixture from refrigerator and let sit at room temperature for 15 minutes. Whisk dressing to recombine, then drizzle 2 tablespoons dressing over chicken. Toss lettuce mixture with scallions, cilantro, and remaining dressing and season with salt and pepper to taste. Transfer lettuce mixture to serving platter and top with chicken and orange segments. Serve.

Creamy Shrimp Salad

SERVES 4 TO 6 • **TO PREP** 40 MINUTES • **STORE** UP TO 24 HOURS • **TO FINISH** 15 MINUTES

WHY THIS RECIPE WORKS: Most shrimp salads suffer from rubbery, overcooked shrimp drowning in too much mayonnaise. We wanted firm yet tender shrimp that would hold up in the fridge overnight and a dressing that wouldn't overpower the delicate flavor of the shrimp. To ensure that the shrimp didn't overcook, we added them to a cold *court-bouillon* (a flavorful poaching liquid of lemon juice, herbs, pepper, and water) and slowly heated them over medium heat until the shrimp were no longer translucent. The gentle cooking enabled the poaching liquid to add flavor to the shrimp while keeping them moist and tender. And since the water was never brought to a simmer, the shrimp didn't overcook. A modest amount of mayonnaise formed the basis for our creamy dressing. Shallot, parsley, tarragon, and lemon juice perked up and rounded out the flavors, and celery added a pleasant crunch. To prevent the celery from releasing moisture and turning the dressing watery, we waited to season the salad with salt until just before serving. This recipe can also be prepared with large shrimp (26 to 30 per pound); the cooking time will be 1 to 2 minutes less. Serve the salad on Bibb lettuce or toasted, buttered hot dog buns.

1½	pounds extra-large shrimp (21 to 25 per pound), peeled, deveined, and tails removed
3	cups water
5	tablespoons lemon juice, spent halves reserved (2 lemons)
5	sprigs fresh parsley, plus 1 teaspoon minced
3	sprigs fresh tarragon, plus 1 teaspoon minced
1	tablespoon sugar
1	teaspoon black peppercorns
	Salt and pepper
⅓	cup mayonnaise
1	shallot, minced
1	celery rib, minced

TO PREP

1. Combine shrimp, water, ¼ cup lemon juice, reserved lemon halves, parsley sprigs, tarragon sprigs, sugar, peppercorns, and 1 teaspoon salt in large saucepan. Place saucepan over medium heat and cook, stirring several times, until shrimp are pink and firm to touch and centers are no longer translucent, 8 to 10 minutes (water should be just bubbling around edge of saucepan and register 165 degrees). Remove saucepan from heat, cover, and let shrimp sit in broth for 2 minutes.

2. Meanwhile, fill large bowl with ice water. Drain shrimp into colander, discarding lemon halves, herbs, and spices. Immediately transfer shrimp to ice water to stop cooking and chill thoroughly, about 3 minutes. Remove shrimp from ice water and thoroughly pat dry with paper towels. Cut shrimp in half lengthwise and then cut each half into thirds.

3. Whisk mayonnaise, shallot, celery, remaining 1 tablespoon lemon juice, minced parsley, and minced tarragon together in medium bowl. Add shrimp and toss to combine; cover.

TO STORE

4. Refrigerate shrimp salad for up to 24 hours.

TO FINISH AND SERVE

5. Remove shrimp salad from refrigerator and let sit at room temperature for 15 minutes. Stir to recombine and season with salt and pepper to taste. Serve.

TEST KITCHEN TIP **DEVEINING SHRIMP**

After removing shell, use paring knife to make shallow cut along back of shrimp so that vein is exposed. Then use tip of knife to lift vein out of shrimp. Discard vein by wiping on paper towel.

Classic Gazpacho

SERVES 6 • **TO PREP** 20 MINUTES • **STORE** 4 HOURS TO 2 DAYS • **TO FINISH** 5 MINUTES

☑ **WHY THIS RECIPE WORKS:** Chilled gazpacho is just about the easiest make-ahead recipe and the perfect way to showcase the flavors of fresh, in-season summer vegetables. Perfectly ripe farm-stand tomatoes, red bell peppers, and cucumbers are the stars of this winning soup. Lots of recipes minimize prep work by having you "chop" the vegetables in a food processor or blender, but we found these methods broke them down beyond recognition, resulting in an unappealing, slushy texture. We preferred hand-chopping the vegetables into consistent ¼-inch pieces. This way, the vegetables retained their individual flavors, and although it took a little more time up front, the benefits to the gazpacho's texture made it worthwhile. Tomato juice, thinned with a small amount of water, gave us a perfectly viscous soup base. For ice-cold gazpacho, we added ice cubes instead of water so they would chill and thin the soup as they melted. The overnight chilling time was convenient as well as crucial for allowing flavors to develop and meld. We found that 4 hours was the minimum time required for the soup to chill and the flavors to blossom. Some extra-virgin olive oil drizzled over each bowl before serving provided some lushness and fruity flavor that nicely countered the fresh, bright flavors of the vegetables. White wine vinegar can be substituted for the sherry vinegar.

12	ounces tomatoes (about 2 medium), cored and cut into ¼-inch pieces
1	red bell pepper, stemmed, seeded, and cut into ¼-inch pieces
1	small cucumber, halved lengthwise, seeded, and cut into ¼-inch pieces
¼	cup minced shallot or sweet onion (such as Vidalia, Maui, or Walla Walla)
2	tablespoons sherry vinegar, plus extra for serving
1	garlic clove, minced
	Salt and pepper
2½	cups tomato juice
½	teaspoon hot sauce (optional)
4	ice cubes

TO SERVE

Extra-virgin olive oil

TO PREP

1. Combine tomatoes, bell pepper, cucumber, shallot, vinegar, garlic, 1 teaspoon salt, and pepper to taste in large nonreactive bowl. Let sit until vegetables just begin to release their juice, about 5 minutes. Stir in tomato juice, hot sauce, if using, and ice cubes; cover.

TO STORE

2. Refrigerate gazpacho for at least 4 hours or up to 2 days.

TO FINISH AND SERVE

3. Remove gazpacho from refrigerator and discard any unmelted ice cubes. Season with vinegar, salt, and pepper to taste. Serve cold, drizzling each portion with about 1 teaspoon extra-virgin olive oil.

TEST KITCHEN TIP SEEDING CUCUMBERS

To seed cucumber, halve cucumber lengthwise. Run small spoon down length of each half to scoop out seeds and surrounding liquid.

24-Hour Chopped Salad

SERVES 6 • **TO PREP** 50 MINUTES • **STORE** UP TO 24 HOURS • **TO FINISH** 15 MINUTES

☑ **WHY THIS RECIPE WORKS:** We liked the idea of a salad that could be assembled in advance, with all the ingredients attractively layered and covered with a creamy dressing, put in the fridge for a night, and simply tossed and served the next day. But our early attempts produced overdressed salads with soggy vegetables—until we got the ingredients and proportions just right. We tried several varieties of lettuce, but iceberg retained the best crunch after sitting with the dressing for a day. Salting the lettuce pulled moisture out, helping it to keep its crunch; we used the released moisture to thin our creamy dressing to the perfect consistency. Soft ingredients like mushrooms and spinach wilted into mush, but crunchy vegetables like celery, bell peppers, and cucumbers stayed crisp in the salad overnight. To make this salad hearty enough for dinner, we crisped a whole pound of bacon and crumbled it over the top along with a generous amount of tangy blue cheese. For a creamy dressing with a subtle kick, we thinned mayonnaise with a little cider vinegar and spiked it with hot sauce. Frank's RedHot is our favorite brand of hot sauce. If using a hotter brand, such as Tabasco, reduce the amount to 1 tablespoon.

1	pound bacon
1	head iceberg lettuce (9 ounces), cored and chopped coarse
	Salt and pepper
½	red onion, sliced thin
6	hard-cooked eggs, chopped
1½	cups frozen peas
4	celery ribs, sliced thin
1	red bell pepper, stemmed, seeded, and chopped
1	cucumber, halved lengthwise, seeded, and sliced thin
6	ounces blue cheese, crumbled (1½ cups)
1½	cups mayonnaise
3	tablespoons cider vinegar
2	tablespoons hot sauce
2	teaspoons sugar

TO PREP

1. Cook half of bacon in 12-inch skillet over medium-high heat until crisp, about 10 minutes. Transfer to paper towel–lined plate. Repeat with remaining bacon and let cool. Crumble bacon into bite-size pieces; set aside.

2. Place half of lettuce in large serving bowl and sprinkle with ½ teaspoon salt. Rinse onion under cold water; pat dry with paper towels. Layer onion, eggs, peas, celery, bell pepper, and cucumber over lettuce. Add remaining lettuce to bowl, sprinkle with ½ teaspoon salt, and top with bacon and cheese.

3. Combine mayonnaise, vinegar, hot sauce, sugar, and 1½ teaspoons pepper in bowl, then spread evenly over top of salad.

TO STORE

4. Cover salad and refrigerate for up to 24 hours.

TO FINISH AND SERVE

5. Remove salad from refrigerator and let sit at room temperature for 15 minutes. Toss until salad is evenly coated with dressing. Season with salt and pepper to taste and serve.

EASY HARD-COOKED EGGS   MAKES 6 EGGS
Place 6 large eggs in medium saucepan, cover with 1 inch of water, and bring to boil over high heat. Remove pan from heat, cover, and let sit for 10 minutes. Meanwhile, fill medium bowl with 1 quart water and 1 tray of ice cubes (or equivalent). Transfer eggs to ice water bath with slotted spoon; let sit for 5 minutes. Peel and use as desired.

ALL ABOUT Making Great Ready-to-Serve Meals

Across this chapter you'll find a variety of dishes, all designed to be prepared a day or two ahead of time so that they can be pulled straight from the fridge and served without cooking. In this chapter you'll find lots of appealing ready-to-serve options perfect to bring to a picnic or potluck or to pull from the fridge when you're pressed for time (or if you simply want to avoid heating up your oven on a hot day). Because these recipes are stashed in the fridge and served cold or at room temperature, we had to find creative ways to ensure that everything tasted bright, fresh, and flavorful. Here's what we learned.

Take Off the Chill

While all the dishes in this chapter are designed to be served chilled, we found that they taste better when allowed to warm up slightly than when served straight from the fridge. For most dishes this was simple—just let them sit on the counter for a few minutes—but for pasta salads, we were surprised to find that it actually took a few hours for the pasta to come to the ideal temperature. To speed this process up, we simply stirred in ¼ cup of boiling water before serving. This step refreshed the pasta and helped to loosen the dressing as well, ensuring that our make-ahead pasta salads tasted just as good as fresh.

Season Aggressively

Research has shown that our ability to taste is dramatically affected by temperature, leaving flavors in cold food harder to recognize than in warm food. The solution? Dishes served chilled or at room temperature should be aggressively seasoned to make up for the flavor-dulling effects of cold temperatures. In this chapter you'll see that we use hefty amounts of fresh herbs, vinegars, and citrus juices as well as flavorful oils (extra-virgin olive oil or sesame oil) to ensure that our ready-to-serve dishes never taste dull.

Reserve Some Dressing

To use the lengthy hands-off refrigerating time to our advantage, we tossed many of our salad components with dressing before storing to infuse them with flavor as they sat. However, we found that the salads absorbed much of the dressing overnight, leaving us with flavorful but underdressed salads the next day. To solve this problem, we reserved some of the dressing and stored it separately to toss with the salad before serving, ensuring that our salads would be perfectly dressed. We also brightened the reserved dressing with some extra lemon juice or vinegar to help reawaken the flavors of the dish on the second day.

Break the Usual Pasta Rules

While we normally recommend cooking pasta until al dente to achieve the proper texture, we found it was best to cook pasta further—until fully tender—for pasta salads. That's because as the pasta cools, its starches firm up, giving the pasta a chewy, slightly hard texture. Cooking the pasta beyond al dente ensures that it stays tender once cooled. We also rinse the cooked pasta to remove excess starches that would make the pasta stick together and clump when stored overnight.

Make Sure Your Herbs Stay Fresh

Chopped fresh herbs are key to finishing many of the dishes in this chapter, so along with storing the salad components carefully, it's important to store the herbs properly so they look and taste fresh. To store herbs, gently rinse them and dry them in a salad spinner, then wrap them in a damp paper towel and store in a partially open zipper-lock bag in the crisper drawer. Basil is the exception; because it's particularly perishable, do not wash it until you are ready to use it or the added moisture will decrease its shelf life. Simply wrap it in clean paper towels, place it in a partially open zipper-lock bag, and refrigerate.

Overnight Kale Salad with Roasted Sweet Potatoes and Pomegranate Vinaigrette

SERVES 4 • **TO PREP** 1 HOUR 10 MINUTES • **STORE** UP TO 24 HOURS • **TO FINISH** 20 MINUTES

✓ **WHY THIS RECIPE WORKS:** We love the earthy, nutty flavor of uncooked kale, which has become a star salad ingredient on menus everywhere. But unless we're using hard-to-find baby kale, its texture can be a little tough. We wanted to find a way to tenderize standard supermarket kale without subjecting it to heat. Many recipes call for tossing kale with oil or salad dressing and letting it sit to tenderize in the refrigerator overnight. We found an improvement in the texture of the kale with this method, but it didn't quite deliver the tender leaves we were after. In addition to storing the dressed kale overnight, we found another technique that got great results: a quick massage. Kneading and squeezing the kale broke down the cell walls in much the same way that heat would, darkening the leaves and turning them silky. We found that it took a rubdown of about 5 minutes to soften one bunch of green curly-leaf kale. To complement the earthy kale, we made a tangy dressing with pomegranate molasses and cider vinegar balanced by a touch of honey. Caramelized roasted sweet potatoes, shredded radicchio, and crunchy pecans plus a sprinkling of Parmesan cheese and pomegranate seeds turned our salad into a hearty meal. Green curly kale, Tuscan kale (also known as dinosaur or Lacinato kale), or red kale can be used in this recipe; do not use baby kale. Pomegranate molasses can be found in the international aisle of well-stocked supermarkets; if you can't find it, substitute 2 tablespoons of lemon juice, 2 teaspoons of mild molasses, and 1 teaspoon of honey.

1½ pounds sweet potatoes, peeled, quartered lengthwise, and cut crosswise into ½-inch pieces
⅓ cup plus 1 tablespoon extra-virgin olive oil
Salt and pepper
2 tablespoons water
1½ tablespoons pomegranate molasses
1 shallot, minced
1 tablespoon honey
1 tablespoon cider vinegar
12 ounces kale, stemmed and sliced into 1-inch strips
½ head radicchio (5 ounces), cored and sliced thin

TO FINISH AND SERVE
½ cup pecans, toasted and chopped
⅓ cup pomegranate seeds (optional)
1 ounce Parmesan cheese, shaved

TO PREP

1. Adjust oven rack to middle position and heat oven to 400 degrees. Toss sweet potatoes with 1 tablespoon oil, ½ teaspoon salt, and ½ teaspoon pepper until evenly coated. Arrange in single layer in rimmed baking sheet and roast until bottom edges of potatoes are browned, about 15 minutes. Flip potatoes and continue to roast until second side is spotty brown, 10 to 15 minutes. Transfer potatoes to large plate and let cool to room temperature, about 20 minutes.

2. Meanwhile, whisk water, pomegranate molasses, shallot, honey, vinegar, ¼ teaspoon salt, and ¼ teaspoon pepper together in medium bowl. Whisking constantly, drizzle in remaining ⅓ cup oil.

3. Vigorously knead and squeeze kale with hands until leaves are uniformly darkened and slightly wilted, about 5 minutes. Toss kale, roasted potatoes, and radicchio with ⅓ cup vinaigrette in large bowl; cover. Cover remaining vinaigrette.

TO STORE

4. Refrigerate kale mixture and vinaigrette separately for up to 24 hours.

TO FINISH AND SERVE

5. Remove kale mixture and vinaigrette from refrigerator and let sit at room temperature for 15 minutes. Whisk vinaigrette to recombine, then drizzle over kale mixture. Add pecans and pomegranate seeds, if using, and toss to combine. Season with salt and pepper to taste and top with Parmesan. Serve.

TENDERIZE THE KALE

For a raw kale salad with greens that were fresh and crisp—but not tough—we needed to find a way to tenderize the kale. The trick turned out to be a quick massage; we kneaded the kale vigorously for 5 minutes until the leaves were darkened and slightly wilted. Then we tossed the salad with a vinai-grette and refrigerated it overnight to tenderize the greens further.

Quinoa, Black Bean, and Mango Salad with Lime Vinaigrette

SERVES 4 TO 6 • **TO PREP** 1 HOUR • **STORE** UP TO 2 DAYS • **TO FINISH** 20 MINUTES

✔ **WHY THIS RECIPE WORKS:** Hearty quinoa is a great choice for a make-ahead recipe because its nutty taste and delicate texture complement a variety of flavors and are not compromised by an extended stay in the fridge. Our challenge was to pair the tasty quinoa with bold flavors that would stay bright overnight and to make the salad hearty enough for a main course. We started by toasting the quinoa to bring out its flavor, then we added liquid to the pan and simmered the grains until nearly tender. We then spread the quinoa in a rimmed baking sheet so that the residual heat would finish cooking it as it sat, giving us perfectly cooked and fluffy—but not waterlogged—grains. Black beans, mango, and bell pepper lent the salad heartiness, bright flavor, and color. A simple but intense vinaigrette with lime juice, jalapeño, cumin, and cilantro gave this dish the acidity needed to keep its flavors fresh overnight. To preserve their color and texture, we added scallions and avocado the next day. If you buy unwashed quinoa, rinse the grains in a fine-mesh strainer, drain them, spread them in a rimmed baking sheet lined with a dish towel, and let them dry for 15 minutes before proceeding with the recipe.

1½ cups prewashed quinoa
2¼ cups water
    Salt and pepper
  5 tablespoons lime juice (3 limes)
  ½ jalapeño chile, stemmed and seeded
  ¾ teaspoon ground cumin
  ½ cup extra-virgin olive oil
  ⅓ cup fresh cilantro leaves
  1 red bell pepper, stemmed, seeded, and chopped
  1 mango, peeled, pitted, and cut into ¼-inch pieces
  1 (15-ounce) can black beans, rinsed

TO FINISH AND SERVE
  2 scallions, sliced thin
  1 avocado, sliced thin

TO PREP

1. Toast quinoa in large saucepan over medium-high heat, stirring often, until quinoa is very fragrant and makes continuous popping sound, 5 to 7 minutes. Stir in water and ½ teaspoon salt and bring to simmer. Cover, reduce heat to low, and continue to simmer until quinoa has absorbed most of water and is nearly tender, about 15 minutes. Spread quinoa in rimmed baking sheet and set aside until quinoa is tender, all water has been absorbed, and quinoa has cooled, about 20 minutes.

2. Meanwhile, process ¼ cup lime juice, jalapeño, cumin, and 1 teaspoon salt in blender until jalapeño is finely chopped, about 15 seconds. Add oil and cilantro and continue to process until smooth and emulsified, about 20 seconds. Transfer ¼ cup vinaigrette to small bowl and stir in remaining 1 tablespoon lime juice; cover.

3. When quinoa is cool, transfer to large bowl. Stir in bell pepper, mango, black beans, and remaining vinaigrette; cover.

TO STORE

4. Refrigerate quinoa mixture and vinaigrette separately for up to 2 days.

TO FINISH AND SERVE

5. Remove quinoa mixture and vinaigrette from refrigerator and let sit at room temperature for 15 minutes. Whisk vinaigrette to recombine, then drizzle over salad. Stir in scallions and season with salt and pepper to taste. Arrange sliced avocado over top and serve.

GETTING PERFECT QUINOA
To ensure that the quinoa for this salad came out perfectly cooked, we started by toasting the grains over medium-high heat to bring out their flavor. Then we simmered the quinoa until nearly tender before spreading it on a baking sheet to let the residual heat finish cooking the grains as they cooled. This method gave us tender and fluffy grains every time.

Wheat Berry, Chickpea, and Arugula Salad

SERVES 4 TO 6 • **TO PREP** 1 HOUR 25 MINUTES • **STORE** UP TO 24 HOURS • **TO FINISH** 20 MINUTES

✓ **WHY THIS RECIPE WORKS:** Chewy, nutty wheat berries lend themselves well to a make-ahead dish because soaking up the dressing overnight doesn't compromise their texture; it actually enhances it. Wheat berries often turn out tough and too chewy, especially when chilled, but an overnight rest in an acidic dressing tenderizes them, improving their texture as they sit. Cooking the wheat berries like pasta in a large amount of water, then draining and rinsing them under cold water to stop the cooking gave us the chewy, tender berries we were after. A simple lemon and cilantro dressing spiked with cumin, paprika, and cayenne provided the perfect amount of spice and brightness. We added chickpeas and roasted red peppers to give the salad a little more heft, nutty flavor, and sweetness. Reserving some of the dressing and brightening it with some extra lemon juice helped to reawaken the flavors of the dish the next day. For a leafy green component, peppery arugula paired well with the nutty wheat berries. Creamy feta lent the right richness and salty bite to round out this hearty salad.

1	cup wheat berries, rinsed
	Salt and pepper
¼	cup lemon juice (2 lemons)
3	tablespoons minced fresh cilantro
1½	teaspoons honey
2	garlic cloves, minced
½	teaspoon ground cumin
¼	teaspoon paprika
	Pinch cayenne pepper
5	tablespoons extra-virgin olive oil
1	(14-ounce) can chickpeas, rinsed
½	cup jarred roasted red peppers, drained, patted dry, and chopped

TO FINISH AND SERVE

6	ounces (6 cups) baby arugula
2	ounces feta cheese, crumbled (½ cup)

TO PREP

1. Bring 4 quarts water to boil in Dutch oven. Add wheat berries and ½ teaspoon salt, partially cover, and cook, stirring often, until tender but still chewy, about 1 hour. Drain wheat berries and rinse under cold running water until cool. Transfer wheat berries to large bowl.

2. Meanwhile, whisk 3 tablespoons lemon juice, cilantro, honey, garlic, cumin, ½ teaspoon salt, paprika, and cayenne together in medium bowl. Whisking constantly, drizzle in oil. Transfer ¼ cup dressing to small bowl and whisk in remaining 1 tablespoon lemon juice; cover.

3. Stir chickpeas and red peppers into cooled wheat berries. Whisk remaining dressing to recombine, then drizzle over wheat berry mixture and toss to combine; cover.

TO STORE

4. Refrigerate wheat berry mixture and dressing separately for up to 24 hours.

TO FINISH AND SERVE

5. Remove wheat berry mixture and dressing from refrigerator and let sit at room temperature for 15 minutes. Whisk dressing to recombine, then drizzle over wheat berry mixture. Add arugula and feta and gently toss to combine. Season with salt and pepper to taste and serve.

Tofu Salad with Vegetables

SERVES 4 • **TO PREP** 50 MINUTES • **STORE** UP TO 24 HOURS • **TO FINISH** 20 MINUTES

✓ **WHY THIS RECIPE WORKS:** Our goal in creating this recipe was a light and easy Asian-inspired vegetarian salad that boasted plenty of vegetables in a fresh, bright vinaigrette. First we sought out a mix of vegetables that, along with the tofu, would give our salad enough heft to make it a main course. We settled on napa cabbage, snow peas, red bell pepper, bean sprouts, and carrots. But when we dressed the salad and stored it overnight, the cabbage leached water and the salad ended up waterlogged. To avoid this soggy mess, we decided not to dress the salad until the day it was eaten. Next we considered the tofu. We preferred soft tofu for its creamy, custard-like texture, and we pan-fried it to give it a slightly crispy outside. Draining the tofu on a paper towel–lined baking sheet before cooking helped to create the light golden crust we were after. And storing the mild tofu in the dressing overnight allowed it to soak up the dressing's bold flavors. For a vinaigrette with extra punch, we combined acidic rice vinegar and lime juice and added depth with fish sauce and rich, nutty flavor with toasted sesame oil. A sprinkling of cilantro and toasted sesame seeds before eating were the perfect accents to our salad.

28	ounces soft tofu, cut into ¾-inch pieces
3	tablespoons lime juice (2 limes)
3	tablespoons honey
2	tablespoons rice vinegar
2	tablespoons fish sauce, plus extra as needed
1	tablespoon grated fresh ginger
1½	teaspoons Sriracha sauce
6	tablespoons vegetable oil
3	tablespoons toasted sesame oil
4	cups shredded napa cabbage
6	ounces snow peas, strings removed, cut in half lengthwise
1	red bell pepper, stemmed, seeded, and cut into ½-inch pieces
1	cup bean sprouts
2	carrots, peeled and shredded
2	scallions, sliced thin on bias

TO FINISH AND SERVE

3	tablespoons minced fresh cilantro
1	tablespoon sesame seeds, toasted

TO PREP

1. Spread tofu on paper towel–lined baking sheet and let drain for 20 minutes. Gently press tofu dry with paper towels. Meanwhile, combine lime juice, honey, vinegar, fish sauce, ginger, and Sriracha in medium bowl. Whisking constantly, drizzle in ¼ cup vegetable oil and sesame oil. Transfer ¼ cup vinaigrette to small bowl; cover.

2. Heat 1 tablespoon vegetable oil in 12-inch non-stick skillet over medium-high heat until shimmering. Add half of tofu to skillet and brown lightly on all sides, about 5 minutes; transfer to bowl with remaining vinaigrette. Repeat with remaining 1 tablespoon vegetable oil and remaining tofu; transfer to bowl with tofu and vinaigrette. Gently toss tofu to coat with vinaigrette. Let cool to room temperature, about 10 minutes; cover.

3. Combine cabbage, snow peas, bell pepper, bean sprouts, carrots, and scallions in large bowl; cover.

TO STORE

4. Refrigerate tofu mixture, vegetable mixture, and vinaigrette separately for up to 24 hours.

TO FINISH AND SERVE

5. Remove tofu mixture, vegetable mixture, and vinaigrette from refrigerator and let sit at room temperature for 15 minutes. Whisk vinaigrette to recombine, then drizzle over vegetables and toss to combine. Add tofu mixture and toss gently to combine. Season with fish sauce to taste. Sprinkle with cilantro and sesame seeds and serve.

Pesto Pasta Salad with Chicken and Arugula

SERVES 4 TO 6 • **TO PREP** 40 MINUTES • **STORE** UP TO 2 DAYS • **TO FINISH** 20 MINUTES

✔ **WHY THIS RECIPE WORKS:** Marrying pesto with hot pasta is no problem. But try to add pesto to cold pasta salad and you'll end up with a gummy dressing that clumps up and dries out. To ensure that our pesto stayed rich and creamy, we borrowed a common pasta salad ingredient: mayonnaise. Just ¼ cup kept the sauce smooth and luscious, so it coated the pasta perfectly without dulling the flavor of the dressing. Although we normally prefer our pasta cooked until al dente in the test kitchen, we found that when served cold, al dente pasta was chewy and a bit tough. So we broke our own rule and cooked the pasta until fully tender. Leaving the pasta slightly wet after draining it also helped keep the dressing loose. We found that fusilli was the ideal pasta shape for trapping the pesto. Last, to ensure that our pasta wasn't gummy and to loosen the cold dressing, we stirred in a little boiling water to refresh the pasta before serving. We also reserved some of the pesto and added it before serving to keep our pasta salad tasting fresh and vibrant. A final addition of peppery baby arugula and juicy cherry tomatoes lent our pasta salad color and freshness. Cooking the pasta until it is completely tender and leaving it slightly wet after rinsing are important for the texture of the finished salad. Other pasta shapes can be substituted for the fusilli. For an accurate measurement of boiling water, bring a full kettle of water to a boil and then measure out the desired amount.

12 **ounces boneless, skinless chicken breasts, trimmed**
 Salt and pepper
¾ **cup plus 1 tablespoon extra-virgin olive oil**
1½ **cups fresh basil leaves**
¾ **cup pine nuts, toasted**
3 **tablespoons lemon juice**
2 **garlic cloves, minced**
1½ **ounces Parmesan cheese, grated (¾ cup)**
¼ **cup mayonnaise**
1 **pound fusilli**

TO FINISH AND SERVE
¼ **cup boiling water**
12 **ounces cherry tomatoes, halved**
3 **ounces (3 cups) baby arugula**

TO PREP

1. Pat chicken dry with paper towels and season with salt and pepper. Heat 1 tablespoon oil in 12-inch skillet over medium-high heat until just smoking. Brown chicken well on first side, 6 to 8 minutes. Flip chicken, add ½ cup water, and cover. Reduce heat to medium-low and continue to cook until chicken registers 160 degrees, 5 to 7 minutes. Transfer chicken to carving board, let cool slightly, then shred into bite-size pieces; set aside.

2. Process basil, pine nuts, lemon juice, garlic, ½ teaspoon salt, ¼ teaspoon pepper, and remaining ¾ cup oil in food processor until smooth, about 1 minute, scraping down bowl as needed. Add Parmesan and mayonnaise and pulse to incorporate, about 5 pulses. Transfer ¼ cup pesto to small bowl; cover.

3. Meanwhile, bring 4 quarts water to boil in large pot. Add pasta and 1 tablespoon salt and cook, stirring often, until tender. Drain pasta, rinse with cold water, and drain again, leaving pasta slightly wet.

4. Toss cooled pasta, remaining pesto, and shredded chicken together in large bowl until combined; cover.

TO STORE

5. Refrigerate pasta mixture and pesto separately for up to 2 days.

TO SERVE

6. Remove pasta mixture and pesto from refrigerator and let sit at room temperature for 15 minutes. Stir boiling water into pasta to loosen. Whisk pesto to recombine, then stir into pasta. Gently stir in tomatoes and arugula and season with salt and pepper to taste. Serve.

Tortellini Salad with Asparagus and Lemony Dressing

SERVES 4 TO 6 • **TO PREP** 40 MINUTES • **STORE** UP TO 2 DAYS • **TO FINISH** 20 MINUTES

✓ **WHY THIS RECIPE WORKS:** For a satisfying new take on pasta salad, we paired convenient store-bought cheese tortellini with crisp, fresh asparagus and a bright lemon dressing. First, we quickly blanched the asparagus to a perfect crisp-tender texture, then we cooked the tortellini in the same cooking water, which infused the pasta with the asparagus's delicate grassy flavor. Cooking the tortellini until fully tender (rather than al dente) gave it the best texture when served cold. Then we marinated it overnight in a bold but classic dressing of extra-virgin olive oil, fresh lemon juice, shallot, and garlic. To refresh the tortellini on the second day, we stirred in a little boiling water, then tossed it with reserved dressing that we brightened with an extra squeeze of lemon juice. Grated Parmesan, fresh basil, toasted pine nuts, and halved cherry tomatoes rounded out the salad and nicely complemented the rich, cheesy tortellini. Cooking the tortellini until it is completely tender and leaving it slightly wet after rinsing are important for the texture of the finished salad. For an accurate measurement of boiling water, bring a full kettle of water to a boil and then measure out the desired amount.

1	pound thin asparagus, trimmed and cut into 1-inch pieces
	Salt and pepper
1	pound dried cheese tortellini
5	tablespoons lemon juice (2 lemons)
2	garlic cloves, minced
1	shallot, minced
½	cup extra-virgin olive oil

TO FINISH AND SERVE

¼	cup boiling water
12	ounces cherry tomatoes, halved
1	ounce Parmesan cheese, grated (½ cup)
¾	cup chopped fresh basil, mint, or parsley
¼	cup pine nuts, toasted

TO PREP

1. Bring 4 quarts water to boil in large pot. Fill large bowl halfway with ice and water. Add asparagus and 1 tablespoon salt to boiling water and cook until asparagus is crisp-tender, about 2 minutes. Using slotted spoon, transfer asparagus to ice water and let cool, about 2 minutes. Remove asparagus from ice water and thoroughly pat dry with paper towels. Transfer asparagus to storage container; cover.

2. Return pot of water to boil. Add tortellini and cook, stirring often, until tender. Reserve ¼ cup cooking water. Drain tortellini, rinse with cold water, and drain again, leaving tortellini slightly wet.

3. Meanwhile, whisk ¼ cup lemon juice, garlic, shallot, 1 teaspoon salt, and ¾ teaspoon pepper together in large bowl. Whisking constantly, drizzle in oil. Transfer ¼ cup dressing to small bowl and stir in remaining 1 tablespoon lemon juice; cover.

4. Add tortellini to remaining dressing and toss to combine, adding reserved pasta cooking water as needed to adjust consistency; cover.

TO STORE

5. Refrigerate asparagus, tortellini mixture, and dressing separately for up to 2 days.

TO FINISH AND SERVE

6. Remove asparagus, tortellini mixture, and dressing from refrigerator and let sit at room temperature for 15 minutes. Stir boiling water into tortellini to loosen. Whisk dressing to recombine, then drizzle over tortellini. Stir in asparagus, tomatoes, Parmesan, basil, and pine nuts and season with salt and pepper to taste. Serve.

Fusilli Salad with Salami, Provolone, and Sun-Dried Tomato Vinaigrette

SERVES 4 • **TO PREP** 35 MINUTES • **STORE** UP TO 2 DAYS • **TO FINISH** 20 MINUTES

✓ **WHY THIS RECIPE WORKS:** Pasta salad from the deli counter might be convenient, but that's about all it has going for it—the heavy dose of mayo, mushy pasta, and dull, overcooked vegetables translate into a disappointing dish. For a bold and satisfying pasta salad that wouldn't taste like a last-ditch dinner, we were inspired by traditional antipasto flavors. Thickly cut salami and provolone added a salty, savory bite and richness, and a handful of sliced kalamata olives added a brininess that helped to punch up the flavor. With several rich ingredients already in the mix, a mayonnaise-based dressing was overkill, so we swapped it out in favor of a bright olive oil–based vinaigrette accented with tangy sun-dried tomatoes, red wine vinegar, garlic, and basil. Marinating the cooked pasta in the vinaigrette overnight flavored it through and through. To loosen the dressing and quickly take the chill off the pasta, we stirred in a little boiling water on the second day. Chopped baby spinach added just before serving lent extra color and freshness. Cooking the pasta until it is completely tender and leaving it slightly wet after rinsing are important for the texture of the finished salad. Other pasta shapes can be substituted for the fusilli; however, their cup measurements may vary. For an accurate measurement of boiling water, bring a full kettle of water to a boil and then measure out the desired amount.

8	ounces (3 cups) fusilli
	Salt and pepper
¾	cup oil-packed sun-dried tomatoes, rinsed, patted dry, and minced, plus 2 tablespoons packing oil
5	tablespoons red wine vinegar
2	tablespoons chopped fresh basil or parsley
1	garlic clove, minced
¼	cup extra-virgin olive oil
8	ounces thickly sliced salami or pepperoni, cut into matchsticks
8	ounces thickly sliced provolone, cut into matchsticks
½	cup pitted kalamata olives, sliced

TO FINISH AND SERVE

¼	cup boiling water
2	ounces (2 cups) baby spinach, chopped

TO PREP

1. Bring 4 quarts water to boil in large pot. Add pasta and 1 tablespoon salt and cook, stirring often, until tender. Drain pasta, rinse with cold water, and drain again, leaving pasta slightly wet.

2. Meanwhile, whisk sun-dried tomatoes, ¼ cup vinegar, basil, garlic, ¾ teaspoon salt, and ¾ teaspoon pepper together in large bowl. Whisking constantly, drizzle in sun-dried tomato packing oil and extra-virgin olive oil. Transfer ¼ cup vinaigrette to small bowl and stir in remaining 1 tablespoon vinegar; cover.

3. Add pasta, salami, cheese, and olives to remaining vinaigrette and toss to combine; cover.

TO STORE

4. Refrigerate pasta mixture and vinaigrette separately for up to 2 days.

TO FINISH AND SERVE

5. Remove pasta mixture and vinaigrette from refrigerator and let sit at room temperature for 15 minutes. Stir boiling water into pasta to loosen. Whisk vinaigrette to recombine, then drizzle over pasta. Stir in spinach and season with salt and pepper to taste. Serve.

OVERCOOK THE PASTA

When we tried making pasta salad with al dente pasta, we found that the pasta ended up chewy and hard, because the pasta's starches firmed up as the pasta cooled. So to give it the right texture when served cold, we cooked the pasta until fully tender. We also stirred in a little boiling water before serving to refresh the pasta.

Orzo Salad with Broccoli and Radicchio

SERVES 4 • **TO PREP** 40 MINUTES • **STORE** UP TO 2 DAYS • **TO FINISH** 20 MINUTES

✔ **WHY THIS RECIPE WORKS:** In this recipe, we set out to make a hearty orzo salad that was fresh, flavorful, and satisfying. To give the dish a variety of balanced flavors, we included broccoli, bitter radicchio, salty sun-dried tomatoes, and crunchy pine nuts. Cooking the orzo in the same water that we used to quickly blanch the broccoli imparted a delicate vegetal flavor throughout the dish and helped streamline the recipe. To ensure that the orzo was tender even when served cold, we cooked it past al dente. To bring together all the flavors of the dish, we made a bold dressing with balsamic vinegar and honey. Toasting the pine nuts intensified their nutty flavor and brought further dimension to the orzo. Sharp Parmesan added the perfect salty accent, and a hefty dose of chopped basil gave us a fresh finish to lighten this hearty dish. Cooking the pasta until it is completely tender and leaving it slightly wet after rinsing are important for the texture of the finished salad. For an accurate measurement of boiling water, bring a full kettle of water to a boil and then measure out the desired amount.

¾ **pound broccoli florets, cut into 1-inch pieces**
   Salt and pepper
1⅓ **cups orzo**
¼ **cup balsamic vinegar**
1 **garlic clove, minced**
1 **teaspoon honey**
½ **cup sun-dried tomatoes, rinsed, patted dry, and minced, plus 3 tablespoons packing oil**
3 **tablespoons extra-virgin olive oil**
1 **head radicchio (10 ounces), cored and chopped fine**

TO FINISH AND SERVE
¼ **cup boiling water**
2 **ounces Parmesan cheese, grated (1 cup)**
½ **cup pine nuts, toasted**
½ **cup chopped fresh basil**

TO PREP

1. Bring 4 quarts water to boil in large pot. Fill large bowl halfway with ice and water. Add broccoli and 1 tablespoon salt to boiling water and cook until crisp-tender, about 2 minutes. Using slotted spoon, transfer broccoli to ice water and let cool, about 2 minutes. Remove broccoli from ice water and thoroughly pat dry with paper towels. Transfer to storage container; cover.

2. Return water to boil, add orzo, and cook, stirring often, until tender. Drain orzo, rinse with cold water, and drain again, leaving pasta slightly wet.

3. Meanwhile, whisk 3 tablespoons vinegar, garlic, honey, and 1 teaspoon salt together in large bowl. Whisking constantly, drizzle in tomato packing oil and extra-virgin olive oil. Transfer ¼ cup vinaigrette to small bowl and whisk in remaining 1 tablespoon vinegar; cover.

4. Add orzo, tomatoes, and radicchio to remaining vinaigrette and toss to combine; cover.

TO STORE

5. Refrigerate broccoli, orzo mixture, and vinaigrette separately for up to 2 days.

TO FINISH AND SERVE

6. Remove broccoli, orzo mixture, and vinaigrette from refrigerator and let sit at room temperature for 15 minutes. Stir boiling water into orzo to loosen. Whisk vinaigrette to recombine, then drizzle over orzo. Stir in broccoli, Parmesan, pine nuts, and basil and season with salt and pepper to taste. Serve.

Sesame Noodles with Chicken

SERVES 4 • **TO PREP** 1 HOUR • **STORE** UP TO 2 DAYS • **TO FINISH** 20 MINUTES

✓ **WHY THIS RECIPE WORKS:** Our recipe for easy but authentic-tasting cold sesame noodles relies on everyday pantry staples to deliver its characteristic sweet, nutty, addictive flavor. Chunky peanut butter and toasted sesame seeds ground together in the blender made the perfect stand-in for hard-to-find Asian sesame paste. Fresh garlic and ginger plus soy sauce, vinegar, hot sauce, and brown sugar rounded out the sauce. Tossing cooked Chinese noodles with sesame oil kept them from sticking and clumping overnight. For moist, tender chicken, we poached boneless, skinless chicken breasts, then shredded them into bite-size pieces. Scallions, grated carrot, and red bell pepper lent fresh flavor, color, and crunch. We tried tossing the salad with the dressing before storing it, but the noodles absorbed too much liquid and ended up pasty and mushy. Instead, we stored the dressing separately, then loosened it with hot water just before tossing it with the noodles. A garnish of toasted sesame seeds lent crunch and nutty flavor and cilantro added freshness. Creamy peanut butter can be substituted for the chunky peanut butter if necessary. Dried spaghetti or linguine can be substituted for the fresh Chinese noodles. For an accurate measurement of boiling water, bring a full kettle of water to a boil and then measure out the desired amount. Leaving the noodles slightly wet after rinsing is important for the texture of the finished salad.

5	tablespoons soy sauce
¼	~~cup chunky peanut butter~~ *Hesp*
3	tablespoons sesame seeds, toasted
2	garlic cloves, minced
2	tablespoons rice vinegar
2	tablespoons packed light brown sugar
1	tablespoon grated fresh ginger
1	teaspoon hot sauce
1½	pounds boneless, skinless chicken breasts, trimmed
	Salt and pepper
1	tablespoon vegetable oil
1	pound fresh Chinese noodles
2	tablespoons toasted sesame oil
4	scallions, sliced thin on bias
1	carrot, peeled and shredded
1	red bell pepper, stemmed, seeded, and cut into ½-inch pieces

TO FINISH AND SERVE

¼	cup boiling water
2	tablespoons minced fresh cilantro
1	tablespoon sesame seeds, toasted

TO PREP

1. Process soy sauce, peanut butter, sesame seeds, garlic, vinegar, sugar, ginger, and hot sauce in blender until smooth, about 30 seconds. With blender running, add ½ cup hot water, 1 tablespoon at a time, until sauce has consistency of heavy cream (you may not need all of water). Transfer sauce to storage container; cover.

2. Pat chicken dry with paper towels and season with salt and pepper. Heat vegetable oil in 12-inch skillet over medium-high heat until just smoking. Brown chicken well on first side, 6 to 8 minutes. Flip chicken, add ½ cup water, and cover. Reduce heat to medium-low and continue to cook until chicken registers 160 degrees, 5 to 7 minutes. Transfer chicken to carving board, let cool slightly, then shred into bite-size pieces; set aside.

3. Meanwhile, bring 4 quarts water to boil in large pot. Add noodles and cook, stirring often, until just tender. Drain noodles, rinse with cold water, and drain again, leaving noodles slightly wet. Transfer to large bowl and toss with sesame oil. Add shredded chicken, scallions, carrot, and bell pepper and gently toss to combine; cover.

TO STORE

4. Refrigerate noodle mixture and sauce separately for up to 2 days.

TO FINISH AND SERVE

5. Remove noodle mixture and sauce from refrigerator and let sit at room temperature for 15 minutes. Stir boiling water into peanut sauce to loosen, then gently toss with noodles until combined. Season with salt and pepper to taste. Sprinkle with cilantro and sesame seeds and serve.

STORE THE DRESSING SEPARATELY
We found that the delicate fresh Chinese noodles in this dish soaked up dressing when stored overnight, ending up mushy and pasty. So we tossed the noodles with just the chicken, vegetables, and a little oil to prevent sticking and stored the dressing separately. The next day we loosened the dressing with hot water and tossed everything together to serve.

Chilled Somen Noodles with Shrimp

SERVES 4 • **TO PREP** 40 MINUTES • **STORE** 2 TO 24 HOURS • **TO FINISH** 20 MINUTES

✓ **WHY THIS RECIPE WORKS:** For our modern-day take on this refreshing Japanese dish, we tossed chilled somen noodles with a flavorful broth made from the shrimp-poaching liquid and seasoned with soy sauce, mirin, and fresh ginger. Somen noodles are dried noodles made from high-gluten wheat flour and aged for one to two years. After cooking the somen, we rinsed them with cold water to stop the cooking and remove extra starch that would make them gummy. We then tossed the noodles with sesame oil to keep them separated during storage. Gently poaching the shrimp kept them perfectly tender, and spiking the poaching liquid with dried seaweed flavored the shrimp as they cooked. Then we used the poaching liquid, now infused with the shrimp's delicate seafood flavor, as the base for our broth. Steeping potent bonito flakes in the liquid gave it a unique smoky flavor, then we stirred in soy sauce, mirin, and fresh ginger. Just before serving, we tossed the noodles with a portion of the broth to refresh and flavor them before dividing them among individual serving bowls and topping them with the shrimp, broth, and a bright garnish of fresh cilantro and pickled ginger. Kombu (dried seaweed) and dried bonito flakes (bonito is a type of fish) can be found in the international aisle of the supermarket, or at Asian and natural foods markets. Bonito flakes add a distinct smoky flavor to this dish but can be left out if desired.

1	pound medium-large shrimp (31 to 40 per pound), peeled, deveined, tails removed, and sliced in half lengthwise
1	(6-inch) piece kombu
¼	cup dried bonito flakes (optional)
1	small cucumber, halved lengthwise and sliced thin
2	scallions, sliced thin on bias
1	tablespoon toasted sesame oil
⅓	cup soy sauce
⅓	cup mirin
1	tablespoon grated fresh ginger
1½	teaspoons sugar
12	ounces somen noodles

TO SERVE

¼	cup warm tap water
¼	cup pickled ginger
¼	cup fresh cilantro leaves

TO PREP

1. Fill large bowl halfway with ice and water. Combine shrimp, 3 cups cold water, and kombu in large saucepan. Place saucepan over medium heat and cook, stirring several times, until shrimp are pink, firm to touch, and no longer translucent, 8 to 10 minutes (water should be just bubbling around edge of pan and register 165 degrees). Remove pan from heat, cover, and let shrimp sit in broth for 2 minutes.

Using slotted spoon, transfer shrimp to ice water to stop cooking and chill thoroughly, about 3 minutes. Stir bonito flakes (if using) into broth, cover, and let sit for 5 minutes.

2. Remove shrimp from ice water and pat dry with paper towels. Combine shrimp, cucumber, scallions, and 1 teaspoon oil in medium bowl; cover. Strain broth through fine-mesh strainer into separate medium bowl, pressing on solids to extract as much broth as possible; discard solids. Whisk in soy sauce, mirin, ginger, and sugar until sugar is dissolved.

3. Meanwhile, bring 4 quarts water to boil in large pot. Add noodles and cook, stirring often, until just tender. Drain noodles, rinse with cold water, and drain again, leaving noodles slightly wet. Transfer noodles to bowl and toss with remaining 2 teaspoons oil; cover.

TO STORE

4. Refrigerate shrimp mixture, broth mixture, and noodles separately for at least 2 hours or up to 24 hours.

TO SERVE

5. Remove shrimp mixture, broth mixture, and noodles from refrigerator and let sit at room temperature for 15 minutes. Stir warm water into broth. Toss noodles with ½ cup broth. Divide noodles among individual serving bowls and pour remaining broth evenly over noodles. Top with shrimp mixture, pickled ginger, and cilantro. Serve.

Spanish Tortilla with Red Pepper Aïoli

SERVES 4 TO 6 • **TO PREP** 1 HOUR 10 MINUTES • **STORE** UP TO 24 HOURS • **TO FINISH** 30 MINUTES

✓ **WHY THIS RECIPE WORKS:** This Spanish potato and egg cake, similar to an omelet or frittata, is irresistible and easily made ahead of time. Parcooking the potatoes before combining them with the eggs was crucial to ensure that the tortilla was fully cooked. Flipping the tortilla over halfway through cooking ensured that it cooked evenly on both sides. We simply slid it out of the pan onto a plate, placed another plate on top, inverted it, then slid the flipped tortilla back into the pan. This kept all the potato filling safely inside the tortilla. Finally, cooling and storing the tortilla on a clean kitchen towel was key. The towel absorbed steam and ensured that the tortilla didn't turn soggy and fall apart, so it was ready to slice into perfect wedges for serving. Garlicky aïoli is the traditional accompaniment to this dish; we added roasted red peppers for extra flavor and a pop of color.

10 tablespoons plus 1 teaspoon extra-virgin olive oil

1½ pounds Yukon Gold potatoes, peeled, quartered lengthwise, and cut crosswise into ⅛-inch-thick slices

1 onion, halved and sliced thin
Salt and pepper

8 large eggs plus 2 large yolks

2 tablespoons minced fresh chives

¼ cup jarred roasted red peppers, rinsed, patted dry, and chopped

2 teaspoons Dijon mustard

2 teaspoons lemon juice

1 garlic clove, minced

⅔ cup vegetable oil

TO PREP

1. Toss ¼ cup extra-virgin olive oil, potatoes, onion, ½ teaspoon salt, and ¼ teaspoon pepper together in large bowl until potato slices are separated and coated with oil. Heat 2 tablespoons extra-virgin olive oil in 10-inch nonstick skillet over medium-high heat until shimmering. Reduce heat to medium-low and add potato mixture to skillet (set bowl aside without washing). Cover and cook, stirring with rubber spatula every 5 minutes, until potatoes offer no resistance when poked with tip of paring knife, 22 to 28 minutes (some potato slices may break into smaller pieces).

2. Meanwhile, whisk whole eggs and ½ teaspoon salt together in reserved bowl until just combined. Using rubber spatula, fold hot potato mixture and chives into eggs until combined.

3. Return skillet to medium-high heat, add 1 teaspoon extra-virgin olive oil, and heat until just beginning to smoke. Add egg-potato mixture and cook, shaking skillet and folding mixture constantly, for 15 seconds. Smooth top of mixture with rubber spatula. Reduce heat to medium, cover, and cook, gently shaking skillet every 30 seconds, until bottom is golden brown and top is lightly set, about 2 minutes.

4. Using rubber spatula, loosen tortilla from skillet, shaking back and forth until tortilla slides around freely in skillet. Slide tortilla onto large plate. Invert tortilla onto second large plate and slide it, browned side up, back into skillet; lay clean kitchen towel on now-empty plate. Tuck edges of tortilla into skillet with rubber spatula. Return pan to medium heat and continue to cook, gently shaking pan every 30 seconds, until second side is golden brown, about 2 minutes longer. Slide tortilla onto towel-lined plate and allow to cool to room temperature, about 1 hour; cover.

5. Process egg yolks, red peppers, mustard, lemon juice, and garlic in food processor until smooth, about 10 seconds, scraping down bowl as needed. With processor running, slowly drizzle in vegetable oil, about 1 minute. Transfer mixture to medium bowl. Whisking constantly, slowly drizzle in remaining ¼ cup extra-virgin olive oil, about 30 seconds. Season with salt and pepper to taste; cover.

TO STORE

6. Refrigerate tortilla and aïoli separately for up to 24 hours.

TO FINISH AND SERVE

7. Remove tortilla and aïoli from refrigerator and let sit at room temperature for 30 minutes. Cut tortilla into wedges and serve with aïoli.

New Orleans Muffuletta

SERVES 8 • **TO PREP** 2½ HOURS • **STORE** UP TO 24 HOURS • **TO FINISH** 30 MINUTES

✓ **WHY THIS RECIPE WORKS:** Not your typical deli sandwich, a New Orleans muffuletta is an addictive combination of meats, cheese, and the quintessential olive salad. Standard supermarket loaves turned out stale and tough, especially after sitting in the refrigerator, so we decided to bake our own "homemade" bread with store-bought pizza dough. The flavor and texture were spot-on, and the extra effort was worth it to get bread that could hold up in the fridge for a day. For the olive salad, we used twice as many green olives as kalamata, since the latter made the salad too salty, and we liked jarred *giardiniera* for its briny, piquant qualities. Thyme, oregano, garlic, red pepper flakes, and parsley balanced out the flavors of the salad. A few pulses in the food processor gave our mixture the right consistency. We then stirred in plenty of olive oil to help the flavors seep into the bread. Alternating layers of salami, mortadella, capicola, and provolone cheese formed the bulk of our sandwiches. But with so many layers, our sandwiches were unwieldy and hard to eat. Luckily, weighting the sandwiches down for an hour rendered them compact and sliceable. If you can't fit a baking sheet in your refrigerator, you can weight the sandwiches on the counter for 1 hour, then transfer them to the refrigerator.

2	(1-pound) packages store-bought pizza dough
2	cups drained jarred giardiniera
1	cup pimento-stuffed green olives
½	cup pitted kalamata olives
2	tablespoons capers, rinsed
1	tablespoon red wine vinegar
1	garlic clove, minced
½	teaspoon dried oregano
¼	teaspoon red pepper flakes
¼	teaspoon dried thyme
½	cup extra-virgin olive oil
¼	cup chopped fresh parsley
1	large egg, beaten
5	teaspoons sesame seeds
4	ounces thinly sliced Genoa salami
6	ounces thinly sliced aged provolone cheese
6	ounces thinly sliced mortadella
4	ounces thinly sliced hot capicola

TO PREP

1. Form pizza dough into 2 tight round balls on oiled baking sheet, cover loosely with greased plastic wrap, and let sit at room temperature until slightly puffy, about 1 hour.

2. Meanwhile, pulse giardiniera, green and kalamata olives, capers, vinegar, garlic, oregano, pepper flakes, and thyme in food processor until coarsely chopped, about 6 pulses, scraping down bowl as needed. Transfer mixture to medium bowl and stir in oil and parsley. Let sit at room temperature for 30 minutes.

3. Adjust oven rack to middle position and heat oven to 425 degrees. Keeping dough balls on sheet, flatten each into 7-inch disk. Brush top of each disk with egg and sprinkle with sesame seeds. Bake until golden brown and loaves sound hollow when tapped, 18 to 20 minutes, rotating sheet halfway through baking. Transfer loaves to wire rack and let cool to room temperature, about 1 hour.

4. Slice loaves in half horizontally. Spread one-fourth of olive salad on cut side of each top and bottom half, pressing firmly with rubber spatula to compact. Onto bottom half of each loaf, layer ingredients in this order: 2 ounces salami, 1½ ounces provolone, 3 ounces mortadella, another 1½ ounces provolone, and 2 ounces capicola. Cap with loaf tops and wrap individual sandwiches tightly in plastic.

5. Place baking sheet on top of sandwiches and weight down with several heavy cans.

TO STORE

6. Refrigerate weighted sandwiches for up to 24 hours, flipping sandwiches once.

TO FINISH AND SERVE

7. Remove sandwiches from refrigerator and let sit at room temperature for 30 minutes to 1 hour. Unwrap and slice each sandwich into quarters. Serve.

SOBA NOODLES WITH ROASTED EGGPLANT

Shop Smart

ONE GROCERY BAG MAKES THREE DINNERS

THE GROCERY BAG

1½ pounds flank steak

1 pound Italian sausage

8 ounces mozzarella cheese

1½ pounds broccoli florets

2 carrots

6 ounces baby spinach

1 red onion

1 knob fresh ginger

1 (1-pound) package store-bought pizza dough

1¼ cups oil-packed sun-dried tomatoes

¼ cup hoisin sauce

1 tablespoon sesame seeds

CHECK THE PANTRY

Parmesan cheese

Garlic (10 cloves)

Penne

Chicken broth

Soy sauce

Red pepper flakes

Vegetable oil

Extra-virgin olive oil

Beef and Broccoli Stir-Fry

SERVES 4 • **TO PREP AND COOK** 30 MINUTES

✓**WHY THIS RECIPE WORKS:** The key to stir-frying is ensuring that the pan is hot enough to sear the meat, deepen the flavors, and evaporate the excess liquid, all in a matter of minutes. We wanted to take advantage of this technique to make a flavorful beef and broccoli stir-fry. Because a stir-fry comes together so quickly, it was critical to get all the ingredients organized ahead of time. Prepping extra broccoli also helped us save time when we made our Skillet Pizza with Broccoli and Red Onion (page 177) later in the week. Slicing the steak very thin ensured that it was in and out of the skillet quickly, reducing the risk of overcooking. A simple combination of hoisin sauce, water, and soy sauce flavored with sautéed ginger, garlic, and red pepper flakes gave our stir-fry bold flavor without making our ingredient list too long. To make slicing the steak easier, freeze it for 20 minutes first. When toasting the sesame seeds in a dry skillet, be sure to shake the pan frequently to prevent them from burning. Serve this dish with white rice.

¼   **cup hoisin sauce**
½   **cup water**
2   **tablespoons soy sauce**
2   **tablespoons vegetable oil**
1   **tablespoon grated fresh ginger**
2   **garlic cloves, minced**
½   **teaspoon red pepper flakes**
1½ **pounds flank steak, trimmed and sliced thin across grain**
1   **pound broccoli florets, cut into 1-inch pieces**
2   **carrots, peeled and cut into 2-inch-long matchsticks**
½   **red onion, sliced thin**
1   **tablespoon sesame seeds, toasted**

1. Whisk hoisin, ¼ cup water, and soy sauce together in bowl; set aside. Combine 1 teaspoon oil, ginger, garlic, and pepper flakes in small bowl.

2. Heat 1½ teaspoons oil in 12-inch nonstick skillet over high heat until just smoking. Add half of beef, breaking up any clumps, and cook without stirring for 1 minute. Stir beef and continue to cook until beef is browned around edges, about 30 seconds; transfer to separate bowl. Repeat with 1½ teaspoons oil and remaining beef; transfer to bowl.

3. Heat remaining 2 teaspoons oil in now-empty skillet over high heat until shimmering. Add broccoli, carrots, and onion and cook for 30 seconds. Add remaining ¼ cup water, cover skillet, and lower heat to medium. Steam vegetables until crisp-tender, about 2 minutes. Push vegetables to sides of skillet.

Add ginger-garlic mixture to center of skillet and cook, mashing mixture into skillet, until fragrant, 15 to 20 seconds. Stir mixture into vegetables.

4. Return beef with any accumulated juices to skillet and toss to combine. Whisk sauce to recombine, then add to skillet and cook, stirring constantly, until sauce is thickened and evenly distributed, about 30 seconds. Sprinkle with sesame seeds and serve.

TO GET AHEAD

- Cut remaining ½ pound broccoli florets into 1-inch pieces. Refrigerate broccoli in zipper-lock bag for up to 4 days.
- Slice remaining onion thin. Refrigerate onion in zipper-lock bag for up to 4 days. Rinse before using.

TEST KITCHEN TIP SLICING FLANK STEAK THINLY

1. Slice steak lengthwise (with grain) into 2-inch-wide pieces.

2. Cut each piece crosswise (against grain) into very thin slices.

Skillet Penne with Sausage, Sun-Dried Tomatoes, and Spinach

SERVES 4 • **TO PREP AND COOK** 45 MINUTES

✓ **WHY THIS RECIPE WORKS:** For a fast one-dish pasta dinner, we combined penne with hot Italian sausage and ready-to-cook baby spinach. Chopped sun-dried tomatoes provided big, bold flavor (and also came in handy for a simple yet vibrant sauce for our skillet pizza later in the week). We kept cleanup to a minimum by building the sauce and cooking the pasta right in the skillet. A combination of chicken broth and water provided enough liquid to cook the pasta, and leaving the pan uncovered allowed the sauce to reduce, intensifying its flavor. The starch released from the pasta helped to thicken the sauce. Stirring in the spinach at the end kept its color and flavor bright. The spinach may seem like a lot at first, but it wilts down substantially. Other pasta shapes can be substituted for the penne; however, their cup measurements may vary.

 1 tablespoon extra-virgin olive oil
 1 pound hot or sweet Italian sausage,
    casings removed
 3 garlic cloves, minced
2½ cups chicken broth
 2 cups water
 8 ounces (2½ cups) penne
 ½ cup oil-packed sun-dried tomatoes,
    rinsed and chopped fine
    Salt and pepper
 6 ounces (6 cups) baby spinach
    Grated Parmesan cheese

1. Heat oil in 12-inch nonstick skillet over medium-high heat until just smoking. Add sausage and cook, breaking up meat with wooden spoon, until no longer pink, about 4 minutes. Stir in garlic and cook until fragrant, about 30 seconds.

2. Stir in broth, water, pasta, tomatoes, and ½ teaspoon salt. Bring to vigorous simmer and cook, stirring often, until pasta is tender and sauce has thickened, 15 to 18 minutes.

3. Stir in spinach, 1 handful at a time, and cook until wilted, about 3 minutes. Season with salt and pepper to taste and serve with Parmesan.

TEST KITCHEN TIP

REMOVING SAUSAGE FROM ITS CASING

Italian sausage is sold in several forms, including links, bulk-style tubes, and patties. If using links, remove the meat from the casing before cooking so that it can be crumbled into small, bite-size pieces.

To remove sausage from its casing, hold sausage firmly on one end and squeeze sausage out of opposite end.

Skillet Pizza with Broccoli and Red Onion

SERVES 4 • **TO PREP AND COOK** 50 MINUTES

✔ **WHY THIS RECIPE WORKS:** We wanted to come up with an easier, quicker way to make pizza at home. Our idea was to build the pizza in a skillet, giving the crust a jump start with heat from the stovetop, then transfer it to the oven to cook through—no pizza stone required. The broccoli florets left over from our stir-fry were the perfect choice for a hearty vegetable topping. The bold flavors of red onion and garlic paired well with the mild broccoli, and a quick steam in the microwave gave the veggies a head start, so they were perfectly tender atop the finished pizza. Rather than reach for store-bought pizza sauce, we created a simple yet assertive spread using the sun-dried tomatoes we used in our skillet penne dish. To make the oil-packed sun-dried tomatoes serve double duty, we used their flavorful packing oil both in our spread and in the skillet to brown the crust. To ensure the crispest crusts, we cooked the pizzas over high heat on the stovetop just until the bottoms began to brown, then transferred them to a 500-degree oven to melt the cheese and finish cooking through. A mixture of mozzarella and Parmesan cheeses rounded out our hearty veggie pizzas. It's important that the pizza dough be at room temperature so that it will stretch and stay put in the skillet to create an even, crisp crust.

¾ **cup oil-packed sun-dried tomatoes, plus ¼ cup packing oil**

½ **cup warm tap water**

5 **garlic cloves, minced**

¼ **teaspoon salt**

8 **ounces broccoli florets, cut into 1-inch pieces**

½ **red onion, sliced thin**

1 **(1-pound) package store-bought pizza dough**

8 **ounces mozzarella cheese, shredded (2 cups)**

2 **ounces Parmesan cheese, grated (1 cup)**

1. Adjust oven rack to upper-middle position and heat oven to 500 degrees. Process tomatoes, 2 tablespoons tomato packing oil, ¼ cup water, one-third of garlic, and salt in food processor until smooth, about 30 seconds, scraping down sides of bowl as needed.

2. Combine broccoli, onion, remaining ¼ cup water, and remaining garlic in large bowl, cover, and microwave until broccoli is tender, about 2 minutes; drain well.

3. Divide dough in half. Press and roll 1 piece of dough (keep other piece covered) into 11-inch round on lightly floured counter. Grease 12-inch ovensafe skillet with 1 tablespoon tomato packing oil, then lay dough in skillet and reshape as needed. Spread half of tomato mixture on dough, leaving ½-inch border at edge, and sprinkle with half each of mozzarella, broccoli-onion mixture, and Parmesan.

4. Set skillet over high heat and cook until edge of crust has set and bottom is spotty brown, about 3 minutes. Transfer skillet to oven and bake pizza until edges are brown and cheese is melted and spotty brown, 7 to 10 minutes. Carefully remove skillet from oven (skillet handle will be hot) and slide pizza onto wire rack. Let cool slightly before serving. Being careful of hot skillet handle, wipe out skillet using paper towels. Let skillet cool slightly, then repeat with remaining 1 tablespoon tomato packing oil, dough, tomato mixture, mozzarella, broccoli-onion mixture, and Parmesan. Serve.

DINNER 1 Lemon-Herb Cod Fillets with Crispy Garlic Potatoes

DINNER 2 Sirloin Steak with Boursin Mashed Potatoes

DINNER 3 Creamy Penne with Asparagus and Peas

THE GROCERY BAG

4 (6- to 8-ounce) skinless cod fillets, 1 to 1½ inches thick

1 (2-pound) boneless shell sirloin steak, 1 to 1¼ inches thick

1 (5.2-ounce) package Boursin Garlic and Fine Herbs cheese

¾ cup heavy cream

1 small bunch fresh chives

5 sprigs fresh thyme

3½ pounds russet potatoes

1 pound asparagus

2 shallots

2 lemons

CHECK THE PANTRY

Unsalted butter

Parmesan cheese

Frozen peas

Garlic

Penne

Chicken broth

All-purpose flour

Vegetable oil

Extra-virgin olive oil

Lemon-Herb Cod Fillets with Crispy Garlic Potatoes

SERVES 4 • **TO PREP AND COOK** 1 HOUR

✔ **WHY THIS RECIPE WORKS:** This simple dinner features flaky, moist fish roasted on a bed of thinly sliced potatoes. Cooking the fish and potatoes together on a rimmed baking sheet allowed their juices to mingle for more flavor and kept the cleanup to just one pan. We chose fluffy russet potatoes as the base and sliced them thinly so they'd cook through quickly. [And because we could also use russet potatoes later in the week for our Sirloin Steak with Boursin Mashed Potatoes (page 180), we were able to cut down our grocery list too.] After slicing the potatoes and piling them on the baking sheet, we popped them into the oven until they were spotty brown and nearly tender. Then we laid the delicate cod fillets on top and topped them with butter, thyme sprigs, and lemon slices; the butter and lemon juice basted the fish as it baked, and the thyme added subtle seasoning to the mild-tasting cod for a dish with elegant flavor. You can substitute haddock or halibut for the cod. Be sure to remove the skin before cooking if you buy skin-on fillets.

1½ **pounds russet potatoes, unpeeled, sliced into ¼-inch-thick rounds**

2 **tablespoons unsalted butter, melted, plus 3 tablespoons cut into ¼-inch pieces**

3 **garlic cloves, minced**

4 **sprigs fresh thyme, plus 1 teaspoon minced Salt and pepper**

4 **(6- to 8-ounce) skinless cod fillets, 1 to 1½ inches thick**

1 **lemon, thinly sliced**

1. Adjust oven rack to lower-middle position and heat oven to 425 degrees. Toss potatoes, melted butter, garlic, minced thyme, ½ teaspoon salt, and ¼ teaspoon pepper together in bowl.

2. Shingle potatoes into four 6 by 4-inch rectangular piles in parchment paper–lined rimmed baking sheet. Roast potatoes until spotty brown and just tender, 30 to 35 minutes, rotating sheet halfway through roasting.

3. Pat cod dry with paper towels and season with salt and pepper. Lay 1 cod fillet, skinned side down, on top of each potato pile and top evenly with butter pieces, thyme sprigs, and lemon slices. Bake until cod flakes apart when gently prodded with paring knife and registers 140 degrees, about 15 minutes.

4. To serve, slide spatula underneath potatoes and cod and gently transfer to individual plates.

TO GET AHEAD

• Peel and slice remaining 2 pounds potatoes ¾ inch thick. Refrigerate potatoes in water for up to 2 days.

TEST KITCHEN TIP SHINGLING POTATOES

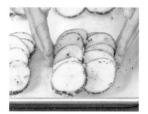

To make neat beds of potatoes for roasting, shingle one-quarter of potato slices into 6 by 4-inch rectangle in each corner of rimmed baking sheet.

Sirloin Steak with Boursin Mashed Potatoes

SERVES 4 • **TO PREP AND COOK** 35 MINUTES

✓ **WHY THIS RECIPE WORKS:** For the complete steakhouse experience at home, we looked to pair a juicy, rosy steak with creamy mashed potatoes flavored with garlic and herbs. Boneless sirloin steak boasted plenty of beefy flavor and a tender texture, and browning it in a smoking-hot pan gave the steak a nicely browned crust. Once the steak was well browned, we flipped it and turned down the heat to cook the meat gently to a perfect rosy medium-rare. As for the potatoes, we kept our ingredient list short by relying on garlicky, herb-spiked Boursin cheese, which provided potent aromatic and herbal flavor and, along with some heavy cream, the richness and silky texture we were after. Half a package of cheese provided plenty of flavor and richness, so we were able to save the rest to make a creamy pasta sauce later in the week. Finally, a sprinkling of minced chives contributed a burst of fresh flavor and bright color. We prefer these steaks cooked to medium-rare, but if you prefer them more or less done, see our guidelines on page 221.

2	pounds russet potatoes, peeled and sliced ¾ inch thick
	Salt and pepper
1	(2-pound) boneless shell sirloin steak, 1 to 1¼ inches thick, trimmed and halved widthwise
1	tablespoon vegetable oil
¾	cup heavy cream
½	(5.2-ounce) package Boursin Garlic and Fine Herbs cheese
2	tablespoons minced fresh chives

1. Place potatoes in large saucepan and add water to cover by 1 inch. Add 1 teaspoon salt and bring to boil. Reduce to gentle simmer and cook until potatoes are tender, 15 to 20 minutes.

2. Meanwhile, pat steaks dry with paper towels and season with salt and pepper. Heat oil in 12-inch skillet over medium-high heat until just smoking. Brown steaks well on first side, 3 to 5 minutes. Flip steaks, reduce heat to medium, and continue to cook until steaks register 120 to 125 degrees (for medium-rare), 5 to 7 minutes. Transfer steaks to carving board, tent loosely with aluminum foil, and let rest for 5 to 10 minutes. Slice steaks thin against grain.

3. Drain potatoes and return to saucepan. Cook over low heat, stirring constantly, until potatoes are thoroughly dried, about 2 minutes. Off heat, mash potatoes with potato masher until smooth. Microwave cream and Boursin together in bowl until hot, about 1 minute, then gently fold into potatoes. Fold chives, ½ teaspoon salt, and ¼ teaspoon pepper into potatoes. Serve with steak.

Creamy Penne with Asparagus and Peas

SERVES 4 TO 6 • **TO PREP AND COOK** 35 MINUTES

✔ **WHY THIS RECIPE WORKS:** We wanted to create a flavorful pasta dish with tender spring vegetables and a tangy, creamy sauce—with just a handful of ingredients. Asparagus and peas provided the perfect mix of quick-cooking, fresh-flavored vegetables. The peas required no prep—we simply stirred them into the sauce to heat through—but to get perfectly crisp-tender asparagus, it was necessary to cook it briefly. To save time, we used the cooking water twice, first to briefly simmer the asparagus and then to cook the pasta. This method had the added bonus of lending the asparagus's subtle flavor to the penne as it cooked. Finally, we needed to build our sauce. The Boursin left over from our mashed potatoes provided both a creamy texture and tangy flavor, plus some herbal and aromatic notes. For even more aromatic flavor, we sautéed garlic and shallots. Then we stirred in some flour for thickening and reduced some chicken broth before whisking in the Boursin along with some Parmesan. A simple sprinkling of chives and lemon zest boosted the flavors even more and gave us the freshness we were after. Other pasta shapes can be substituted for the penne; however, their cup measurements may vary.

2 tablespoons extra-virgin olive oil
2 shallots, sliced thin
3 garlic cloves, minced
1½ tablespoons all-purpose flour
1½ cups chicken broth
½ (5.2-ounce) package Boursin Garlic and Fine Herbs cheese, crumbled
1 ounce Parmesan cheese, grated (½ cup), plus extra for serving
1 cup frozen peas, thawed
1 pound asparagus, trimmed and cut on bias into 1-inch lengths
   Salt and pepper
1 pound penne
2 tablespoons minced fresh chives
1 tablespoon lemon zest

1. Heat oil in 12-inch skillet over medium-high heat until shimmering. Add shallots and cook until softened, about 2 minutes. Stir in garlic and cook until fragrant, about 30 seconds. Stir in flour and cook for 1 minute. Slowly whisk in broth, scraping up any browned bits. Bring to simmer and cook until slightly thickened, about 1 minute. Off heat, whisk in Boursin and Parmesan until smooth. Stir in peas; cover to keep warm.

2. Meanwhile, bring 4 quarts water to boil in large pot. Add asparagus and 1 tablespoon salt and cook, stirring often, until asparagus is crisp-tender, 2 to 4 minutes. Using slotted spoon, transfer asparagus to paper towel–lined plate.

3. Return water to boil, add pasta, and cook, stirring often, until al dente. Reserve ½ cup cooking water, then drain pasta and return it to pot.

4. Add sauce, asparagus, chives, lemon zest, ½ teaspoon salt, and ¼ teaspoon pepper to pasta and toss to coat. Adjust consistency with reserved cooking water as needed and season with salt and pepper to taste. Serve with extra Parmesan.

TEST KITCHEN TIP
TRIMMING ASPARAGUS SPEARS

1. Remove 1 stalk of asparagus from bunch and bend it at thicker end until it snaps.

2. Using chef's knife, trim ends of remaining asparagus with broken asparagus as guide.

THE GROCERY BAG

4 (6- to 8-ounce) skinless halibut fillets, 1 to 1½ inches thick

1½ pounds ground pork

1 pound boneless, skinless chicken breasts

2 ounces Monterey Jack cheese

1 small bunch fresh Thai basil

2 large bunches fresh cilantro

1½ pounds Yukon Gold potatoes

3 mangos

1 red bell pepper

3 limes

12 (6-inch) corn tortillas

CHECK THE PANTRY

Onions

Garlic

Chicken broth

All-purpose flour

Sugar

Cornstarch

Soy sauce

Rice vinegar

Chipotle in adobo

Red pepper flakes

Vegetable oil

Extra-virgin olive oil

Pan-Seared Halibut and Potatoes with Cilantro Sauce

SERVES 4 • **TO PREP AND COOK** 35 MINUTES

✔ **WHY THIS RECIPE WORKS:** For a quick dinner of halibut and potatoes with exceptional flavor, we went in search of the best cooking method. We tested various techniques and found we got much better results when we cooked the two components independently on the stovetop than when we cooked them together. To keep our recipe friendly for a weeknight, we cut the potatoes into chunks and microwaved them with a little oil, salt, and pepper until tender. Then, to give them rich roasted flavor, we quickly browned them on the stovetop over medium-high heat. While the potatoes were microwaving, we seared the halibut on the stovetop, then we transferred it to a serving platter and tented it with foil while we finished cooking the potatoes. To complement the mild flavor of the fish, we made a bright and bold cilantro sauce. To ensure that the flavors of the sauce were well balanced, we toasted the harsh raw garlic before pulsing it in the food processor with the cilantro, lime zest and juice, and a good amount of olive oil to create a rich sauce. You can substitute cod or haddock for the halibut.

2 garlic cloves, unpeeled
1½ cups fresh cilantro leaves
¾ cup extra-virgin olive oil
½ teaspoon grated lime zest plus 2 tablespoons juice
Salt and pepper
1½ pounds Yukon Gold potatoes, unpeeled, cut into 1-inch pieces
4 (6- to 8-ounce) skinless halibut fillets, 1 to 1½ inches thick

1. Toast garlic in 12-inch nonstick skillet over medium heat, shaking skillet occasionally, until fragrant and spotty brown, about 7 minutes; let cool slightly, then peel and chop. Pulse chopped garlic, cilantro, 7 tablespoons oil, lime zest and juice, and ½ teaspoon salt in food processor until cilantro is finely chopped, 10 to 15 pulses, scraping down sides of bowl as needed. Transfer to serving bowl and season with pepper to taste.

2. Combine potatoes, 1 tablespoon oil, ½ teaspoon salt, and ¼ teaspoon pepper in bowl, cover, and microwave until potatoes begin to soften, 6 to 8 minutes. Drain potatoes well.

3. Meanwhile, pat halibut dry with paper towels and season with salt and pepper. Heat 2 tablespoons oil in now-empty skillet over medium-high heat until just smoking. Lay halibut in skillet, skinned side up, and cook until golden, 3 to 5 minutes. Flip halibut, skinned side down, and continue to cook until halibut flakes apart when gently prodded with paring knife and registers 140 degrees, 3 to 5 minutes; transfer to serving platter and tent loosely with aluminum foil.

4. Add remaining 2 tablespoons oil and drained potatoes to now-empty skillet and cook over medium-high heat until potatoes are golden and tender, about 10 minutes; transfer to platter with halibut. Serve with cilantro sauce.

Easy Pork Tacos

SERVES 4 • **TO PREP AND COOK** 25 MINUTES

✓ **WHY THIS RECIPE WORKS:** We set out to create a recipe for easy pork tacos that were moist and flavorful, with subtle heat and the bright notes of juicy mango. Rather than using the traditional pork butt, we started with quick-cooking ground pork. To infuse the pork with rich flavor and a balanced heat, we cooked it with smoky chipotle chile packed in a tomato-based adobo sauce. Because pork is a lean protein, we found that it ended up with a dry texture when cooked on its own. Adding some finely chopped onion to the pork kept the mixture moist. Once the pork was no longer pink, we stirred in Monterey Jack cheese for richness. A simple mango salsa, flavored with onion, cilantro, and lime juice, made the perfect garnish and bright finish to our easy pork tacos. We prefer fresh, ripe mangos here, but you can substitute 1 cup frozen mangos, thawed and chopped as directed. If your mangos are unripe (whether fresh or frozen), add sugar to the salsa in step 1 as needed. Serve with lime wedges.

- 2 mangos, peeled, pitted, and cut into ½-inch pieces
- 1 small onion, chopped fine
- ½ cup minced fresh cilantro
- 2 tablespoons lime juice
    Salt and pepper
- 2 teaspoons vegetable oil
- 2 teaspoons minced canned chipotle chile in adobo sauce
- 1½ pounds ground pork
- 2 ounces Monterey Jack cheese, shredded (½ cup)
- 12 (6-inch) corn tortillas

1. Combine mangos, half of onion, ¼ cup cilantro, 1 tablespoon lime juice, ¼ teaspoon salt, and ¼ teaspoon pepper in bowl; set aside.

2. Heat oil in 12-inch skillet over medium-high heat until shimmering. Add chipotle and remaining onion and cook until onion is softened, about 3 minutes. Add pork and cook, breaking up meat with wooden spoon, until pork is no longer pink, about 5 minutes. Off heat, stir in Monterey Jack, remaining ¼ cup cilantro, and remaining 1 tablespoon lime juice. Season with salt and pepper to taste.

3. Meanwhile, stack tortillas on plate, cover, and microwave until warm and soft, about 2 minutes. Spoon pork mixture into warm tortillas, top with mango salsa, and serve.

TO GET AHEAD

- Peel, pit, and cut remaining 1 mango into ½-inch-thick slices. Refrigerate mango for up to 2 days.

TEST KITCHEN TIP **PREPARING MANGOS**

1. After cutting thin slice from 1 end of mango, rest mango on trimmed bottom and cut off skin in thin strips, top to bottom.

2. Cut down along each side of flat pit to remove flesh, and trim any remaining flesh off sides of pit. Once fruit is peeled and removed from pit, cut or slice it as directed.

Spicy Chicken and Mango Stir-Fry

SERVES 4 • **TO PREP AND COOK** 40 MINUTES

✔ **WHY THIS RECIPE WORKS:** Stir-frying highlights the fresh flavors of seared vegetables and proteins, but it is the sauce that ties it all together and adds a big flavor boost. We wanted a chicken stir-fry with a flavorful spicy chili sauce that we could make with ingredients we already had in our pantry. Chicken broth made the best base as its flavor was savory but not overpowering. Soy sauce, vinegar, red pepper flakes, and a little sugar gave the sauce bold but balanced flavor. A little cornstarch thickened the sauce nicely. Before cooking the chicken, we dipped the pieces in a cornstarch-oil mixture. The cornstarch coating, a modified version of the Chinese technique called velveting, helped the chicken stay moist when cooked over high heat. To accompany the chicken, we balanced the spicy sauce with the fruity flavor of sweet fresh mango plus the crunch of red bell pepper. Thai basil leaves added a bright herbal note to round out the dish. To make slicing the chicken easier, freeze it for 20 minutes first. If you can't find Thai basil, you can substitute regular basil. If you prefer a less spicy dish, decrease the amount of red pepper flakes in step 1 to ½ teaspoon. Serve this dish with white rice.

¾ **cup chicken broth**

3 **tablespoons soy sauce, plus extra for seasoning**

5 **teaspoons cornstarch**

2 **teaspoons rice vinegar**

1½ **teaspoons red pepper flakes**

1 **teaspoon sugar**

¼ **cup plus 1 teaspoon vegetable oil**

4 **garlic cloves, minced**

1 **tablespoon all-purpose flour**

1 **pound boneless, skinless chicken breasts, trimmed and sliced thin**

1 **mango, peeled, pitted, and sliced ½ inch thick**

1 **red bell pepper, stemmed, seeded, and cut into ½-inch-wide strips**

1 **onion, halved and sliced ¼ inch thick**

¼ **cup Thai basil, chopped**

1. Whisk broth, soy sauce, 2 teaspoons cornstarch, vinegar, pepper flakes, and sugar together in bowl until no lumps remain; set aside. Combine 1 teaspoon oil and garlic in small bowl. In medium bowl, combine 2 tablespoons oil, flour, and remaining 1 tablespoon cornstarch; add chicken and stir until evenly coated.

2. Heat 2 teaspoons oil in 12-inch nonstick skillet over high heat until just smoking. Add half of chicken, breaking up any clumps, and cook until lightly browned on all sides but not fully cooked, 2 to 3 minutes; transfer chicken to clean bowl. Repeat with 2 teaspoons oil and remaining chicken; transfer to bowl.

3. Heat remaining 2 teaspoons oil in now-empty skillet over high heat until shimmering. Add mango, bell pepper, and onion and cook until lightly browned and crisp-tender, 3 to 4 minutes. Push mango mixture to sides of skillet. Add garlic mixture to center of skillet and cook, mashing garlic into skillet, until fragrant, about 30 seconds. Stir garlic into mango mixture.

4. Return chicken with any accumulated juices to skillet and toss to combine. Whisk sauce to recombine, then add to skillet and cook, stirring constantly, until chicken is cooked through and sauce is thickened, 1 to 2 minutes. Season with soy sauce to taste. Sprinkle with basil and serve.

TEST KITCHEN TIP
SLICING CHICKEN BREASTS THINLY

Slice breasts across grain into ¼-inch-wide strips that are 1½ to 2 inches long. Cut center pieces in half so they are approximately same length as end pieces.

THE MENU   **DINNER 1** Pan-Roasted
Pork Tenderloin with
Artichokes and Olives

DINNER 2 Lamb Pitas
with Roasted Red
Pepper Sauce

DINNER 3 Skillet Orzo
with Artichokes and
Goat Cheese

THE GROCERY BAG

2 (1-pound) pork
tenderloins

1 pound ground lamb

3 ounces goat cheese

¼ cup marinated feta
cheese

1 large bunch fresh parsley

1 small bunch fresh oregano

1½ pounds frozen
artichoke hearts

1½ pounds cherry
tomatoes

1 lemon

4 (6-inch) pita breads

1½ cups (12 ounces) jarred
roasted red peppers

½ cup pitted niçoise or
kalamata olives

CHECK THE PANTRY

Onions

Garlic

Orzo

Chicken broth

White wine

Ground coriander

Ground cumin

Cayenne pepper

Red pepper flakes

Vegetable oil

Extra-virgin olive oil

Pan-Roasted Pork Tenderloin with Artichokes and Olives

SERVES 4 • **TO PREP AND COOK** 50 MINUTES

✔ **WHY THIS RECIPE WORKS:** Pork tenderloin is quick-cooking and requires almost no prep—perfect for a weeknight meal. But while it has a supremely tender texture, when it comes to flavor, this lean cut needs a little help. To give our pork tenderloin a boost, we rubbed it with coriander, cumin, and cayenne before searing it in a skillet to get good browning. We then transferred the skillet to the oven to cook the pork gently through. To accompany the pork, we added artichoke hearts to the skillet to lightly brown and pick up flavor from the pork's juices. We then stirred sweet cherry tomatoes, briny olives, and lemon zest into the artichokes as a flavorful accompaniment for the pork. A few tablespoons of minced parsley added fresh floral notes to round out the dish. To thaw frozen artichoke hearts quickly, remove them from their package and microwave in a covered bowl for 5 minutes. Be sure to thoroughly dry the thawed artichokes with paper towels; otherwise, their moisture will keep them from browning in the oven.

12   ounces frozen artichoke hearts, thawed, patted dry, and quartered
 3   tablespoons extra-virgin olive oil
     Salt and pepper
 1   teaspoon ground coriander
 1   teaspoon ground cumin
⅛   teaspoon cayenne pepper
 2   (1-pound) pork tenderloins, trimmed
 1   pound cherry tomatoes, halved
½   cup pitted niçoise or kalamata olives, halved
 1   tablespoon grated lemon zest
 2   tablespoons minced fresh parsley

1. Adjust oven rack to lowest position and heat oven to 350 degrees. Combine artichokes, 1 tablespoon oil, ⅛ teaspoon salt, and ⅛ teaspoon pepper in bowl. In separate bowl, combine coriander, cumin, and cayenne.

2. Pat pork dry with paper towels, sprinkle evenly with coriander mixture, and season with salt and pepper. Heat remaining 2 tablespoons oil in 12-inch ovensafe skillet over medium-high heat until just smoking. Place both tenderloins in skillet, alternating thicker end to thinner end and spaced at least 1 inch apart. Cook until well browned on all sides, 8 to 10 minutes. Arrange artichokes around pork. Transfer skillet to oven and roast until pork registers 145 degrees, 15 to 20 minutes.

3. Carefully remove skillet from oven (skillet handle will be hot). Transfer pork to carving board, tent loosely with aluminum foil, and let rest for 5 to 10 minutes. Being careful of hot skillet handle, stir tomatoes, olives, and lemon zest into artichokes. Return skillet to oven and continue to roast until tomatoes are softened, 5 to 10 minutes. Stir in parsley and season with salt and pepper to taste. Slice pork into ½-inch-thick slices and serve with artichoke mixture.

TO GET AHEAD

- Thaw, pat dry, and quarter remaining 12 ounces frozen artichoke hearts. Refrigerate artichokes for up to 4 days.
- Quarter remaining 8 ounces cherry tomatoes. Refrigerate tomatoes for up to 2 days.

Lamb Pitas with Roasted Red Pepper Sauce

SERVES 4 • **TO PREP AND COOK** 35 MINUTES

✓ **WHY THIS RECIPE WORKS:** We wanted a homemade lamb sandwich recipe that would give us the same great flavors as restaurant gyros. We started with convenient ground lamb and formed it into patties flavored with oregano, onion, and minced garlic. To keep the patties juicy, we made an easy panade by processing pita crumbs with the aromatics and adding the mixture to the ground lamb. Then we pan-fried the patties to give them a nicely browned crust. A simple no-cook sauce made with roasted red peppers and marinated feta added a rich flavor to the sandwiches. We found that jarred roasted peppers work just as well as those that have been freshly roasted at home, as long as you give them a thorough rinse to rid them of excess salt from the briny packing liquid. To add some bright flavor and freshness, we made a quick salad with whole parsley leaves and quartered cherry tomatoes tossed with the flavorful oil from the marinated feta. You can substitute 85 percent lean ground beef for the lamb. The skillet may appear crowded when you begin cooking the patties, but they will shrink slightly as they cook.

½ cup jarred roasted red peppers, rinsed and patted dry
¼ cup marinated feta cheese, plus 1 tablespoon packing oil
Salt and pepper
4 (6-inch) pita breads
1 small onion, chopped
1 tablespoon lemon juice
3 garlic cloves, minced
2 teaspoons minced fresh oregano or ½ teaspoon dried
1 pound ground lamb
1 tablespoon vegetable oil
8 ounces cherry tomatoes, quartered
½ cup fresh parsley leaves

1. Process red peppers and feta in food processor until completely smooth, about 20 seconds. Transfer mixture to bowl and season with salt and pepper to taste.

2. Cut top 2 inches from each pita bread round, reserving 2 scrap pieces. Process reserved pita scraps, onion, lemon juice, garlic, oregano, ½ teaspoon salt, and ¼ teaspoon pepper in now-empty food processor to smooth paste, about 30 seconds, scraping down sides of bowl as needed. Transfer mixture to large bowl, add lamb, and mix together using hands until combined. Pinch off and roll mixture into 12 balls, then press into ½-inch-thick patties.

3. Heat vegetable oil in 12-inch nonstick skillet over medium-high heat until just smoking. Brown patties well on first side, 3 to 4 minutes. Flip patties, reduce heat to medium, and continue to cook until well browned and cooked through, about 5 minutes. Transfer patties to paper towel–lined plate and tent loosely with aluminum foil.

4. Combine tomatoes, parsley, and feta packing oil in bowl and season with salt and pepper to taste. Stack pitas on plate and microwave, covered, until warm, about 30 seconds. Nestle 3 lamb patties inside each warm pita, drizzle with red pepper sauce, and top with tomato mixture. Serve.

TO GET AHEAD

• Rinse, pat dry, and cut remaining 1 cup roasted red peppers into ½-inch pieces. Refrigerate peppers for up to 2 days.

TEST KITCHEN TIP **CUTTING THE TOPS OFF PITAS**

Cut top 2 inches off each pita, reserving 2 trimmed pieces to use as binder in lamb patties.

Skillet Orzo with Artichokes and Goat Cheese

SERVES 4 • **TO PREP AND COOK** 50 MINUTES

✔ **WHY THIS RECIPE WORKS:** For a satisfying vegetarian pasta dish, we paired creamy orzo with moist, tender roasted red peppers and artichoke hearts—both ingredients left over from earlier in the week. To give the dish rich, well-rounded flavor, we browned the artichokes and sautéed the aromatics. Garlic and red pepper flakes lent depth of flavor and a subtle heat. We then added the orzo and lightly toasted it to bring out its flavor before stirring in the wine and broth and simmering the orzo until it was al dente. As the orzo simmered, it released its starches, thickening the cooking liquid to create a creamy sauce. Then we stirred in the artichokes and red peppers along with some goat cheese for extra richness and tanginess. Finally, we sprinkled the dish with fresh parsley to add bright color and flavor.

2	tablespoons extra-virgin olive oil
12	ounces frozen artichoke hearts, thawed, patted dry, and quartered
1	onion, chopped fine
4	garlic cloves, minced
½	teaspoon red pepper flakes
	Salt and pepper
1⅓	cups orzo
2½	cups chicken broth
½	cup dry white wine
1	cup jarred roasted red peppers, rinsed, patted dry, and cut into ½-inch pieces
3	ounces goat cheese, crumbled (¾ cup)
2	tablespoons minced fresh parsley

1. Heat 1 tablespoon oil in 12-inch nonstick skillet over medium-high heat until shimmering. Add artichokes and cook until lightly browned, 4 to 6 minutes; transfer to bowl. Heat remaining 1 tablespoon oil in now-empty skillet over medium heat until shimmering. Add onion and cook until softened, about 5 minutes. Stir in garlic, pepper flakes, and ½ teaspoon salt and cook until fragrant, about 30 seconds. Add orzo and cook, stirring frequently, until orzo is coated with oil and lightly browned, about 4 minutes.

2. Stir in broth and wine, bring to vigorous simmer, and cook, stirring occasionally, until orzo is al dente, 12 to 14 minutes. Stir in browned artichokes and red peppers, then stir in goat cheese until completely incorporated. Continue to cook until vegetables are warmed through, about 2 minutes. Sprinkle with parsley and season with salt and pepper to taste. Serve.

DINNER 1 Oven-Roasted Salmon with Orange and Radish Salad

DINNER 2 Orange-Glazed Chicken with Couscous

DINNER 3 Soba Noodles with Roasted Eggplant

THE GROCERY BAG

4 (6- to 8-ounce) skin-on salmon fillets, about 1½ inches thick

4 (12-ounce) bone-in split chicken breasts

1 large bunch fresh cilantro

1 small bunch fresh mint

2 pounds Italian or Japanese eggplant

6 radishes

2 shallots

5 oranges

1 lemon

12 ounces dried soba noodles

1½ cups couscous

½ cup sliced almonds

CHECK THE PANTRY

Unsalted butter

Garlic

Sugar

Cornstarch

Chicken broth

Barbecue sauce

Soy sauce

Rice vinegar

Cayenne pepper

Red pepper flakes

Vegetable oil

Extra-virgin olive oil

Toasted sesame oil

Oven-Roasted Salmon with Orange and Radish Salad

SERVES 4 • **TO PREP AND COOK** 30 MINUTES

✓ **WHY THIS RECIPE WORKS:** Roasting salmon fillets can create a beautiful bronzed, flavorful crust, but often the price is a dry, chalky interior. To get the best of both worlds, we developed a hybrid roasting method. For salmon with a nicely browned exterior, we preheated the oven to 500 degrees but then turned the heat down to 275 degrees just before moving the fish to the oven. The initial blast of high heat browned the exterior and rendered some excess fat, then the fish gently cooked through as the temperature of the oven slowly dropped. This method kept the salmon moist without any extra hands-on effort. Making slashes in the salmon's skin before roasting further helped the fat to render. A fresh citrus salad served with the salmon provided acidity that balanced the richness of the fish. The bright flavors of orange and mint were a refreshing combination; shallots added a savory note, and radishes added crunch and a peppery bite. To ensure uniform pieces of fish that will cook at the same rate, look for evenly sized fillets, or buy a whole center-cut fillet and cut it into four equal pieces. If your knife is not sharp enough to easily cut through the skin, try a serrated knife. It is important to keep the skin on during cooking to protect the flesh; remove it afterward if you choose not to serve it.

- 3   **oranges**
- 4   **(6- to 8-ounce) skin-on salmon fillets, about 1½ inches thick**
- 2   **tablespoons extra-virgin olive oil**
      Salt and pepper
- 6   **radishes, trimmed and sliced thin**
- 3   **tablespoons chopped fresh mint**
- 1   **shallot, minced**
- 2   **teaspoons lemon juice**

1. Adjust oven rack to lowest position, place rimmed baking sheet on rack, and heat oven to 500 degrees. Cut away peel and pith from oranges and cut into ½-inch pieces. Place orange pieces in fine-mesh strainer set over medium bowl and let drain for 15 minutes.

2. Meanwhile, make 4 or 5 shallow slashes about 1 inch apart along skin side of each piece of salmon, being careful not to cut into flesh. Pat salmon dry with paper towels. Rub fillets evenly with 1 tablespoon oil and season with salt and pepper.

3. Reduce oven temperature to 275 degrees and remove baking sheet. Carefully place salmon, skin side down, on sheet and roast until center of salmon is still translucent when checked with tip of paring knife and registers 125 degrees (for medium-rare), 9 to 13 minutes.

4. Pour off all but 2 tablespoons orange juice from bowl, then stir in radishes, mint, shallot, lemon juice, and remaining 1 tablespoon oil. Stir in orange pieces and season with salt and pepper to taste. Serve with salmon.

TO GET AHEAD

- Remove peel and pith from 1 more orange and cut into ½-inch pieces. Refrigerate orange for up to 2 days.

TEST KITCHEN TIP
REMOVING THE PEEL AND PITH FROM AN ORANGE

To easily remove peel and pith from orange, slice off top and bottom of orange, then cut away peel and pith using paring knife. Cut peeled orange into pieces.

Orange-Glazed Chicken with Couscous

SERVES 4 • **TO PREP AND COOK** 45 MINUTES

✔ **WHY THIS RECIPE WORKS:** For this easy weeknight chicken recipe, we wanted perfectly moist chicken with a sweet glaze that would cling to the chicken and taste fruity but not cloying. We already had oranges on hand from our roasted salmon, so we chose to make a bright orange glaze. We whisked fresh orange juice with a bit of sugar and cornstarch to create a nicely viscous sauce and added a pinch of cayenne pepper to balance the sweetness. Bone-in split chicken breasts had great flavor and stayed moist and juicy. We browned the chicken on the stovetop briefly to crisp the skin, then transferred it to the oven. Halving the chicken breasts crosswise helped them to cook through faster. While the chicken finished baking, we made a quick side of couscous. Toasted almonds and fresh cilantro added texture and brightness to the couscous, and pieces of orange lent a burst of fresh citrus and tied the dish together. Try to buy chicken breasts of similar size so that they will cook at the same rate.

1	orange plus ½ cup juice
2	tablespoons sugar
1	teaspoon cornstarch
⅛	teaspoon cayenne pepper
4	(12-ounce) bone-in split chicken breasts, trimmed and halved crosswise
	Salt and pepper
1	tablespoon vegetable oil
2	tablespoons unsalted butter
1½	cups couscous
1	shallot, minced
1	cup chicken broth
1	cup water
½	cup sliced almonds, toasted
2	tablespoons minced fresh cilantro

1. Adjust oven rack to middle position and heat oven to 475 degrees. Whisk orange juice, sugar, cornstarch, and cayenne together in bowl until no lumps remain; set aside.

2. Pat chicken dry with paper towels and season with salt and pepper. Heat oil in 12-inch ovensafe skillet over medium-high heat until just smoking. Lay chicken, skin side down, in skillet and cook until well browned, about 5 minutes. Flip chicken skin side up and transfer skillet to oven. Cook until chicken is deep golden brown and registers 160 degrees, 15 to 18 minutes.

3. Meanwhile, cut away peel and pith from orange and cut into ½-inch pieces. Melt butter in medium saucepan over medium-high heat. Add couscous and cook, stirring frequently, until grains are just beginning to brown, about 5 minutes. Stir in shallot, broth, water, and ½ teaspoon salt and bring to brief simmer. Off heat, cover and let sit until grains are tender, about 7 minutes. Uncover, fluff couscous with fork, and gently fold in orange pieces, almonds, and cilantro. Season with salt and pepper to taste.

4. Carefully remove skillet from oven (skillet handles will be hot). Transfer chicken to plate and tent loosely with aluminum foil. Being careful of hot skillet handle, pour off fat from skillet and discard. Whisk orange juice mixture to recombine, then add to now-empty skillet and bring to boil over medium heat. Return chicken, skin side up, to skillet along with any accumulated juices and simmer until sauce is thick and glossy, 2 to 3 minutes. Turn chicken to coat evenly. Serve with couscous.

TO GET AHEAD

• Pick additional ¾ cup cilantro leaves. Place cilantro in storage container, top with damp paper towel, and refrigerate, covered, for up to 1 day.

Soba Noodles with Roasted Eggplant

SERVES 4 • **TO PREP AND COOK** 45 MINUTES

✓ **WHY THIS RECIPE WORKS:** The creamy texture and mild flavor of eggplant make it the perfect complement to rich, nutty soba noodles in this recipe. Roasting was an easy, hands-off way to cook the eggplant. Tossing it with soy sauce and vegetable oil before cooking helped to season the vegetable and draw out its moisture for better browning. For a rich, flavorful sauce, we started with more soy sauce and added toasted sesame oil to bring out the nuttiness of the noodles. We wanted to enhance our sauce with a smoky flavor, which pairs well with eggplant, but instead of shopping for a specialty Asian ingredient, we reached for barbecue sauce to provide smokiness and thicken our sauce. Just 2 tablespoons did the trick without giving our dish a distinct barbecue flavor. A bit of sugar, garlic, and red pepper flakes provided a nice balance of sweet and spicy flavors, and rice vinegar lent some acidity. A hearty sprinkling of fresh cilantro leaves (left over from our orange-glazed chicken) was the perfect bright finishing touch. The sweetness of the sauce will vary depending on the sweetness of the barbecue sauce. The test kitchen's favorite brand of barbecue sauce is Bull's Eye Original. Do not substitute other types of noodles for the soba noodles here.

2	pounds Italian or Japanese eggplant, cut into 1-inch pieces
3	tablespoons vegetable oil
5	tablespoons soy sauce
2	tablespoons barbecue sauce
2	tablespoons toasted sesame oil
2	tablespoons rice vinegar
1	tablespoon sugar
2	garlic cloves, minced
¼	teaspoon red pepper flakes
12	ounces dried soba noodles
¾	cup fresh cilantro leaves

1. Adjust oven rack to middle position and heat oven to 450 degrees. Line rimmed baking sheet with aluminum foil and spray with vegetable oil spray. Toss eggplant with vegetable oil and 1 tablespoon soy sauce, then spread in prepared sheet. Roast until well browned and tender, 25 to 30 minutes, stirring halfway through roasting.

2. Combine remaining ¼ cup soy sauce, barbecue sauce, sesame oil, vinegar, sugar, garlic, and pepper flakes in small saucepan and cook over medium heat until sugar has dissolved, about 1 minute.

3. Meanwhile, bring 4 quarts water to boil in large pot. Add noodles and cook, stirring often, until tender. Reserve ½ cup cooking water, then drain noodles and return them to pot.

4. Add sauce and roasted eggplant to noodles and toss to combine. Adjust consistency with reserved cooking water as needed. Sprinkle with cilantro and serve.

TEST KITCHEN TIP CUTTING UP AN EGGPLANT

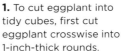

1. To cut eggplant into tidy cubes, first cut eggplant crosswise into 1-inch-thick rounds.

2. Cut rounds into tidy 1-inch cubes.

<table>
<tr><td>THE MENU</td><td>**DINNER 1** Braised Cod with Leeks and Cherry Tomatoes</td><td>**DINNER 2** Pan-Roasted Chicken with Tomatoes and Israeli Couscous</td><td>**DINNER 3** Rustic Potato-Leek Soup with Kielbasa and Garlic Toast</td></tr>
</table>

THE GROCERY BAG

4 (6- to 8-ounce) skinless cod fillets, 1 to 1½ inches thick

4 (12-ounce) bone-in split chicken breasts

8 ounces kielbasa sausage

1 small bunch fresh parsley

1 small bunch fresh rosemary

3 pounds leeks

2¼ pounds cherry tomatoes

½ pound red potatoes

1 cup Israeli couscous

1 (12-inch) baguette

½ cup pitted kalamata olives

CHECK THE PANTRY

Unsalted butter

Garlic

Chicken broth (6¼ cups)

Dry white wine or dry vermouth

Ground fennel

Extra-virgin olive oil

Braised Cod with Leeks and Cherry Tomatoes

SERVES 4 • **TO PREP AND COOK** 35 MINUTES

✔ **WHY THIS RECIPE WORKS:** Braising is a great way to add flavor to a mild-tasting fish like cod—plus it's mess-free (no oil splattering on the stovetop). Pairing our cod with juicy tomatoes and a white wine sauce added brightness and freshness. Cherry tomatoes required little prep and became meltingly tender when braised (and we could buy extra to roast alongside our pan-roasted chicken later in the week). Thinly sliced leeks provided a subtle, earthy flavor that complemented the tomatoes. (The remaining leeks played a starring role in our rustic potato-leek soup.) After sautéing the leeks in butter until they were tender, we stirred in a good amount of minced garlic and the cherry tomatoes plus ½ cup of wine, then we sprinkled the cod with ground fennel and nestled it into the pan. To ensure that the cod cooked through gently and evenly, we turned down the heat and covered the skillet with a tight-fitting lid so that the fish partially simmered and partially steamed. A pat of butter stirred into the vegetables at the end contributed just the right amount of richness. You can substitute haddock or halibut for the cod.

3 tablespoons unsalted butter
1 pound leeks, white and light green parts only, halved lengthwise, sliced ¼ inch thick, and washed thoroughly
  Salt and pepper
4 garlic cloves, minced
12 ounces cherry tomatoes, halved
½ cup dry white wine or dry vermouth
4 (6- to 8-ounce) skinless cod fillets, 1 to 1½ inches thick
1 teaspoon ground fennel

1. Melt 2 tablespoons butter in 12-inch nonstick skillet over medium-high heat. Add leeks and ¼ teaspoon salt and cook until softened, about 5 minutes. Stir in garlic and cook until fragrant, about 30 seconds. Add tomatoes, wine, and ¼ teaspoon pepper and bring to simmer.

2. Pat cod dry with paper towels, sprinkle with fennel, and season with salt and pepper. Nestle cod, skinned side down, into skillet and spoon some vegetables and sauce over top. Cover, reduce heat to medium-low, and cook until cod flakes apart when gently prodded with paring knife and registers 140 degrees, 10 to 12 minutes.

3. Carefully transfer cod to serving platter. Stir remaining 1 tablespoon butter into vegetables and season with salt and pepper to taste. Spoon sauce and vegetables over cod and serve.

TO GET AHEAD

• Halve remaining 1½ pounds cherry tomatoes. Refrigerate tomatoes for up to 2 days.
• Halve remaining 2 pounds leeks lengthwise, slice white and light green parts 1 inch thick, and wash thoroughly. Refrigerate leeks for up to 4 days.

DINNER 2 | # Pan-Roasted Chicken with Tomatoes and Israeli Couscous

SERVES 4 • **TO PREP AND COOK** 1 HOUR

☑ **WHY THIS RECIPE WORKS:** To take humble pan-roasted chicken breasts up a notch, we paired them with tomatoes, olives, and large-grained Israeli couscous for a rustic supper with a Mediterranean flair. We first browned the chicken in a skillet to crisp its skin, then set it aside. Then we combined the cherry tomatoes with kalamata olives in the pan, tucked in our chicken, and moved the skillet to the oven to roast. For rich aromatic flavor, we added fresh rosemary and thinly sliced garlic, which melted into the tomatoes as they roasted. Once the chicken was done cooking and the tomatoes had exuded their juice, we set the chicken aside and simmered the couscous with the juicy tomatoes and some chicken broth until it was tender and flavorful. Be sure to use Israeli couscous in this dish; regular (or fine-grain) couscous won't work here.

4	**(12-ounce) bone-in split chicken breasts, trimmed**
	Salt and pepper
2	**tablespoons extra-virgin olive oil**
1½	**pounds cherry tomatoes, halved**
½	**cup pitted kalamata olives, halved**
3	**garlic cloves, sliced thin**
2	**teaspoons minced fresh rosemary**
1¼	**cups chicken broth**
1	**cup Israeli couscous**
2	**tablespoons minced fresh parsley**

1. Adjust oven rack to middle position and heat oven to 450 degrees. Pat chicken dry with paper towels and season with salt and pepper. Heat 1 tablespoon oil in 12-inch ovensafe skillet over medium-high heat until just smoking. Lay chicken, skin side down, in skillet and cook until well browned and crisp, 6 to 8 minutes; transfer chicken to plate.

2. Add tomatoes, olives, garlic, rosemary, ¼ teaspoon salt, ¼ teaspoon pepper, and remaining 1 tablespoon oil to now-empty skillet. Nestle chicken, skin side up, into skillet. Transfer skillet to oven and bake until chicken registers 160 degrees, 25 to 30 minutes.

3. Carefully remove skillet from oven (skillet handle will be hot). Transfer chicken to cutting board and tent loosely with aluminum foil. Being careful of hot skillet handle, stir broth and couscous into skillet. Bring to simmer over medium-high heat and cook, stirring often, until couscous is tender, 10 to 12 minutes. Sprinkle parsley over couscous and serve with chicken.

Rustic Potato-Leek Soup with Kielbasa and Garlic Toast

SERVES 4 • **TO PREP AND COOK** 45 MINUTES

✓ **WHY THIS RECIPE WORKS:** In this rustic soup, chunks of sweet, tender leeks lighten a hearty soup of potatoes and kielbasa sausage. Most of the potato-leek soups we tried lacked strong leek presence, tasting more like thin mashed potatoes, so we used a full 2 pounds of leeks to ensure that their delicate flavor permeated the soup. For intense savoriness, we lightly browned the kielbasa, then we added the leeks and cooked them down in a covered pot until they were meltingly tender and had a concentrated, subtle onion flavor. To prevent the leeks from breaking down into the broth entirely, we cut them into large 1-inch pieces. For the potatoes, we found that red potatoes were the best at holding their shape. To prevent the potatoes from breaking down into the soup, we simmered them until almost tender then removed the pot from the heat to let the residual heat gently finish cooking them through. Cutting them slightly smaller than the leeks, into ¾-inch pieces, kept them from being unwieldy to eat. To accompany our hearty soup, we sliced a baguette, flavored it with garlic, and toasted it quickly in the oven.

- 1 **(12-inch) baguette, sliced 1 inch thick on bias**
- 1 **garlic clove, peeled**
- 2 **tablespoons extra-virgin olive oil**
- 4 **tablespoons unsalted butter**
- 8 **ounces kielbasa sausage, halved lengthwise and sliced ½ inch thick**
- 2 **pounds leeks, white and light green parts only, halved lengthwise, sliced 1 inch thick, and washed thoroughly**
- 5 **cups chicken broth**
- ½ **pound red potatoes, unpeeled, cut into ¾-inch pieces**
   Salt and pepper

1. Adjust oven rack to middle position and heat oven to 400 degrees. Arrange bread in single layer in rimmed baking sheet and bake until dry and crisp, about 10 minutes, turning slices over halfway through baking. While still hot, rub each slice of bread with garlic and drizzle with oil; set aside.

2. Meanwhile, melt butter in Dutch oven over medium heat. Cook kielbasa until lightly browned, 2 to 3 minutes. Stir in leeks, cover, and cook, stirring occasionally, until leeks are tender but not mushy, 10 to 15 minutes.

3. Stir in broth, scraping up any browned bits. Stir in potatoes and bring to simmer. Cover, reduce heat to medium-low, and simmer gently until potatoes are almost tender, 5 to 7 minutes.

4. Off heat, let sit until potatoes are tender and flavors meld, 10 to 15 minutes. Season with salt and pepper to taste and serve with garlic toast.

TEST KITCHEN TIP PREPARING LEEKS

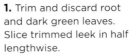

1. Trim and discard root and dark green leaves. Slice trimmed leek in half lengthwise.

2. Cut halves into pieces as directed. Rinse cut leeks thoroughly to remove dirt and sand.

THE GROCERY BAG

11 ounces goat cheese

6 ounces whole-milk
ricotta cheese

1 small bunch fresh basil

3 fennel bulbs

12 ounces Swiss chard

10 ounces frozen spinach

6 scallions

2 lemons

1 box (14 by 9-inch) phyllo
sheets

1 (9½ by 9-inch) sheet
puff pastry

½ cup pitted oil-cured
black olives

2 tablespoons coarsely
chopped walnuts

CHECK THE PANTRY

Unsalted butter

Parmesan cheese

Onion

Garlic

Arborio rice

Vegetable broth (4 cups)

Dry white wine or dry
vermouth

Fennel seeds

Nutmeg

Dried oregano

Red pepper flakes

Extra-virgin olive oil

Risotto with Fennel and Swiss Chard

SERVES 4 TO 6 • **TO PREP AND COOK** 1 HOUR

✓ **WHY THIS RECIPE WORKS:** Classic risotto can demand half an hour of stovetop tedium for the best creamy results. To make risotto feasible on a busy weeknight, our goal was 5 minutes of stirring, tops. First, we swapped out the saucepan for a Dutch oven, which has a thick, heavy bottom, deep sides, and a tight-fitting lid ideal for trapping and distributing heat as evenly as possible. We sautéed our aromatics, onion, and two whole fennel bulbs along with garlic and fennel seeds to build layers of flavor, then added the rice. Typical recipes dictate adding the broth in small increments (and stirring constantly after each addition), but we added most of the broth at once and covered the pan, allowing the rice to simmer gently until almost all the broth had been absorbed, and stirred just twice. After adding the second and final portion of broth, along with a few handfuls of Swiss chard, we stirred the pot for a few minutes to ensure that the bottom didn't cook more quickly than the top, then we turned off the heat and let the risotto sit until it was perfectly tender. Without sitting over a direct flame, the sauce turned out smooth and velvety and the rice was just barely chewy. All the risotto needed to finish was a little butter for richness and a sprinkling of minced fennel fronds for a hit of fresh flavor. This more hands-off method requires precise timing, so we strongly recommend using a timer.

4	cups vegetable broth
3	cups water
4	tablespoons unsalted butter
2	fennel bulbs, stalks discarded, 2 tablespoons fronds minced, bulbs halved, cored, and chopped fine
1	small onion, chopped fine
	Salt and pepper
2	garlic cloves, minced
1	teaspoon fennel seeds
2	cups Arborio rice
1	cup dry white wine or dry vermouth
12	ounces Swiss chard, stemmed, leaves cut into 1-inch pieces
2	ounces Parmesan cheese, grated (1 cup)

1. Bring broth and water to boil in large saucepan over high heat. Reduce heat to medium-low to maintain gentle simmer.

2. Melt 2 tablespoons butter in Dutch oven over medium heat. Add chopped fennel, onion, and ½ teaspoon salt and cook, stirring occasionally, until vegetables are softened, 10 to 12 minutes. Stir in garlic and fennel seeds and cook until fragrant, about 30 seconds. Add rice and cook, stirring frequently, until grains are translucent around edges, about 3 minutes.

3. Add wine and cook, stirring constantly, until fully absorbed, 2 to 3 minutes. Stir 5 cups hot broth mixture into rice; cover, reduce heat to medium-low, and simmer until almost all liquid has been absorbed and rice is just al dente, 16 to 19 minutes, stirring twice during cooking.

4. Stir in chard and ¾ cup hot broth mixture and stir gently without stopping until risotto becomes creamy, about 3 minutes. Stir in Parmesan. Remove pot from heat, cover, and let sit for 5 minutes. Stir in remaining 2 tablespoons butter and fennel fronds. Adjust consistency of risotto with remaining broth mixture as needed. Season with salt and pepper to taste and serve immediately.

TO GET AHEAD

• Halve, core, and thinly slice remaining fennel bulb. Refrigerate fennel for up to 4 days.

Spinach Strudel

SERVES 4 • **TO PREP AND COOK** 50 MINUTES

✓ **WHY THIS RECIPE WORKS:** Sweet strudels might be better known, but savory strudels have a long, delicious history. Our starting point for this recipe was a filling of frozen spinach (thawed and squeezed dry to remove excess moisture) with creamy goat and ricotta cheeses. We added crunchy walnuts for contrasting texture and scallions, garlic, and oregano for aromatic flavor. For the assembly, we kept the process simple: We stacked the sheets of phyllo, brushing each one with extra-virgin olive oil. Then we spread the filling into a narrow log at the base of the sheets and rolled the phyllo around the filling. After 20 minutes in the oven, the filling was hot and the phyllo was golden brown and flaky. Phyllo dough is also available in larger 18 by 14-inch sheets; if using, cut them in half to make 14 by 9-inch sheets. Don't thaw the phyllo in the microwave; let it sit in the refrigerator overnight or on the counter for 4 to 5 hours.

10	ounces frozen spinach, thawed, squeezed dry, and chopped coarse
6	ounces (¾ cup) whole-milk ricotta cheese
3	ounces goat cheese, crumbled (¾ cup)
6	scallions, sliced thin
2	tablespoons coarsely chopped walnuts, toasted
2	tablespoons lemon juice
2	garlic cloves, minced
1	teaspoon dried oregano
	Salt and pepper
¼	teaspoon ground nutmeg
	Pinch red pepper flakes
10	(14 by 9-inch) phyllo sheets, thawed
3	tablespoons extra-virgin olive oil

1. Adjust oven rack to middle position and heat oven to 400 degrees. Line rimmed baking sheet with parchment paper. Mix spinach, ricotta, goat cheese, scallions, walnuts, lemon juice, garlic, oregano, ½ teaspoon salt, ¼ teaspoon pepper, nutmeg, and pepper flakes together in bowl. Season with salt and pepper to taste.

2. Lay 1 phyllo sheet on counter, with long side parallel to counter edge; brush thoroughly with oil. Layer with remaining phyllo and oil, 1 sheet at a time.

Mound spinach mixture into narrow log along bottom edge of phyllo, leaving 2-inch border at bottom and ½-inch border on sides. Fold bottom edge of dough over filling, then continue rolling dough tightly around filling, leaving ends open.

3. Transfer strudel, seam side down, to prepared sheet. Cut four 1½-inch vents diagonally across top of strudel. Bake until strudel is golden brown, 20 to 25 minutes. Let strudel cool slightly on sheet, then slice and serve.

TEST KITCHEN TIP MAKING SPINACH STRUDEL

1. Mound spinach mixture into narrow log along bottom edge of layered phyllo, leaving 2-inch border at bottom and ½-inch border on sides.

2. Fold bottom edge of dough over filling, then continue to roll dough around filling into tight log, leaving ends open.

Fennel, Olive, and Goat Cheese Tarts

SERVES 4 • **TO PREP AND COOK** 45 MINUTES

✔ **WHY THIS RECIPE WORKS:** We wanted to make elegant savory tarts inspired by the flavors of the Mediterranean. To keep the dish easy enough for a weeknight, we pulled store-bought puff pastry from the freezer to form the base. For the filling, fresh, anise-flavored fennel and briny cured olives made a light but flavorful combination. We sautéed the fennel briefly to drive off moisture and encourage browning. Tangy goat cheese brightened with fresh basil contrasted nicely with the rich, flaky pastry and helped bind the vegetables and pastry together. Parbaking the pastry without the weight of the filling allowed it to puff up nicely. To keep the filling firmly in place, we cut a border around the edges of the baked crusts and lightly pressed down the centers to make neat beds for the vegetables. Just 5 minutes more in the oven heated the filling through and browned the crusts beautifully. To thaw frozen puff pastry, let it sit either in the refrigerator for 24 hours or on the counter for 30 minutes to 1 hour.

1 **(9½ by 9-inch) sheet puff pastry, thawed and cut in half**
3 **tablespoons extra-virgin olive oil**
1 **fennel bulb, stalks discarded, bulb halved, cored, and sliced thin**
3 **garlic cloves, minced**
½ **cup dry white wine or dry vermouth**
½ **cup pitted oil-cured black olives, chopped**
1 **teaspoon grated lemon zest plus 1 tablespoon juice**
   Salt and pepper
8 **ounces goat cheese, softened**
⅓ **cup chopped fresh basil**

1. Adjust oven rack to middle position and heat oven to 425 degrees. Lay puff pastry halves on parchment paper–lined baking sheet and poke all over with fork. Bake until puffed and golden brown, about 15 minutes, rotating sheet halfway through baking. Using tip of paring knife, cut ½-inch-wide border around top edge of each pastry, then press down centers with fingertips.

2. Meanwhile, heat 1 tablespoon oil in 12-inch skillet over medium heat until shimmering. Add fennel and cook until softened and browned, 10 to 12 minutes. Stir in garlic and cook until fragrant, about 30 seconds.

Stir in wine, cover, and cook for 5 minutes. Uncover and continue to cook until liquid has evaporated and fennel is soft, 5 to 7 minutes. Off heat, stir in olives and lemon juice and season with salt and pepper to taste.

3. Mix goat cheese, ¼ cup basil, lemon zest, ¼ teaspoon pepper, and remaining 2 tablespoons oil together in bowl. Spread cheese mixture evenly in center of baked pastry shells. Spoon fennel mixture over top. Bake tarts until cheese is heated through and crust is deep golden, 5 to 7 minutes. Sprinkle with remaining basil and serve.

TEST KITCHEN TIP
MAKING PUFF PASTRY TART SHELLS

1. Lay pastry rectangles on parchment paper–lined baking sheet and poke them all over with fork.

2. After baking, use tip of paring knife to cut ½-inch-wide border around top edge of each pastry, then press centers down with fingertips to create beds for filling.

THE GROCERY BAG

10 ounces feta cheese

1 small bunch fresh basil

1½ pounds kale

8 (4- to 5-inch) portobello mushroom caps

1 ounce baby arugula

1 red onion

1 lemon

1 (14-ounce) can chickpeas

1 cup oil-packed sun-dried tomatoes

½ cup jarred roasted red peppers

4 kaiser rolls

CHECK THE PANTRY

Parmesan cheese

Onions

Garlic

Gemelli or penne

Quinoa

Mayonnaise

Dry white wine or dry vermouth

Red wine vinegar

Extra-virgin olive oil

Baked Quinoa with Roasted Kale and Chickpeas

SERVES 4 • **TO PREP AND COOK** 50 MINUTES

☑ **WHY THIS RECIPE WORKS:** Quinoa makes a great starting point for a vegetarian dinner: Not only is it a nutritional powerhouse, but it is also easy to prepare. For this unique pilaf-style dish, we combined the quinoa with protein-rich chickpeas. Hearty kale, which we roasted briefly with some sun-dried tomato oil to boost its earthy flavor, made our casserole seem more complete (and this versatile green was easy to incorporate into another dish later in the week). To give our casserole a bright, robust flavor, we stirred in chopped sun-dried tomatoes, lemon zest, and a squeeze of lemon juice. Topped with a generous sprinkling of tangy feta cheese, this hearty baked quinoa was fresh and satisfying. Be sure to rinse the quinoa to remove its bitter coating (known as saponin). For an accurate measurement of boiling water, bring a full kettle of water to a boil and then measure out the desired amount.

8 ounces kale, stemmed and chopped

½ cup oil-packed sun-dried tomatoes, chopped coarse, plus 3 tablespoons packing oil

1 (14-ounce) can chickpeas, rinsed

1 cup quinoa, rinsed

1 teaspoon grated lemon zest plus 2 teaspoons juice

¼ teaspoon salt

¼ teaspoon pepper

1½ cups plus 2 tablespoons boiling water

6 ounces feta cheese, crumbled (1½ cups)

1. Adjust oven rack to middle position and heat oven to 450 degrees. Toss kale with 1 tablespoon tomato packing oil and spread in even layer in aluminum foil–lined rimmed baking sheet. Roast until crisp and lightly browned at edges, 6 to 8 minutes. Combine roasted kale, chickpeas, quinoa, lemon zest, salt, pepper, and remaining 2 tablespoons tomato packing oil in large bowl. Transfer to 8-inch square baking dish.

2. Pour 1½ cups boiling water over quinoa mixture and cover dish tightly with double layer of foil. Bake until quinoa is tender and no liquid remains, 20 to 25 minutes.

3. Remove dish from oven and fluff quinoa with fork. Gently fold in tomatoes, lemon juice, and remaining 2 tablespoons water, then sprinkle with feta. Bake casserole, uncovered, until feta is heated through, 6 to 8 minutes. Serve.

TO GET AHEAD

• Stem remaining 1 pound kale and cut into 1-inch pieces. Refrigerate kale for up to 4 days.

• Pat dry and chop remaining ½ cup sun-dried tomatoes. Refrigerate tomatoes for up to 4 days.

Gemelli with Caramelized Onions, Kale, and Mushrooms

SERVES 4 TO 6 • **TO PREP AND COOK** 45 MINUTES

✔ **WHY THIS RECIPE WORKS:** Glossy caramelized onions, braised kale, and earthy portobello mushrooms give this hearty pasta dish a sweet, savory, and addictive flavor profile. Not only is this dish satisfying, it also comes together quickly. Caramelizing onions gives them a rich, complex flavor, but it can take upward of 40 minutes to achieve. To speed things up, we jump-started the process by cooking them covered so they'd release their moisture, then we removed the lid and sautéed them for 15 minutes until the liquid had evaporated and the onions were deeply browned and meltingly tender. We found that the portobellos could be added with the onions. As they released their moisture and browned, they lent a deep, umami-rich flavor to the dish. Because we were using a full pound of kale, adding it in batches was important to keep it from overflowing the pan. Adding some boiling water with the second batch helped to wilt the greens further without fear of scorching. Once the kale was tender, we tossed it with the pasta. A cup of grated Parmesan and a final drizzle of olive oil were all we needed to create a rich, creamy sauce. For an accurate measurement of boiling water, bring a full kettle of water to a boil and then measure out the desired amount.

6	tablespoons extra-virgin olive oil
3	onions, halved and sliced thin
4	(4- to 5-inch) portobello mushroom caps, gills removed, cut into ½-inch pieces
	Salt and pepper
4	garlic cloves, minced
1	pound kale, stemmed and cut into 1-inch pieces
1½	cups boiling water
½	cup dry white wine or dry vermouth
1	pound gemelli or penne
2	ounces Parmesan cheese, grated (1 cup), plus extra for serving

1. Heat 2 tablespoons oil in 12-inch nonstick skillet over medium heat until shimmering. Add onions, mushrooms, and ½ teaspoon salt, cover, and cook until softened, 5 to 8 minutes. Uncover and continue to cook, stirring often, until well browned, 15 to 20 minutes.

2. Stir in garlic and cook until fragrant, about 30 seconds. Stir in half of kale and cook until kale begins to wilt, about 2 minutes. Add remaining kale, boiling water, and wine (skillet will be very full). Cover and simmer, tossing occasionally, until kale is tender, about 15 minutes.

3. Meanwhile, bring 4 quarts water to boil in large pot. Add pasta and 1 tablespoon salt and cook, stirring often, until al dente. Reserve ½ cup cooking water, then drain pasta and return it to pot. Add kale mixture, remaining ¼ cup oil, and Parmesan and toss to combine. Season with salt and pepper to taste. Adjust consistency with reserved cooking water as needed. Serve with extra Parmesan.

TO GET AHEAD

• Remove gills from remaining 4 portobello mushroom caps. Refrigerate mushrooms for up to 2 days.

TEST KITCHEN TIP **REMOVING PORTOBELLO GILLS**

To remove mushroom gills, simply scrape them off using spoon before cutting mushroom.

Grilled Portobello Burgers

SERVES 4 • **TO PREP AND COOK** 1 HOUR

✔ WHY THIS RECIPE WORKS: Grilled portobello burgers are a great alternative to the traditional barbecue fare, but they can easily fall flat. The grill adds great charred flavor, but plain grilled mushrooms can be downright boring. For a boldly flavored portobello burger we'd have to up the ante. First, we wanted to marinate our mushrooms in a few pantry staples. A little oil and vinegar seasoned simply with garlic, salt, and pepper gave the mushrooms a big flavor boost. We let the mushrooms rest in the marinade while we set up the grill. As for the standard, plain-Jane burger toppings, we had other ideas. Since we had already used feta cheese and sun-dried tomatoes in our baked quinoa recipe, we decided to use the leftovers here. The domed shape of a portobello is perfect for stuffing, so once the mushrooms were nicely charred, we filled them with the sun-dried tomatoes and feta along with some chopped roasted red peppers. Then they went back on the grill to warm the filling through. For the condiments, we created an aromatic herb mayonnaise to spread on the buns before serving. A little baby arugula added fresh flavor. If the mushrooms absorb all of the marinade, brush the onions with olive oil before grilling in step 3. For information on setting up a single-level fire, see page 51.

4	(4- to 5-inch) portobello mushroom caps, gills removed
½	cup extra-virgin olive oil
3	tablespoons red wine vinegar
1	garlic clove, minced
1	teaspoon salt
½	teaspoon pepper
4	ounces feta cheese, crumbled (1 cup)
½	cup jarred roasted red peppers, patted dry and chopped
½	cup oil-packed sun-dried tomatoes, patted dry and chopped
½	cup mayonnaise
½	cup chopped fresh basil
4	(½-inch-thick) slices red onion
4	kaiser rolls, split
1	cup baby arugula

1. Using tip of paring knife, cut ½-inch crosshatch pattern on tops of mushroom caps, 1/16 inch deep. Combine oil, vinegar, garlic, salt, and pepper in 1-gallon zipper-lock bag. Add mushrooms, seal bag, turn to coat, and let sit for at least 30 minutes or up to 1 hour.

2. Combine feta, red peppers, and tomatoes in bowl. Whisk mayonnaise and basil together in separate bowl. Push 1 toothpick horizontally through each onion slice to keep rings intact while grilling.

3. Remove mushrooms from marinade, reserving excess marinade. Brush onions all over with reserved mushroom marinade. Place mushrooms, gilled side up, and onions over hot, single-level fire. Grill (covered if using gas) until mushrooms have released their liquid and vegetables are charred on first side, 4 to 6 minutes. Flip mushrooms and onions and continue to cook (covered if using gas) until vegetables are charred on second side, 3 to 5 minutes.

4. Transfer onions to serving platter; remove toothpicks. Transfer mushrooms, gilled side up, to platter and divide feta mixture evenly among caps, packing down with hand. Return mushrooms to grill, feta side up, and cook, covered, until heated through, about 3 minutes.

5. Return mushrooms to platter and tent loosely with aluminum foil. Grill rolls, cut sides down, until lightly charred, about 1 minute. Spread basil mayonnaise on bottom halves of rolls and top each with 1 mushroom and 1 onion slice. Divide arugula evenly among burgers, then cap with top halves of rolls. Serve.

TEST KITCHEN TIP SCORING PORTOBELLO CAPS

To help mushrooms release excess moisture, use tip of sharp paring knife to lightly score top of each mushroom cap on the diagonal in crosshatch pattern.

TURKEY AND GREEN CHILE ENCHILADAS

The Sunday Cook

BIG ROASTS PLUS CREATIVE SECOND MEALS

THE MENU

THE BIG ROAST Two Roast Chickens with Roasted Garlic and Herb Jus

THE SECOND MEAL Chicken and Bread Salad with Hazelnuts and Roasted Garlic **OR** Penne with Tuscan Chicken

Two Roast Chickens with Roasted Garlic and Herb Jus

SERVES 4 WITH LEFTOVERS • TO PREP 1 HOUR FOR BRINING • TO COOK 1 HOUR 40 MINUTES

✔ **WHY THIS RECIPE WORKS:** Cooking two whole chickens at once is as simple as arranging them side by side on a rack in a roasting pan, and leftover roast chicken offers a host of possibilities for second meals. To guarantee juicy, well-seasoned chicken we turned to a brine. Adding sugar along with the salt encouraged browning during roasting. Arranging the chickens in opposite directions on a V-rack in a large roasting pan ensured even airflow between the two birds so they cooked and browned evenly. We started cooking the chickens at 375 degrees to keep the delicate breast meat from drying out, then turned up the oven to 450 degrees to crisp and brown the skin. Brushing the skin with melted butter gave it a beautiful bronze color. For the finishing touch, we roasted a hefty amount of garlic alongside the chicken to form the base of a deeply flavorful pan sauce. If using kosher chickens, do not brine.

Salt and pepper
¾ cup sugar
2 (4- to 4½-pound) whole chickens, giblets discarded
5 garlic heads, outer papery skins removed and top third of each head cut off and discarded
1 tablespoon extra-virgin olive oil
2 tablespoons unsalted butter, melted, plus 2 tablespoons chilled
1 cup chicken broth
¾ cup dry white wine or dry vermouth
½ cup water
2 large shallots, minced
2 bay leaves
1 sprig fresh thyme or rosemary
2 tablespoons minced fresh parsley

TO PREP

1. Dissolve ¾ cup salt and sugar in 3 quarts cold water in large container. Submerge chickens in brine, cover, and refrigerate for 1 hour.

TO COOK

2. Adjust oven rack to middle position and heat oven to 375 degrees. Place garlic heads cut side up on piece of aluminum foil, drizzle with oil, and wrap tightly. Set V-rack in roasting pan and spray with vegetable oil spray.

3. Remove chickens from brine and pat dry with paper towels. Brush chickens all over with melted butter and season with pepper. Place chickens breast side up in prepared V-rack, with legs facing in opposite directions. Pour broth into roasting pan and transfer pan to oven. Place prepared garlic directly on oven rack. Roast for 40 minutes.

4. Increase oven temperature to 450 degrees, rotate pan, and continue to roast until breasts register 160 degrees and thighs register 175 degrees, 20 to 30 minutes.

5. Transfer chickens to carving board and let rest, uncovered, while making jus. Open garlic package and let cool slightly. Squeeze garlic from skins into bowl, then mash smooth with fork. Set aside 2 tablespoons garlic paste.

6. Using large spoon, skim excess fat from juices in roasting pan, then transfer juices to medium saucepan. Stir in wine, water, shallots, bay leaves, and thyme sprig and simmer over medium-high heat until flavors meld, about 10 minutes. Strain jus through fine-mesh strainer, discarding solids, then return jus to pot and bring to simmer. Whisk in parsley, remaining garlic paste, and chilled butter. Season with salt and pepper to taste.

7. Set aside 10 ounces boneless, skinless chicken. Carve remaining chicken and serve with jus.

SAVE IT

Reserved 10 ounces chicken and 2 tablespoons garlic paste can be used to make either Chicken and Bread Salad with Hazelnuts and Roasted Garlic (page 210) or Penne with Tuscan Chicken (page 211). Refrigerate chicken and garlic paste separately for up to 2 days.

Chicken and Bread Salad with Hazelnuts and Roasted Garlic

SERVES 4 TO 6 • **TO PREP AND COOK** 35 MINUTES

✔ **WHY THIS RECIPE WORKS:** To transform leftover roast chicken into a new and interesting meal, we turned to *panzanella*. This classic Italian bread salad features chunks of hearty bread, tomatoes, and basil tossed with a bright vinaigrette. We sought to make it a hearty dinner salad by incorporating our shredded roast chicken and a few new ingredients. Tomatoes and basil are traditional, but we liked cherry tomatoes because they guaranteed bright flavor even in the dead of winter. We also swapped the usual basil for the sharp, peppery flavor of baby arugula. Toasted hazelnuts paired nicely with the chicken, and finishing with shaved Parmesan added savory richness. To achieve just the right amount of crunch in the bread pieces, we relied on a high oven temperature to crisp just the edges of the bread, then tossed them, while still warm, with a couple of tablespoons of the vinaigrette. Thanks to the roasted garlic we had reserved, it was a snap to make a deeply flavored roasted garlic vinaigrette to round out the dish. The cooked chicken and the garlic paste in this recipe are from Two Roast Chickens with Roasted Garlic and Herb Jus on page 209.

¼ cup red wine vinegar
2 tablespoons Dijon mustard
2 tablespoons garlic paste
  Salt and pepper
½ cup extra-virgin olive oil
10 ounces rustic Italian bread, cut or torn into 1-inch cubes (5 cups)
10 ounces cooked chicken, shredded (2 cups)
8 ounces cherry tomatoes, halved
¼ cup hazelnuts, toasted, skinned, and chopped coarse
1 shallot, sliced thin
6 ounces (6 cups) baby arugula
2 ounces Parmesan cheese, shaved

1. Adjust oven rack to middle position and heat oven to 400 degrees. Whisk vinegar, mustard, garlic paste, and ½ teaspoon salt together in bowl. Whisking constantly, drizzle in 6 tablespoons oil; set aside.

2. Toss bread pieces with remaining 2 tablespoons oil, ¼ teaspoon salt, and ¼ teaspoon pepper; arrange bread in single layer in rimmed baking sheet. Bake until light golden brown and edges are crisp, 12 to 15 minutes, stirring halfway through baking. Transfer warm bread pieces to large bowl, add 2 tablespoons vinaigrette, and toss to coat; set aside and let cool slightly.

3. Add shredded chicken, tomatoes, hazelnuts, shallot, and remaining vinaigrette to bread and toss to combine. Just before serving, add arugula, season with salt and pepper to taste, and top with Parmesan. Serve.

TEST KITCHEN TIP SKINNING HAZELNUTS

1. To remove hazelnut skins easily, transfer hot toasted nuts to center of clean dish towel. Gather towel around nuts.

2. Rub nuts together in towel to scrape off as much skin as possible. Open towel to check that skins have come away from nuts; a few patches of skin may remain.

Penne with Tuscan Chicken

SERVES 4 TO 6 • **TO PREP AND COOK** 45 MINUTES

✔ **WHY THIS RECIPE WORKS:** Traditionally, Tuscan chicken is a combination of mild, tender chicken, garlic, and lemon that creates an intensely flavored dish. We decided to add penne and use our delicious leftover roast chicken to turn this Italian classic into an easy weeknight pasta supper. For a quick pasta sauce with mellow but bold garlic flavor, we sautéed the leftover roasted garlic paste in oil with lots of thinly sliced shallots to draw out its sweet, nutty notes. Then we stirred in red pepper flakes for a subtle heat, white wine and chicken broth to serve as the base of the sauce, and a little flour to thicken things up. A hefty amount of peppery arugula added a fresh flavor dimension and color. We reserved the requisite lemon juice for a finishing touch to keep its flavor bright. The lemon juice brought the flavors of our dish into balance, and a generous amount of grated Parmesan cheese created a rich and creamy sauce. Other pasta shapes can be substituted for the penne. The cooked chicken and the garlic paste in this recipe are from Two Roast Chickens with Roasted Garlic and Herb Jus on page 209.

1	tablespoon extra-virgin olive oil
2	tablespoons garlic paste
3	shallots, sliced thin
1	tablespoon all-purpose flour
	Pinch red pepper flakes
¾	cup dry white wine
3	cups chicken broth
1	pound penne
	Salt and pepper
10	ounces cooked chicken, shredded (2 cups)
5	ounces (5 cups) baby arugula
1½	ounces Parmesan cheese, grated (¾ cup), plus extra for serving
1	tablespoon lemon juice

1. Heat oil in large saucepan over medium-low heat until shimmering. Add garlic paste and shallots and cook until softened and beginning to brown, about 3 minutes. Stir in flour and pepper flakes and cook for 30 seconds. Whisk in wine and broth until smooth. Increase heat to medium-high, bring to simmer, and cook until sauce is slightly thickened and measures 2½ cups, about 15 minutes; cover to keep warm.

2. Meanwhile, bring 4 quarts water to boil in large pot. Add pasta and 1 tablespoon salt and cook, stirring often, until al dente. Reserve ½ cup cooking water, then drain pasta and return it to pot.

3. Add sauce, shredded chicken, arugula, Parmesan, and lemon juice to pasta and toss until arugula is slightly wilted. Before serving, adjust consistency with reserved cooking water as needed. Season with salt and pepper to taste. Serve with extra Parmesan.

THE MENU

THE BIG ROAST Turkey Breast
en Cocotte with Pan Gravy

THE SECOND MEAL Thai-Style
Turkey and Jasmine Rice Soup
OR Turkey and Green Chile
Enchiladas

Turkey Breast en Cocotte with Pan Gravy

SERVES 4 WITH LEFTOVERS • **TO PREP** 35 MINUTES • **TO COOK** 2 HOURS 45 MINUTES

✔ **WHY THIS RECIPE WORKS:** Around Thanksgiving, recipes using moist, tender leftover turkey abound—then quickly disappear until the next holiday, because roasting a whole turkey is impractical unless you're feeding a crowd. But a whole turkey breast is a great alternative; it's easy to cook and provides enough leftovers for a creative second-day meal. To ensure that our turkey breast would be super moist and tender (a must when using leftovers for another meal), we turned to a French technique called cooking *en cocotte* where the bird is cooked with aromatics at very low heat with no added liquid. This method traps all the steam released by the meat during cooking, essentially braising it in its own juices. It gave us perfectly cooked turkey, plus the flavorful liquid left in the pot made a delicious and easy pan gravy. Avoid "hotel-style" turkey breasts if possible; they still have the wings and rib cage attached. If this is the only type of breast you can find, remove the wings and cut away the rib cage with kitchen shears before proceeding with the recipe. You will need at least a 7-quart Dutch oven for this recipe. Don't buy a turkey breast larger than 7 pounds; it won't fit in the pot.

1 **(6- to 7-pound) whole bone-in turkey breast, trimmed**
  Salt and pepper
2 **tablespoons extra-virgin olive oil**
1 **onion, chopped**
1 **carrot, peeled and chopped**
1 **celery rib, chopped**
6 **garlic cloves, lightly crushed and peeled**
2 **sprigs fresh thyme**
1 **bay leaf**
2 **tablespoons all-purpose flour**
2 **cups chicken broth**

TO PREP

1. Adjust oven rack to lowest position and heat oven to 250 degrees. Pat turkey dry with paper towels and season with salt and pepper. Heat oil in Dutch oven over medium-high heat until just smoking. Brown turkey on all sides, about 12 minutes; transfer to large plate.

2. Pour off all but 2 tablespoons fat from pot and heat over medium heat until shimmering. Add onion, carrot, and celery and cook, stirring occasionally, until softened, about 5 minutes. Stir in garlic, thyme sprigs, and bay leaf and cook until fragrant, about 30 seconds. Off heat, return turkey, breast side up, to pot along with any accumulated juices.

TO COOK

3. Fit large piece of aluminum foil over pot, pressing to seal, then cover tightly with lid. Transfer pot to oven and cook until turkey registers 160 degrees, about 2 hours.

4. Carefully remove pot from oven. Transfer turkey to carving board, tent loosely with foil, and let rest while making gravy.

5. Being careful of hot pot handles, bring remaining juices and vegetables to simmer over medium-high heat and cook until nearly all liquid has evaporated, about 15 minutes. Add flour and cook, stirring constantly, until browned, 1 to 3 minutes. Slowly add broth, whisking constantly to smooth out any lumps. Bring to simmer and cook, stirring often, until gravy is thickened and measures about 1½ cups, about 10 minutes. Strain gravy through fine-mesh strainer and season with salt and pepper to taste.

6. Set aside 1 pound boneless, skinless turkey. Carve remaining turkey and serve, passing gravy separately.

SAVE IT

Reserved 1 pound turkey can be used to make either Thai-Style Turkey and Jasmine Rice Soup (page 214) or Turkey and Green Chile Enchiladas (page 215). Refrigerate reserved turkey for up to 2 days.

Thai-Style Turkey and Jasmine Rice Soup

SERVES 4 • **TO PREP AND COOK** 50 MINUTES

✔ **WHY THIS RECIPE WORKS:** A hearty soup is a great way to use up extra turkey, but we wanted something a little more exciting than a humdrum soup with egg noodles and carrots. For a turkey soup boasting the bright, fresh flavors of Thai cuisine, we started by simmering chicken broth with aromatic ginger, lemon grass, and garlic for just 10 minutes. After straining the broth, we stirred in half a cup of jasmine rice, a Thai variety of long-grain rice. To avoid tough turkey, we waited until our rice was tender and fully cooked, then stirred in the turkey along with a handful of delicate, crunchy snow peas and thinly sliced jalapeños. The vegetables took just a few minutes to turn crisp-tender, at which point the turkey was heated through. A generous amount of coconut milk gave our broth body and a velvety texture and imparted a delicate sweetness that worked well with the bright notes of the lemon grass and ginger. The cooked turkey in this recipe is from Turkey Breast en Cocotte with Pan Gravy on page 213.

4 cups chicken broth

1½ cups water

3 lemon grass stalks, trimmed to bottom 6 inches and bruised with back of knife

1 (2-inch) piece ginger, peeled and sliced into ½-inch-thick rounds

4 garlic cloves, unpeeled, smashed

¼ teaspoon salt

½ cup jasmine rice

2 (13.5-ounce) cans coconut milk

1 pound cooked turkey, shredded (4 cups)

4 ounces snow peas, strings removed, cut into 1-inch pieces

2 jalapeño chiles, stemmed, seeded, and sliced thin

3 tablespoons fish sauce, plus extra for seasoning

2 tablespoons minced fresh cilantro

Lime wedges

1. Bring broth, water, lemon grass, ginger, garlic, and salt to simmer in large saucepan over medium-high heat. Cover, reduce heat to medium, and simmer until broth is fragrant and flavorful, about 10 minutes. Using slotted spoon, remove lemon grass, ginger, and garlic.

2. Add rice to broth and bring to boil. Cover, reduce heat to medium, and simmer until rice is tender, about 15 minutes. Stir in coconut milk, shredded turkey, snow peas, jalapeños, and fish sauce and cook until turkey is heated through and snow peas and jalapeños are crisp-tender, 2 to 3 minutes. Stir in cilantro and season with extra fish sauce to taste. Serve with lime wedges.

TEST KITCHEN TIP **BRUISING LEMON GRASS**

To release flavor from lemon grass, trim and discard all but bottom 6 inches of stalk. Peel off discolored outer layer, then, using back of chef's knife, lightly smash stalk.

Turkey and Green Chile Enchiladas

SERVES 4 TO 6 • **TO PREP AND COOK** 1 HOUR

✓ **WHY THIS RECIPE WORKS:** To give our turkey leftovers a bold makeover, we looked south of the border to saucy, spicy enchiladas. For the filling, we sautéed sliced onion with garlic, cumin, and chili powder, then stirred in our shredded cooked turkey, corn, green chiles, Monterey Jack cheese, and enchilada sauce. Canned enchilada sauce provided great flavor and kept this dish easy enough for a weeknight. Fresh cilantro brought an herbal note to the filling. We softened corn tortillas in the microwave, then wrapped them around the filling and arranged them in a 13 by 9-inch baking dish. To keep the tortillas from drying out and cracking while baking, we lightly coated them with vegetable oil spray before pouring more enchilada sauce over the top and sprinkling on more cheese. After just 20 minutes in the oven, our enchiladas were piping hot and the cheese was gooey and bubbling. Serve with lime wedges, sour cream, thinly sliced scallion, and hot sauce. The cooked turkey in this recipe is from Turkey Breast en Cocotte with Pan Gravy on page 213.

3   tablespoons vegetable oil
1   onion, halved and sliced thin
4   garlic cloves, minced
1   teaspoon ground cumin
½   teaspoon chili powder
2   (10-ounce) cans green enchilada sauce
1   pound cooked turkey, shredded (4 cups)
1   cup canned chopped green chiles, drained
8   ounces Monterey Jack cheese, shredded
     (2 cups)
½   cup frozen corn
½   cup minced fresh cilantro
12   (6-inch) corn tortillas
     Vegetable oil spray

1. Adjust oven rack to middle position and heat oven to 450 degrees. Heat 1 tablespoon oil in 12-inch skillet over medium heat until shimmering. Add onion and cook until softened and lightly browned, 5 to 7 minutes. Stir in garlic, cumin, and chili powder and cook until fragrant, about 30 seconds. Off heat, stir in half of enchilada sauce, shredded turkey, chiles, ½ cup Monterey Jack, corn, and cilantro.

2. Brush both sides of tortillas with remaining 2 tablespoons oil. Stack tortillas, wrap in damp dish towel, and place on plate; microwave until warm and pliable, about 1 minute. Working with 1 warm tortilla at a time, spread ⅓ cup filling across center of tortilla, roll tortilla tightly around filling, and place seam side down in greased 13 by 9-inch baking dish.

3. Spray tops of enchiladas with vegetable oil spray. Pour remaining enchilada sauce over enchiladas, covering tortillas completely, then sprinkle remaining 1½ cups Monterey Jack across center of enchiladas. Cover dish tightly with greased aluminum foil and bake until enchiladas are hot throughout and bubbling around edges, about 15 minutes. Remove foil and continue to bake until cheese is completely melted, about 5 minutes. Serve.

THE MENU

THE BIG ROAST Slow-Roasted
Pork with Peach Sauce

THE SECOND MEAL Pork
Fried Rice
OR Pork Ragu with Easy
Polenta

Slow-Roasted Pork with Peach Sauce

SERVES 6 TO 8 WITH LEFTOVERS • **TO PREP** 12 TO 24 HOURS FOR SALTING • **TO COOK** 6½ TO 7½ HOURS

✔ **WHY THIS RECIPE WORKS:** A pork butt roast is a relatively fatty cut that becomes meltingly tender when braised or slow-roasted. It's a great candidate for a Sunday roast that delivers moist, tender leftovers perfect for making a quick weeknight meal. We started with bone-in pork butt because the bone helps the meat to cook evenly. Then we crosshatched the thick fat cap, rubbed the exterior with brown sugar and salt, and let the roast rest overnight. The long rest allowed the salt to penetrate the surface and restructure the meat's proteins, helping them retain moisture, while the sugar dried out the exterior, boosting browning. Roasting the pork on a V-rack at a low temperature for 5 to 6 hours allowed the pork's collagen to break down and render the interior meltingly tender yet still sliceable. Finally, a sweet-and-sour peach sauce with mustard and thyme cut the richness and nicely complemented the pork. For a couple of clever options to use up the tender, flavorful leftovers without requiring a lot of time or ingredients, we developed easy recipes for pork ragu with polenta and pork fried rice. Add more water to the roasting pan as necessary during the last hours of cooking to prevent the fond from burning. We prefer natural to "enhanced" pork, though both will work in this recipe. Pork butt roast is often labeled Boston butt in the supermarket.

1	**(6- to 8-pound) bone-in pork butt roast**
⅓	**cup packed light brown sugar**
	Kosher salt and pepper
2	**cups fresh or frozen peaches, cut into ½-inch pieces**
2	**cups dry white wine**
½	**cup granulated sugar**
2	**tablespoons plus ½ teaspoon rice vinegar**
2	**sprigs fresh thyme**
1	**tablespoon whole-grain mustard**

TO PREP

1. Using sharp knife, cut slits spaced 1 inch apart in crosshatch pattern in fat cap of roast, being careful to cut down to but not into meat. Combine brown sugar and ⅓ cup salt, then rub mixture over entire roast and into slits. Wrap roast tightly in double layer of plastic wrap, place on large plate, and refrigerate for at least 12 hours or up to 24 hours.

TO COOK

2. Adjust oven rack to lowest position and heat oven to 325 degrees. Spray V-rack with vegetable oil spray and set inside large roasting pan. Unwrap roast, brush any excess salt mixture from surface, and season with pepper. Place roast in prepared V-rack and pour 4 cups water into roasting pan.

3. Cook roast, basting twice during cooking, until meat is extremely tender and registers 190 degrees, 5 to 6 hours. Transfer roast to carving board, tent loosely with aluminum foil, and let rest for 1 hour. Pour liquid from roasting pan into fat separator. Let jus settle for 5 minutes, then pour off and reserve 2 tablespoons defatted juices.

4. Bring reserved juices, peaches, wine, granulated sugar, 2 tablespoons vinegar, and thyme sprigs to simmer in small saucepan over medium-high heat. Cook, stirring occasionally, until reduced to ¾ cup, 20 to 30 minutes. Stir in mustard and remaining ½ teaspoon vinegar. Off heat, remove thyme sprigs and cover sauce to keep warm.

5. Using sharp paring knife, cut around inverted T-shaped bone and, using clean kitchen towel, pull bone free from roast. Set aside 1 pound trimmed pork. Using serrated knife, slice remaining roast. Serve, passing sauce separately.

SAVE IT

Reserved 1 pound pork can be used to make either Pork Fried Rice (page 218) or Pork Ragu with Polenta (page 219). Refrigerate reserved pork for up to 2 days.

Pork Fried Rice

SERVES 4 TO 6 • **TO PREP AND COOK** 1 HOUR

✓ **WHY THIS RECIPE WORKS:** Fried rice is the perfect solution to what to do with leftover pork, but it often ends up a soggy mess of greasy rice doused in too much soy sauce. We wanted a quick weeknight supper that boasted firm grains of rice, tender pork, and well-seasoned vegetables that tasted light, fresh, and flavorful—not heavy and greasy. To achieve rice with a firm, distinct texture, we found it essential to start with rice that had been cooked, then cooled. For a balanced sauce, we mixed salty soy sauce with sweet hoisin and spicy, garlicky Sriracha. A combination of shiitake mushrooms, baby bok choy, scallions, and shallots freshened the dish and made it feel like a complete meal. Cooking the vegetables before adding the rice and leftover pork ensured that everything was cooked to perfection—no rubbery meat or mushy vegetables. To get rich flavor without excess grease, we sautéed the vegetables with just a little bit of oil. Finally, we added a small amount of sugar for sweetness and folded in scrambled eggs and scallion greens. You can substitute 6 cups of cooked long-grain rice for the raw rice; omit steps 1 and 2. The cooked pork in this recipe is from Slow-Roasted Pork with Peach Sauce on page 217.

2	tablespoons vegetable oil
1¼	cups long-grain white rice, rinsed
1¾	cups water
½	teaspoon salt
3	tablespoons hoisin sauce
1	tablespoon soy sauce, plus extra for seasoning
1½	teaspoons Sriracha sauce
2	large eggs, lightly beaten
8	ounces shiitake mushrooms, stemmed and quartered
1	head baby bok choy (4 ounces), halved and sliced 1 inch thick
8	scallions, white parts minced, green parts sliced thin
2	shallots, sliced thin
4	teaspoons grated fresh ginger
2	garlic cloves, minced
1	teaspoon sugar
1	pound cooked pork, shredded (3 cups)

1. Heat 1 tablespoon oil in medium saucepan over medium heat until shimmering. Stir in rice and cook until edges of grains begin to turn translucent, about 2 minutes. Stir in water and salt, increase heat to high, and bring to boil. Cover, reduce heat to low, and simmer until all liquid is absorbed, about 18 minutes.

2. Off heat, uncover saucepan and place clean kitchen towel folded in half over saucepan, then replace lid. Let rice sit for 10 minutes, then spread in rimmed baking sheet and let cool to room temperature, about 20 minutes.

3. Combine hoisin, soy sauce, and Sriracha in bowl; set aside. Heat 1 teaspoon oil in 12-inch nonstick skillet over medium heat until shimmering. Add eggs and cook, without stirring, until just beginning to set, about 20 seconds, then scramble until eggs are cooked through but not browned, about 1 minute. Transfer eggs to bowl. Wipe skillet clean with paper towels.

4. Heat remaining 2 teaspoons oil in now-empty skillet over medium heat until shimmering. Add mushrooms and bok choy and cook until tender and lightly browned, about 5 minutes. Stir in scallion whites, shallots, ginger, garlic, and sugar and cook until fragrant, about 30 seconds. Stir in rice and cook until fragrant, about 30 seconds. Stir in shredded pork and hoisin mixture and cook until rice and pork are coated with sauce and heated through, 2 to 4 minutes.

5. Off heat, stir in scallion greens and scrambled eggs and season with soy sauce to taste. Serve.

Pork Ragu with Easy Polenta

SERVES 4 TO 6 • **TO PREP AND COOK** 40 MINUTES

✓ **WHY THIS RECIPE WORKS:** A classic pork ragu normally takes hours to make, but with the tender leftover pork from our slow-roasted pork butt, we already had a jump start on the process. We just needed to build a hearty red sauce with long-simmered flavor. To build an aromatic base, we browned an onion, followed by garlic, red pepper flakes, and savory tomato paste. Then we deglazed the pan with red wine to add brightness and loosen the rich, flavorful fond. We tested a variety of tomato products, and in the end we liked the ease and fresh taste of diced tomatoes. To quickly thicken the sauce, we mashed the tomatoes with a potato masher until we had our desired saucy consistency. Thanks to our flavorful base and our meltingly tender leftover pork, we were able to cut the usual hours-long simmering time down to just 15 minutes. Polenta was the perfect accompaniment for this hearty ragu. To help break down the cornmeal's tough endosperm, we added a pinch of baking soda to the pot along with the salt. This simple trick gave us tender, creamy polenta in less time. The cooked pork in this recipe is from Slow-Roasted Pork with Peach Sauce on page 217.

PORK RAGU

- 2 tablespoons vegetable oil
- 1 onion, chopped fine
- Salt and pepper
- 2 tablespoons tomato paste
- 4 garlic cloves, minced
- ¼ teaspoon red pepper flakes
- 1 cup dry red wine
- 2 (14.5-ounce) cans diced tomatoes
- ½ cup water
- 1 pound cooked pork, shredded (3 cups)
- ¼ cup chopped fresh basil

POLENTA

- 4 cups water
- Salt and pepper
- ⅛ teaspoon baking soda
- 1 cup coarse-ground polenta
- 2 tablespoons unsalted butter
- Grated Parmesan cheese

1. FOR THE PORK RAGU: Heat oil in medium saucepan over medium heat until shimmering. Add onion, ½ teaspoon salt, and ½ teaspoon pepper and cook until softened and lightly browned, 5 to 7 minutes. Stir in tomato paste, garlic, and pepper flakes and cook until fragrant, about 30 seconds.

2. Stir in wine and cook until it has nearly evaporated, 3 to 5 minutes. Stir in tomatoes and their juice and water and mash with potato masher until tomatoes break into small pieces. Stir in shredded pork, bring to simmer, and cook, stirring often, until sauce is thickened, 15 to 20 minutes. Stir in basil and season with salt and pepper to taste.

3. FOR THE POLENTA: Meanwhile, bring water to boil in large saucepan over medium-high heat. Stir in 1 teaspoon salt and baking soda, then very slowly pour polenta into boiling water while stirring constantly in circular motion with wooden spoon. Bring mixture to boil, stirring constantly, about 30 seconds. Reduce heat to lowest possible setting and cover.

4. After 5 minutes, whisk polenta to smooth out lumps, scraping down sides and bottom of saucepan. Cover and continue to cook, without stirring, until grains of polenta are tender but slightly al dente, 8 to 10 minutes. (Polenta should be loose and barely hold its shape; it will continue to thicken as it cools.)

5. Off heat, stir in butter and season with salt and pepper to taste. Let stand, covered, for 5 minutes. Spoon polenta into individual serving bowls and top with pork ragu. Sprinkle with Parmesan and serve.

TEST KITCHEN TIP IMPROVISING A FLAME TAMER

A flame tamer diffuses the heat from the burner, keeping dishes from simmering too briskly. To improvise one, shape a long sheet of heavy-duty aluminum foil into an even 1-inch-thick ring.

ALL ABOUT Making Great Roasts

For time-crunched cooks, double-duty cooking can be a great strategy—spend a relaxing Sunday making a big roast, then use the flavorful leftovers to assemble an easy meal on a busy weeknight. But to be worthwhile, the roast needs to come out perfectly and the leftover recipes need to be fresh and exciting— reheated slices of chicken or beef just don't cut it. So we filled this chapter with six foolproof roast recipes, then for each roast we came up with two options for creative recipes that took advantage of the tender, flavorful leftovers. To set you up for success, here are some tips for buying and cooking great roasts.

Whole Chicken

When buying a whole chicken, avoid birds that are "enhanced" (injected with broth and flavoring) or "water-chilled" (soaked in a water bath in which they absorb up to 14 percent of their weight in water); these chickens have an unnaturally spongy texture. Instead, look for those that are labeled air-chilled. Without the excess water weight, we find these chickens to have a better texture and richer, meatier flavor.

Bone-In Turkey Breast

Most supermarkets offer two different styles of whole bone-in turkey breast: regular or true cut and hotel or country-style. We prefer to avoid hotel-style turkey breasts, which come with the wings attached. We also try to avoid turkey breasts that have been injected with a saline solution (a brine of sorts)—these are often called self-basters. We found the solution masks the natural flavor of the turkey.

Bone-In Pork Butt

This large, flavorful cut is often labeled Boston butt or pork shoulder and sold bone-in or boneless. Pork butt is sold "natural" or "enhanced" (injected with water, salt, and sodium phosphate to season the pork and prevent it from drying out). We prefer natural pork; enhanced pork tends to be salty and can have an artificial flavor. However, both styles of pork can be used in our recipes.

Beef Eye-Round Roast

Falling between top round (which we enthusiastically seek) and bottom round (which we usually avoid) on the cow, this boneless roast has a nice, mild flavor. It is inexpensive and has a shape that slices neatly, making it a better choice than other round or rump roasts. To make this lean cut tender, we roast it slowly in a very low oven.

Beef Chuck-Eye Roast

This roast can be labeled boneless chuck roll or boneless chuck fillet at the market. It is very tender and juicy but also contains a large amount of fat, which should be trimmed away before cooking. We like the chuck-eye roast for its compact, uniform shape, deep flavor, and meltingly tender texture.

Boneless Leg of Lamb

When buying lamb, we prefer the milder flavor and larger size of domestic or American lamb over gamier imported lamb from Australia or New Zealand. For our roast leg of lamb recipe (page 231), we opt to use a boneless leg that has been butterflied to an even thickness; whole, bone-in legs of lamb are tricky to cook evenly.

Taking the Temperature of Meat and Poultry

An instant-read thermometer is the most accurate way to determine the doneness of meat and poultry. Take the temperature at the center of the roast, avoid touching any bones (if present), and check large roasts in multiple places. The temperature of the meat will continue to rise as it rests, an effect called carryover cooking, so it's best to remove it from the heat when it's 5 to 10 degrees below the desired serving temperature. Carryover cooking doesn't apply to poultry, so it should be cooked to a safe serving temperature. The following temperatures should be used to determine when to stop cooking.

BEEF/LAMB	
Rare	115 to 120 degrees (120 to 125 degrees after resting)
Medium-Rare	120 to 125 degrees (125 to 130 degrees after resting)
Medium	130 to 135 degrees (135 to 140 degrees after resting)
Medium-Well	140 to 145 degrees (145 to 150 degrees after resting)
Well-Done	150 to 155 degrees (155 to 160 degrees after resting)
PORK	
Medium	140 to 145 degrees (145 to 150 degrees after resting)
Well-Done	150 to 155 degrees (155 to 160 degrees after resting)
POULTRY	
White Meat	160 degrees
Dark Meat	175 degrees

Let It Rest

We rest all roasts (as well as most smaller cuts of meat and poultry) after cooking. As meat cooks, its proteins tighten, driving its juices to the center of the meat. Allowing the meat to sit undisturbed for a time before serving allows the juices to redistribute themselves more evenly throughout the meat. As a result, meat that has rested will shed much less juice than meat sliced straight after cooking, which in turn makes for much juicier and more tender meat.

Secure Pot Roasts with Twine

Most roasts are unevenly shaped, which leads to uneven cooking. For our Pot Roast in Foil (page 227), we divide the pot roast into two smaller roasts and give each a neater shape by tying them with twine at about 1-inch intervals.

Carving a Whole Chicken

1. Using chef's knife, cut chicken where leg meets breast. Pull leg quarter away from chicken and cut through joint to remove leg quarter. Repeat with other leg.

2. Cut through joint that connects drumstick to thigh. Repeat with second leg.

3. Cut down along each side of breastbone, pulling meat away from bone. Cut through wing joint to remove wing from each breast. Slice breasts crosswise.

THE MENU

THE BIG ROAST Slow-Roasted
Beef with Horseradish Sauce

THE SECOND MEAL Beef and
Vegetable Fajitas
OR Vietnamese Rice Noodle
Soup with Beef

Slow-Roasted Beef with Horseradish Sauce

SERVES 4 WITH LEFTOVERS • **TO PREP** 18 TO 24 HOURS FOR SALTING • **TO COOK** 2½ TO 3 HOURS

✔ **WHY THIS RECIPE WORKS:** With its beefy flavor and moderate price tag, the eye round is an appealing choice for a big roast that makes a great dinner and yields versatile leftovers. But cooking it so it would remain tender proved challenging. First, to flavor the meat and to improve its ability to hold on to its juices, we salted the roast overnight. The next day, we browned the roast on the stovetop to create a flavorful crust before roasting. We tried roasting the beef in a 225-degree oven until it reached the correct doneness, but this resulted in a tough and dry roast. We needed a more gentle method to give the connective tissue enough time to break down and tenderize. The key turned out to be shutting off the oven partway through cooking. When the meat reached 115 degrees, we turned off the oven to allow the roast to finish cooking gently as the oven cooled, resulting in a tender and very juicy roast. A simple horseradish sauce was the perfect complement to our rich and juicy roast. Now that we had perfect roast beef, we had a jump start on a second flavorful dinner for later in the week. Beef and vegetable fajitas and Vietnamese rice noodle soup with beef were easy recipes that took advantage of the leftover meat because they require just warming the meat through, keeping the rosy beef from overcooking. We don't recommend cooking this roast past medium. Open the oven door as little as possible and remove the roast from the oven while taking its temperature. If the roast has not reached the desired temperature in the time specified in step 3, heat the oven to 225 degrees for 5 minutes, shut it off, and continue to cook the roast to the desired temperature.

1 **(3½- to 4½-pound) boneless eye-round roast, trimmed**
  Kosher salt and pepper
⅓ **cup sour cream**
1 **tablespoon mayonnaise**
1 **tablespoon prepared horseradish**
2 **teaspoons lemon juice**
¼ **teaspoon garlic powder**
1 **tablespoon plus 2 teaspoons vegetable oil**

TO PREP

1. Season roast evenly with 4 teaspoons salt, wrap tightly with plastic wrap, and refrigerate for at least 18 hours or up to 24 hours.

2. Combine sour cream, mayonnaise, horseradish, lemon juice, and garlic powder in small bowl. Season with salt and pepper to taste and add water as needed to thin sauce to desired consistency. Cover and refrigerate until needed.

TO COOK

3. Adjust oven rack to middle position and heat oven to 225 degrees. Pat roast dry with paper towels, then rub with 2 teaspoons oil and sprinkle evenly with pepper. Heat remaining 1 tablespoon oil in 12-inch skillet over medium-high heat until just smoking. Brown roast on all sides, about 12 minutes. Transfer roast to wire rack set in rimmed baking sheet. Roast until meat registers 115 degrees (for medium-rare), 1¼ to 1¾ hours, or 125 degrees (for medium), 1¾ to 2¼ hours.

4. Turn oven off; leave roast in oven, without opening door, until meat registers 130 degrees (for medium-rare) or 140 degrees (for medium), 30 to 50 minutes longer. Transfer roast to carving board and let rest for 15 minutes.

5. Set aside 1 pound beef. Slice remaining roast as thin as possible and serve with horseradish sauce.

SAVE IT

Reserved 1 pound beef can be used to make either Beef and Vegetable Fajitas (page 224) or Vietnamese Rice Noodle Soup with Beef (page 225). Reserved beef can be refrigerated for up to 2 days.

Beef and Vegetable Fajitas

SERVES 4 • **TO PREP AND COOK** 30 MINUTES

✔ **WHY THIS RECIPE WORKS:** This classic Tex-Mex favorite is a simple combination of juicy, flavorful meat and crisp-tender sweet peppers tucked into a warm, chewy flour tortilla. From-scratch beef fajita recipes often require marinating the beef for at least 30 minutes before cooking, but we were able to skip this step by taking advantage of our savory leftover roast beef. To lend bold Tex-Mex flavor to the dish, we bloomed chili powder and cumin in a skillet before sautéing the peppers and onion. To avoid overcooking the perfectly medium-rare meat, we added it to the skillet once the vegetables were tender and just warmed it through. Finishing the steak and vegetables with a drizzle of lime juice brightened the dish's flavor. Serve the fajitas with salsa, sour cream, avocado, queso fresco, and/or lime wedges. The cooked beef in this recipe is from Slow-Roasted Beef with Horseradish Sauce on page 223.

1   **tablespoon vegetable oil**
1   **teaspoon chili powder**
½   **teaspoon ground cumin**
1   **red onion, halved and sliced ¼ inch thick**
2   **red bell peppers, stemmed, seeded, and cut into ¼-inch-wide strips**
2   **teaspoons Worcestershire sauce**
1½   **teaspoons minced canned chipotle chile in adobo sauce**
½   **teaspoon salt**
1   **pound cooked roast beef, sliced thin and cut into 1-inch-wide strips (2 cups)**
1   **tablespoon lime juice**
½   **cup chopped fresh cilantro**
12   **(6-inch) flour tortillas, warmed**

Heat oil in 12-inch skillet over medium-high heat until shimmering. Add chili powder and cumin and cook, stirring constantly, until fragrant, about 1 minute. Add onion, bell peppers, Worcestershire, chipotle, and salt and cook until vegetables are crisp-tender and lightly browned, 5 to 7 minutes. Stir in sliced beef and cook until heated through, 2 to 3 minutes. Off heat, stir in lime juice and sprinkle with cilantro. Serve with warmed tortillas and garnishes.

TEST KITCHEN TIP
CUTTING BELL PEPPERS INTO STRIPS

1. To cut bell pepper into strips, slice off top and bottom of pepper and remove seeds and stem. Slice down through sides of pepper.

2. Lay pepper flat on cutting board, trim away any remaining ribs and seeds, then slice pepper into ¼-inch-thick strips.

Vietnamese Rice Noodle Soup with Beef

SERVES 4 • **TO PREP AND COOK** 1 HOUR

✔ **WHY THIS RECIPE WORKS:** Vietnamese noodle soup is the perfect vehicle for leftover roast beef because this dish traditionally features tender, medium-rare slices of steak. To serve the soup, hot broth is poured over thin slices of raw beef so that the heat from the broth cooks the meat just enough. We already had perfectly cooked beef, so we just needed to develop a rich, flavorful broth. To achieve complex flavor without any fuss, we fortified store-bought chicken broth with onion, garlic, lemon grass, fish sauce, soy sauce, star anise, and cloves. We simmered the broth and aromatics for just 10 minutes to allow the flavors to infuse. To serve the dish, we portioned cooked rice noodles into individual bowls before ladling the broth and leftover sliced beef over the noodles, so that the hot broth just warmed the beef through. To add a fresh note to our dish, we topped the bowls with bean sprouts and whole basil and cilantro leaves. Flat rice noodles come in a variety of widths, but the thinner (¼-inch-wide) noodles are traditional for this recipe. Be ready to serve the soup immediately after adding the beef in step 4; if the beef sits in the hot broth for too long it will become tough. The cooked beef in this recipe is from Slow-Roasted Beef with Horseradish Sauce on page 223.

BROTH

- 2 teaspoons vegetable oil
- 1 onion, chopped fine
- 4 garlic cloves, minced
- 2 lemon grass stalks, trimmed to bottom 6 inches, halved lengthwise, and sliced thin
- ¼ cup fish sauce, plus extra for serving
- 8 cups chicken broth
- 2 cups water
- 2 tablespoons soy sauce
- 2 tablespoons sugar
- 4 star anise pods
- 4 whole cloves

NOODLES, BEEF, GARNISH

- 8 ounces (¼-inch-wide) rice noodles
- 1 pound cooked roast beef, sliced thin and cut into 1-inch-wide strips (2 cups)
- 1 cup fresh cilantro leaves
  Bean sprouts
  Sprigs fresh Thai or Italian basil
  Lime wedges
  Hoisin sauce
  Sriracha sauce

1. FOR THE BROTH: Heat oil in large saucepan over medium heat until shimmering. Add onion, garlic, lemon grass, and 2 tablespoons fish sauce and cook, stirring often, until onion is softened but not browned, about 5 minutes.

2. Stir in broth, water, soy sauce, sugar, star anise, cloves, and remaining 2 tablespoons fish sauce and bring to simmer. Cover, reduce heat to low, and simmer until flavors have blended, about 10 minutes. Strain broth through fine-mesh strainer, discarding solids, and return to saucepan.

3. FOR THE NOODLES, BEEF, AND GARNISH: Bring 4 quarts water to boil in large pot. Remove boiling water from heat, add rice noodles, and let sit, stirring occasionally, until noodles are tender, 12 to 14 minutes. Drain immediately and divide noodles among individual bowls.

4. Bring broth to rolling boil over high heat. Divide sliced beef among individual bowls, shingling slices on top of noodles, and sprinkle with cilantro. Ladle hot broth into each bowl. Serve immediately, passing bean sprouts, basil sprigs, lime wedges, hoisin, Sriracha, and extra fish sauce separately.

THE MENU

THE BIG ROAST Pot Roast
in Foil

THE SECOND MEAL Rigatoni
with Beef Ragu
OR Hearty Beef and Barley
Soup

Pot Roast in Foil

SERVES 4 WITH LEFTOVERS • **TO PREP** 30 MINUTES • **TO COOK** 5 HOURS

✔ **WHY THIS RECIPE WORKS:** Traditionally, this lazy cook's pot roast involves rubbing a chuck roast with onion soup mix, wrapping it in foil, and cooking it in the oven until tender. While we liked the ease of this dish, we weren't fans of its artificial, salty taste. We wanted to transform pot roast in foil into a homey meal worthy of a special-occasion supper. To elevate this dish, we created our own flavorful spice rub, starting with the basics: onion and garlic powder. To bring the rub into balance, we added brown sugar, which lent sweetness and depth. A surprise ingredient—a little instant espresso powder—provided toasty complexity. Dividing the roast into two smaller ones allowed us to apply more of the flavorful spice rub to its exterior. To make this dish a complete meal, we included carrots and potatoes. Drizzling the vegetables with soy sauce before roasting enhanced the dish's beefy flavor, and placing the roast on top allowed the vegetables to baste in the beef's rich juices. Use small red potatoes measuring 1 to 2 inches in diameter. You will need an 18-inch-wide roll of heavy-duty aluminum foil for this recipe. For more information on tying a pot roast, see page 221.

- 3 **tablespoons cornstarch**
- 4 **teaspoons onion powder**
- 1 **tablespoon minced fresh thyme or 1 teaspoon dried**
- 2 **teaspoons packed brown sugar**
- 2 **teaspoons salt**
- 1 **teaspoon pepper**
- 1 **teaspoon garlic powder**
- 1 **teaspoon instant espresso powder**
- ½ **teaspoon celery seeds**
- 1 **(4-pound) boneless beef chuck-eye roast, pulled into 2 pieces at natural seam and trimmed of large pieces of fat**
- 2 **onions, quartered**
- 1 **pound small red potatoes, unpeeled, quartered**
- 4 **carrots, peeled and cut into 1½-inch pieces**
- 2 **bay leaves**
- 2 **tablespoons soy sauce**

TO PREP

1. Adjust oven rack to lower-middle position and heat oven to 300 degrees. Combine cornstarch, onion powder, thyme, sugar, salt, pepper, garlic powder, espresso powder, and celery seeds in bowl.

2. Season roasts evenly with spice rub. Tie roasts crosswise with kitchen twine at 1-inch intervals and pat dry with paper towels.

3. Crisscross two 30 by 18-inch sheets of heavy-duty aluminum foil inside large roasting pan. Place onions, potatoes, carrots, and bay leaves in center of foil and drizzle with soy sauce. Set roasts on top of vegetables. Fold opposite corners of foil toward each other and crimp edges tightly to seal.

TO COOK

4. Cook roasts until meat is completely tender and fork slips easily in and out of meat, about 4½ hours.

5. Remove roasts from foil pouch and transfer to carving board. Tent meat loosely with foil and let rest for 20 minutes. Discard onions and bay leaves. Using slotted spoon, place potatoes and carrots on serving platter. Strain contents of roasting pan through fine-mesh strainer into fat separator. Let liquid settle for 5 minutes, then pour 1 cup defatted pan juices into storage container; set aside.

6. Remove kitchen twine from roasts and set aside 1 pound trimmed beef. Slice remaining roasts thin against grain and transfer to platter with vegetables. Pour remaining defatted pan juices over meat and serve.

SAVE IT

Reserved 1 pound beef and 1 cup pan juices can be used to make either Rigatoni with Beef Ragu (page 228) or Hearty Beef and Barley Soup (page 229). Refrigerate reserved beef and pan juices separately for up to 2 days.

Rigatoni with Beef Ragu

SERVES 4 • **TO PREP AND COOK** 35 MINUTES

✔ **WHY THIS RECIPE WORKS:** Rustic, Italian-style ragu is all about low-and-slow simmering—it relies on lots of time to turn an inexpensive, tough cut of meat meltingly tender. Since we were starting with leftover pot roast and pan juices that already had a silky, fall-apart-tender texture and big beefy flavor, we were able to skip the long simmering time without sacrificing flavor. We just needed to make a quick tomato sauce. We started by sautéing garlic, tomato paste, and oregano in a good amount of olive oil to bring out their flavors, then we stirred in crushed tomatoes, broth, and the reserved pan juices. After just 15 minutes of simmering, we stirred in the shredded pot roast and we had a full-fledged beef ragu. A little heavy cream enriched the sauce further. A sprinkling of parsley and some grated Parmesan cheese finished the dish. Other pasta shapes can be substituted for the rigatoni. The cooked pot roast and pan juices in this recipe are from Pot Roast in Foil on page 227.

2 tablespoons extra-virgin olive oil
6 garlic cloves, minced
4 teaspoons tomato paste
¾ teaspoon minced fresh oregano or
   ¼ teaspoon dried
1 (28-ounce) can crushed tomatoes
1 cup chicken broth
1 cup pot roast pan juices
   Salt and pepper
1 pound cooked pot roast, shredded (4 cups)
½ cup heavy cream
1 pound rigatoni
2 tablespoons chopped fresh parsley
   Grated Parmesan cheese

1. Cook oil, garlic, tomato paste, and oregano in large saucepan over medium heat until fragrant, about 1 minute. Stir in tomatoes, broth, pot roast pan juices, and ½ teaspoon salt. Bring to simmer and cook until sauce has thickened and flavors have melded, about 15 minutes. Stir in shredded beef and cream and cook until heated through, about 2 minutes. Season with salt and pepper to taste.

2. Meanwhile, bring 4 quarts water to boil in large pot. Add pasta and 1 tablespoon salt and cook, stirring often, until al dente. Reserve ½ cup cooking water, then drain pasta and return it to pot.

3. Add sauce and parsley to pasta and toss to combine. Before serving, adjust consistency with reserved cooking water as needed. Serve with Parmesan.

TEST KITCHEN TIP **MINCING GARLIC TO A PASTE**

1. Mincing garlic to a paste helps to distribute its flavor evenly throughout a dish. To make garlic paste, first finely mince garlic cloves.

2. Sprinkle minced garlic with pinch salt, then scrape blade of knife back and forth over garlic until it forms sticky paste.

Hearty Beef and Barley Soup

SERVES 4 • **TO PREP AND COOK** 1 HOUR

✔ **WHY THIS RECIPE WORKS:** What better way to use leftover beef and pot roast jus than to make a hearty shortcut soup? Beef and barley soup boasts rich, deeply beefy broth that often requires hours of cooking to achieve. Our leftover pot roast juices and tender, meaty shredded beef delivered the same satisfying results without all the work. The reserved pan juices from the pot roast beefed up convenient store-bought chicken broth; to add even more depth of flavor, we turned to umami-rich ingredients like tomato paste and soy sauce. Browning onion and thinly sliced white mushrooms gave us a flavorful fond and bulked up our soup. To cut down on cooking time, we used instant barley, which takes just 20 minutes to cook compared to an hour or more for traditional barley. Carrots added welcome sweetness and fresh vegetal flavor, and a sprinkling of parsley gave the soup a fresh finish. Instant barley is sometimes labeled quick barley. The cooked pot roast and pan juices in this recipe are from Pot Roast in Foil on page 227.

1	tablespoon vegetable oil
8	ounces white mushrooms, trimmed and sliced thin
1	onion, chopped
	Salt and pepper
1	tablespoon tomato paste
¾	teaspoon minced fresh thyme or ¼ teaspoon dried
7	cups chicken broth
1	cup pot roast pan juices
4	carrots, peeled and cut into ¼-inch pieces
¾	cup instant barley
2	tablespoons soy sauce
1	pound cooked pot roast, shredded (4 cups)
2	tablespoons chopped fresh parsley

1. Heat oil in Dutch oven over medium heat until shimmering. Add mushrooms and cook, stirring occasionally, until released liquid has evaporated and mushrooms are softened, 5 to 8 minutes. Stir in onion and ½ teaspoon salt and cook until onion is softened and vegetables are lightly browned, 5 to 8 minutes.

2. Stir in tomato paste and thyme and cook until fragrant, about 30 seconds. Stir in broth, pot roast pan juices, carrots, barley, and soy sauce and bring to simmer. Cover, reduce heat to medium-low, and cook until carrots and barley are tender, about 20 minutes.

3. Stir in shredded beef and cook until heated through, about 2 minutes. Stir in parsley and season with salt and pepper to taste. Serve.

TEST KITCHEN TIP TRIMMING MUSHROOMS

White mushrooms have tender stems that can be sliced and cooked alongside the mushroom caps. Simply trim off a thin slice from the bottom of the stem.

THE MENU

THE BIG ROAST Roast
Butterflied Leg of Lamb
with Coriander, Cumin, and
Mustard Seeds

THE SECOND MEAL Lamb
Shawarma
OR Greek Salad with Lamb

Roast Butterflied Leg of Lamb with Coriander, Cumin, and Mustard Seeds

SERVES 6 WITH LEFTOVERS • **TO PREP** 1 HOUR 15 MINUTES • **TO COOK** 1 HOUR

✔ **WHY THIS RECIPE WORKS:** Swapping in a butterflied leg of lamb for the usual bone-in or boned, rolled, and tied leg-of-lamb options provided us with a number of benefits: the ability to season it thoroughly, a great ratio of crust to meat, and faster, more even cooking. Salting the roast for an hour before cooking seasoned the meat and kept it moist. By first roasting the lamb in a 250-degree oven, we were able to cook the meat gently, keeping it juicy; then a quick blast under the broiler crisped and browned the exterior to give the lamb a flavorful crust. We ditched the usual dry spice rub (which had a tendency to scorch under the broiler) in favor of a slow-cooked, spice-infused oil that flavored the lamb as it cooked. To give spiced oil Mediterranean flavors, we chose a combination of coriander, cumin, mustard seeds, and lemon. The leftover roast lamb was moist and deeply flavored—perfect for making lamb shawarma or a Greek salad without a lot of extra work. We prefer the subtler flavor and larger size of lamb labeled domestic or American for this recipe. The amount of salt (2 tablespoons) in step 1 is for a 6-pound leg. If using a larger leg (7 to 8 pounds), add an additional teaspoon of salt for every pound.

- 1 **(6- to 8-pound) butterflied leg of lamb**
- 2 **tablespoons kosher salt**
- ⅓ **cup vegetable oil**
- 3 **shallots, sliced thin**
- 4 **garlic cloves, peeled and smashed**
- 1 **(1-inch) piece ginger, sliced into ½-inch-thick rounds and smashed**
- 1 **tablespoon coriander seeds**
- 1 **tablespoon cumin seeds**
- 1 **tablespoon mustard seeds**
- 3 **bay leaves**
- 2 **(2-inch) strips lemon zest**

TO PREP

1. Place lamb on cutting board with fat cap facing down. Using sharp knife, trim any pockets of fat and connective tissue from underside of lamb. Flip lamb over, trim fat cap so it's between ⅛ and ¼ inch thick, and pound roast to even 1-inch thickness. Cut slits, spaced ½ inch apart, in fat cap in crosshatch pattern, being careful to cut down to but not into meat. Rub salt over entire roast and into slits in fat. Let sit, uncovered, at room temperature for 1 hour.

2. Meanwhile, adjust oven racks to lower-middle position and 4 to 5 inches from broiler element; heat oven to 250 degrees. Stir together oil, shallots, garlic, ginger, coriander seeds, cumin seeds, mustard seeds, bay leaves, and lemon zest in rimmed baking sheet and bake on lower rack until spices are softened and fragrant and shallots and garlic turn golden, about 1 hour. Remove sheet from oven and discard bay leaves.

TO COOK

3. Thoroughly pat lamb dry with paper towels and transfer, fat side up, to sheet (directly on top of spices). Roast on lower rack until lamb registers 120 degrees, 30 to 40 minutes. Remove sheet from oven and heat broiler. Broil lamb on upper rack until surface is well browned and charred in spots and lamb registers 125 degrees (for medium-rare), 3 to 8 minutes.

4. Remove sheet from oven and, using 2 pairs of tongs, transfer lamb to carving board (some spices will cling to bottom of roast); tent loosely with aluminum foil and let rest for 20 minutes.

5. Set aside 1 pound trimmed lamb. Slice remaining lamb with grain into 2 equal pieces. Turn each piece and slice across grain into ¼-inch-thick slices. Serve.

> ### SAVE IT
>
> Reserved 1 pound lamb can be used to make either Lamb Shawarma (page 232) or Greek Salad with Lamb (page 233). Refrigerate reserved lamb for up to 2 days.

Lamb Shawarma

SERVES 4 • **TO PREP AND COOK** 35 MINUTES

✔ **WHY THIS RECIPE WORKS:** When we crave Turkish lamb shawarma—sandwiches of spiced lamb, parsley, lettuce, and cucumber-yogurt sauce wrapped in a warm pita—we usually head for the nearest Middle Eastern restaurant. But with juicy leftover roast lamb on hand, we could easily create a flavorful alternative at home. Shawarma is traditionally slices of crispy meat with a moist, tender interior shaved from a vertical rotisserie. We were able to create a great home-style version using a hot oiled skillet. We thinly sliced the leftover lamb and pan-fried it with ground cumin, coriander, and cardamom. Topped with lettuce, tomato, parsley, and yogurt sauce, these home-style shawarma are a satisfying version of the classic. If you don't have tahini, you can make the sauce without it, but you may need to increase the amount of seasonings. Cumin seeds and coriander seeds are both used in the roast leg of lamb; you can grind the whole spices in a spice grinder or a coffee grinder to make ground cumin and coriander for this recipe. For easier slicing, place the lamb in the freezer for 15 minutes before slicing. The cooked lamb in this recipe is from Roast Butterflied Leg of Lamb with Coriander, Cumin, and Mustard Seeds on page 231.

YOGURT-TAHINI SAUCE

- ¼ cup plain yogurt
- 2 tablespoons tahini
- 2 tablespoons lemon juice
- 2 teaspoons minced fresh parsley
- 1 garlic clove, minced
  Salt and pepper

SANDWICHES

- 3 tablespoons vegetable oil
- 1 teaspoon ground cumin
- 1 teaspoon ground coriander
- ½ teaspoon ground cardamom
- 1 pound cooked lamb, sliced thin (1¾ cups)
- ¼ cup minced fresh parsley
  Salt and pepper
- 4 (6-inch) pita breads, warmed
- 2 cups chopped iceberg or romaine lettuce
- 2 plum tomatoes, cored and chopped
- 2 shallots, sliced thin

1. FOR THE YOGURT-TAHINI SAUCE: Combine yogurt, tahini, lemon juice, parsley, garlic, and ¼ teaspoon salt in bowl. Season with salt and pepper to taste, cover, and refrigerate until needed.

2. FOR THE SANDWICHES: Heat oil in 12-inch non-stick skillet over medium-high heat until shimmering. Add cumin, coriander, and cardamom and cook, stirring constantly, until spices are fragrant and just beginning to brown, about 1 minute. Add sliced lamb, breaking up any clumps, and cook until just beginning to crisp, 2 to 3 minutes. Off heat, stir in 2 tablespoons parsley and season with salt and pepper to taste.

3. Spread ¼ cup yogurt-tahini sauce in center of each warmed pita, then divide lamb mixture evenly among pitas. Top with remaining 2 tablespoons parsley, lettuce, tomatoes, and shallots. Wrap pitas around filling and serve.

Greek Salad with Lamb

SERVES 4 • **TO PREP AND COOK** 35 MINUTES

✓ **WHY THIS RECIPE WORKS:** Searching for another recipe where our fragrant spiced leftover lamb could take center stage, we turned to an Americanized Greek classic: Greek salad. We wanted to breathe new life into this salad by adding our fragrant leftover cooked lamb. But first we needed to perfect the salad and eliminate its main problems: pale lettuce, watery vegetables, and a greasy pool of dressing at the bottom of the bowl. To reduce the amount of liquid released from the vegetables, we seeded the cucumbers and used fleshy cherry tomatoes rather than the larger (and juicier) tomatoes traditionally called for in Greek salad recipes. To blend the flavors of the salad, we marinated the sliced shallots and cucumbers in the dressing for 20 minutes before tossing together the rest of the salad. Fresh mint, crumbled feta cheese, and briny kalamata olives rounded out the traditional flavors. When the salad was tossed with our juicy roast lamb, we had a flavorful, hearty dinner. The cooked lamb in this recipe is from Roast Butterflied Leg of Lamb with Coriander, Cumin, and Mustard Seeds on page 231.

DRESSING

- ¼ **cup red wine vinegar**
- 1 **garlic clove, minced**
- 1 **teaspoon minced fresh oregano or ¼ teaspoon dried**
- ½ **teaspoon salt**
- ⅛ **teaspoon sugar**
- ⅓ **cup extra-virgin olive oil**

SALAD

- 2 **cucumbers, peeled, halved lengthwise, seeded, and sliced ½ inch thick**
- 2 **shallots, sliced thin**
- 1 **pound cooked lamb, sliced thin (1¾ cups)**
- 2 **romaine lettuce hearts (12 ounces), torn into bite-size pieces**
- 12 **ounces grape or cherry tomatoes, halved**
- 2 **tablespoons minced fresh mint or parsley Salt and pepper**
- 4 **ounces feta cheese, crumbled (1 cup)**
- ½ **cup pitted kalamata olives, quartered**

1. FOR THE DRESSING: Whisk vinegar, garlic, oregano, salt, and sugar together in large bowl. Whisking constantly, drizzle in oil.

2. FOR THE SALAD: Stir cucumbers and shallots into bowl with dressing and let sit at room temperature until flavors blend, about 20 minutes. Add sliced lamb, lettuce, tomatoes, and mint and gently toss to combine. Season with salt and pepper to taste. Sprinkle with feta and olives and serve.

TEST KITCHEN TIP **CRUMBLING FETA CHEESE**

To crumble feta cheese neatly, place in bowl and use fork to break off small pieces from block. Continue to break up pieces with fork until crumbles are desired size.

SLOW-COOKER SICILIAN CHICKPEA AND ESCAROLE SOUP

Come Home
to Dinner

EASY SLOW-COOKER FAVORITES

Slow-Cooker Beef and Barley Soup

SERVES 6 TO 8 • **TO PREP** 25 MINUTES • **TO COOK** 9 TO 10 HOURS ON LOW OR 6 TO 7 HOURS ON HIGH
TO FINISH 15 MINUTES

✓ **WHY THIS RECIPE WORKS:** To build a flavorful base for this simple but comforting soup in a slow cooker, we started by microwaving the aromatics with some oil to help bloom their flavors. This simple step made a world of difference in the soup's flavor and allowed us to skip the tedious process of browning the meat. To further simplify things we used trimmed beef blade steak, which we shredded after it had become meltingly tender in the slow cooker—no need to cut the meat into pieces to start. A mix of equal parts beef and chicken broth balanced this soup perfectly, and, as with all our slow-cooker beef soups and stews, soy sauce added a surprising amount of flavor. Since pearl barley can absorb two to three times its volume of cooking liquid, we needed to be judicious in the quantity we added to the soup. A modest ¼ cup was all that was needed to lend a pleasing velvety texture without overfilling the slow cooker with swollen grains. You will need a 5½- to 7-quart slow cooker for this recipe.

3	onions, chopped fine
2	tablespoons tomato paste
2	tablespoons vegetable oil
1	tablespoon minced fresh thyme or 1 teaspoon dried
1	(28-ounce) can crushed tomatoes
2	cups beef broth
2	cups chicken broth
2	carrots, peeled and chopped
⅓	cup soy sauce
¼	cup dry red wine
¼	cup pearl barley
2	pounds beef blade steaks, trimmed
	Salt and pepper

TO FINISH AND SERVE

¼	cup minced fresh parsley

TO PREP

1. Microwave onions, tomato paste, oil, and thyme in bowl, stirring occasionally, until onions are softened, about 5 minutes; transfer to slow cooker. Stir in tomatoes, beef broth, chicken broth, carrots, soy sauce, wine, and barley. Season beef with salt and pepper and nestle into slow cooker.

TO COOK

2. Cover and cook until beef is tender, 9 to 10 hours on low or 6 to 7 hours on high.

TO FINISH AND SERVE

3. Transfer beef to cutting board, let cool slightly, then shred into bite-size pieces using 2 forks, discarding excess fat. Skim excess fat from surface of soup.

4. Stir in shredded beef and let sit until heated through, about 5 minutes. Stir in parsley, season with salt and pepper to taste, and serve.

NIGHT TIME PREP

- Carrots can be chopped; refrigerate.
- Blade steaks can be trimmed and seasoned; refrigerate.
- Onion mixture can be microwaved; cool to room temperature and refrigerate.

Slow-Cooker Turkey and Wild Rice Soup

SERVES 8 • **TO PREP** 25 MINUTES • **TO COOK** 9 TO 10 HOURS ON LOW OR 6 TO 7 HOURS ON HIGH
TO FINISH 45 MINUTES

✓ **WHY THIS RECIPE WORKS:** Turkey soup is a dish perfectly suited for a slow cooker. The hearty flavor of turkey translates easily into a full-flavored soup without requiring any tricks, and turkey thighs (which we prefer for soup) seem to have been designed for the slow cooker's low and steady cooking environment. Turkey thighs, which are made up entirely of dark meat, are quite big and thick, which means they are nearly impossible to overcook and have lots of flavor to spare. (As a bonus, they're cheap, too!) Do not substitute a turkey breast for the thighs; the breast will not cook at the same rate as the thighs and will produce too much meat for the soup. We like the flavor of a wild and white rice blend in this soup; however, you can substitute ½ cup of long-grain white rice. You will need a 5½- to 7-quart slow cooker for this recipe.

2   onions, chopped fine
4   garlic cloves, minced
1   tablespoon vegetable oil
1   tablespoon tomato paste
2   teaspoons minced fresh thyme or
     ½ teaspoon dried
8   cups chicken broth
3   carrots, peeled and sliced ¼ inch thick
2   celery ribs, sliced ¼ inch thick
2   bay leaves
2   (1-pound) bone-in turkey thighs, skin
     removed, thighs trimmed
     Salt and pepper

TO FINISH AND SERVE
½   cup long-grain white rice and wild rice blend
2   tablespoons minced fresh parsley

TO PREP

1. Microwave onions, garlic, oil, tomato paste, and thyme in bowl, stirring occasionally, until onions are softened, about 5 minutes; transfer to slow cooker. Stir in broth, carrots, celery, and bay leaves. Season turkey with salt and pepper and nestle into slow cooker.

TO COOK

2. Cover and cook until turkey is tender, 9 to 10 hours on low or 6 to 7 hours on high.

TO FINISH AND SERVE

3. Transfer turkey to cutting board, let cool slightly, then shred into bite-size pieces using 2 forks, discarding bones. Skim excess fat from surface of soup. Discard bay leaves.

4. Stir in rice, cover, and cook on high until rice is tender, 30 to 40 minutes. Stir in shredded turkey and let sit until heated through, about 5 minutes. Stir in parsley, season with salt and pepper to taste, and serve.

NIGHT TIME PREP

- Carrots and celery can be sliced; refrigerate.
- Turkey thighs can be trimmed and seasoned; refrigerate.
- Onion mixture can be microwaved; cool to room temperature and refrigerate.

USE TURKEY THIGHS

We use large turkey thighs for this soup because they have great flavor and are impossible to overcook. Removing the skin keeps the soup from becoming greasy. Once the turkey is cooked, we remove the thighs and shred the meat, then we add the rice and let it cook through before returning the meat to the soup to warm through.

Slow-Cooker Japanese Pork and Ramen Soup

SERVES 8 • **TO PREP** 20 MINUTES • **TO COOK** 7 TO 8 HOURS ON LOW OR 4 TO 5 HOURS ON HIGH
TO FINISH 25 MINUTES

✔ **WHY THIS RECIPE WORKS:** A great ramen soup requires a great broth, and to accomplish this in a slow cooker we enhanced store-bought chicken broth with onions, garlic, and ginger at the beginning of cooking, then stirred in white miso (fermented soybean paste), soy sauce, mirin (Japanese rice wine), and sesame oil at the end. The combination of slow-cooked boneless country-style pork ribs, which are easy to shred after cooking, and hearty shiitakes imparted an intense, meaty flavor to the finished soup. Fresh spinach, stirred in at the end, added an earthy flavor, and supermarket ramen noodles cooked perfectly in the same amount of time as the spinach. You will need a 5½- to 7-quart slow cooker for this recipe.

2	onions, chopped fine
6	garlic cloves, minced
2	tablespoons grated fresh ginger
1	tablespoon vegetable oil
8	cups chicken broth
12	ounces shiitake mushrooms, stemmed and sliced thin
1½	pounds boneless country-style pork ribs, trimmed
	Salt and pepper

TO FINISH AND SERVE

2	(3-ounce) packages ramen noodles, seasoning packets discarded
6	ounces (6 cups) baby spinach
2	tablespoons white miso, plus extra for serving
2	tablespoons soy sauce, plus extra for serving
1	tablespoon mirin
1	teaspoon toasted sesame oil
2	scallions, sliced thin
1	tablespoon sesame seeds, toasted

TO PREP

1. Microwave onions, garlic, ginger, and vegetable oil in bowl, stirring occasionally, until onions are softened, about 5 minutes; transfer to slow cooker. Stir in broth and mushrooms. Season pork with salt and pepper and nestle into slow cooker.

TO COOK

2. Cover and cook until pork is tender, 7 to 8 hours on low or 4 to 5 hours on high.

TO FINISH AND SERVE

3. Transfer pork to cutting board, let cool slightly, then shred into bite-size pieces using 2 forks, discarding excess fat. Skim excess fat from surface of soup.

4. Stir in noodles and spinach, cover, and cook on high until noodles are tender, about 8 minutes. Stir in shredded pork, miso, soy sauce, mirin, and sesame oil and let sit until heated through, about 5 minutes. Season with extra miso and extra soy sauce to taste. Sprinkle individual portions with scallions and sesame seeds before serving.

NIGHT TIME PREP

- Mushrooms can be sliced; refrigerate.
- Pork can be trimmed and seasoned; refrigerate.
- Onion mixture can be microwaved; cool to room temperature and refrigerate.

A FRESH FINISH IS KEY
For a Japanese-style soup that lived up to its name, we added the ramen noodles and spinach at the end of the long cooking time—after just 8 minutes they were the right texture. Meanwhile, we shredded the tender pork ribs and returned them to the slow cooker along with miso, soy sauce, mirin, and sesame oil.

Slow-Cooker Southern Black-Eyed Pea Soup

SERVES 6 • **TO PREP** 15 MINUTES • **TO COOK** 9 TO 10 HOURS ON LOW OR 6 TO 7 HOURS ON HIGH
TO FINISH 35 MINUTES

✔ **WHY THIS RECIPE WORKS:** The slow cooker is the perfect environment for turning dried beans into a creamy, flavorful soup. We wanted to take advantage of this with a classic Southern-style black-eyed pea soup. To give our soup plenty of kick, we added Cajun seasoning and kielbasa sausage. To build flavor, we browned the sausage in a skillet and then sautéed the onions, garlic, and Cajun seasoning, transferring them to the slow cooker to simmer away with the beans and a combination of chicken broth and water. The only prep the black-eyed peas needed was to be quickly picked over (to remove any small stones or debris) and rinsed. Then we added them right into the slow cooker where they gently simmered, absorbing the flavors of the sausage, aromatics, and seasonings, until they were perfectly cooked. Collard greens and rice, stirred in during the final 30 minutes of cooking, turned perfectly tender and added color and heft. Because kielbasa can be quite salty, be careful when seasoning the soup with additional salt.

1 tablespoon vegetable oil
8 ounces kielbasa sausage, halved lengthwise and sliced ½ inch thick
2 onions, chopped
3 garlic cloves, minced
1 teaspoon Cajun seasoning
6 cups chicken broth
2 cups water
8 ounces (1¼ cups) dried black-eyed peas, picked over and rinsed

TO FINISH AND SERVE
1 pound collard greens, stemmed and cut into 1-inch pieces
½ cup long-grain white rice and wild rice blend
1 teaspoon hot sauce
   Salt and pepper

TO PREP

1. Heat oil in 12-inch skillet over medium-high heat until shimmering. Brown sausage on all sides, about 5 minutes; transfer to slow cooker.

2. Add onions to now-empty skillet and cook until softened and lightly browned, 5 to 7 minutes. Stir in garlic and Cajun seasoning and cook until fragrant, about 30 seconds; transfer to slow cooker. Stir in broth, water, and peas.

TO COOK

3. Cover and cook until peas are tender, 9 to 10 hours on low or 6 to 7 hours on high.

TO FINISH AND SERVE

4. Stir in collard greens and rice, cover, and cook on high until rice is tender, 30 to 40 minutes. Stir in hot sauce and season with salt, pepper, and extra hot sauce to taste.

NIGHT TIME PREP

• Sausage and onion mixture can be cooked; transfer to bowl, cool to room temperature, and refrigerate.
• Collard greens can be cut; refrigerate.

Slow-Cooker Sicilian Chickpea and Escarole Soup

SERVES 6 • **TO PREP** 20 MINUTES • **TO COOK** 10 TO 11 HOURS ON LOW OR 7 TO 8 HOURS ON HIGH
TO FINISH 20 MINUTES

✓ **WHY THIS RECIPE WORKS:** Most Italian soups usually feature cannellini beans, but in Sicily, chickpeas are the favored legume for soup. To create a Sicilian-style bean soup in our slow cooker, we started with some classic flavors of the region: olive oil, garlic, oregano, and red pepper flakes. Fennel, which grows wild throughout much of the Mediterranean and is common in Sicilian cooking, made a great addition; its mild anise bite complemented the nutty chickpeas. A couple of minced anchovies added a subtle meatiness (without adding fishiness). We also incorporated a leftover Parmesan rind, simmering it in the broth so that it could lend a richness and complexity that bolstered the broth's flavor. We preferred dried chickpeas over canned; by the time the flavors of the soup had melded, the chickpeas were just tender. Escarole, stirred in at the end, perfectly rounded out our Sicilian soup, adding freshness and a nice light crunch. You will need a 5½- to 7-quart slow cooker for this recipe.

2   fennel bulbs, stalks discarded, bulbs halved, cored, and chopped
1   tablespoon extra-virgin olive oil, plus extra for seasoning
3   garlic cloves, minced
2   teaspoons minced fresh oregano or ½ teaspoon dried
2   anchovy fillets, rinsed and minced
¼   teaspoon red pepper flakes
7   cups chicken broth
8   ounces (1¼ cups) dried chickpeas, picked over and rinsed
1   Parmesan cheese rind (optional)

TO FINISH AND SERVE
½   head escarole (8 ounces), trimmed and chopped coarse
    Salt and pepper
    Grated Parmesan cheese

TO PREP
1. Microwave fennel, oil, garlic, oregano, anchovies, and pepper flakes in bowl, stirring occasionally, until fennel is softened, about 5 minutes; transfer to slow cooker. Stir in broth, chickpeas, and Parmesan rind, if using.

TO COOK
2. Cover and cook until chickpeas are tender, 10 to 11 hours on low or 7 to 8 hours on high.

TO FINISH AND SERVE
3. Discard Parmesan rind. Stir in escarole, cover, and cook on high until tender, about 15 minutes. Season with salt and pepper to taste. Drizzle individual portions with extra oil and serve with grated Parmesan.

NIGHT TIME PREP
- Fennel mixture can be microwaved; cool to room temperature and refrigerate.
- Escarole can be chopped; refrigerate.

TEST KITCHEN TIP CORING FENNEL

Trim thin slice from base of fennel bulb. Remove tough or blemished outer layers, then cut bulb in half through base. Using small, sharp knife, cut into base of fennel to remove pyramid-shaped core.

Slow-Cooker Garden Minestrone

SERVES 8 • **TO PREP** 15 MINUTES • **TO COOK** 9 TO 10 HOURS ON LOW OR 6 TO 7 HOURS ON HIGH
TO FINISH 25 MINUTES

✔ **WHY THIS RECIPE WORKS:** Creating anything garden-fresh in a slow cooker is a tall order, but we were willing to try to beat the odds and develop a recipe for a bright, lively tasting minestrone that married a flavorful tomato broth with fresh vegetables, beans, and pasta. The base of our soup would be our broth, and after microwaving the aromatics with oil and some tomato paste, we added store-bought chicken broth and dried beans—which could sustain a long stay in a slow cooker. Sliced zucchini and chopped chard were added during the last 30 minutes of cooking along with the pasta. Be sure to finish this soup with additional olive oil and freshly grated Parmesan for a final burst of flavor. You will need a 5½- to 7-quart slow cooker for this recipe.

1   onion, chopped fine
2   tablespoons tomato paste
4   garlic cloves, minced
1   tablespoon extra-virgin olive oil, plus extra for serving
1½ teaspoons minced fresh oregano or ½ teaspoon dried
⅛   teaspoon red pepper flakes
7   cups chicken broth
1   cup dried great Northern or cannellini beans, picked over and rinsed

TO FINISH AND SERVE
1   zucchini, quartered lengthwise and sliced ¼ inch thick
8   ounces Swiss chard, cut into 1-inch pieces
½   cup small pasta, such as ditalini, tubettini, or elbow macaroni
1   pound tomatoes, cored and cut into ½-inch pieces
¼   cup minced fresh basil
    Salt and pepper
    Grated Parmesan cheese

TO PREP

1. Microwave onion, tomato paste, garlic, oil, oregano, and pepper flakes in bowl, stirring occasionally, until onion is softened, about 5 minutes; transfer to slow cooker. Stir in broth and beans.

TO COOK

2. Cover and cook until beans are tender, 9 to 10 hours on low or 6 to 7 hours on high.

TO FINISH AND SERVE

3. Stir in zucchini, chard, pasta, and tomatoes; cover and cook on high until vegetables and pasta are tender, 20 to 30 minutes. Stir in basil, season with salt and pepper to taste, and serve with Parmesan and extra oil.

NIGHT TIME PREP

- Onion mixture can be microwaved; cool to room temperature and refrigerate.
- Zucchini and Swiss chard can be prepared; refrigerate.

TEST KITCHEN TIP **PREPARING SWISS CHARD**

Cut away leafy green portion from either side of stem using chef's knife. Then stack several leaves on top of one another and slice crosswise into strips.

Slow-Cooker Wheat Berry and Wild Mushroom Stew

SERVES 6 • **TO PREP** 20 MINUTES • **TO COOK** 10 TO 11 HOURS ON LOW OR 7 TO 8 HOURS ON HIGH
TO FINISH 10 MINUTES

✓ **WHY THIS RECIPE WORKS:** For a vegetarian stew that was so flavorful and substantial even carnivores would be satisfied, we started with sweet, nutty wheat berries and added mushrooms for earthy, meaty depth. The wheat berries were hearty enough to withstand the long cooking time of the slow cooker, yet still maintain their chewy texture. Including two types of mushrooms—sliced cremini and dried porcini—ensured that our stew had tender bites of mushroom and intense, earthy flavor. To reinforce the woodsy notes of the mushrooms, we included thyme. Vegetable broth worked well for the cooking liquid and provided a subtly sweet backbone. To give it a boost, we stirred in some Madeira; adding more of the fortified wine at the end of cooking contributed brightness to our hearty stew. Baby spinach provided some color and freshness. Finally, for a hint of richness, we stirred in a couple of pats of butter. The wheat berries will retain a chewy texture once fully cooked. You can substitute dry sherry for the Madeira if desired.

2	pounds cremini mushrooms, trimmed and sliced
1	tablespoon vegetable oil
3	garlic cloves, minced
2	teaspoons minced fresh thyme or ½ teaspoon dried
6	cups vegetable broth, plus extra as needed
1½	cups wheat berries
½	cup dry Madeira
½	ounce dried porcini mushrooms, rinsed and minced
	Salt and pepper

TO FINISH AND SERVE

6	ounces (6 cups) baby spinach
2	tablespoons unsalted butter

TO PREP

1. Microwave cremini mushrooms, oil, garlic, and thyme in bowl, stirringly occasionally, until mushrooms are softened, about 5 minutes; transfer to slow cooker. Stir in broth, wheat berries, 6 tablespoons Madeira, porcini mushrooms, and ½ teaspoon salt.

TO COOK

2. Cover and cook until wheat berries are tender, 10 to 11 hours on low or 7 to 8 hours on high.

TO FINISH AND SERVE

3. Stir in spinach, 1 handful at a time, and let sit until wilted, about 5 minutes. (Adjust stew consistency with extra hot broth as needed.) Stir in butter and remaining 2 tablespoons Madeira and season with salt and pepper to taste. Serve.

NIGHT TIME PREP

• Porcini mushrooms can be minced; refrigerate.
• Cremini mushroom mixture can be microwaved; cool to room temperature and refrigerate.

ALL ABOUT Using a Slow Cooker

The slow cooker is a great tool for making meals ahead—with a modest investment of up-front prep time, you can come home to a hot and ready meal with rich, complex flavor thanks to hours of gentle simmering. For slow-cooker recipes that cater to the make-ahead cook, we focused on recipes that we could get into the slow cooker quickly (some in just 15 minutes) and that could cook all day without worry of drying out or overcooking. To make mornings even easier, we figured out what prep work can be done the night before so that in the morning we could just dump and go. We also include several big-batch pasta sauces perfect for stashing in the freezer; they're great recipes to make in a slow cooker because they can simmer for hours unattended, developing great flavor completely hands-off.

Choosing a Slow Cooker

Today's slow cookers come in a wide array of sizes with lots of different features. In our recipe testing for this book, we found 5½- to 7-quart slow cookers to be the most versatile because they could accommodate generous batches of soups, stews, and pasta sauces as well large roasts.

To find out which models performed best and which features really mattered, we tested seven large (6-quart capacity or more) slow cookers to prepare pot roast, meaty tomato sauce, and French onion soup. In short, the features we liked included programmable timers, warming modes, and clear glass lids (which allow the cook to assess the food as it cooks). Inserts that have handles, which make it easy to remove the insert from the slow cooker, and that can be washed in the dishwasher earned extra points.

We rated each slow cooker on cooking ability and design. We also devised a test to measure the maximum temperatures of the models on high and low settings; we found that some models didn't get hot enough, whereas others hovered around or hit the boiling point. The best models quickly brought food into the safe zone (above 140 degrees), then climbed slowly to the boiling point or just below it over a period of hours rather than reaching the boiling point right away and overcooking food.

In the end, the **KitchenAid 6-Quart Slow Cooker with Solid Glass Lid**, $99.99, was our favorite. We found its control panel extremely easy to use, and the timer counted up to 20 hours, even on high. Sunday gravy thickened to the correct consistency, pot roast was tender and sliceable, and onions caramelized perfectly every time.

Get to Know Your Slow Cooker

Some models run hot and fast, while others heat more slowly and gently. Most models perform best on low, but it's hard to make blanket statements that will apply to all slow cookers. In our testing, we have found that some slow cookers run hot or cool on just one of the settings (either low or high). This is where the cook's experience comes into play. If you have been using a slow cooker for some time, ask yourself if recipes are generally done at the low or high end of the cooking times provided in recipes. The answer should tell you whether you have a "fast" slow cooker or a "slow" model. If you are just getting started with your slow cooker, check all recipes at the beginning of the time range but allow some extra time to cook food longer if necessary.

Keeping Food Safe

For safety reasons, the internal temperature of meat and poultry should reach 140 degrees (the temperature at which bacteria cannot grow) by the 2-hour mark in the cooking time. When you first start using your slow cooker, we suggest that you check the temperature of meat or chicken at this stage to be sure this is happening. If your food doesn't reach this safety zone when cooking on low, you might be able to solve the problem by using the high setting. Note that putting frozen meat or other frozen food into any slow cooker is dangerous as it will dramatically increase the amount of time it takes your food to reach this safe zone.

Speed Up Prep with the Microwave

Oddly enough, the fastest appliance in your kitchen, your microwave, can come in handy when using the slowest appliance in your kitchen, your slow cooker. When browning meat isn't necessary, we often turn to the microwave to save time (and dirty skillets) and to create dishes that are fresher-tasting, with vegetables that are cooked to perfection. Rather than cook aromatics and spices on the stovetop to bloom their flavors, we simply microwave them for a few minutes. We also use the microwave to parcook delicate vegetables before adding them to the slow cooker at the end of cooking to ensure that they remain colorful and crisp-tender.

Place aromatics (such as onions, garlic, celery, and ginger) and any spices along with vegetable oil in bowl and microwave, stirring occasionally, until softened, about 5 minutes.

Don't Skimp on the Aromatics

Because the moist heat environment and long cooking times that come with the slow cooker tend to dull flavors, we call for generous amounts of onions, garlic, herbs, and other flavorful ingredients in our recipes. We also use umami-rich ingredients like tomato paste, soy sauce, and anchovies to ramp up the meaty richness of everything from soups and stews to pasta sauces. And to give the recipes a bright flavor boost at the end of the cooking time, we often finish with fresh herbs, lemon or lime juice, or other flavorful ingredients.

Finish with Quick-Cooking Ingredients

To ensure that our slow-cooker recipes would fit into a busy schedule, we wanted recipes that could cook all day and be ready in time for dinner. However, some ingredients like delicate vegetables, pasta, and grains can't hold up to hours of cooking without ending up mushy and blown out. So we add them at the end, crank the heat up to high, and cook them until tender. For a perfect garden minestrone, we simmer the broth and hearty vegetables for hours to develop complex flavor, then add zucchini, Swiss chard, and pasta; in just 20 minutes, the vegetables and pasta are perfectly tender. More delicate vegetables like spinach and artichokes need just 10 minutes to cook. For slightly firmer vegetables like bell peppers, a quick stint in the microwave before adding them to the slow cooker ensures that they remain colorful and crisp-tender.

Making a Foil Packet

During the long cooking time in the slow cooker, even hearty vegetables can begin to break down and lose their shape. To prevent this, we place the vegetables in a foil packet and nestle it into the slow cooker. The packet helps to protect the vegetables so that they turn tender but remain distinct.

Place vegetables on one side of large piece of aluminum foil. Fold foil over vegetables and crimp edges to seal packet. Place packet on top of ingredients in slow cooker, pressing packet gently as needed to help it fit.

Slow-Cooker Hearty Beef Stew

SERVES 6 TO 8 • **TO PREP** 45 MINUTES • **TO COOK** 9 TO 10 HOURS ON LOW OR 6 TO 7 HOURS ON HIGH
TO FINISH 10 MINUTES

✔ **WHY THIS RECIPE WORKS:** Achieving big, bold, beefy flavor in a beef stew typically starts with browning the meat, but we wanted maximum flavor without all the labor. To avoid browning the meat and still achieve a blue-ribbon beef stew, we enlisted the help of tomato paste—which we browned with the other aromatics—to create a rich, complex base. A combination of chicken and beef broths also helped pump up the meaty notes, though it was the unlikely addition of soy sauce that finally took this stew to the next level. We kept the potatoes and carrots tender but distinct during the long cooking time by placing them in a foil packet on top of the stew. For more information on making a foil packet, see page 249. You will need a 5½- to 7-quart slow cooker for this recipe.

3	tablespoons vegetable oil
3	onions, chopped
¼	cup tomato paste
6	garlic cloves, minced
1	tablespoon minced fresh thyme or 1 teaspoon dried
⅓	cup all-purpose flour
1½	cups chicken broth, plus extra as needed
1½	cups beef broth
⅓	cup soy sauce
2	bay leaves
4	pounds boneless beef chuck-eye roast, trimmed and cut into 1½-inch pieces
	Salt and pepper
1½	pounds red potatoes, unpeeled, cut into 1-inch pieces
1	pound carrots, peeled, halved lengthwise, and sliced 1 inch thick

TO FINISH AND SERVE

2	cups frozen peas

TO PREP

1. Heat 2 tablespoons oil in 12-inch skillet over medium heat until shimmering. Add onions and cook until softened and lightly browned, 8 to 10 minutes. Stir in tomato paste, garlic, and thyme and cook until fragrant, about 1 minute. Stir in flour and cook for 1 minute. Slowly whisk in chicken broth, scraping up any browned bits and smoothing out any lumps; transfer to slow cooker.

2. Stir in beef broth, soy sauce, and bay leaves. Season beef with salt and pepper and stir into slow cooker. Toss potatoes and carrots with remaining 1 tablespoon oil, season with salt and pepper, and wrap in foil packet. Lay foil packet on top of stew.

TO COOK

3. Cover and cook until beef is tender, 9 to 10 hours on low or 6 to 7 hours on high.

TO FINISH AND SERVE

4. Transfer foil packet to plate. Skim excess fat from surface of stew. Discard bay leaves.

5. Carefully open foil packet (watch for steam) and stir vegetables into stew along with any accumulated juices. Stir in peas and let sit until heated through, about 5 minutes. (Adjust stew consistency with extra hot chicken broth as needed.) Season with salt and pepper to taste. Serve.

NIGHT TIME PREP

• Potatoes and carrots can be prepared. Cover potatoes with water and refrigerate vegetables separately; drain potatoes before using.
• Beef can be cut and seasoned; refrigerate.
• Onion mixture can be cooked; transfer to bowl, cool to room temperature, and refrigerate.

MAKE A FOIL PACKET

Most stews emerge from the slow cooker with mushy, overcooked vegetables. To solve this problem, we wrapped the potatoes and carrots in a foil packet and placed it on top of the stew (we stirred the vegetables in at the end). To ensure a deeply flavorful stew, we found we needed to get out a skillet, sauté the aromatics, make a roux, and deglaze the pan with broth.

Slow-Cooker Mexican-Style Pork and Hominy Stew

SERVES 6 TO 8 • **TO PREP** 30 MINUTES • **TO COOK** 9 TO 10 HOURS ON LOW OR 6 TO 7 HOURS ON HIGH
TO FINISH 10 MINUTES

✔ **WHY THIS RECIPE WORKS:** Known as *pozole*, this fragrant and spicy stew is all about the combination of hominy, spices, and tender chunks of pork. To thicken this stew we pureed a can of hominy at the outset with chicken broth—this also added a nice base of corn flavor. A hefty amount of onions microwaved with equally generous amounts of aromatics and spices ensured that this was one flavorful stew. Soy sauce deepened the meaty flavor of the stew without calling any attention to itself. For more information on making a foil packet, see page 249. You will need a 5½- to 7-quart slow cooker for this recipe.

- 3 **(15-ounce) cans white or yellow hominy, rinsed**
- 3 **cups chicken broth, plus extra as needed**
- 3 **onions, chopped**
- ¼ **cup tomato paste**
- ¼ **cup vegetable oil**
- 6 **garlic cloves, minced**
- 2 **tablespoons chili powder**
- 2 **tablespoons minced fresh oregano or 2 teaspoons dried**
- 1 **(14.5-ounce) can diced tomatoes**
- ⅓ **cup soy sauce**
- 4 **pounds boneless pork butt roast, trimmed and cut into 1½-inch pieces**
  Salt and pepper
- 1 **pound carrots, peeled, halved lengthwise, and sliced 1 inch thick**

TO FINISH AND SERVE
- ¼ **cup minced fresh cilantro**
- 1 **tablespoon lime juice**

TO PREP

1. Process one-third of hominy and 2 cups broth in blender until smooth, about 1 minute; transfer to slow cooker.

2. Microwave onions, tomato paste, 3 tablespoons oil, garlic, chili powder, and oregano in bowl, stirring occasionally, until onions are softened, about 5 minutes; transfer to slow cooker. Stir in remaining hominy, remaining 1 cup broth, tomatoes and their juice, and soy sauce. Season pork with salt and pepper and stir into slow cooker.

3. Toss carrots with remaining 1 tablespoon oil, season with salt and pepper, and wrap in foil packet. Lay foil packet on top of stew.

TO COOK

4. Cover and cook until pork is tender, 9 to 10 hours on low or 6 to 7 hours on high.

TO FINISH AND SERVE

5. Transfer foil packet to plate. Skim excess fat from surface of stew. Carefully open foil packet (watch for steam) and stir carrots into stew along with any accumulated juice. (Adjust stew consistency with extra hot broth as needed.) Stir in cilantro and lime juice, season with salt and pepper to taste, and serve.

NIGHT TIME PREP

- Hominy can be rinsed and hominy mixture can be processed; refrigerate processed mixture and remaining unprocessed hominy together.
- Pork can be cut and seasoned; refrigerate.
- Carrots can be sliced, tossed with oil, seasoned, and wrapped in foil packet; refrigerate.
- Onion mixture can be microwaved; cool to room temperature and refrigerate.

Slow-Cooker Chickpea Tagine

SERVES 6 • **TO PREP** 20 MINUTES • **TO COOK** 10 TO 11 HOURS ON LOW OR 7 TO 8 HOURS ON HIGH
TO FINISH 25 MINUTES

✔️ **WHY THIS RECIPE WORKS:** This tagine (aka Moroccan-style stew) gets its complex flavor from a combination of sweet paprika and garam masala (a blend of warm spices), along with onions, garlic, and lemon zest, all of which perfume the sauce. Since many vegetables would be obliterated after hours in a slow cooker, we opted to stir in softened bell peppers and thawed frozen artichokes at the end, cooking them just enough to heat through. (Frozen artichokes are generally packaged already quartered; if yours are not, cut the artichoke hearts into quarters before using.) To continue with the Mediterranean flavor profile we added chopped kalamata olives and Greek-style yogurt to the stew. Golden raisins added a touch of sweetness, and fresh cilantro brightened up the dish before serving. You will need a 5½- to 7-quart slow cooker for this recipe.

2   **onions, chopped**
3   **tablespoons extra-virgin olive oil, plus extra for serving**
8   **garlic cloves, minced**
4   **teaspoons paprika**
2   **teaspoons garam masala**
¼   **teaspoon cayenne pepper**
7   **cups chicken broth, plus extra as needed**
2   **cups water**
1   **pound dried chickpeas (2½ cups), picked over and rinsed**
4   **(3-inch) strips lemon zest**
2   **bay leaves**

TO FINISH AND SERVE
2   **red or yellow bell peppers, stemmed, seeded, and cut into 1-inch pieces**
18   **ounces frozen artichoke hearts, thawed**
½   **cup pitted kalamata olives, chopped coarse**
½   **cup golden raisins**
½   **cup plain whole Greek yogurt**
½   **cup minced fresh cilantro**
    Salt and pepper

TO PREP

1. Microwave onions, 2 tablespoons oil, garlic, paprika, garam masala, and cayenne in bowl, stirring occasionally, until onions are softened, about 5 minutes; transfer to slow cooker. Stir in broth, water, chickpeas, lemon zest, and bay leaves.

TO COOK

2. Cover and cook until chickpeas are tender, 10 to 11 hours on low or 7 to 8 hours on high.

TO FINISH AND SERVE

3. Discard lemon zest and bay leaves. Transfer 2 cups chickpeas to bowl and mash with potato masher until mostly smooth, then return to slow cooker. Microwave bell peppers with remaining 1 tablespoon oil in bowl, stirring occasionally, until tender, about 5 minutes. Stir bell peppers, artichokes, olives, and raisins into stew, cover, and cook on high until heated through, about 10 minutes.

4. In bowl, combine ¼ cup hot stew liquid with yogurt (to temper), then stir mixture into stew with cilantro. (Adjust stew consistency with extra hot broth as needed.) Season with salt and pepper to taste. Drizzle individual portions with extra oil before serving.

NIGHT TIME PREP

• Onion mixture can be microwaved; cool to room temperature and refrigerate.
• Bell peppers and olives can be prepared; refrigerate.

Slow-Cooker Vegetarian Black Bean Chili

SERVES 6 TO 8 • **TO PREP** 25 MINUTES • **TO COOK** 9 TO 10 HOURS ON LOW OR 6 TO 7 HOURS ON HIGH
TO FINISH 15 MINUTES

WHY THIS RECIPE WORKS: Black bean chili is a hearty, satisfying dish and a great option for the slow cooker. But vegetarian versions are a bit trickier since there are no ham products, like meaty, smoky ham hocks, to build flavor over the long cooking time. To achieve the full flavors we expected from a traditional black bean chili, we started by microwaving generous amounts of aromatics and spices. This step was promising but got us only so far—the chili still seemed pretty lean. Though a bit odd for a chili, mustard seeds added an appealing pungency and the level of complexity we were looking for. To bulk up the chili, we added bell peppers, white mushrooms, and canned tomatoes. We added the tomatoes at the end because when added at the beginning, their acidity prevented the beans from cooking through fully. And while canned diced tomatoes were convenient, they took more time to turn tender than hand-cut whole canned tomatoes, so we chose whole instead. To make this dish spicier, add the chile seeds. Serve with your favorite chili garnishes.

2	onions, chopped
2	red bell peppers, stemmed, seeded, and chopped
2	jalapeño chiles, stemmed, seeded, and minced
3	tablespoons vegetable oil
9	garlic cloves, minced
3	tablespoons chili powder
4	teaspoons mustard seeds
1	tablespoon minced canned chipotle chile in adobo sauce
1	tablespoon ground cumin
1	tablespoon dried oregano
2½	cups vegetable broth
2½	cups water
1	pound (2½ cups) dried black beans, picked over and rinsed
10	ounces white mushrooms, trimmed and halved if small or quartered if large
2	bay leaves

TO FINISH AND SERVE

1	(28-ounce) can whole peeled tomatoes, drained and cut into ½-inch pieces
2	tablespoons minced fresh cilantro
	Salt and pepper

TO PREP

1. Microwave onions, bell peppers, jalapeños, oil, garlic, chili powder, mustard seeds, chipotle, cumin, and oregano in bowl, stirring occasionally, until vegetables are softened, about 5 minutes; transfer to slow cooker. Stir in broth, water, beans, mushrooms, and bay leaves.

TO COOK

2. Cover and cook until beans are tender, 9 to 10 hours on low or 6 to 7 hours on high.

TO FINISH AND SERVE

3. Discard bay leaves. Transfer 1 cup cooked beans to bowl and mash smooth with potato masher. Stir mashed beans and tomatoes into chili and let sit until heated through, about 5 minutes. Stir in cilantro, season with salt and pepper to taste, and serve.

NIGHT TIME PREP

- Mushrooms can be prepared; refrigerate.
- Onion mixture can be microwaved; cool to room temperature and refrigerate.
- Tomatoes can be cut into pieces; refrigerate.

Slow-Cooker Texas Chili

SERVES 8 TO 10 • **TO PREP** 30 MINUTES • **TO COOK** 9 TO 10 HOURS ON LOW OR 6 TO 7 HOURS ON HIGH
TO FINISH 5 MINUTES

✔ **WHY THIS RECIPE WORKS:** Texans are famous for their style of chili featuring big chunks of beef slowly simmered in a chile-infused sauce. For our slow-cooker version we chose generous chunks of beef chuck, which remained moist while still turning impressively tender. To achieve the characteristic rich and smooth sauce, we used tomato puree and seasoned it with hefty amounts of onions and garlic mixed with equally generous amounts of aromatics and spices. Canned chipotle chile and a little soy sauce added even more complexity of flavor. While beans are traditionally served alongside this chili, we liked the creaminess they provided when cooked with the meat, so we included them in the mix. You will need a 5½- to 7-quart slow cooker for this recipe. Serve with your favorite chili garnishes.

3	onions, chopped
¼	cup chili powder
¼	cup tomato paste
3	tablespoons vegetable oil
8	garlic cloves, minced
2	tablespoons ground cumin
1	tablespoon minced fresh oregano or 1 teaspoon dried
2	(15-ounce) cans dark red kidney beans, rinsed
1	(28-ounce) can tomato puree
2	cups chicken broth
¼	cup instant tapioca
3	tablespoons soy sauce
2	tablespoons minced canned chipotle chile in adobo sauce
2	tablespoons packed brown sugar, plus extra for seasoning
2	bay leaves
5	pounds boneless beef chuck-eye roast, trimmed and cut into 1½-inch pieces
	Salt and pepper

TO PREP

1. Microwave onions, chili powder, tomato paste, oil, garlic, cumin, and oregano in bowl, stirring occasionally, until onions are softened, about 5 minutes; transfer to slow cooker. Stir in beans, tomato puree, broth, tapioca, soy sauce, chipotle, sugar, and bay leaves. Season beef with salt and pepper and stir into slow cooker.

TO COOK

2. Cover and cook until beef is tender, 9 to 10 hours on low or 6 to 7 hours on high.

TO FINISH AND SERVE

3. Skim excess fat from surface of chili. Discard bay leaves. Season with salt, pepper, and extra sugar to taste and serve.

NIGHT TIME PREP

- Chipotle can be minced; refrigerate.
- Beef can be cut and seasoned; refrigerate.
- Onion mixture can be microwaved; cool to room temperature and refrigerate.

TEST KITCHEN TIP
TRIMMING AND CUTTING CHUCK-EYE ROAST

Pull apart roast at major seams delineated by lines of fat, using knife as necessary. Then trim off excess fat and silverskin and cut meat into cubes or chunks as directed in recipe.

Slow-Cooker New Mexican Red Pork Chili

SERVES 6 TO 8 • **TO PREP** 25 MINUTES • **TO COOK** 9 TO 10 HOURS ON LOW OR 6 TO 7 HOURS ON HIGH
TO FINISH 10 MINUTES

✔ **WHY THIS RECIPE WORKS:** Inspired by the traditional New Mexican stew *carne adovada*, this chili features meltingly tender chunks of pork in an intense, richly flavored red chile sauce. For this long-simmered chili, we found that the considerable marbling of fat in pork butt (also known as Boston butt) produced supremely tender chunks of meat that didn't dry out. As for the sauce, traditional recipes called for toasting and grinding dried chiles—nearly two dozen—to achieve the recipe's distinct bitter, dried-fruit flavor, but we wanted a simpler, more pantry-friendly alternative. Chili powder, oregano, and chipotle chile provided a solid baseline of warmth and depth, and fresh coffee brought a balance of robust, bittersweet flavors. And, since the flavor of dried chiles is sometimes described as raisiny, we went to the source, adding raisins before serving to achieve the desired fruity nuance. Fresh cilantro, lime zest, and lime juice stirred in at the end helped to brighten this earthy dish. You will need a 5½- to 7-quart slow cooker for this recipe. Serve with your favorite chili garnishes.

2 onions, chopped
¼ cup chili powder
2 tablespoons vegetable oil
6 garlic cloves, minced
2 tablespoons tomato paste
1 tablespoon minced fresh oregano or
   1 teaspoon dried
2 cups chicken broth
½ cup brewed coffee
¼ cup instant tapioca
1 tablespoon minced canned chipotle chile
   in adobo sauce
1 tablespoon packed brown sugar, plus extra
   for seasoning
2 bay leaves
4 pounds boneless pork butt roast, trimmed
   and cut into 1½-inch pieces
   Salt and pepper

TO FINISH AND SERVE
½ cup raisins
¼ cup minced fresh cilantro
1 tablespoon lime juice, plus extra for
   seasoning
1 teaspoon grated lime zest

TO PREP

1. Microwave onions, chili powder, oil, garlic, tomato paste, and oregano in bowl, stirring occasionally, until onions are softened, about 5 minutes; transfer to slow cooker. Stir in broth, coffee, tapioca, chipotle, sugar, and bay leaves. Season pork with salt and pepper and stir into slow cooker.

TO COOK

2. Cover and cook until pork is tender, 9 to 10 hours on low or 6 to 7 hours on high.

TO FINISH AND SERVE

3. Skim excess fat from surface of chili. Discard bay leaves. Stir in raisins and let sit until heated through and tender, about 5 minutes. Stir in cilantro, lime juice, and lime zest. Season with salt, pepper, extra sugar, and extra lime juice to taste. Serve.

NIGHT TIME PREP

• Chipotle can be minced; refrigerate.
• Pork can be cut and seasoned; refrigerate.
• Onion mixture can be microwaved; cool to
  room temperature and refrigerate.

Slow-Cooker Atlanta Brisket

SERVES 6 • **TO PREP** 25 MINUTES • **TO COOK** 8 TO 9 HOURS ON LOW OR 5 TO 6 HOURS ON HIGH
TO FINISH 20 MINUTES

✓ **WHY THIS RECIPE WORKS:** Atlanta brisket is a braised Southern dish featuring boxed onion soup mix, ketchup, and Atlanta's own Coca-Cola. For a slow-cooker version of this regional classic, we replaced the artificial-tasting soup mix with our own aromatic blend of softened onions, onion powder, garlic, and thyme. We stirred this into the slow cooker along with the ketchup and cola. We also included some instant tapioca to help thicken the braising liquid into a sweet yet savory sauce with caramelized complexity. The low, even heat of the slow cooker was perfect for getting meltingly tender brisket. Once the brisket was done, we simply sliced it and served it with the sweet and tangy sauce. You will need a 5½- to 7-quart oval slow cooker for this recipe.

1	pound onions, halved and sliced ½ inch thick
1	tablespoon vegetable oil
2	garlic cloves, minced
1	tablespoon minced fresh thyme or 1 teaspoon dried
1	(3-pound) beef brisket, flat cut preferred, fat trimmed to ¼ inch
	Salt and pepper
1	cup cola
¾	cup ketchup
2	tablespoons instant tapioca
4	teaspoons onion powder

TO PREP

1. Microwave onions, oil, garlic, and thyme in bowl, stirring occasionally, until onions are softened, about 5 minutes; transfer to slow cooker. Season brisket with salt and pepper and nestle fat side up into slow cooker. Whisk cola, ketchup, tapioca, onion powder, 1 teaspoon salt, and 1 teaspoon pepper together in bowl, then pour over brisket.

TO COOK

2. Cover and cook until brisket is tender and fork slips easily in and out of meat, 8 to 9 hours on low or 5 to 6 hours on high.

TO FINISH AND SERVE

3. Transfer brisket to carving board, tent loosely with aluminum foil, and let rest for 15 minutes. Skim excess fat from surface of sauce. Season with salt and pepper to taste. Slice brisket against grain into ¼-inch-thick slices, trimming and discarding any excess fat, if desired. Shingle slices on serving platter. Pour 1 cup sauce over brisket and serve with remaining sauce.

NIGHT TIME PREP

- Brisket can be trimmed and seasoned; refrigerate.
- Onion mixture can be microwaved; cool to room temperature and refrigerate.

TEST KITCHEN TIP SLICING BRISKET

It's important to slice brisket thin (about ¼ inch) and against the grain in order for the meat to taste tender. If the slices are cut too thick, the meat will have a tougher, chewy texture.

Slow-Cooker Shredded Barbecued Beef

SERVES 8 • **TO PREP** 45 MINUTES • **TO COOK** 9 TO 10 HOURS ON LOW OR 6 TO 7 HOURS ON HIGH
TO FINISH 40 MINUTES

✓ **WHY THIS RECIPE WORKS:** Piled high on soft buns, saucy barbecued shredded beef is a real crowd-pleaser. We chose a boneless chuck roast for the beef since we knew it would become tender and shreddable after hours in a slow cooker. For a richly flavored sauce, we got out our skillet, first browning bacon for smoky flavor and then sautéing onions and spices in the rendered bacon fat. We then added ketchup, mustard, and brown sugar plus a somewhat unusual ingredient—coffee—which when reduced along with all the other sauce ingredients lent just the complexity we were seeking. You will need a 5½- to 7-quart slow cooker for this recipe.

4	slices bacon, chopped
2	onions, chopped
2	tablespoons chili powder
1	tablespoon paprika
1½	cups ketchup
1½	cups brewed coffee
¼	cup packed dark brown sugar
2	tablespoons brown mustard
1	(5-pound) boneless beef chuck-eye roast, trimmed and quartered
	Salt and pepper

TO FINISH AND SERVE

1	tablespoon hot sauce
1	tablespoon cider vinegar
1	teaspoon liquid smoke
8	hamburger buns

TO PREP

1. Cook bacon in 12-inch skillet over medium heat until crisp, 5 to 7 minutes. Stir in onions and cook until softened and lightly browned, 8 to 10 minutes. Stir in chili powder and paprika and cook until fragrant, about 1 minute. Stir in ketchup, coffee, sugar, and 1 tablespoon mustard. Bring to simmer and cook until mixture is thickened and measures 4 cups, about 10 minutes. Transfer 2 cups mixture to slow cooker; reserve remaining mixture separately.

2. Season beef with salt and pepper and nestle into slow cooker.

TO COOK

3. Cover and cook until beef is tender, 9 to 10 hours on low or 6 to 7 hours on high.

TO FINISH AND SERVE

4. Using slotted spoon, transfer beef to bowl and let cool slightly. Shred beef into bite-size pieces using 2 forks, discarding excess fat. Skim excess fat from surface of braising liquid.

5. Strain braising liquid into saucepan, bring to simmer over medium heat, and cook until thickened and measures 1 cup, 20 to 30 minutes. Whisk in reserved ketchup mixture, remaining 1 tablespoon mustard, hot sauce, vinegar, and liquid smoke and bring to simmer. Stir 1½ cups sauce into shredded beef; add more sauce as needed to keep meat moist. Season with salt and pepper to taste. Serve shredded beef on buns with remaining sauce.

NIGHT TIME PREP

• Beef can be cut and seasoned; refrigerate.
• Sauce can be cooked and divided; cool to room temperature and refrigerate.

BUILD SMOKY FLAVOR
We built a flavor-packed foundation for our sauce by first cooking bacon in a skillet until crisp; 2 cups of the sauce went into the slow cooker, and we saved the rest to whisk into the braising liquid at the end, which we reduced on the stovetop and then combined with the shredded beef. Brewed coffee and liquid smoke helped lend this sauce smoky complexity.

Slow-Cooker Asian Braised Beef Short Ribs

SERVES 4 TO 6 • **TO PREP** 15 MINUTES • **TO COOK** 9 TO 10 HOURS ON LOW OR 6 TO 7 HOURS ON HIGH
TO FINISH 10 MINUTES

✓ **WHY THIS RECIPE WORKS:** For a boldly flavored, ultrasatisfying dinner, we slow-cooked short ribs until meltingly tender in an Asian-style sauce that tasted sweet, spicy, and savory all at once. The well-marbled ribs cooked down significantly, so to compensate we started with 5 pounds of ribs for four to six diners. The duo of hoisin sauce and chili-garlic sauce provided an intensely flavored sauce with a nice sweetness and subtle heat, and a small amount of chicken broth worked to thin the mixture slightly. To ensure an ultraclingy sauce by the end of the cooking time, we stirred in 1 tablespoon of tapioca. Thinly sliced scallion whites gave the sauce an aromatic presence. Once the ribs were tender, we defatted the sauce and sprinkled the finished dish with scallion greens for freshness and a burst of color. You will need a 5½- to 7-quart slow cooker for this recipe. Serve with egg noodles or rice.

¼   cup chicken broth
¾   cup hoisin sauce
3   scallions, white parts minced, green parts sliced thin
4   teaspoons Asian chili-garlic sauce
1   tablespoon instant tapioca
5   pounds bone-in English-style short ribs, trimmed
      Salt and pepper

TO PREP

1. Combine broth, hoisin, scallion whites, chili-garlic sauce, and tapioca in slow cooker. Season short ribs with salt and pepper and nestle into slow cooker.

TO COOK

2. Cover and cook until beef is tender, 9 to 10 hours on low or 6 to 7 hours on high.

TO FINISH AND SERVE

3. Transfer short ribs to serving platter, tent loosely with aluminum foil, and let rest for 5 minutes. Skim excess fat from surface of sauce. Pour sauce over short ribs and sprinkle with scallion greens. Serve.

NIGHT TIME PREP

• Scallions can be prepared; refrigerate.
• Short ribs can be trimmed and seasoned; refrigerate.

TEST KITCHEN TIP **TRIMMING BONE-IN SHORT RIBS**

To prevent dish from turning out greasy, trim excess fat and silverskin from both sides of each short rib using chef's knife.

Slow-Cooker Southwestern Pork Roast

SERVES 4 TO 6 • **TO PREP** 20 MINUTES • **TO COOK** 8 TO 9 HOURS ON LOW OR 5 TO 6 HOURS ON HIGH
TO FINISH 20 MINUTES

✓ **WHY THIS RECIPE WORKS:** To put a Southwestern spin on a slow-cooker pork roast, we started with a well-marbled pork butt and seasoned it liberally with chili powder, oregano, salt, and pepper. We also added some of the spices to a mixture of canned tomato sauce and spicy chipotle chile to make a boldly flavored braising liquid. Blooming the spices in oil in the microwave gave them deeper, more complex flavors. As the roast cooked, it lent its juices to the braising liquid, transforming it into a meaty, spicy sauce. We simply skimmed off the excess fat and stirred in some cilantro while the roast rested, then sliced the roast and served it with the bold sauce. Boneless pork butt roast is often labeled Boston butt in the supermarket. You will need a 5½- to 7-quart slow cooker for this recipe. Serve with rice.

1½ tablespoons chili powder
1 tablespoon minced fresh oregano or
   1 teaspoon dried
   Salt and pepper
2 onions, chopped
1 tablespoon vegetable oil
1 (15-ounce) can tomato sauce
2 teaspoons minced canned chipotle chile in
   adobo sauce
1 (4-pound) boneless pork butt roast, trimmed

TO FINISH AND SERVE
3 tablespoons minced fresh cilantro

TO PREP

1. Mix chili powder, oregano, 1 teaspoon salt, and 1 teaspoon pepper together in bowl. Microwave onions, oil, and half of spice mixture in separate bowl, stirring occasionally, until onions are softened, about 5 minutes; transfer to slow cooker. Stir in tomato sauce and chipotle.

2. Tie roast around circumference with kitchen twine, season with remaining spice mixture, and nestle into slow cooker.

TO COOK

3. Cover and cook until pork is tender, 8 to 9 hours on low or 5 to 6 hours on high.

TO FINISH AND SERVE

4. Transfer roast to carving board, tent loosely with aluminum foil, and let rest for 15 minutes. Skim excess fat from surface of sauce. Stir in cilantro and season with salt and pepper to taste. Remove twine from roast and slice against grain into ½-inch-thick slices. Serve with sauce.

NIGHT TIME PREP

- Chipotle can be minced; refrigerate.
- Pork can be trimmed, tied, and seasoned; refrigerate.
- Onion mixture can be microwaved; cool to room temperature and refrigerate.

INFUSE ROAST WITH FLAVOR
A robust spice mixture does double duty in this recipe: We use half as a spice rub for the pork butt roast, and the other half is micro-waved with the aromatics and oil to build a flavor base along with tomato sauce and chipotle chile. To keep the roast intact during the long cooking time, we simply tied it with kitchen twine before nestling it into the slow cooker.

Slow-Cooker Smoky Chipotle Beef Tacos

SERVES 4 TO 6 • **TO PREP** 25 MINUTES • **TO COOK** 9 TO 10 HOURS ON LOW OR 6 TO 7 HOURS ON HIGH
TO FINISH 15 MINUTES

✓ **WHY THIS RECIPE WORKS:** Weeknight tacos are usually limited to quick-cooking fillings like ground beef, but the slow cooker makes it easy to use cuts like beef chuck that take several hours to turn tender. We wanted to make easy pulled beef tacos and pair them with a rich, smoky chipotle sauce. For starters, we braised boneless chuck roast in a tomato-based sauce along with aromatics, spices, canned chipotle chile (dried and smoked jalapeños in piquant adobo sauce), and a fresh jalapeño. The chipotle imparted sweet and smoky notes and a warm, lingering heat to the finished dish, and the fresh jalapeño intensified the moderate, but not overwhelming, spiciness. This shredded beef filling was intensely flavorful, but since the essence of chipotle mellows during cooking, it lacked the distinct smokiness we were after. Adding a splash of liquid smoke to the sauce ensured a lasting smoky flavor. You will need a 5½- to 7-quart slow cooker for this recipe. To make this dish spicier, add the jalapeño seeds. Serve with sour cream, chopped onion, chopped cilantro, thinly sliced radishes, and/or lime wedges.

2	onions, chopped
⅓	cup chili powder
3	tablespoons minced canned chipotle chile in adobo sauce
2	tablespoons vegetable oil
6	garlic cloves, minced
1	jalapeño chile, stemmed, seeded, and minced
1	tablespoon tomato paste
1	tablespoon ground cumin
1	(15-ounce) can tomato sauce
2	teaspoons packed light brown sugar
½	teaspoon liquid smoke
1	(3-pound) boneless beef chuck-eye roast, trimmed and halved
	Salt and pepper

TO FINISH AND SERVE
12–18 (6-inch) corn tortillas, warmed

TO PREP
1. Microwave onions, chili powder, chipotle, oil, garlic, jalapeño, tomato paste, and cumin in bowl, stirring occasionally, until onions are softened, about 5 minutes; transfer to slow cooker. Stir in tomato sauce, sugar, and liquid smoke. Season beef with salt and pepper and nestle into slow cooker.

TO COOK
2. Cover and cook until beef is tender, 9 to 10 hours on low or 6 to 7 hours on high.

TO FINISH AND SERVE
3. Using slotted spoon, transfer beef to bowl and let cool slightly. Shred beef into bite-size pieces using 2 forks, discarding excess fat. Skim excess fat from surface of sauce.

4. Stir 1 cup sauce into shredded beef; add more sauce as needed to keep meat moist. Season with salt and pepper to taste. Serve with warm tortillas and remaining sauce.

> **NIGHT TIME PREP**
> • Beef can be halved and seasoned; refrigerate.
> • Onion mixture can be microwaved; cool to room temperature and refrigerate.

TEST KITCHEN TIP **WARMING TORTILLAS**

To warm tortilla over gas burner, place directly on cooking grate over medium flame. Heat until slightly charred around edges, 15 to 30 seconds per side. Wrap in clean dish towel to keep warm.

Slow-Cooker Classic Marinara Sauce

MAKES ABOUT 8 CUPS, ENOUGH TO SAUCE 2 POUNDS OF PASTA • **TO PREP** 30 MINUTES
TO COOK 9 TO 10 HOURS ON LOW OR 6 TO 7 HOURS ON HIGH • **TO FINISH** 10 MINUTES

✔ **WHY THIS RECIPE WORKS:** A rich and full-bodied marinara sauce usually takes a couple of hours of stovetop simmering, so we wanted to develop a hands-off slow-cooker version—a bit of a challenge since the slow cooker doesn't provide any chance for evaporation and reduction. The biggest hurdle was choosing the right tomato products, as many of our tests produced sauces that were either too watery or too thick and overpowering. Our solution was a combination of four different tomato products (paste, crushed, diced, and sauce). The concentrated products (tomato paste and tomato sauce) provided lots of strong, complex flavor without unwanted water—no need for evaporation. For more layers of flavor, we sautéed a few anchovies with our aromatics and deglazed the pan with red wine before stirring everything together with 2 tablespoons of soy sauce—the anchovies and soy sauce added much-needed meaty flavor to the sauce. You will need a 5½- to 7-quart slow cooker for this recipe. Leftover sauce can be refrigerated for up to 3 days or frozen for up to 1 month.

2   tablespoons extra-virgin olive oil
2   onions, chopped fine
6   garlic cloves, minced
2   tablespoons tomato paste
2   tablespoons minced fresh oregano or
    2 teaspoons dried
2   anchovy fillets, rinsed and minced
    Pinch red pepper flakes
1   cup dry red wine
1   (28-ounce) can crushed tomatoes
1   (28-ounce) can diced tomatoes, drained
1   (28-ounce) can tomato sauce
2   tablespoons soy sauce

TO FINISH AND SERVE
½   cup chopped fresh basil
2   teaspoons sugar, plus extra for seasoning
    Salt and pepper

TO PREP

1. Heat oil in 12-inch skillet over medium heat until shimmering. Add onions and cook until softened and lightly browned, 8 to 10 minutes. Stir in garlic, tomato paste, oregano, anchovies, and pepper flakes and cook until fragrant, about 1 minute. Stir in wine, scraping up any browned bits. Bring to simmer and cook until thickened, about 5 minutes; transfer to slow cooker. Stir in crushed tomatoes, diced tomatoes, tomato sauce, and soy sauce.

TO COOK

2. Cover and cook until sauce is deeply flavored, 9 to 10 hours on low or 6 to 7 hours on high.

TO FINISH AND SERVE

3. Stir in basil and sugar and season with salt, pepper, and extra sugar to taste. Before draining pasta, reserve some pasta cooking water to adjust sauce consistency when tossed with pasta.

NIGHT TIME PREP

• Onion mixture can be cooked; transfer to bowl, cool to room temperature, and refrigerate.

BUILD FLAVOR IN A SKILLET FIRST
To re-create the flavor of a long-cooked and rich-tasting marinara sauce in the slow cooker, we found it necessary to sauté the onions and aromatics in a skillet until browned and then deglaze the pan with red wine to capture all the flavorful browned bits. Four different tomato products combined to give our sauce complex flavor and rich texture.

Slow-Cooker Meaty Tomato Sauce

MAKES ABOUT 12 CUPS, ENOUGH TO SAUCE 3 POUNDS OF PASTA • **TO PREP** 20 MINUTES
TO COOK 9 TO 10 HOURS ON LOW OR 6 TO 7 HOURS ON HIGH • **TO FINISH** 10 MINUTES

✔ **WHY THIS RECIPE WORKS:** Nothing could be more welcoming on a cold night than coming home to a rustic, flavor-packed meat sauce ready to toss with some stick-to-your-ribs pasta. For our slow-cooker version, we relied on pork butt, which turned meltingly tender during the long cooking because of its considerable marbling. To limit the amount of preparation, we cut the raw roast into four large pieces instead of cutting it into cubes, then placed it in the slow cooker. Once the pork was fully cooked, it was easy to break it into shreds using tongs. To prevent the sauce from turning out watery, we relied on a trio of tomato products: tomato paste, diced tomatoes, and tomato puree. A dose of soy sauce further enhanced the sauce's meaty flavor. No one would ever guess that this rich-tasting and meaty sauce was so easy to make. Boneless pork butt roast is often labeled Boston butt in the supermarket. You will need a 5½- to 7-quart slow cooker for this recipe. Leftover sauce can be refrigerated for up to 3 days or frozen for up to 1 month.

2   onions, chopped
12 garlic cloves, minced
¼   cup tomato paste
2   tablespoons extra-virgin olive oil
2   tablespoons minced fresh oregano or
    2 teaspoons dried
¼   teaspoon red pepper flakes
1   (28-ounce) can diced tomatoes, drained
1   (28-ounce) can tomato puree
¾   cup dry red wine
⅓   cup soy sauce
2   bay leaves
3   pounds boneless pork butt roast, trimmed
    and quartered
    Salt and pepper

TO FINISH AND SERVE
¼   cup minced fresh parsley

TO PREP

1. Microwave onions, garlic, tomato paste, oil, oregano, and pepper flakes in bowl, stirring occasionally, until onions are softened, about 5 minutes; transfer to slow cooker. Stir in tomatoes, tomato puree, wine, soy sauce, and bay leaves. Season pork with salt and pepper and nestle into slow cooker.

TO COOK

2. Cover and cook until pork is tender, 9 to 10 hours on low or 6 to 7 hours on high.

TO FINISH AND SERVE

3. Skim excess fat from surface of sauce. Discard bay leaves. Break pork into bite-size pieces with tongs. Stir in parsley and season with salt and pepper to taste. Before draining pasta, reserve some pasta cooking water to adjust sauce consistency when tossed with pasta.

NIGHT TIME PREP

• Pork can be trimmed, quartered, and seasoned; refrigerate.
• Onion mixture can be microwaved; cool to room temperature and refrigerate.

Slow-Cooker Spicy Sausage Ragu with Red Peppers

MAKES ABOUT 12 CUPS, ENOUGH TO SAUCE 3 POUNDS OF PASTA • **TO PREP** 45 MINUTES
TO COOK 9 TO 10 HOURS ON LOW OR 6 TO 7 HOURS ON HIGH • **TO FINISH** 15 MINUTES

✓ **WHY THIS RECIPE WORKS:** Spicy Italian sausages and sweet bell peppers are a classic pairing that we thought would translate perfectly into a bright, slightly sweet, and deeply flavored slow-cooker pasta sauce. We liked the flavorful heat that hot Italian sausages imparted, and a few minutes spent browning them and breaking them up in a skillet gave the sauce an even deeper and richer flavor. Since we had our skillet out, we sautéed our aromatics (onions, garlic, oregano, and red pepper flakes) and deglazed the pan with red wine. Tomato paste, crushed tomatoes, diced tomatoes, and tomato sauce were the perfect combination of tomato products with which to build our sauce—neither too watery nor too thick. As for the bell peppers, which rounded out the flavors and cut a little of the heat, we simply softened them in the microwave and stirred them into the sauce just before serving. You will need a 5½- to 7-quart slow cooker for this recipe. To remove the sausage from its casing, cut it open at the end and simply squeeze out the ground sausage. Leftover sauce can be refrigerated for up to 3 days or frozen for up to 1 month.

2   **tablespoons extra-virgin olive oil**
2   **pounds hot Italian sausage, casings removed**
2   **onions, chopped**
6   **garlic cloves, minced**
2   **tablespoons tomato paste**
2   **tablespoons minced fresh oregano or**
       2 teaspoons dried
1   **teaspoon red pepper flakes**
1   **cup dry red wine**
1   **(28-ounce) can crushed tomatoes**
1   **(28-ounce) can diced tomatoes, drained**
1   **(28-ounce) can tomato sauce**

TO FINISH AND SERVE
2   **red bell peppers, stemmed, seeded, and cut into ½-inch pieces**
½   **cup minced fresh parsley**
       Salt and pepper

TO PREP

1. Heat 1 tablespoon oil in 12-inch skillet over medium-high heat until just smoking. Brown sausage well, breaking up large pieces with wooden spoon, about 5 minutes; transfer to slow cooker.

2. Pour off all but 2 tablespoons fat from skillet, add onions, and cook over medium heat until softened and lightly browned, 8 to 10 minutes. Stir in garlic, tomato paste, oregano, and pepper flakes and cook until fragrant, about 1 minute. Stir in wine, scraping up any browned bits. Bring to simmer and cook until thickened, about 5 minutes; transfer to slow cooker. Stir in crushed tomatoes, diced tomatoes, and tomato sauce.

TO COOK

3. Cover and cook until sauce is deeply flavored, 9 to 10 hours on low or 6 to 7 hours on high.

TO FINISH AND SERVE

4. Microwave bell peppers with remaining 1 tablespoon oil in bowl, stirring occasionally, until tender, about 5 minutes. Skim excess fat from surface of sauce. Stir in bell peppers and parsley and season with salt and pepper to taste. Before draining pasta, reserve some pasta cooking water to adjust sauce consistency when tossed with pasta.

NIGHT TIME PREP

- Sausage and onion mixture can be cooked; transfer to bowl, cool to room temperature, and refrigerate.
- Bell peppers can be cut; refrigerate.

Slow-Cooker Italian Sunday Gravy

MAKES ABOUT 16 CUPS, ENOUGH TO SAUCE 3 POUNDS OF PASTA • **TO PREP** 30 MINUTES
TO COOK 9 TO 10 HOURS ON LOW OR 6 TO 7 HOURS ON HIGH • **TO FINISH** 20 MINUTES

✔ **WHY THIS RECIPE WORKS:** Traditional "Sunday gravy" is more than just meat sauce—it's a labor of love, an all-day kitchen affair involving several types of meat and lots of work at the stove. We wanted to honor this meaty extravaganza but simplify it for the slow cooker and eliminate most of the work. Instead of browning six or seven types of meat, we found that we could cut the meat down to three different types: country-style pork ribs, Italian sausages, and flank steak. In more traditional versions the flank steak is stuffed and rolled into *braciole*, but for simplicity we left it whole and shredded it along with the pork ribs after cooking. Because of the juices released from all the meat, we opted to use concentrated tomato products—tomato paste, drained diced tomatoes, and tomato sauce—to prevent the sauce from turning out watery. You will need a 5½- to 7-quart slow cooker for this recipe. Leftover sauce can be refrigerated for up to 3 days or frozen for up to 1 month.

2 onions, chopped
1 (6-ounce) can tomato paste
12 garlic cloves, minced
2 tablespoons vegetable oil
2 tablespoons minced fresh oregano or
2 teaspoons dried
1 (28-ounce) can diced tomatoes, drained
1 (28-ounce) can tomato sauce
½ cup dry red wine
1½ pounds bone-in country-style pork ribs, trimmed
1 (1½-pound) flank steak, trimmed
Salt and pepper
2 pounds hot or sweet Italian sausage

TO FINISH AND SERVE
3 tablespoons minced fresh basil

TO PREP

1. Microwave onions, tomato paste, garlic, oil, and oregano in bowl, stirring occasionally, until onions are softened, about 5 minutes; transfer to slow cooker. Stir in tomatoes, tomato sauce, and wine. Season pork and flank steak with salt and pepper and nestle into slow cooker along with sausage.

TO COOK

2. Cover and cook until meat is tender, 9 to 10 hours on low or 6 to 7 hours on high.

TO FINISH AND SERVE

3. Transfer pork, flank steak, and sausage to cutting board and let cool slightly. Shred pork and flank steak into bite-size pieces using 2 forks, discarding excess fat; slice sausage in half crosswise. Skim excess fat from surface of sauce.

4. Stir shredded pork, shredded flank steak, and sausage into sauce and let sit until heated through, about 5 minutes. Stir in basil and season with salt and pepper to taste. Before draining pasta, reserve some pasta cooking water to adjust sauce consistency when tossed with pasta.

NIGHT TIME PREP

- Pork and flank steak can be trimmed and seasoned; refrigerate.
- Onion mixture can be microwaved; cool to room temperature and refrigerate.

USE THREE TYPES OF MEAT
For our slow-cooker version of this Italian classic, we kept work to a minimum by relying on prep-free country-style pork ribs, Italian sausage, and flank steak. At the end we shredded the pork and the flank steak and sliced the sausage into pieces; after stirring the meat back into the slow cooker, we simply let it heat through for 5 minutes.

MEATY LASAGNA

Stock the Freezer

BIG-BATCH SUPPERS

Creamy Macaroni and Cheese

MAKES 2 CASSEROLES, EACH SERVING 4 • **TO PREP** 1 HOUR 10 MINUTES
STORE UP TO 1 MONTH • **TO FINISH** 1 HOUR 20 MINUTES

✓**WHY THIS RECIPE WORKS:** At its best, macaroni and cheese emerges from the oven with a golden, crisp topping and an indulgent cheese sauce. When made ahead and reheated, however, it's more likely to end up dry, bland, and underwhelming. To make a macaroni and cheese that could survive a stint in the freezer and still bake up rich and creamy, we first had to focus on creating a never-fail sauce. Egg-based sauces were out: By the time the center of the casserole was heated through, the outer edge was overbaked and the sauce curdled and separated. A béchamel, on the other hand, thickened the sauce without risk of curdling. Using a combination of chicken broth and whole milk made a rich-tasting sauce that stayed loose; a loose sauce going into the freezer was key to ensuring a creamy, not pasty, sauce coming out of the oven. Rinsing the pasta ensured that it wouldn't clump and removed extra starch that would otherwise make the sauce gloppy. For a crunchy topping, we tossed panko bread crumbs with melted butter and toasted them to ensure that they would stay crisp in the freezer. To keep the crumbs from burning, we cooked the casserole covered and then removed the aluminum foil toward the end of cooking to recrisp and brown the topping. Finally, with our topping golden and our sauce creamy, we knew our macaroni and cheese would satisfy any cheesy craving. You will need two 8-inch square disposable aluminum pans for this recipe.

1	cup panko bread crumbs
2	tablespoons unsalted butter, melted, plus
	6 tablespoons unsalted butter
	Salt and pepper
1	pound elbow macaroni
6	tablespoons all-purpose flour
2	teaspoons dry mustard
1	garlic clove, minced
⅛	teaspoon cayenne pepper
4	cups whole milk
2¾	cups chicken broth
1	pound Colby cheese, shredded (4 cups)
8	ounces extra-sharp cheddar cheese, shredded (2 cups)
1	ounce Parmesan cheese, grated (½ cup)

TO PREP

1. Adjust oven rack to middle position and heat oven to 350 degrees. Toss panko with melted butter and season with salt and pepper. Spread evenly on rimmed baking sheet and bake until golden brown, about 10 minutes; set aside.

2. Bring 4 quarts water to boil in large pot. Add macaroni and 1 tablespoon salt and cook, stirring often, until nearly al dente. Drain pasta, rinse with cold water, and drain again, leaving pasta slightly wet; leave in colander.

3. Dry now-empty pot, add remaining 6 tablespoons butter, and melt over medium heat. Stir in flour, mustard, garlic, and cayenne and cook for 1 minute. Slowly whisk in milk and broth until smooth. Bring to simmer and cook, whisking often, until thickened, about 15 minutes.

4. Off heat, gradually whisk in Colby, cheddar, Parmesan, 1 teaspoon salt, and pinch pepper. Let cool to room temperature, about 30 minutes. Stir pasta into sauce, breaking up any clumps. Divide pasta mixture evenly between 2 greased, 8-inch square disposable aluminum pans. Sprinkle evenly with toasted panko. (To serve 1 casserole right away, bake uncovered on aluminum foil–lined rimmed baking sheet in 375-degree oven until sauce is bubbling around edges, 20 to 25 minutes. Let cool for 10 minutes before serving.)

TO STORE

5. Wrap pans tightly with plastic wrap and cover with foil. Freeze for up to 1 month. (Do not thaw before reheating.)

TO FINISH AND SERVE

6. Unwrap casserole, cover with greased foil, and place on foil-lined rimmed baking sheet. Place casserole on middle rack of cold oven, turn oven to 375 degrees, and bake until casserole is hot throughout, about 70 minutes. Uncover and continue to bake until topping is crisp and sauce is bubbling around edges, about 10 minutes. Let cool for 10 minutes before serving.

MAKE A LOOSE SAUCE
To ensure our cheese sauce stayed creamy through freezing and reheating, we made a simple béchamel that resisted breaking. A combination of whole milk and chicken broth tasted rich while still being thin enough to stay loose when reheated. And rinsing the pasta thoroughly washed away excess starch that otherwise made the sauce gloppy.

Shepherd's Pie

MAKES 2 CASSEROLES, EACH SERVING 4 • **TO PREP** 1 HOUR 45 MINUTES
STORE UP TO 1 MONTH • **TO FINISH** 1 HOUR 15 MINUTES

WHY THIS RECIPE WORKS: Traditional shepherd's pie, with slow-cooked stewed lamb and gravy topped with mashed potatoes, is delicious but time-consuming to make. We wanted a streamlined recipe with flavorful meat. The most common shortcut is to use ground meat, so we began by swapping the lamb for ground beef. To keep the meat tender even when frozen and reheated, we skipped browning it and just cooked it until no longer pink. To replace the missing flavor from the browned meat, we sautéed the onions, carrots, and tomato paste to create a flavorful fond in the pot. Then we deglazed the pot with red wine and boosted the filling's flavor with thyme and Worcestershire sauce. The Worcestershire lent the gravy depth, color, and a subtle savory note. Finally, we added chicken broth to the filling to make sure it stayed moist and saucy. For the mashed potato topping, we needed enough cream and butter for a topping that could be frozen and reheated without becoming gluey and dry. Reheating the assembled pie proved tricky; because the filling reheated faster than the topping, it overflowed the pan. To fix this problem, we made a small vent in the center of the pie to allow steam to escape before briefly broiling the pie until the potatoes were golden brown. Do not use ground beef that is fattier than 93 percent lean or the dish will be greasy. You will need two 8-inch square disposable aluminum pans for this recipe.

1	tablespoon vegetable oil
2	onions, chopped fine
5	carrots, peeled and sliced ¼ inch thick
	Salt and pepper
2	pounds 93 percent lean ground beef
4	garlic cloves, minced
4	teaspoons tomato paste
⅓	cup all-purpose flour
½	cup dry red wine
2	cups chicken broth
2	teaspoons minced fresh thyme or
	½ teaspoon dried
¾	teaspoon Worcestershire sauce
3	pounds russet potatoes, peeled and cut into
	1-inch pieces
¾	cup heavy cream, warmed
4	tablespoons unsalted butter, softened
⅔	cup frozen peas

TO PREP

1. Heat oil in Dutch oven over medium heat until shimmering. Add onions, carrots, 1 teaspoon salt, and ½ teaspoon pepper and cook until softened, 8 to 10 minutes. Add ground beef, breaking up meat with wooden spoon, and cook until no longer pink, about 5 minutes. Stir in garlic and tomato paste and cook until fragrant, about 30 seconds. Stir in flour and cook for 2 minutes.

2. Slowly stir in wine and cook until slightly reduced, about 2 minutes. Stir in broth, thyme, and Worcestershire, scraping up any browned bits. Bring to simmer and cook, stirring occasionally, until mixture is slightly thickened, 6 to 8 minutes. Divide beef mixture evenly between 2 greased, 8-inch square disposable aluminum pans; set aside.

3. Place potatoes and 1 tablespoon salt in large saucepan and add water to cover by 1 inch. Bring to boil, then reduce to simmer and cook until potatoes are tender, about 20 minutes; drain potatoes. Return to now-empty saucepan over low heat, stirring constantly, to evaporate any remaining moisture, about 1 minute. Off heat, mash potatoes smooth with potato masher. Stir in cream, followed by butter, and season with salt and pepper to taste.

4. Spread frozen peas evenly over each pan, gently pressing them into filling. Dollop potatoes evenly over filling, then spread into even layer, making sure to push potatoes to edges of pans. Let cool to room temperature, about 20 minutes. (To serve 1 casserole right away, skip cooling and follow serving instructions, baking uncovered in preheated 400-degree oven for 35 to 40 minutes before broiling.)

TO STORE

5. Wrap pans tightly with plastic wrap and cover with aluminum foil. Freeze for up to 1 month. (Do not thaw before reheating.)

TO FINISH AND SERVE

6. Unwrap casserole, cover with greased foil, and place on foil-lined rimmed baking sheet. Place casserole on upper-middle rack of cold oven, turn oven to 400 degrees, and bake until meat mixture is hot throughout, about 1 hour. Remove casserole from oven and heat broiler. Uncover casserole, then, using butter knife, create 1-inch vent hole in center of potatoes. Broil, uncovered, until potatoes are spotty brown, 12 to 14 minutes, rotating sheet halfway through broiling. Let cool for 10 minutes before serving.

Beef Tamale Pie

MAKES 2 CASSEROLES, EACH SERVING 4 • **TO PREP** 1 HOUR
STORE UP TO 1 MONTH • **TO FINISH** 1½ HOURS

☑ **WHY THIS RECIPE WORKS:** An ideal tamale pie contains a juicy, spicy mixture of meat and vegetables topped with a cornmeal crust. A favorite of adults and children alike, this casserole makes a hearty dinner, but preparing both a filling and a topping on a busy weeknight is a nonstarter for most. We wanted to be able to pull this casserole from the freezer and have it bake up with a moist, cheesy filling topped with tender cornbread. We tackled the filling first, knowing it would need more liquid to hold up during the reheating process. To add moisture, we preferred canned crushed tomatoes to diced; their thicker liquid evaporated less during baking than the thin juice of the diced tomatoes. Plenty of cheese in the filling ensured that we had a rich and creamy base. As for the topping, we were hesitant to pour a raw batter over the filling and then let it sit in the freezer. Sure enough, the batter soaked up moisture from the filling and ended up soggy. Our solution was to use a sheet of aluminum foil to make a barrier between the topping and filling, allowing them to be stored and baked together without direct contact. For the reheat, we found that starting the pie in a cold oven gave the casserole time as the oven warmed up to defrost gently without burning the bottom of the pan or drying out the casserole. This method gave us a saucy, flavorful filling and a tender cornbread topping. You will need two 8-inch square disposable aluminum pans for this recipe. For more information on removing the foil barrier, see page 283. Serve with lime wedges.

FILLING

- 1 tablespoon vegetable oil
- 1 onion, chopped fine
- 1 jalapeño chile, stemmed, seeded, and minced
  Salt and pepper
- 1½ pounds 85 percent lean ground beef
- 2 tablespoons chili powder
- 4 garlic cloves, minced
- 1 teaspoon ground cumin
- 1 (28-ounce) can crushed tomatoes
- 1 (15-ounce) can black beans, rinsed
- 1½ cups frozen corn
- 8 ounces Monterey Jack cheese, shredded (2 cups)
- ¼ cup minced fresh cilantro

CORNBREAD

- 1½ cups (7½ ounces) all-purpose flour
- 1 cup (5 ounces) cornmeal
- ¼ cup (1¾ ounces) sugar
- 2 teaspoons baking powder
- ¼ teaspoon baking soda
- ¾ teaspoon salt
- 1 cup buttermilk
- 8 tablespoons unsalted butter, melted and cooled
- 2 large eggs, lightly beaten

TO PREP

1. FOR THE FILLING: Heat oil in Dutch oven over medium heat until shimmering. Add onion, jalapeño, and 1 teaspoon salt and cook until softened and lightly browned, 5 to 7 minutes. Add ground beef, breaking up meat with wooden spoon, and cook until no longer pink, 3 to 5 minutes.

2. Stir in chili powder, garlic, and cumin and cook until fragrant, about 30 seconds. Stir in tomatoes and their juice, scraping up any browned bits. Off heat, stir in beans, corn, Monterey Jack, and cilantro. Season with salt and pepper to taste.

3. Divide filling evenly between 2 greased, 8-inch square disposable aluminum pans and let cool to room temperature, about 10 minutes. Cut out two 12 by 8-inch sheets of aluminum foil and grease both sides lightly. Press sheet of foil flush to surface of each filling, letting excess hang over edges of pans.

4. FOR THE CORNBREAD: Whisk flour, cornmeal, sugar, baking powder, baking soda, and salt together in large bowl. In separate bowl, whisk buttermilk, melted butter, and eggs together until butter forms small clumps. Stir buttermilk mixture into flour mixture with rubber spatula until combined. Divide batter evenly between pans, spreading it evenly to pan edges. (To serve 1 casserole right away, bake,

uncovered, on foil-lined rimmed baking sheet in pre-heated 375-degree oven until crust is golden, 40 to 45 minutes. Holding cornbread in place, gently pull foil out from underneath. Let cool for 10 minutes before serving.)

TO STORE

5. Wrap pans tightly with plastic wrap and cover with foil. Freeze for up to 1 month. (Do not thaw before reheating.)

TO FINISH AND SERVE

6. Unwrap casserole, cover with greased foil, and place on foil-lined rimmed baking sheet. Place casserole on middle rack of cold oven, turn oven to 375 degrees, and bake until topping has thawed, 30 to 40 minutes. Uncover and continue to bake until casserole is hot throughout and crust is golden, 45 to 50 minutes longer. Holding cornbread in place, gently pull foil out from underneath. Let cool for 10 minutes before serving.

ALL ABOUT Stashing Food in the Freezer

Throughout this chapter you'll find casseroles, stews, pasta sauces, and dinner options like veggie burgers, chicken fingers, and meat pies, all engineered to withstand freezing for up to one month and to go from freezer to oven to table, putting lots of appealing dinner options within reach. Apart from making sure that these recipes would come to the table as vibrant and flavorful as when they were freshly made (which often meant boosting the flavor or making a dish more saucy), we learned a few tricks for freezing them well.

Freezer Philosophy

Unlike your fridge, where the coldest setting is normally too cold, the optimal temperature for your freezer is below 0 degrees. To maintain the coldest temperature, adjust the freezer to the coldest possible setting and periodically vacuum the filters and coils to promote efficiency. To help keep food as cold as possible, make sure to store it close to the rear center of the freezer and maximize cold air circulation by not blocking freezer vents. And though it may seem like a good shortcut for cooling foods, never put hot food in the freezer immediately after cooking. This may cause the temperature of your freezer to rise, which will potentially cause other food to partially thaw. Instead, cool food on the counter to room temperature (about 75 degrees) before transferring it to the freezer.

How Long Can I Freeze It?

From a safety standpoint, food that is frozen properly and kept at a constant temperature of 0 degrees or lower will be safe to eat for a very long time. In our experience, however, "safe to eat" is not the same as "at its best." Moisture loss and the activity of enzymes and other chemical processes that are slowed, but not stopped, by freezing cause the quality of frozen food to diminish over time, usually a matter of months. Exactly how much time depends on the freshness of the food when frozen; the age, efficiency, and type of freezer; how full the freezer is; the frequency with which the freezer door is opened; and various other factors. To avoid storing dishes past their prime, label and date them clearly with a permanent marker. For the best results, we recommend eating them within a month of storing.

Pick the Right Container

Whether you are preparing assembled casseroles, stews, sauces, or single-serving meals for the freezer, the container you choose to store them in has a big effect on their overall success. We find disposable aluminum pans to be ideal for casseroles since they are inexpensive and convenient (so you easily can keep a bunch on hand). And they are lighter than glass casserole dishes and much easier to store in the freezer. We like to make smaller-size casseroles in 8-inch square or 9-inch round pans; they heat through faster, and these pans make it easy to make two casseroles for four or six, giving you more serving options and multiple dinners. For stews and sauces, we stick to freezer-safe storage containers, which make it easy to divide these big-batch recipes into convenient portions. And when it comes to single-serving items, we find it best to store them together in tightly sealed zipper-lock freezer bags or wrapped individually in plastic wrap and foil. For information on our favorite brands of storage equipment, see page 8–11.

Preventing a Soggy Topping

We learned that when freezing a casserole with a cornbread topping or a pastry crust, the topping emerges from the oven broken or soggy. To prevent this, we use an aluminum foil shield to protect the topping from soaking up liquid from the moist filling, then simply slide it out from underneath the topping before serving.

1. Form foil shield by pressing sheet of greased foil flush to surface of filling, letting excess hang over edges.

2. Spread batter over foil or place pastry on foil before wrapping and freezing casserole.

3. Once casserole is fully baked, hold cornbread or pastry in place with 1 hand and gently pull foil out from underneath.

A Space-Saving Way to Store Stews and Sauces

The simplest way to store stews or sauces for the freezer is to portion them into storage containers. But if your freezer is tight on room, try this method instead. Line a container with a quart-size zipper-lock freezer bag and pour the stew or sauce into the bag. Seal the bag, place it flat on a baking sheet, and freeze. Once the contents are frozen, you can stack the bags or store them upright wherever there is room.

The Right Wrap

We stick to three basic rules when wrapping food for the freezer. First, wrap food tightly in plastic wrap. This prevents the moisture loss that causes frozen foods to become dry and discolored, a condition known as freezer burn. Second, wrap the food again—this time with aluminum foil. Frozen foods easily pick up odors and off-flavors, and the second wrap will prevent this. Third, wrap larger, single-serving items, such as burritos, separately. They will freeze more quickly and can then be defrosted individually. When freezing food in zipper-lock bags, always use bags specifically designed for freezer storage; they are engineered to prevent freezer burn and lock out odors. And be sure to squeeze out as much air as possible before sealing the bag. For information on our favorite brands of plastic wrap and zipper-lock freezer bags, see page 8.

Thaw Carefully (When Necessary)

Many of the recipes in this chapter are engineered to go directly from the freezer to a cold oven. As the oven heats up, it warms the food gently, preserving its texture. However, stews, chilis, and pasta sauces require thawing before they can be reheated on the stovetop. Thawing should always be done in the refrigerator, not on the counter at room temperature where bacteria can multiply readily. However, if you forget to plan ahead, you can always thaw them quickly in the microwave at 50 percent power (but note that the texture of meat and vegetables may suffer slightly).

Chicken Pot Pie

MAKES 2 PIES, EACH SERVING 4 • **TO PREP** 1½ HOURS
STORE UP TO 1 MONTH • **TO FINISH** 1½ HOURS

✔ **WHY THIS RECIPE WORKS:** With its flaky pastry topping and velvety rich filling, it's easy to understand why chicken pot pie is a family favorite, but it's not a weeknight-friendly recipe. Looking for an alternative to the pot pies in the freezer aisle, we set out to create a better-tasting make-ahead version that would hold up to freezing and reheating. We followed the classic method for building the sauce, lightly browning the aromatics in butter before adding tomato paste for color and flavor. We added some flour to thicken things up before stirring in the chicken broth. A looser sauce was important so it did not become overly thick and gummy during cooling and reheating. For the chicken, we began by poaching a combination of chicken breasts and thighs in the sauce, but while the thighs remained moist and flavorful, the breasts ended up dry and stringy, so we decided to use all chicken thighs. Once the chicken was tender, we removed it from the pot, shredded it, and returned it to the sauce along with heavy cream for richness and sherry for a deeper flavor. For the topping, we turned to convenient store-bought pie dough, which comes in packages of two and was easy to trim to fit over the filling. But during baking, the filling bubbled up through the vents in the crust, making it wet and gummy. To ensure a crisp crust, we took a tip from our tamale pie and created an aluminum foil barrier so the filling could heat through while the crust thawed and baked. The pie needed both covered and uncovered baking time to ensure that it was defrosted before browning the crust. You will need two 9½-inch disposable aluminum deep-dish pie pans for this recipe. For information on removing the foil barrier, see page 283.

1	tablespoon unsalted butter
2	onions, chopped fine
1	pound carrots, peeled and sliced ¼ inch thick
2	celery ribs, sliced ¼ inch thick
	Salt and pepper
2	teaspoons tomato paste
2	teaspoons minced fresh thyme or
	½ teaspoon dried
½	cup all-purpose flour
2½	cups chicken broth
3	pounds boneless, skinless chicken thighs, trimmed
½	cup heavy cream
2	tablespoons dry sherry
1	cup frozen peas
¼	cup minced fresh parsley
1	package store-bought pie dough

TO FINISH AND SERVE

1	large egg, lightly beaten

TO PREP

1. Melt butter in Dutch oven over medium heat. Add onions, carrots, celery, 1 teaspoon salt, and ½ teaspoon pepper and cook until softened and lightly browned,

8 to 10 minutes. Stir in tomato paste and thyme and cook until browned, about 2 minutes. Stir in flour and cook for 1 minute.

2. Slowly whisk in chicken broth, scraping up any browned bits and smoothing out any lumps. Add chicken and bring to simmer. Reduce heat to medium-low, cover, and simmer, stirring occasionally, until chicken registers 175 degrees and sauce is thickened, 25 to 30 minutes. Off heat, transfer chicken to cutting board, let cool slightly, then shred into bite-size pieces using 2 forks.

3. Stir heavy cream and sherry into sauce, then stir in shredded chicken with any accumulated juices. Season with salt and pepper to taste. Divide filling evenly between 2 greased, 9½-inch disposable aluminum deep-dish pie pans and let cool to room temperature, about 30 minutes. Divide peas and parsley evenly between pans and stir into fillings.

4. Cut out two 12-inch square sheets of aluminum foil and grease both sides lightly. Press sheet of foil flush to surface of each filling, letting excess hang over edges of pans. Unroll each pie dough round, trim to 9-inch round (if necessary), and cut four 2-inch vents in center. Gently place 1 pie dough round on each pan. (To bake 1 casserole right away, skip cooling in step 3.

Brush pastry top with beaten egg, place pot pie on foil-lined rimmed baking sheet, and bake, uncovered, in preheated 400-degree oven until crust is golden, 35 to 40 minutes. Let cool for 15 minutes. Loosen foil from edges of pan. Holding pie crust in place, gently pull foil out from underneath. Serve.)

TO STORE

5. Wrap pans tightly with plastic wrap and cover with foil. Freeze casseroles for up to 1 month. (Do not thaw before reheating.)

TO FINISH AND SERVE

6. Unwrap pot pie, brush top with beaten egg, cover with greased foil, and place on foil-lined rimmed baking sheet. Place pot pie on middle rack of cold oven, turn oven to 400 degrees, and bake for 40 minutes. Uncover and continue to bake until crust is golden, 35 to 40 minutes. Let cool for 15 minutes. Loosen foil from edges of pan. Holding pie crust in place, gently pull foil out from underneath. Serve.

Meaty Lasagna

MAKES 2 CASSEROLES, EACH SERVING 4 • **TO PREP** 1 HOUR
STORE UP TO 1 MONTH • **TO FINISH** 1 HOUR 35 MINUTES

✔ **WHY THIS RECIPE WORKS:** Making and freezing your favorite lasagna ahead of time seems like a good idea, but reheated lasagna usually turns out dry and bland. We wanted a lasagna with tender noodles, a rich sauce, and creamy filling—straight from the freezer. No-boil lasagna noodles didn't require any prep and baked up just as tender as traditional noodles. For the meat sauce, we chose a saucy recipe that would stand up to the drying effects of the freezer. For the cheese, we started with a good dose of mozzarella and added more mozzarella and Parmesan right before serving to ensure a cheesy top. We loved the creaminess of ricotta, but the flavor left tasters unimpressed, so we added eggs for richness, Parmesan cheese, and fresh basil. Meatloaf mix is a prepackaged mix of ground beef, pork, and veal; if it's unavailable, use 8 ounces each of ground pork and 85 percent lean ground beef. Note that some no-boil lasagna noodle packages contain only 12 noodles; this recipe requires 16 noodles. You will need two 8-inch square disposable aluminum pans for this recipe.

1	tablespoon extra-virgin olive oil
1	onion, chopped fine
6	garlic cloves, minced
¼	teaspoon red pepper flakes
1	pound meatloaf mix
	Salt and pepper
¼	cup heavy cream
2	(28-ounce) cans crushed tomatoes
½	cup chopped fresh basil
1	pound (2 cups) whole-milk ricotta cheese
2	ounces Parmesan cheese, grated (1 cup)
2	large eggs, lightly beaten
16	no-boil lasagna noodles
1	pound mozzarella cheese, shredded (4 cups)

TO FINISH AND SERVE (PER CASSEROLE)

2½	ounces mozzarella cheese, shredded (⅔ cup)
¼	cup grated Parmesan cheese
2	tablespoons chopped fresh basil

TO PREP

1. Heat oil in Dutch oven over medium heat until shimmering. Add onion and cook until softened, about 5 minutes. Stir in garlic and pepper flakes and cook until fragrant, about 30 seconds. Add meatloaf mix, ½ teaspoon salt, and ¼ teaspoon pepper and cook, breaking up meat with wooden spoon, until no longer pink, about 3 minutes. Stir in cream and simmer until liquid evaporates and only fat remains, about 4 minutes. Stir in tomatoes, bring to simmer, and cook until flavors blend, about 5 minutes. Off heat, stir in ¼ cup basil and season with salt and pepper to taste. Let cool to room temperature, 30 to 45 minutes.

2. Meanwhile, combine ricotta, Parmesan, eggs, 1 teaspoon salt, ½ teaspoon pepper, and remaining ¼ cup basil in bowl.

3. Grease two 8-inch square disposable aluminum pans. Spread 1 cup sauce over bottom of each prepared pan. Assemble 2 lasagnas by layering ingredients as follows: lay 2 noodles in pan, spread generous ⅓ cup ricotta mixture over noodles, sprinkle with ⅔ cup mozzarella, and top with ⅔ cup sauce; repeat layering 2 more times. Lay remaining 4 noodles in pans, 2 noodles per pan, and top evenly with remaining sauce. (To serve 1 casserole right away, follow serving instructions, baking in preheated 400-degree oven and reducing covered baking time to 45 minutes.)

TO STORE

4. Wrap pans tightly with plastic wrap and cover with aluminum foil. Freeze for up to 1 month. (Do not thaw before reheating.)

TO FINISH AND SERVE

5. Unwrap casserole, cover with greased foil, and place on foil-lined rimmed baking sheet. Place on upper-middle rack of cold oven, turn oven to 400 degrees, and bake until casserole is hot throughout, about 75 minutes. Remove casserole from oven and heat broiler. Uncover, sprinkle with mozzarella and Parmesan, and broil until cheese is melted and spotty brown, 5 to 7 minutes. Let cool for 10 minutes, sprinkle with basil, and serve.

Spinach Manicotti

MAKES 2 CASSEROLES, EACH SERVING 4 • **TO PREP** 40 MINUTES
STORE UP TO 1 MONTH • **TO FINISH** 1 HOUR 15 MINUTES

✓ **WHY THIS RECIPE WORKS:** Baked manicotti is one of our favorite dinners, but it can be a chore to make. We wanted an easier recipe that we could pull from the freezer without compromising on flavor. We started with the ricotta filling. Eggs helped to bind the filling and added richness. Parmesan lent flavor, and parsley and frozen spinach added freshness. Next we tackled filling the manicotti. Store-bought manicotti tubes were awkward to fill when parcooked, and when we filled the raw tubes and then baked them, they cooked unevenly. No-boil lasagna noodles were our answer: Soaking them in hot water made them pliable enough to wrap around the filling. We liked the convenience of freezing the manicotti in easy-to-store bundles of four. Note that some no-boil lasagna noodle packages contain only 12 noodles; this recipe requires 16 noodles. We like to use our Easy Marinara Sauce (recipe follows), but you can substitute your favorite homemade or store-bought marinara sauce.

24 ounces (3 cups) whole-milk ricotta cheese
8 ounces whole-milk mozzarella cheese, shredded (2 cups)
10 ounces frozen spinach, thawed, squeezed dry, and chopped fine
2 ounces Parmesan cheese, grated (1 cup)
2 large eggs, lightly beaten
2 tablespoons minced fresh parsley
½ teaspoon salt
½ teaspoon pepper
16 no-boil lasagna noodles

TO FINISH AND SERVE (PER CASSEROLE)
3 cups marinara sauce
1 ounce Parmesan cheese, grated (½ cup)
1 ounce whole-milk mozzarella cheese, shredded (¼ cup)
2 tablespoons chopped fresh basil

TO PREP

1. Line rimmed baking sheet with parchment paper. Combine ricotta, mozzarella, spinach, Parmesan, eggs, parsley, salt, and pepper in bowl.

2. Pour 1 inch boiling water into 13 by 9-inch baking dish and slip noodles into water, one at a time. Let noodles soak until pliable, about 5 minutes, separating noodles with tip of knife to prevent sticking. Remove noodles from water and place in single layer on clean dish towels with short ends facing you; discard water.

3. Spread heaping ¼ cup ricotta mixture evenly over bottom three-quarters of each noodle. Roll noodles up around filling and place seam side down on prepared sheet, spaced 1 inch apart. (To serve 1 casserole right away, follow serving instructions, reducing covered baking time to 30 to 35 minutes.)

TO STORE

4. Cover manicotti loosely with plastic wrap and freeze until firm, about 1 hour. Tightly wrap in bundles of 4, first in plastic and then in aluminum foil. Freeze for up to 1 month. (Do not thaw before reheating.)

TO FINISH AND SERVE

5. Adjust oven rack to middle position and heat oven to 400 degrees. Spread 1 cup sauce over bottom of 13 by 9-inch baking dish; place 8 manicotti over sauce. Pour 1 cup sauce over top, cover with foil, and bake until hot throughout, about 40 minutes. Uncover, pour remaining 1 cup sauce over top, and sprinkle with Parmesan and mozzarella. Continue to bake, uncovered, until sauce is bubbling and cheese is melted, about 10 minutes. Let cool for 5 minutes, sprinkle with basil, and serve.

EASY MARINARA SAUCE MAKES 6 CUPS
Heat 2 tablespoons vegetable oil, 3 minced garlic cloves, and pinch red pepper flakes in large saucepan over medium heat until garlic turns golden but not brown, 1 to 2 minutes. Stir in one 28-ounce can diced tomatoes, one 28-ounce can tomato puree, and 1 teaspoon salt and bring to brief simmer. Off heat, stir in 2 tablespoons chopped fresh basil and season with salt and pepper to taste. (Marinara can be refrigerated for up to 3 days or frozen for up to 1 month.)

FREEZE THEN BUNDLE MANICOTTI
When we tried freezing a fully assembled manicotti casserole, we ended up with noodles that stuck together and fell apart. To ensure the manicotti stayed intact all the way to the table, we froze them individually first and stored them in bundles, then simply layered the frozen manicotti and sauce in a baking dish before baking.

Hearty Beef Stew

MAKES 12 TO 14 SERVINGS • **TO PREP** 4 HOURS 50 MINUTES
STORE UP TO 1 MONTH • **TO FINISH** ABOUT 30 MINUTES

✓ **WHY THIS RECIPE WORKS:** Beef stew is the perfect make-ahead dish: It freezes and reheats well, it's easy to scale up into large batches, and it can be fancy enough to serve to company. Unfortunately, many recipes we tested produced tough, dry meat in a thin, bland sauce. To find the best cut of beef, we tested the gamut of cuts available at the supermarket. The winner was chuck-eye roast, which boasts flavorful, tender meat and a moderate price tag (especially significant for a big batch of stew). For the most flavor possible, even after freezing and reheating, browning the beef turned out to be a must, but we discovered that browning half of the beef was all we needed for deep flavor. Using vegetable oil during browning was important to ensure that the pan was hot enough to develop plenty of fond, but switching to butter for the onions and aromatics gave our sauce a rich, flavorful base. Finally, baking the stew in a roasting pan ensured that we could make a big batch without risk of overflowing the pot.

7	pounds boneless beef chuck-eye roast, pulled apart at seams, trimmed, and cut into 1½-inch pieces
	Salt and pepper
2	tablespoons vegetable oil, plus extra as needed
1¾	pounds carrots, peeled and sliced 1 inch thick
3	bay leaves
1½	tablespoons minced fresh thyme or 1½ teaspoons dried
4	tablespoons unsalted butter
2	pounds onions, chopped
5	garlic cloves, minced
¾	cup all-purpose flour
2	tablespoons tomato paste
1½	cups dry red wine
4	cups chicken broth
2⅔	pounds red potatoes, unpeeled, cut into 1-inch pieces

TO FINISH AND SERVE
    Frozen peas
    Minced fresh parsley

TO PREP

1. Adjust oven rack to lower-middle position and heat oven to 325 degrees. Pat beef dry with paper towels and season with salt and pepper; transfer half of beef to large roasting pan. Heat oil in Dutch oven over medium-high heat until just smoking. Working in 2 batches, brown remaining beef on all sides, about 8 minutes, adding extra oil if pot looks dry; transfer to roasting pan. Add carrots, bay leaves, and thyme to roasting pan.

2. Melt butter in now-empty pot over medium-low heat. Add onions and 1 teaspoon salt and cook, stirring often, until softened, 7 to 10 minutes. Stir in garlic and cook until fragrant, about 30 seconds. Stir in flour and tomato paste and cook, stirring constantly, until golden, about 1 minute. Slowly whisk in wine, scraping up any browned bits. Gradually whisk in broth until smooth and bring to simmer. Transfer broth mixture to roasting pan with meat mixture. Cover roasting pan tightly with aluminum foil and bake for 1½ hours.

3. Stir in potatoes and continue to cook, covered, until meat is just tender, 2 to 2½ hours longer.

4. Discard bay leaves and season with salt and pepper to taste. Let stew cool to room temperature, about 1½ hours, stirring occasionally.

TO STORE

5. Divide stew among freezer-safe storage containers and freeze for up to 1 month. (Plan on about 2 cups per person.)

TO FINISH AND SERVE

6. Thaw stew in refrigerator overnight. Skim fat from surface of stew and transfer to saucepan. Cover saucepan, bring stew to gentle simmer over low heat, and cook, stirring occasionally, until heated through; adjust consistency with water as needed. Off heat, stir in ½ cup peas and 2 tablespoons parsley for every 4 servings and let heat through, about 5 minutes. Season with salt and pepper to taste and serve.

All-American Beef Chili

MAKES 12 TO 14 SERVINGS • **TO PREP** 3 HOURS 40 MINUTES
STORE UP TO 1 MONTH • **TO FINISH** ABOUT 30 MINUTES

✔ **WHY THIS RECIPE WORKS:** Chili is a natural make-ahead meal—the longer the chili sits, the more its flavors meld and complement each other. It's also incredibly handy to have a big batch of chili ready to pull out of your freezer for the next game day or to stretch over a few cold winter nights. To make our chili taste as good from the freezer as fresh, we found that a combination of tomato puree and diced tomatoes and their juice provided just the right consistency for our base. Using all diced tomatoes created a chunky but watery sauce, but adding tomato puree thickened our chili just enough to feel hearty and substantial. We also found that a heavy hand with seasonings was important for a flavorful chili that could survive a trip to the freezer, though we were surprised to find that we needed a relatively small amount of cayenne and red pepper flakes for the right amount of heat. We found that our chili thickened during freezing; adding water while reheating loosened the chili enough to compensate for evaporation during freezing and allowed us to control the final consistency. You will need at least a 12-quart pot for this recipe. Serve with your favorite chili toppings.

¼ cup vegetable oil
2 pounds onions, chopped
2 red bell peppers, stemmed, seeded, and cut into ½-inch pieces
12 garlic cloves, minced
½ cup chili powder
2 tablespoons ground cumin
4 teaspoons ground coriander
2 teaspoons red pepper flakes
2 teaspoons dried oregano
¾ teaspoon cayenne pepper
Salt and pepper
4 pounds 85 percent lean ground beef
4 (15-ounce) cans red kidney beans, rinsed
2 (28-ounce) cans diced tomatoes
2 (28-ounce) cans tomato puree

TO PREP

1. Heat oil in large pot over medium heat until shimmering. Add onions, bell peppers, garlic, chili powder, cumin, coriander, pepper flakes, oregano, cayenne, and 1 teaspoon salt and cook, stirring often, until vegetables are softened, about 15 minutes.

2. Increase heat to medium-high. Add ground beef, 1 pound at a time, and cook, breaking up meat with wooden spoon, until no longer pink, about 10 minutes.

3. Stir in beans, tomatoes and their juice, and tomato puree and bring to simmer. Reduce heat to low, cover, and simmer, stirring occasionally, until flavors blend, about 1 hour.

4. Uncover and continue to simmer, stirring occasionally, until beef is tender and chili is dark and thickened slightly, about 1½ hours. (If chili begins to stick to bottom of pot, stir in ½ cup water and continue to simmer.) Season with salt to taste. Let chili cool to room temperature, 1½ to 2 hours, stirring occasionally.

TO STORE

5. Divide chili among freezer-safe storage containers and freeze for up to 1 month. (Plan on about 2 cups per person.)

TO FINISH AND SERVE

6. Thaw chili in refrigerator overnight. Skim fat from surface of chili and transfer to saucepan. Cover saucepan, bring chili to gentle simmer over low heat, and cook, stirring occasionally, until heated through; adjust consistency with water as needed. Season with salt and pepper to taste and serve.

Vegetarian Chili

MAKES 6 TO 8 SERVINGS • **TO PREP** 3 HOURS 40 MINUTES
STORE UP TO 1 MONTH • **TO FINISH** ABOUT 30 MINUTES

✓ **WHY THIS RECIPE WORKS:** We wanted a vegetarian chili so good we'd want to keep quarts of it stashed in the freezer. To create a true chili—not just a bean and vegetable stew—we had to find replacements for the different ways in which meat adds richness and flavor to chili. We looked to umami-rich ingredients to lend depth and meatiness to our chili: A combination of shiitake mushrooms, soy sauce, and ground walnuts added texture, savory flavor, and richness. Next, we needed to bulk up our chili. Diced vegetables ended up overcooked and they watered down the dish, rice turned to mush, and pearl barley was chewy and gummy. Finally, we hit on bulgur—precooked wheat kernels—which gave the chili a satisfying textural dimension and chew plus a great nutty flavor. To ensure that the bulgur maintained its distinctive chew, we undercooked it slightly before freezing so that it would finish cooking to just the right consistency as the chili reheated. For the beans, we wanted to use a mix of beans with different characteristics to give our chili further complexity. We singled out sweet, nutty cannellini beans and meaty black beans as our favorites. Dried beans offered the best texture; we used a quick salt-soaking method to ensure soft, creamy beans that were well seasoned and evenly cooked. Taking a tip from earlier recipes, we found that adding a little baking soda to the salt soak sped up their cooking. The alkali helped break down the cell structure of the beans, resulting in tender beans in less time. For a spicier chili, use both jalapeños. Serve with your favorite chili toppings.

8	ounces (1¼ cups) dried black beans, picked over and rinsed
8	ounces (1¼ cups) dried cannellini beans, picked over and rinsed
	Salt
1	teaspoon baking soda
½	ounce dried shiitake mushrooms, rinsed and chopped coarse
4	teaspoons dried oregano
½	cup walnuts, toasted
1	(28-ounce) can diced tomatoes, drained with juice reserved
3	tablespoons tomato paste
1–2	jalapeño chiles, stemmed, seeded, and coarsely chopped
6	garlic cloves, minced
3	tablespoons soy sauce
¼	cup vegetable oil
2	pounds onions, chopped
¼	cup chili powder
1	tablespoon ground cumin
7	cups water
⅔	cup medium-grind bulgur

TO FINISH AND SERVE
Chopped fresh cilantro

TO PREP

1. Bring 4 quarts water, beans, 3 tablespoons salt, and baking soda to boil in Dutch oven over high heat. Off heat, cover and let stand for 1 hour. Drain beans and rinse well. Wipe out pot.

2. Adjust oven rack to middle position and heat oven to 300 degrees. Process mushrooms and oregano in food processor until finely ground, about 1 minute; transfer to bowl and set aside. Process walnuts in now-empty food processor until finely ground, about 30 seconds; transfer to separate bowl. Process drained tomatoes, tomato paste, jalapeño(s), garlic, and soy sauce in now-empty food processor until tomatoes are finely chopped, about 45 seconds, scraping down sides of bowl as needed.

3. Heat oil in now-empty Dutch oven over medium heat until shimmering. Add onions and 1¼ teaspoons salt and cook, stirring occasionally, until softened and beginning to brown, 8 to 10 minutes. Reduce heat to medium, stir in ground mushroom mixture, chili powder, and cumin, and cook, stirring constantly, until fragrant, about 1 minute. Add rinsed beans and water and bring to boil. Cover pot, transfer to oven, and cook for 45 minutes.

4. Remove pot from oven. Stir in bulgur, ground walnuts, tomato mixture, and reserved tomato juice. Cover pot and return to oven. Cook until beans are fully tender, about 1 hour.

5. Remove pot from oven, stir chili well, and let cool to room temperature, 1½ to 2 hours, gently stirring occasionally. (To serve right away, increase cooking time to 1½ hours in step 4. Remove pot from oven, stir chili well, and let sit, uncovered, for 20 minutes. Stir in ¼ cup cilantro.)

TO STORE

6. Divide chili among freezer-safe storage containers and freeze for up to 1 month. (Plan on about 2 cups per person.)

TO FINISH AND SERVE

7. Thaw chili in refrigerator overnight. Transfer to saucepan. Cover saucepan, bring chili to gentle simmer over low heat, and cook, stirring occasionally, until heated through; adjust consistency with water as needed. Season with salt and pepper to taste. Stir in 2 tablespoons cilantro for every 4 servings. Serve.

Marinara Sauce

MAKES ABOUT 12 CUPS, ENOUGH TO SAUCE 3 POUNDS OF PASTA • **TO PREP** 1 HOUR 20 MINUTES
STORE UP TO 1 MONTH • **TO FINISH** ABOUT 30 MINUTES

✔ **WHY THIS RECIPE WORKS:** When it comes to making a big batch of tomato sauce to stash in your freezer, the choice is clear. A complex and well-balanced marinara sauce, one that has simmered long enough for its flavors to deepen and meld, beats a fast tomato sauce any day. But there are many theories about how to make a great marinara sauce, one that can be served simply with pasta and cheese or layered into a lasagna or manicotti recipe. The first decision was which tomatoes to use. We chose canned diced tomatoes for their bright flavor and because they're already chopped into small pieces, allowing them to soften and break down quickly. Since consistency is a big issue with sauce, we gained control by draining the tomatoes first and reserving a portion of the juice to add later in the cooking process. We also reserved a small amount of the drained tomatoes to add at the end for bright flavor and texture. To develop a multidimensional sauce rich with tomato flavor, we browned the drained tomatoes until they became glazed and nearly caramelized, then we added the reserved juice from the canned tomatoes. Red wine was a quick way to add depth and complexity, and plenty of minced onion lent our sauce aromatic flavor to balance the acidity of the tomatoes. Chopped basil and a drizzle of olive oil just before serving added a bright, fresh finish. If you prefer a chunkier sauce, give it fewer pulses in the food processor in step 3.

6   (28-ounce) cans diced tomatoes, drained
     with 6 cups juice reserved
5   tablespoons extra-virgin olive oil, plus extra
     as needed
3   onions, chopped fine
     Salt and pepper
12 garlic cloves, minced
3   tablespoons minced fresh oregano or
     1 tablespoon dried
1   cup dry red wine
     Sugar

TO FINISH AND SERVE
     Chopped fresh basil

TO PREP

1. Set aside 2¼ cups drained tomatoes in small bowl. Heat 3 tablespoons oil in Dutch oven over medium heat until shimmering. Add onions and 1 teaspoon salt and cook until onions are softened and lightly browned, 10 to 15 minutes. Stir in garlic and oregano and cook until fragrant, about 30 seconds.

2. Stir in remaining drained tomatoes and increase heat to medium-high. Cook, stirring occasionally, until liquid has evaporated, tomatoes begin to stick to bottom of pot, and brown glaze forms around edges, 20 to 25 minutes. Stir in wine, scraping up any browned bits, and cook until thick and syrupy, about 1 minute. Stir in reserved tomato juice and bring to simmer. Reduce heat to low and cook, stirring often, until sauce is thickened, about 20 minutes.

3. Working in batches, process sauce with reserved 2¼ cups tomatoes in food processor until slightly chunky, about 30 seconds. Transfer sauce to large bowl, stir in remaining 2 tablespoons oil, and season with salt, pepper, and sugar to taste. Let sauce cool to room temperature, 1½ to 2 hours, stirring occasionally.

TO STORE

4. Divide sauce among freezer-safe storage containers and freeze for up to 1 month. (Plan on about 4 cups sauce for every pound of pasta, which will serve 4 to 6.)

TO FINISH AND SERVE

5. Thaw sauce in refrigerator overnight. Transfer to saucepan. Cover saucepan, bring sauce to gentle simmer over low heat, and cook, stirring occasionally, until heated through. Season with salt, pepper, extra sugar, and extra oil to taste. Stir in 2 tablespoons basil for every 4 cups sauce. Before draining pasta, reserve some pasta cooking water to adjust sauce consistency when tossed with pasta.

Easy Meat Sauce

MAKES ABOUT 12 CUPS, ENOUGH TO SAUCE 3 POUNDS OF PASTA • **TO PREP** 1 HOUR 25 MINUTES
STORE UP TO 1 MONTH • **TO FINISH** ABOUT 30 MINUTES

✔ WHY THIS RECIPE WORKS: Most quick meat sauces involve nothing more than throwing ground beef, aromatics, and canned tomatoes into a pot and simmering it all for half an hour. We wanted an easy version that would taste as if it had been simmered for hours, a version worthy of being stacked up in the freezer for busy nights to come. In our quest for such a sauce, we discovered a few tricks. Browning the meat can dry it out and toughen it, so we skipped this step. Instead, we browned a small amount of white mushrooms, which we had ground in the food processor. Cooking the mushrooms for about 10 minutes left browned bits on the bottom of the pan that instilled our sauce with deep, savory flavor. To further ensure that the meat stayed tender, we blended it with a panade (a mixture of bread and milk) before cooking it just until it lost its color. The bread's starches absorbed liquid from the milk to form a gel that coated and lubricated the meat. Finally, for good tomato flavor, we added tomato paste to the browned vegetables and deglazed the pan with a little tomato juice before adding the canned tomatoes. Using two varieties of canned tomatoes struck a nice balance; diced tomatoes lent a chunky texture, and crushed tomatoes provided a smooth foundation.

8	ounces white mushrooms, trimmed and halved if small or quartered if large
2	slices hearty white sandwich bread, torn into quarters
¼	cup whole milk
	Salt and pepper
2	pounds 85 percent lean ground beef
2	tablespoons extra-virgin olive oil
2	large onions, chopped fine
12	garlic cloves, minced
½	teaspoon red pepper flakes
2	tablespoons tomato paste
1	(28-ounce) can diced tomatoes, drained with ½ cup juice reserved
2	tablespoons minced fresh oregano or 2 teaspoons dried
2	(28-ounce) cans crushed tomatoes

TO SERVE
Grated Parmesan cheese

TO PREP

1. Pulse mushrooms in food processor until finely chopped, about 8 pulses, scraping down sides of bowl as needed; transfer to bowl. Add bread, milk, 1 teaspoon salt, and 1 teaspoon pepper to now-empty food processor and pulse until paste forms, about 8 pulses. Add ground beef and process until mixture is well combined, about 30 seconds.

2. Heat oil in Dutch oven over medium-high heat until just smoking. Add processed mushrooms and onions and cook until vegetables are softened and well browned, 8 to 10 minutes. Stir in garlic, pepper flakes, and tomato paste and cook until fragrant, about 1 minute. Stir in ½ cup reserved tomato juice and oregano, scraping up any browned bits. Add meat mixture and cook, breaking up meat with wooden spoon, until no longer pink, about 5 minutes.

3. Stir in drained diced tomatoes and crushed tomatoes, bring to gentle simmer, and cook until sauce is thickened and flavors blend, about 30 minutes. Season with salt and pepper to taste. Let sauce cool to room temperature, 1½ to 2 hours, stirring occasionally.

TO STORE

4. Divide sauce among freezer-safe storage containers and freeze for up to 1 month. (Plan on about 4 cups sauce for every pound of pasta, which will serve 4 to 6.)

TO FINISH AND SERVE

5. Thaw sauce in refrigerator overnight. Transfer to saucepan. Cover saucepan, bring sauce to gentle simmer over low heat, and cook, stirring occasionally, until heated through. Season with salt and pepper to taste. Stir in ½ cup grated Parmesan cheese for every 4 cups sauce. Before draining pasta, reserve some pasta cooking water to adjust sauce consistency when tossed with pasta.

Meatballs and Marinara

MAKES ABOUT 7 CUPS SAUCE AND 30 MEATBALLS, ENOUGH TO SAUCE 2 POUNDS OF PASTA
TO PREP 1 HOUR 40 MINUTES • **STORE** UP TO 1 MONTH • **TO FINISH** ABOUT 30 MINUTES

✔ **WHY THIS RECIPE WORKS:** Tender, flavorful meatballs served over pasta with a long-simmered marinara sauce make a great dinner for company or for family. But it takes some time and effort to do this dish right, which is why making a big batch and freezing it is so appealing. To build a sauce with a long-simmered flavor, we started by sautéing onions, then added a healthy dose of garlic, oregano, and red pepper flakes. Reserving half of this mixture to season the meatballs streamlined our recipe. With tomato paste for richness and red wine to deglaze the pan, we had a strong flavor foundation for our sauce. Next, we decided to use canned crushed tomatoes for their ease and for their packing liquid, which prevented the sauce from overreducing during the reheat. For hearty meatballs, we combined lean ground beef with boldly flavored sweet Italian sausage. This lean mixture held its shape well, but to compensate for the decreased amount of fat, we added a panade of sandwich bread and milk. This kept the meat moist and prevented it from getting tough. To boost the flavor further, a good dose of Parmesan and parsley did the trick. An egg was also important for texture and flavor; its rich fats and emulsifiers added moistness, richness, and structure to our meatballs. For a golden brown crust without the hassle of frying, we baked our meatballs on baking sheets in a superhot oven. While reheating the sauce, make sure that you stir very gently or the meatballs will start to break down.

MARINARA

- ¼ cup extra-virgin olive oil
- 3 onions, chopped fine
- 8 garlic cloves, minced
- 1 tablespoon dried oregano
- ¾ teaspoon red pepper flakes
- 1 (6-ounce) can tomato paste
- 1 cup dry red wine
- 1 cup water
- 4 (28-ounce) cans crushed tomatoes
- 1 ounce Parmesan cheese, grated (½ cup)
  Salt and pepper

MEATBALLS

- 4 slices hearty white sandwich bread, torn into pieces
- ¾ cup milk
- 8 ounces sweet Italian sausage, casings removed
- 2 ounces Parmesan cheese, grated (1 cup)
- ½ cup chopped fresh parsley
- 2 large eggs
- 2 garlic cloves, minced
- 1½ teaspoons salt
- 2½ pounds 80 percent lean ground chuck

TO FINISH AND SERVE
  Chopped fresh basil

TO PREP

1. FOR THE MARINARA: Heat oil in Dutch oven over medium heat until shimmering. Add onions and cook until softened and lightly browned, 10 to 15 minutes. Stir in garlic, oregano, and pepper flakes and cook until fragrant, about 30 seconds. Transfer half of onion mixture to large bowl and set aside.

2. Add tomato paste to remaining onion mixture in pot and cook over medium-high heat until fragrant, about 1 minute. Stir in wine, scraping up any browned bits, and cook until slightly thickened, about 2 minutes. Stir in water and tomatoes and bring to simmer. Reduce heat to low and simmer until sauce is no longer watery, 45 to 60 minutes. Stir in Parmesan and season with salt and pepper to taste. Let sauce cool to room temperature, 1½ to 2 hours, stirring occasionally.

3. FOR THE MEATBALLS: Meanwhile, adjust oven racks to upper-middle and lower-middle positions and heat oven to 475 degrees. Line 2 rimmed baking sheets with aluminum foil and spray with vegetable oil spray.

4. Mash bread and milk in bowl with reserved onion mixture until smooth. Add sausage, Parmesan, parsley, eggs, garlic, and salt and mash with hands to combine. Mix in ground beef with hands until uniform. Pinch off and roll mixture into 2-inch round meatballs (about 30 meatballs total). Arrange meatballs

evenly on prepared sheets. Bake until well browned, about 20 minutes, switching and rotating sheets halfway through baking. Let meatballs cool to room temperature.

TO STORE

5. Divide meatballs and sauce among freezer-safe storage containers and freeze for up to 1 month. (Plan on 3½ cups sauce and 15 meatballs for every pound of pasta, which will serve 4 to 6.)

TO FINISH AND SERVE

6. Thaw meatballs and sauce in refrigerator overnight. Transfer to saucepan. Cover saucepan, bring sauce to very gentle simmer over low heat, and cook, gently stirring occasionally, until meatballs are heated through. Season with salt to taste. Stir in 2 tablespoons basil for every 3½ cups sauce. Before draining pasta, reserve some pasta cooking water to adjust sauce consistency when tossed with pasta.

Bolognese Sauce

MAKES ABOUT 12 CUPS, ENOUGH TO SAUCE 3 POUNDS OF PASTA • **TO PREP** 8 HOURS
STORE UP TO 1 MONTH • **TO FINISH** ABOUT 30 MINUTES

✔ **WHY THIS RECIPE WORKS:** A good Bolognese sauce should be thick and meaty with rich, complex flavor. Achieving that complexity requires a lengthy simmer, making this sauce perfect for preparing on a lazy Sunday afternoon. Unlike other meat sauces in which tomatoes dominate, Bolognese sauce is about the meat, with the tomatoes playing a supporting role. We discovered that meatloaf mix—a prepackaged combination of ground beef, veal, and pork—made this sauce especially complex and rich tasting. Once we had chosen our meat, we had to decide whether or not to brown it. Although browning meat builds flavor, we found the browned meat became tough during its stay in the freezer, so we preferred cooking the meat just until it lost its pink color. This way we didn't need a lengthy simmer when reheating to retenderize the meat. Next, we needed to decide which type of tomato product made the best Bolognese. After testing whole tomatoes, pureed tomatoes, and diced tomatoes, we found that the packing juice in diced tomatoes made a looser sauce, which helped to keep the pot from scorching during the reheating process. Finally, to make a classic Bolognese sauce, we also needed to add dairy—butter, milk, and/or cream. We chose milk to give the beef a subtly sweet, appealing flavor. This tasty sauce is perfect for stocking the freezer, and the results are definitely worth the (mostly hands-off) cooking time. If meatloaf mix is unavailable, use 1½ pounds each of ground pork and 85 percent lean ground beef.

5   **tablespoons unsalted butter**
1   **onion, chopped**
2   **carrots, peeled and chopped**
2   **celery ribs, chopped fine**
     Salt and pepper
3   **pounds meatloaf mix**
3   **cups whole milk**
1   **(750-ml) bottle dry white wine**
4   **(28-ounce) cans diced tomatoes, drained with 3½ cups juice reserved**

TO PREP

1. Melt butter in Dutch oven over medium heat. Add onion, carrots, celery, and 1 tablespoon salt and cook until softened, 8 to 10 minutes. Add meatloaf mix and cook, breaking up meat with wooden spoon, until no longer pink, 6 to 8 minutes.

2. Stir in milk, bring to simmer, and cook until liquid evaporates and only fat remains, about 1 hour. Stir in wine, bring to simmer, and cook until wine has evaporated, about 1 hour.

3. Meanwhile, working in batches, pulse drained tomatoes in food processor until slightly chunky, about 8 pulses. Add drained tomatoes and reserved tomato juice to pot and bring to gentle simmer. Reduce heat to low and simmer gently, stirring occasionally, until liquid has evaporated, 5 to 5½ hours. Season with salt and pepper to taste. Let sauce cool to room temperature, 1½ to 2 hours, stirring occasionally.

TO STORE

4. Divide sauce among freezer-safe storage containers and freeze for up to 1 month. (Plan on about 4 cups sauce for every pound of pasta, which will serve 4 to 6.)

TO FINISH AND SERVE

5. Thaw sauce in refrigerator overnight. Transfer to saucepan. Cover saucepan, bring to gentle simmer over low heat, and cook, stirring occasionally, until heated through. Season with salt to taste. Before draining pasta, reserve some pasta cooking water to adjust sauce consistency when tossed with pasta.

Classic Pesto

MAKES ABOUT 2¼ CUPS, ENOUGH TO SAUCE 3 POUNDS PASTA • **TO PREP** 30 MINUTES
STORE UP TO 1 MONTH • **TO FINISH** ABOUT 30 MINUTES

✔ **WHY THIS RECIPE WORKS:** There are good reasons why pesto has gone from obscure Italian sauce to American favorite. As a no-cook sauce, it is quick and easy to make and so flavorful and versatile it can transform plain pasta, chicken, or a sandwich into something great. Because pesto has so many uses, making a big batch that can be stored in the freezer and used at a moment's notice makes a lot of sense. We started with a recipe of standard ratios to dress a pound of pasta—2 cups of basil, 3 garlic cloves, ½ cup of extra-virgin olive oil, and ¼ cup of pine nuts—and pureed everything in the food processor, which combined the ingredients quickly and easily. The result was a very raw, spicy garlic sauce with a hint of basil. To bring out the basil's flavor, we gently pounded it with a mallet before tossing it into the food processor; this helped to release its flavorful oils. To tame the garlic, we toasted it. Since we already had the skillet out, we toasted the nuts as well to give them more flavor. Once we had a simple and balanced recipe, we scaled it up to make enough to stash in the freezer. To serve the pesto with pasta, we found that thinning out the mixture with a little pasta water before tossing it with the pasta allowed for good distribution throughout the pasta, softened the flavors, and highlighted the creaminess of the cheese and nuts. For sharper flavor, use Pecorino Romano cheese in place of the Parmesan.

¾	**cup pine nuts**
7	**garlic cloves, unpeeled**
6	**cups fresh basil leaves**
6	**tablespoons fresh parsley leaves**
1¼	**cups extra-virgin olive oil, plus extra as needed**
1½	**ounces Parmesan cheese, grated (¾ cup)**
	Salt and pepper

TO PREP

1. Toast pine nuts in 12-inch skillet over medium heat, stirring often, until golden and fragrant, 4 to 5 minutes; transfer to plate and let cool. Toast garlic in now-empty skillet over medium heat, shaking skillet occasionally, until fragrant and spotty brown, about 7 minutes; let cool slightly, then peel and chop.

2. Place basil and parsley in 1-gallon zipper-lock bag and pound lightly with meat pounder or rolling pin until leaves are bruised. Process pine nuts, garlic, bruised herbs, oil, Parmesan, and 1½ teaspoons salt in food processor until smooth, 60 to 90 seconds, scraping down sides of bowl as needed. Season with salt and pepper to taste.

TO STORE

3. Divide pesto among freezer-safe storage containers and smooth tops. Pour ¼ inch of oil over pesto. Freeze for up to 1 month. (Plan on about ¾ cup sauce for every pound of pasta, which will serve 4 to 6.)

TO FINISH AND SERVE

4. Thaw pesto in refrigerator overnight. Stir pesto to recombine and season with salt and pepper to taste. Before draining pasta, reserve some pasta cooking water to adjust sauce consistency when tossed with pasta.

Cheese Pizza

MAKES TWO 12-INCH PIZZAS • **TO PREP** 1 HOUR 25 MINUTES
STORE UP TO 1 MONTH • **TO FINISH** 50 MINUTES

✔ **WHY THIS RECIPE WORKS:** The appeal of store-bought frozen pizza is undeniable, but it always pales in comparison to freshly made pizza. Freezing our favorite homemade recipe seemed like an easy solution, but our first tests resulted in a flat, tough crust. The reason is that as the dough froze, ice crystals formed, inhibiting the yeast's ability to rise the dough. Drawing on some test kitchen tricks to solve this problem, we added baking powder, which gave the dough extra lift, creating air pockets during baking that resulted in a lighter crust with more rise. To ensure tenderness, we swapped out a little of the all-purpose flour for cornstarch, which has less protein, translating to less gluten production and a more tender dough. Using half-and-half in place of some of the water further tenderized the dough and added richness. To prevent the cheeses from drying out in the freezer, we tossed them with more half-and-half. To bake the pizza, a preheated baking stone was a must for crispness, and baking the pizza on the upper-middle rack (the hottest part) of the oven browned the cheese and further ensured a crisp crust. To make the pizzas easy to shape and store, we simply patted the dough out into 12-inch disposable aluminum pizza pans. Finally, this pizza offered the best of both worlds: great homemade flavor with the convenience of coming straight from the freezer. If you do not have a baking stone, you can use an inverted rimmed baking sheet. You will need two 12-inch disposable aluminum pizza pans for this recipe.

DOUGH

- 1½ cups warm half-and-half (110 degrees)
- ½ cup warm water (110 degrees)
- 2 tablespoons extra-virgin olive oil
- 4 cups (20 ounces) all-purpose flour
- ¼ cup cornstarch
- 2¼ teaspoons instant or rapid-rise yeast
- 1½ teaspoons salt
- ½ teaspoon baking powder
- ½ teaspoon sugar

SAUCE AND TOPPINGS

- 1 (14.5-ounce) can diced tomatoes, drained with ½ cup juice reserved
- 1 tablespoon extra-virgin olive oil
- 1 tablespoon tomato paste
- 2 garlic cloves, minced
- 1 tablespoon minced fresh oregano or 1 teaspoon dried
- ¼ teaspoon red pepper flakes
  Salt and pepper
- 8 ounces mozzarella cheese, shredded (2 cups)
- 1 ounce Parmesan cheese, grated (½ cup)
- ¼ cup half-and-half

TO FINISH AND SERVE (PER PIZZA)

- 2 tablespoons extra-virgin olive oil

TO PREP

1. FOR THE DOUGH: Spray large bowl with vegetable oil spray and set aside. Combine half-and-half, water, and oil in 4-cup liquid measuring cup. Using stand mixer fitted with dough hook, mix flour, cornstarch, yeast, salt, baking powder, and sugar together on medium-low speed until combined. Slowly add half-and-half mixture and mix until dough comes together, about 1 minute. Continue mixing until sticky strands form around exterior but center of dough is uniform in texture, about 5 minutes. (Dough will be wet and cling to sides of bowl.) Transfer dough to prepared bowl, cover with plastic wrap, and let rise at room temperature until doubled in size, about 1 hour.

2. FOR THE SAUCE AND TOPPINGS: Meanwhile, pulse drained tomatoes and reserved juice in food processor until coarsely ground, about 5 pulses. Heat oil in large saucepan over medium heat until shimmering. Add tomato paste and cook, stirring frequently, until just beginning to brown, about 2 minutes. Stir in garlic, oregano, and pepper flakes and cook until fragrant, about 30 seconds. Add pulsed tomatoes, bring to simmer, and cook until reduced to 1 cup, about 10 minutes. Season with salt and pepper to taste and let cool to room temperature, about 30 minutes.

3. Mix mozzarella, Parmesan, and half-and-half together in separate bowl until well combined.

4. Divide dough equally between two 12-inch disposable aluminum pizza pans. Using well-oiled hands, press dough out evenly toward edges of pans. Spread ½ cup sauce over each dough round, leaving ½-inch border around edge, then sprinkle cheese mixture evenly over sauce.

TO STORE

5. Wrap each pizza tightly with plastic and cover with aluminum foil. Freeze pizzas for up to 1 month. (Do not thaw before reheating.)

TO FINISH AND SERVE

6. Thirty minutes before baking, adjust oven rack to upper-middle position (rack should be 4 to 5 inches from broiler), set baking stone on rack, and heat oven to 500 degrees. Unwrap 1 pizza and remove from aluminum pan. Transfer pizza to pizza peel and brush edges of dough with oil. Carefully slide pizza onto baking stone and bake until crust is well browned and cheese is bubbling and beginning to brown, 15 to 25 minutes, rotating pizza halfway through baking. Transfer pizza to wire rack and let cool for 5 minutes before slicing and serving.

Beef and Bean Burritos

MAKES 8 BURRITOS • **TO PREP** 1½ HOURS • **STORE** UP TO 1 MONTH • **TO FINISH** 15 MINUTES

✔ **WHY THIS RECIPE WORKS:** Whether as a quick lunch on the go or an easy dinner when the refrigerator is bare, frozen burritos may satisfy our hunger pangs, but not much else. We set out to create freezer burritos minus the bland flavors, mushy fillings, and chewy wraps. To streamline our filling, we swapped the traditional stewed and shredded meat for easy ground beef and nixed the idea of soaking and cooking dried beans in favor of convenient canned beans. Mashing half of the beans gave our filling a creamy consistency, and cumin, oregano, chile powder, tomato paste, and lime juice contributed bold flavor. White rice (cooked in chicken broth with garlic), a good amount of fresh cilantro, and sharp cheddar cheese rounded out our flavorful filling. Reheating these burritos in the oven took almost an hour, but we found that wrapping a burrito in a paper towel and microwaving it for a few minutes heated it through, and a quick run under the broiler melted and browned the cheesy topping.

2⅔ cups chicken broth
1 cup long-grain white rice
8 garlic cloves, minced
  Salt
⅓ cup minced fresh cilantro
1 (15-ounce) can pinto beans, rinsed
1 tablespoon vegetable oil
1 onion, chopped fine
¼ cup tomato paste
1 tablespoon ground cumin
1 teaspoon dried oregano
1 teaspoon chipotle chile powder
1 pound 90 percent lean ground beef
4 teaspoons lime juice
8 (10-inch) flour tortillas
8 ounces sharp cheddar cheese, shredded
  (2 cups)

TO FINISH AND SERVE
  Shredded sharp cheddar cheese
  Sour cream

TO PREP

1. Bring 2 cups broth, rice, half of garlic, and 1 teaspoon salt to boil in small saucepan over medium-high heat. Reduce heat to low, cover, and cook until rice is tender and all liquid has been absorbed, about 20 minutes. Off heat, let sit, covered, for 10 minutes. Add cilantro, fluff rice with fork, and set aside to cool.

2. Meanwhile, using potato masher, coarsely mash half of beans with remaining ⅔ cup broth in medium bowl. Heat oil in 12-inch nonstick skillet over medium heat until shimmering. Add onion and cook until softened, about 5 minutes. Stir in tomato paste, cumin, oregano, chile powder, and remaining garlic and cook until fragrant, about 1 minute. Add ground beef and cook, breaking up meat with wooden spoon, until no longer pink, 8 to 10 minutes.

3. Add mashed bean mixture and cook, stirring constantly, until combined, about 1 minute. Stir in lime juice, 1 teaspoon salt, and remaining whole beans. Let filling cool to room temperature, about 20 minutes.

4. Wrap tortillas in clean dish towel; microwave until soft and pliable, about 90 seconds. Arrange tortillas on counter. Divide rice, beef-and-bean filling, and cheddar evenly over bottom halves of tortillas, leaving 1- to 2-inch border at edge. Fold sides of each tortilla over filling, fold bottom of tortilla over sides and filling, and roll tightly into burrito. (To serve burrito right away, follow serving instructions, eliminating use of microwave.)

TO STORE

5. Wrap each burrito tightly with plastic wrap, then wrap with aluminum foil. Freeze burritos for up to 1 month. (Do not thaw before reheating.)

TO FINISH AND SERVE

6. Adjust oven rack to middle position and heat broiler. Line rimmed baking sheet with foil. Unwrap burrito(s) and wrap with paper towels. Microwave burrito(s) until softened and heated through, about 5 minutes. Discard paper towels and transfer burrito(s) to prepared sheet. Sprinkle top of each with 2 tablespoons cheddar and broil until cheese is melted and starting to brown, 3 to 5 minutes, rotating sheet halfway through broiling. Serve with sour cream.

FINISH UNDER THE BROILER
Frozen burritos usually give options for either microwaving or baking, but the microwave produces lackluster results and the oven takes 30 minutes or more. We combined the methods to get the best of both. Just 5 minutes in the microwave, wrapped in paper towels, defrosted the burritos, then we topped them with extra cheese and broiled them until it was gooey and browned.

Meat Hand Pies

MAKES 16 PIES • **TO PREP** 3½ HOURS • **STORE** UP TO 1 MONTH • **TO FINISH** 35 MINUTES

✓ **WHY THIS RECIPE WORKS:** Meat pies are a meal in and of themselves: Pull a few half-moon-shaped pies of flaky dough filled with a savory meat filling from the freezer, and all you need is a salad for a well-rounded meal. The dough falls somewhere between pastry and pasta dough. Shortening, eggs, baking powder, and chicken broth all combine to create a flavorful dough that bakes up into a flaky, savory casing for the filling. And these pies are a great make-ahead option; they're just as good when made ahead of time and frozen. Plus, with all the work that goes into making the dough, assembling the pies, and baking them, it made sense to make a big batch and freeze them. Many recipes called for frying the pies, but we thought that seemed unnecessarily fussy, requiring cooking in several batches, so instead we mimicked pan frying in the oven. Preheating a baking sheet in a hot oven, drizzling a couple of tablespoons of vegetable oil on the sheet, and baking the pies on the hot oiled sheet gave us crisp, golden brown crusts as good as fried ones without all the mess. And reheating the pies was even simpler—all they needed was a quick stint in the oven before serving. Meatloaf mix is a prepackaged mix of ground beef, pork, and veal; if it's unavailable, use 12 ounces each of ground pork and 85 percent lean ground beef.

FILLING

- 1 tablespoon vegetable oil
- 1 onion, chopped fine
- 1 green bell pepper, stemmed, seeded, and minced
- 6 scallions, white parts minced, green parts sliced thin
- 3 garlic cloves, minced
- ¼ teaspoon cayenne pepper
- 1½ pounds meatloaf mix
  Salt and pepper
- 2 tablespoons all-purpose flour
- 1 cup chicken broth
- 4 ounces Monterey Jack cheese, shredded (1 cup)

DOUGH

- 4 cups (20 ounces) all-purpose flour
- 2 teaspoons salt
- 1 teaspoon baking powder
- 8 tablespoons vegetable shortening, cut into ½-inch pieces
- 1 cup chicken broth
- 2 large eggs, lightly beaten
- 5 tablespoons vegetable oil

TO PREP

1. FOR THE FILLING: Heat oil in 12-inch skillet over medium heat until shimmering. Add onion, bell pepper, and scallion whites and cook until softened, about 5 minutes. Stir in garlic and cayenne and cook until fragrant, about 30 seconds. Add meatloaf mix, 1 teaspoon salt, and ½ teaspoon pepper and cook, breaking up meat with wooden spoon, until no longer pink, 5 to 8 minutes.

2. Sprinkle flour over meat and cook, stirring constantly, until evenly coated, about 1 minute. Stir in broth, bring to boil, and cook until mixture is thickened, about 5 minutes. Transfer filling to large bowl, stir in Monterey Jack and scallion greens, and let cool to room temperature, about 30 minutes. Refrigerate until completely cool, about 1 hour.

3. FOR THE DOUGH: Meanwhile, process flour, salt, and baking powder in food processor until combined, about 3 seconds. Add shortening and pulse until mixture resembles coarse cornmeal, 6 to 8 pulses. Add broth and eggs and pulse until dough just comes together, about 5 pulses. Transfer dough to lightly floured counter and knead by hand until dough forms smooth ball, about 20 seconds. Divide dough into 16 equal pieces. With cupped palms, form each piece into smooth, tight ball.

4. Adjust oven racks to upper-middle and lower-middle positions, place 1 rimmed baking sheet on each rack, and heat oven to 425 degrees. Working with 1 dough ball at a time, roll into 6-inch circle on lightly floured counter. Place ¼ cup cooled filling in center of dough round. Brush edges of dough with water and

fold dough over filling. Press to seal, trim any ragged edges, and crimp edges with tines of fork.

5. Drizzle 2 tablespoons oil on each hot sheet, then return to oven for 2 minutes. Gently brush tops of meat pies with remaining 1 tablespoon oil. Carefully place 8 meat pies on each prepared sheet and cook until golden brown, 35 to 40 minutes, switching and rotating sheets halfway through baking. Transfer meat pies to wire rack and let cool to room temperature, about 30 minutes.

TO STORE

6. Transfer cooled meat pies to zipper-lock freezer bags, press out air, and seal. Freeze for up to 1 month. (Do not thaw before reheating.)

TO FINISH AND SERVE

7. Adjust oven rack to middle position and heat oven to 350 degrees. Place meat pies on wire rack set in rimmed baking sheet and bake until heated through, 20 to 30 minutes. Serve.

Chicken Fingers

MAKES 16 FINGERS • **TO PREP** 1 HOUR 20 MINUTES • **STORE** UP TO 1 MONTH • **TO FINISH** 45 MINUTES

✔ **WHY THIS RECIPE WORKS:** When we looked at the ingredient list on prepackaged chicken fingers, we were surprised to discover so many preservatives we couldn't pronounce. We liked the idea of having something as simple and adaptable as chicken fingers on hand, so we wondered if we could stock our freezer with kid-friendly, great-tasting chicken fingers with minimal effort. The freezer has a drying effect on food, and lean chicken breast is no exception. We had a hunch that all those preservatives were helping to keep the chicken moist during the reheat, so we started by thinking about how to keep the chicken as moist as possible. Brining turned out to be the best solution: It makes the chicken very juicy so it doesn't dry out as it cooks. To give our chicken fingers great flavor, we added a dash of Worcestershire sauce to the brine and onion and garlic powder to the breading. To get a crisp coating on our chicken even after reheating, we swapped traditional bread crumbs for ultracrisp panko bread crumbs and tried a few different cooking techniques. Deep-frying the chicken fingers was a lot of work for little payoff. Next, we tried to mimic frying by tossing the breading with oil and baking the chicken, but on the reheat the chicken was dry and the coating was sandy. Sautéing turned out to be the winning technique: By the time the breading fried up supercrisp and golden, the chicken was cooked through but still tender and moist, and we avoided all the mess and waste of deep frying. These chicken fingers were good enough to please kids and adults alike. Don't brine the chicken for longer than 30 minutes or it will be too salty.

Salt and pepper
2 tablespoons Worcestershire sauce
1½ pounds boneless, skinless chicken breasts, trimmed and cut lengthwise into ¾-inch-wide strips
½ cup all-purpose flour
1 tablespoon onion powder
1 teaspoon granulated garlic
3 large eggs
2 cups panko bread crumbs, toasted
¾ cup vegetable oil

TO PREP

1. Dissolve 1 tablespoon salt and Worcestershire in 2 cups cold water in large bowl. Submerge chicken in brine, cover, and refrigerate for 30 minutes.

2. Remove chicken from brine and pat dry with paper towels. Combine flour, onion powder, granulated garlic, ¼ teaspoon salt, and ¾ teaspoon pepper in shallow dish. Lightly beat eggs in second shallow dish. Spread panko in third shallow dish. Working in batches, dredge chicken in flour mixture, dip in eggs, then coat with panko, pressing gently to adhere; transfer to large plate.

3. Set wire rack in rimmed baking sheet. Heat ¼ cup oil in 12-inch nonstick skillet over medium heat until shimmering. Lay one-third of chicken in skillet and cook until golden brown, about 3 minutes per side. Transfer to prepared rack and wipe out skillet. Repeat shallow frying twice more with remaining oil and chicken. Let chicken cool to room temperature, about 30 minutes.

TO STORE

4. Transfer cooled chicken fingers to zipper-lock freezer bags, press out air, and seal. Freeze for up to 1 month. (Do not thaw before reheating.)

TO FINISH AND SERVE

5. Adjust oven rack to middle position and heat oven to 350 degrees. Place chicken fingers on wire rack set in rimmed baking sheet and bake until heated through and crisp, about 30 minutes, flipping chicken halfway through baking. Serve.

BRINE THE CHICKEN

To protect the chicken for our chicken fingers from drying out in the freezer, we started by cutting boneless, skinless chicken breasts into large strips, rather than small nuggets. To further ensure juiciness, we brined the chicken before breading it; adding some Worcestershire sauce to the brine gave the chicken even more meaty flavor.

Ultimate Veggie Burgers

MAKES 12 BURGERS • **TO PREP** 2½ HOURS • **STORE** UP TO 1 MONTH • **TO FINISH** 25 MINUTES

✓ **WHY THIS RECIPE WORKS:** Store-bought veggie burgers are notoriously inedible, yet really great homemade versions are time-consuming. In our minds, this made them an exceptionally appealing recipe to develop for our from-the-freezer chapter. To get the texture of our burgers right we tried a variety of meat alternatives, from tempeh to tofu to something called "textured vegetable protein," but none had a texture that tasters liked in a burger. When we turned to a more traditional base for veggie burgers we had better luck. Legumes, specifically lentils, had the best flavor, and bulgur and panko absorbed the excess moisture the lentils retained even after thorough drying. Adding aromatic vegetables was a no-brainer; onions, celery, leek, and garlic provided depth of flavor without being overwhelming. We knew that cremini mushrooms would give our burgers a meaty flavor, but adding ground cashews took them to the next level. Pulsing everything together in the food processor made for a more cohesive and even-textured mix, and mayonnaise provided the necessary fat and binding qualities. As for cooking, searing the burgers on the stovetop and then transferring them to the oven prevented them from scorching by the time they were heated through while also developing a crunchy, charred exterior for veggie burgers that were far better than anything you can find in the freezer aisle. Serve with your favorite burger toppings.

¾   cup brown lentils, picked over and rinsed
     Salt and pepper
1   tablespoon vegetable oil
1   pound cremini mushrooms, trimmed and
     sliced thin
2   onions, chopped fine
1   celery rib, minced
1   small leek, white and light green parts only,
     chopped fine and washed thoroughly (½ cup)
2   garlic cloves, minced
¾   cup medium-grind bulgur, rinsed
1   cup raw cashews
⅓   cup mayonnaise
2   cups panko bread crumbs

TO FINISH AND SERVE
     Vegetable oil
     Burger buns

TO PREP

1. Bring 3 cups water, lentils, and 1 teaspoon salt to boil in medium saucepan over high heat. Reduce heat to medium-low and simmer, stirring occasionally, until lentils just begin to fall apart, about 25 minutes. Drain well and transfer to paper towel–lined baking sheet; gently pat lentils dry.

2. Meanwhile, heat oil in 12-inch nonstick skillet over medium heat until shimmering. Add mushrooms and cook, stirring occasionally, until released liquid has evaporated and mushrooms are softened, about 8 minutes. Add onions, celery, leek, and garlic and cook until vegetables are softened and just beginning to brown, 10 to 15 minutes. Transfer to sheet with lentils and let mixture cool to room temperature, about 30 minutes.

3. Combine 2 cups water, bulgur, and ¼ teaspoon salt in large bowl and microwave, covered, until bulgur is softened, about 5 minutes. Drain well, using rubber spatula to press out excess moisture, and return to now-empty bowl; let cool slightly.

4. Pulse cashews in food processor until finely ground, about 25 pulses, scraping down sides of bowl as needed. Stir ground cashews, cooled lentil-vegetable mixture, and mayonnaise into bowl with bulgur until combined. Transfer half of mixture to now-empty food processor and pulse until coarsely ground, about 15 pulses; mixture should be cohesive but roughly textured. Transfer processed mixture to separate large bowl; repeat with remaining bulgur mixture. Stir in panko, 1 teaspoon salt, and pepper to taste until uniform.

5. Line 2 clean baking sheets with parchment paper. Divide mixture into 12 equal portions (about ½ cup each) and place on prepared sheets; tightly pack each portion into ½-inch-thick patty. (To serve right away, follow serving instructions.)

TO STORE

6. Cover sheets loosely with plastic wrap and freeze patties until firm, about 1 hour. Wrap patties with plastic in bundles of 4, with small sheets of parchment paper between patties. Transfer bundles to zipper-lock freezer bags, press out air, and seal. Freeze for up to 1 month. (Do not thaw before reheating.)

TO FINISH AND SERVE

7. Adjust oven rack to middle position and heat oven to 350 degrees. Line baking sheet with aluminum foil. Heat 2 tablespoons oil in 12-inch nonstick skillet over medium heat until shimmering. Add up to 4 burgers to skillet and cook until well browned on first side, about 4 minutes. Flip burgers, add additional oil if skillet looks dry, and cook until well browned on second side, about 4 minutes longer; transfer burgers to prepared sheet. Bake until heated through, about 10 minutes. Serve on burger buns.

Conversions & Equivalencies

Some say cooking is a science and an art. We would say that geography has a hand in it, too. Flour milled in the United Kingdom and elsewhere will feel and taste different from flour milled in the United States. So we cannot promise that the loaf of bread you bake in Canada or England will taste the same as a loaf baked in the States, but we can offer guidelines for converting weights and measures. We also recommend that you rely on your instincts when making our recipes. Refer to the visual cues provided. If the bread dough hasn't "come together in a ball," as described, you may need to add more flour—even if the recipe doesn't tell you to. You be the judge.

The recipes in this book were developed using standard U.S. measures following U.S. government guidelines. The charts below offer equivalents for U.S., metric, and imperial (U.K.) measures. All conversions are approximate and have been rounded up or down to the nearest whole number.

EXAMPLE:

| 1 teaspoon | = | 4.9292 milliliters, rounded up to 5 milliliters |
| 1 ounce | = | 28.3495 grams, rounded down to 28 grams |

VOLUME CONVERSIONS

U.S.	METRIC
1 teaspoon	5 milliliters
2 teaspoons	10 milliliters
1 tablespoon	15 milliliters
2 tablespoons	30 milliliters
¼ cup	59 milliliters
⅓ cup	79 milliliters
½ cup	118 milliliters
¾ cup	177 milliliters
1 cup	237 milliliters
1¼ cups	296 milliliters
1½ cups	355 milliliters
2 cups (1 pint)	473 milliliters
2½ cups	591 milliliters
3 cups	710 milliliters
4 cups (1 quart)	0.946 liter
1.06 quarts	1 liter
4 quarts (1 gallon)	3.8 liters

WEIGHT CONVERSIONS

OUNCES	GRAMS
½	14
¾	21
1	28
1½	43
2	57
2½	71
3	85
3½	99
4	113
4½	128
5	142
6	170
7	198
8	227
9	255
10	283
12	340
16 (1 pound)	454

CONVERSIONS FOR INGREDIENTS COMMONLY USED IN BAKING

Baking is an exacting science. Because measuring by weight is far more accurate than measuring by volume, and thus more likely to achieve reliable results, in our recipes we provide ounce measures in addition to cup measures for many ingredients. Refer to the chart below to convert these measures into grams.

INGREDIENT	OUNCES	GRAMS
1 cup all-purpose flour*	5	142
1 cup cake flour	4	113
1 cup whole-wheat flour	5½	156
1 cup granulated (white) sugar	7	198
1 cup packed brown sugar (light or dark)	7	198
1 cup confectioners' sugar	4	113
1 cup cocoa powder	3	85
4 tablespoons butter† (½ stick, or ¼ cup)	2	57
8 tablespoons butter† (1 stick, or ½ cup)	4	113
16 tablespoons butter† (2 sticks, or 1 cup)	8	227

* U.S. all-purpose flour, the most frequently used flour in this book, does not contain leaveners, as some European flours do. These leavened flours are called self-rising or self-raising. If you are using self-rising flour, take this into consideration before adding leavening to a recipe.

† In the United States, butter is sold both salted and unsalted. We generally recommend unsalted butter. If you are using salted butter, take this into consideration before adding salt to a recipe.

OVEN TEMPERATURES

FAHRENHEIT	CELSIUS	GAS MARK (IMPERIAL)
225	105	¼
250	120	½
275	135	1
300	150	2
325	165	3
350	180	4
375	190	5
400	200	6
425	220	7
450	230	8
475	245	9

CONVERTING TEMPERATURES FROM AN INSTANT-READ THERMOMETER

We include doneness temperatures in many of the recipes in this book. We recommend an instant-read thermometer for the job. Refer to the above table to convert Fahrenheit degrees to Celsius. Or, for temperatures not represented in the chart, use this simple formula:

Subtract 32 degrees from the Fahrenheit reading, then divide the result by 1.8 to find the Celsius reading.

EXAMPLE:
"Roast chicken until thighs register 175 degrees." To convert:

175°F – 32 = 143°
143° ÷ 1.8 = 79.44°C, rounded down to 79°C

Index